Native Claims

Native Claims

Indigenous Law against Empire,

1500–1920

Edited by Saliha Belmessous

OXFORD
UNIVERSITY PRESS

OXFORD
UNIVERSITY PRESS

Oxford University Press is a department of the University of Oxford.
It furthers the University's objective of excellence in research, scholarship,
and education by publishing worldwide.

Oxford   New York
Auckland   Cape Town   Dar es Salaam   Hong Kong   Karachi
Kuala Lumpur   Madrid   Melbourne   Mexico City   Nairobi
New Delhi   Shanghai   Taipei   Toronto

With offices in
Argentina   Austria   Brazil   Chile   Czech Republic   France   Greece
Guatemala   Hungary   Italy   Japan   Poland   Portugal   Singapore
South Korea   Switzerland   Thailand   Turkey   Ukraine   Vietnam

Oxford is a registered trade mark of Oxford University Press
in the UK and certain other countries.

Published in the United States of America by
Oxford University Press
198 Madison Avenue, New York, NY 10016

© Oxford University Press 2012

First issued as an Oxford University Press paperback, 2014.

Library of Congress Cataloging-in-Publication Data
Native claims : indigenous law against empire, 1500–1920 / edited by Saliha Belmessous.
p.   cm.
Includes bibliographical references and index.
ISBN 978-0-19-979485-0 (hardcover : alk. paper); 978-0-19-938611-6 (paperback : alk. paper)
1. Indigenous people—Legal status, laws, etc.—History.
2. Indigenous people—Claims—History. I. Belmessous, Saliha.
K3248.L36N38   2011
346.04'3208997—dc22   2011007319

CONTENTS

ACKNOWLEDGMENTS

I am deeply grateful to the Faculty of Arts and the School of Philosophical and Historical Inquiry at the University of Sydney for their financial support. I am particularly indebted to Professor Stephen Garton who took up the project so keenly.

My thanks also go to Oxford University Press for its diligent support, to Nancy Toff for her enthusiasm and confidence, to Sonia Tycko for her invaluable editorial assistance, and to the Press's anonymous readers for their comments.

Finally, I wish to thank all the contributors for their dedication to the book.

Saliha Belmessous

Native Claims

INTRODUCTION
THE PROBLEM OF INDIGENOUS
CLAIM MAKING IN COLONIAL HISTORY

Saliha Belmessous

Since the 1990s, the relationship between law and colonization has generated an enormous and dynamic scholarly literature that has appealed to readers in political and legal circles even beyond academe. Accounts of indigenous rights have been dominated by two perspectives. On the one hand, we have histories of European legal arguments regarding colonized lands.[1] We are led to believe that because these literate arguments are presented from a European perspective, they are in their very nature not amenable to indigenous cultures. On the other hand, anthropologists have, for several generations, provided accounts of indigenous claims to land based on customary law. These accounts tell us the role the claims performed within indigenous cultures. Additionally, there is a deep engagement in the present between indigenous and colonial cultures on the level of legal argument. But this, it is assumed, is something new. History and anthropology tell us little about indigenous peoples engaging in legal argument with colonizing powers prior to the World War II period and would, on the whole, lead us to believe that such engagement did not occur.[2]

The aim of this book is to bring indigenous claims to the heart of the debate over colonial property by showing that indigenous peoples extensively employed legal arguments to oppose dispossession by European colonizers from the moment colonization was launched. The story of indigenous resistance to European colonization is, of course, well known. But legal resistance has been wrongly understood to be a relatively recent phenomenon. Whether in North or South America, Africa or Australasia, indigenous peoples made claims to territory and forced Europeans to make rival claims, from the moment European expansion commenced in the fifteenth century through to the final great expansion of the nineteenth century.

There have been valuable attempts by colonial historians to go behind the European history of dispossession and consider the history of native peoples' legal resistance to the appropriation of their lands immediately following colonization.[3] These studies, important though they are, were written as individual colonial experiences, and they consequently have not aimed to reveal the range of native resistance. Taking a broader spatial and temporal perspective—which only a collective work can provide—our book shows the continuities between individual experiences separated by geographical and temporal gulfs.

The hidden legal record of indigenous claims and counterclaims confounds common assumptions about the nature of indigenous resistance. Indeed, it is generally assumed that legal argumentation concerning dispossession was a product of European culture that indigenous peoples appropriated in the twentieth century. Yet evidence presented in this book shows that native and European legal arguments could be strikingly parallel; it also shows that European arguments need to be reconsidered in the context of indigenous claims. Contrary to common perception, European justifications of colonization should be understood not as an original and originating legal discourse but, at least in part, as a form of counterclaim.

The perception that we cannot use legal concepts to discuss indigenous claims has been one of the strongest obstacles to the historical recognition of those claims. Could we, as historians, use concepts such as sovereignty and property to characterize the type of claims indigenous peoples made in the first decades following colonization? Since the "linguistic turn" in the humanities in the 1960s, '70s, and '80s, the emphasis of historical research has been upon showing subjects in their historical contexts, revealing myth, and demonstrating the historical construction of law. "Sovereignty" and "property" being European legal concepts that the Europeans themselves were constantly redefining, it might seem awkward, not to say Eurocentric and even anachronistic, to translate indigenous notions with such heavily laden concepts. The issue at stake is whether we can translate indigenous notions of land rights into a European language at a time when native peoples were not employing those concepts. Is it even helpful to characterize indigenous claims as legal?

There is ample evidence, both in the primary and secondary literature, showing that Europeans generally acknowledged that native peoples had laws; that they thought these laws were brutal is irrelevant to the present discussion. Native peoples themselves represented their societies in terms of law when their claims were translated on first contact with Europeans. They had, whether in America, Africa, or Australasia, "means to force people to act in ways they would not otherwise choose. (. . .) They remedied wrongs, through restitution or punishment, in ways that were bound by rule."[4]

Native peoples stood by these conventions and enforced them whenever possible, whether it was in relation to other native communities or with Europeans. Their claims could therefore be considered as legal. Their translation is a further problem, and the essays presented in this volume show that characterizing legal titles such as conquest and inheritance as "European" could be problematic. Many titles put forward by Europeans had comparable forms in indigenous law pointing to the permeability between legal languages. Law was a language that European and native peoples could share more easily than scholars have previously understood. In emphasizing the permeability between legal languages, we are not, however, suggesting that European law and indigenous law were easily exchangeable. Indeed, it was precisely the difference between European law and indigenous law that made translation between the systems necessary.

In translating native claims, Europeans were not just, as some scholars have suggested, simplifying their content: they were showing their ability to bring those claims to the reach of their understanding; they were able to do so because these claims had counterparts, however approximate, in the Europeans' own legal world. Different cultures coming together find it necessary to translate across the divide. This need points to the possibility of shared meanings rather than absolute cultural incommensurability.[5] Mutual understanding, as colonist Thomas Morton explained, "is commonly seene where 2 nations traffique together, the one indevouring to understand the others meaning makes the both many times speak a mixed language, as is approoved by the Natives of New England, through the coveteous desire they have, to commerce with our nation, and wee with them."[6] Cultural boundaries were porous, allowing indigenous and European peoples to translate each other's legal arguments, to draw parallels, and to understand what kind of titles they could use to make recognizable and valid claims to land. Europeans often, although not always, understood the nature of the claims put forward by their native competitors: they understood that when indigenous communities made claims to ownership (hence British insistence, for example, upon purchasing the land), they were distinct from when they made claims that resembled sovereignty: that is, when they made claims to a particular territory with delimited borders and upon which they had established the law of the land, determining, for example, who could come and live on that territory. The exercise of control over such territory is described by Europeans as "sovereignty." One question addressed in this book is whether non-Europeans perceived their claims in comparable terms.

It is not possible, even in a collective work, to catalogue the history of indigenous legal resistance to colonization, and it is not our intention to undertake such a massive task. Rather, we have delved into several moments in different colonial contexts and on different continents, from the sixteenth century to the end of the nineteenth century. Each moment was a relatively short time after first contact or predated the establishment of colonial sovereignty. The land disputes we have recovered opposed European colonizers to Tlaxcalans in sixteenth-century Mexico; the Andeans in late-sixteenth and early seventeenth-century Peru; the Powhatans in early-seventeenth-century Virginia; the Narragansetts in seventeenth-century New England; the Wabanaki, the Mohegans, and the Mashpee in northeastern North America in the eighteenth century; the Māori in nineteenth-century New Zealand; the Flinders Islanders, the Kulin, the Kaurna, the

Ngarrindjeri, the Yorta Yorta, and the Pangerang in nineteenth-century Australia; and the Lagosians in nineteenth-century Western Africa. These cases point to a common, although buried, story of legal resistance to early colonization.

Contextualism in Legal History

Recovering indigenous claims is not, as one would expect, an easy methodological task. Whereas ideologies of dispossession have been discussed largely in relation to Europeans—"this blessedly uncomplicated view" denounced by Brian Slattery twenty-five years ago—dispossession itself has prevented generations of scholars from questioning colonial narratives.[7] In focusing on the outcome of colonial ventures, namely, dispossession, scholars have overlooked the historical developments that shaped these enterprises and simplified the dynamics of relations between native peoples and Europeans. The essays in this book show that indigenous and European peoples were engaged in a continuing political conversation using legal arguments and sometimes force to advance their claims to territory. And it was not always clear, neither for the natives nor the Europeans, that the former would eventually be dispossessed by the latter.

The pitfalls of not employing a contextual methodology have also been evident in the legal histories of colonization. Legal history has too often been written to discover current legal principles in past legal practice and so anachronistically imposes present concerns on the past. History has been used to resolve postcolonial political issues and initiate or support "postcolonial campaigns of redress."[8] There have been relatively few attempts to consider indigenous claims in a historical perspective, and yet historical inquiry is necessary to explain how and why those claims were articulated.[9] Although our book is linked to concerns in the present, it attempts to understand past peoples on their own terms and does not allow present concerns to generate conclusions about the past.

The Paucity of Evidence

One of the principal obstacles the historian encounters in recovering the history of indigenous claims is the paucity of evidence. Historians have generally considered that such a history concerning the early periods of colonization was impossible to write. Legal resistance may have occurred, they concede, but no evidence has survived. These concerns were greater in particular contexts such as Australia.

Although a few cases of legal opposition are relatively well known—for example, the Mohegans in eighteenth-century New England—much of the evidence has been buried for the reason that Europeans were not willing to acknowledge rejection of their imperial ventures.[10] To shed light on those obscured sources, James C. Scott's theory of "public and hidden transcripts" is invaluable. Scott has shown that, while "public transcripts" emphasize the effectiveness of coercion, "hidden transcripts" dispute that account and reveal how weak groups are able to challenge hegemonic control.[11] Public transcripts highlighted acceptance by indigenous peoples of European expansion. The extraordinarily long list of treaties made throughout the centuries of European colonization provides an outstanding example of this public record.[12]

Only rarely was indigenous peoples' rejection of territorial dispossession brought to public light. Particular circumstances allowed such claims to become public. In seventeenth- and eighteenth-century North America, for example, colonial rivalry between France and England over Wabanaki lands provided an opportunity for native claims to be heard: while the French kept silent on native opposition to their own claims, they nonetheless happily recorded native rejection of English claims to weaken the English case for title. The records of these claims by the Wabanaki function as what Scott describes as hidden transcripts of opposition: that is, the French unwittingly recorded Wabanaki opposition to French as well as English title because the Wabanaki stated their right to their land against *all* European invaders. It is by revealing such hidden transcripts of resistance, as Scott argues, that offstage players can be brought to center stage. In this instance, the identification of these hidden transcripts helps us to discover a legal resistance that was previously believed not to exist.

In most circumstances, it is only through working contextually and digging deep into the colonial archive that it is possible to unearth the evidence for indigenous legal arguments. Jessie Mitchell and Ann Curthoys have belied common assumptions about the absence of early indigenous legal counterstrategies to the loss of Australian aboriginal land.[13] Their study shows that familiarity with well-known sources has blinded historians who either could not imagine what was in these archives or have failed to identify legal resistance even when it was perceptible in the documents they were handling. Yet a document's answer depends on the question the historian has asked.

Authorship and Ventriloquism

A further challenge for this kind of study concerns the issue of authorship. Many of the sources for indigenous legal claims rely largely, but not exclusively, on contemporary reports of European officials. In some cases, European individuals were even involved in drafting native claims and counterclaims. Already in the early-modern era, the accusation of ventriloquism was used to cast doubt on the veracity of native claims. This accusation was sometimes justified, but it was also used as a political instrument to silence indigenous challengers to European claims. When, however, indigenous authorship is not established, historians have to assess the claims keeping in mind that they could be examples of ethnological ventriloquism. Who was talking? The native speaker? The European writer? The European counsel?

Andrew Fitzmaurice has suggested that dismissing translated indigenous claims as European projections can be more problematic than working with them. There are ways to examine the authenticity of indigenous claims. Cross-examining rival colonial transcripts is the first way. Wabanaki claims, for example, are reported in both French and English archives. Evidence provided by other perspectives, particularly anthropology and archaeology, can support archival evidence.[14] Finally, indigenous peoples' oral history has also recorded some claims and brought them to light in later times.

Colonial authorities unwittingly established the authorship of some claims. For more than a decade, in late-nineteenth-century Victoria (Australia), the Kulin people wrote letters and petitions to secure the land upon which their reserve was established. The "Central Board to Watch Over the Interests of the Aborigines" believed that some Europeans were behind those claims. Accordingly, it twice employed detectives to prove that the Kulin were not the authors of their letters and petitions. Yet, what the detectives found was that the Kulin documents were authentic. Curthoys and Mitchell have also shown that assistance in framing written claims could also come from indigenous groups: for example, Kulin individuals involved in making claims to their own reserve traveled to New South Wales to assist the Yorta Yorta people in preparing further petitions.

Besides the ventriloquism of content, we face what has been described as the "ventriloquism of forms." To make their claims, indigenous peoples sometimes framed their arguments according to European legal conventions. Mark Hickford has shown how the Māori contested British claims to political authority and jurisdiction and asserted their own rights to exert that jurisdiction. This contestation was made clear during land disputes that opposed Māori to each other and during which the English and the Māori argued about the kind of evidence needed to establish a legitimate claim. A failure to accommodate Māori and English land tenure systems, combined with intra-Māori politics, led the English to believe that Māori and English concepts of land were incommensurable. Yet, in order to access territorial space for settlements, it became necessary to adapt Māori to English land tenure.

As Christopher Hilliard has shown, the Native Land Court represented one experiment established for the purpose of converting Māori land into individually owned tracts. This allotment policy obliged the Māori willing to participate in this Court's process to establish their rights to territory in order to be given shares of the land—in this instance, indigenous rights were encouraged by the colonial authority. Given the fluidity and complexity of Māori societies and their intersecting claims in land, any reform of customary tenure or its conversion to an English equivalent was fraught with difficulty. Both authors claim that colonial attempts at tenure reform necessarily rendered fixed, certain, and simple what was fluid and complex. The Court attempted to weigh arguments using Māori custom and usage (though they were distorted). Europeans tended to express land tenure as a list of sources for Māori title—conquest and occupation, for example—giving each basis the same sort of weighing, which had the effect, according to Hickford, of objectifying land as an asset away from its political and social connotations in Māori communities.[15]

Kristin Mann's analysis of nineteenth-century West Africa provides a contrasting analysis of indigenous adaptation to legal developments.[16] Her study of African strategies to contest British land claims emphasizes cultural change and reinvention rather than the distortion of indigenous claims or the ventriloquism of forms. Mann's "messy and contested history of land tenure in colonial Lagos" has brought to light the central role played by Africans in the transformation of land tenure over time. After having first initiated and conducted the development of private property rights in land before and immediately after colonization, they then reverted to indigenous practices and imposed the transformation of privately owned land to family-owned land upon the British authorities. Lagosians also used custom as a way to legitimate new types of ownership over land and slaves. The invention of what constituted Lagosian customary laws to challenge and counteract British concepts of ownership is the most intriguing aspect of Mann's essay.

Did the use of European forms force indigenous legal claims into the processes and assumptions of European legal framework in such a way that the legal battle was lost before it had begun? Before taking for granted that the forms indigenous peoples used were borrowed, it is necessary to look ethnohistorically at the documents recording their claims. Algonquian peoples, for example, used a diplomatic language based on metaphors of submission in their dealings with each other. In their representations to the English, they used the same language. That the Europeans used a comparable language in their petitions testifies to cultural parallels. We can also assume that the Algonquians' own diplomatic language may have facilitated their understanding of English legal processes. It is therefore prudent to handle carefully the language of subjecthood as it is used in petitions and not to make generalizations about indigenous submission to colonial sovereignty: that is, historians should not assume that the language employed in these petitions, which appears to be "European," is necessarily so.

Even in cases where indigenous groups submitted to the colonizing authority, relations were often more complicated than they seemed. Jovita Baber shows that indigenous use of petitions and other European legal forms can be seen as an ingenious move to advance claims. Petitions are particularly interesting documents because they were directed to the Crown. In the Spanish Empire, the Tlaxcalans used petitions strategically to appeal to the Crown when land disputes opposed them to settlers or colonial governments, and they framed their claims in response to changing imperial politics, adjusting the rhetoric throughout the sixteenth century.[17] In northeastern North America, the Narragansetts in 1644 and the Mohegans throughout the first half of the eighteenth century appealed similarly to the British Crown to oppose colonial encroachments. By asking the Crown to defend their interests and contesting settlers' respect of European rules, indigenous peoples from Mexico and New England suggested that an alliance would benefit both themselves and the Crown. If requesting royal protection implied, for the Tlaxcalans and the Mohegans, surrendering sovereignty, they nonetheless claimed autonomy and property rights over their territory. The Crown, on the other hand, valued its special relationships with the natives as this kind of alliance enabled the exercise of its royal authority as well as helped to maintain a counterbalance to settlers' power.

Whether a European counselor converted indigenous claims to European forms, or native peoples framed their claims according to European conventions, does not ultimately invalidate these claims. As New South Wales' first Attorney General (1824–1826) and long-time advocate of indigenous rights, Saxe Bannister, once observed, the suspicion of ventriloquism was a product of a European perception that indigenous peoples were legally inarticulate. Bannister had worked for three years on civil and criminal cases concerning the South African Khoikhoi, for whom he wrote letters to support their legal claims against dispossession. In translating the letter the Chief Adam Kok and nine of his councillors wrote to the Governor of the Cape of Good Hope in January 1829, Bannister explicitly addressed the problem of ventriloquism: "It may be alledged [sic] that such documents are *got up* by the friends of the native people; unquestionably those friends assist them, but the writer of these notes has had some experience of the feelings of the Hottentots, and can safely testify that those instruments are genuine in every sense." He added that, "A few points of form excepted, there are Hottentots perfectly capable of preparing them; and in January last the writer was requested by one at Bethelsdorp, to supply him with a proper form of address to the governor. He also possesses a ms. memoir written by a Griqua chief, in defence of his political life."[18]

Bannister's conclusion was that mediation, cultural permeability, or intermingling should not be used to discount indigenous voices. We would suggest that denying the validity of these claims for the reason that they had allegedly been altered reveals a failure to overcome the essentialist view of native cultures as either pure or corrupted.

European Responses

Even when authorship was contested, Europeans understood anyway that native peoples were making claims. "A claim," as James Sheehan has explained, "is neither a request nor a demand." To make a claim suggests an "appeal to some standard of justice, some sort of right" and the ability to back up these claims with the use of force.[19] Europeans were perfectly aware of these implications. They also recognized the validity of indigenous claims and responded accordingly. In the sixteenth and seventeenth centuries, Spain and Portugal negotiated their expansion in the Indian and Atlantic Oceans by adapting their methods for claiming possession to each other's claims and to the strategies of the indigenous peoples. According to Lauren Benton, Iberians emphasized the argument of possession in claiming new territories because it was a claim more easily substantiated and less easily challenged than a claim to title.[20]

A dialogue over possession and dispossession was similarly being held between the Virginia Company and the Powhatans in the early seventeenth century. Andrew Fitzmaurice's argument concerns traces of indigenous claims in early accounts of the Powhatans that were published in 1609 and 1610 to publicize the Company's right to the territory it was engaged in settling. Confronted with Powhatan legal claims, based on arguments such as custom, occupation, and conquest, the English issued counterclaims employing parallel arguments. A hundred years later, the English of New England found themselves in a similar situation. As my essay shows, powerful Wabanaki claims to their own territory in 1721 forced the government of New England to make counterclaims. Here, too, the arguments used by both peoples were parallel and testify to a shared legal understanding of what a title was.[21]

Sovereignty and Property Rights

Indigenous and European claims can be difficult to investigate as they mixed, and sometimes confused, claims to sovereignty with claims to property rights. Whereas some peoples were exclusively concerned with property (the Tlaxcalans, for example), others were also making claims for their own absolute political autonomy or sovereignty, and yet others again moved between these claims. Rolena Adorno has shown that after having failed to establish his family property rights on ancestral lands against another native group, the Quechua Felipe Guaman Poma de Ayala wrote a legal chronicle of Spanish conquest of Peru, addressed to the Spanish king, in which he rejected Spanish title. According to Guaman Poma, the Spanish could not own Peru by right of conquest as they had not conquered it. He then called for the restoration of Andean sovereignty "as an act of Christian restitution."[22]

There is a crucial difference, therefore, between the indigenous legal claims uncovered in this study and the post–World War II claims that have previously been the focus of scholarly attention. Largely out of the necessity of dealing with the fait accompli, which is the colonial state, modern indigenous legal claims have been mainly (although not exclusively—there are important exceptions) focused on questions of property in land rather than sovereignty. By contrast, the indigenous legal claims made in the generations after first contact concerned both land and sovereignty.

Whereas Europeans and natives generally agreed that territory acquired by conquest fell under the sovereignty of the conqueror, the status of territories acquired by cession, purchase, possession, or occupation remains unclear. Historians have asserted that sovereignty did not carry property rights in the early European law of nations.[23] Nineteenth-century civil lawyer Charles Salomon argued, on the other hand, that early-modern Europeans did not always distinguish the notion of sovereignty from the idea of property. Through his commissioned agents, the King acquired, according to Salomon, the full sovereignty of the territories they "discovered," that is, that they explored. The Crown usually kept the sovereign title to those lands and granted, as a reward, the property rights to its agents.[24] Lauren Benton maintains that, in the sixteenth and seventeenth centuries, when indigenous polities ceded the right to construct trading posts and accepted European jurisdiction over settlers, they did not cede sovereignty—a fact that Europeans were aware of.[25] Allowing the construction of trading posts or even the settlement of Europeans did not limit indigenous authority on territory that could be, as in northeastern America, for example, physically marked with natural and artificial signs such as painted posts, marked trees, and stone heaps.[26]

Yet, Europeans claimed that they had acquired territorial sovereignty as well as property rights.[27] Such presumption could, as Benton has explained in this volume, be justified by the status of European agents. These agents were either Crown appointees or employees of trading companies, which were "acting as states in the sense that they were authorized by charters to make war and peace, acquire territory, and exercise legal authority over subordinates and subjects of the crown."[28] Endorsed with this kind of authority, these agents may have assumed that they could pretend to full sovereignty over the territories they were acquiring even though they recognized that indigenous peoples were constituted in polities and that no cession of sovereignty had taken place. By the nineteenth century, stadial evolutionary models, which informed anthropology, presented native peoples as savages or barbarians unable to conceive of land as a sovereign territory. Stadial theory informed policies that ignored native rights and confiscated both sovereignty and ownership over newly explored territories. Australia was one of the most striking examples of that colonial ideology. The same stadial theory, combined with international law, provided, on the other hand, the theoretical background that allowed the British to acknowledge Māori sovereignty in the first years of their settlement.[29]

The British used a variety of legal forms to acquire indigenous territories that changed in different contexts. The annexation of the kingdom of Lagos to Britain in 1861 was achieved by forcing the king's hand and formalized by a treaty of cession. Treaties of (forced) cession would be used throughout the Pacific in the nineteenth century.[30] In

Lagos, the cession did not proceed smoothly. As Kristin Mann has shown, a number of eminent chiefs contested the transfer of sovereignty and property within months of the signature of the treaty, arguing that they, and not the king, owned Lagos. The chiefs declared that the king owned what had been granted to him and his family and he could not, consequently, have ceded all of Lagos' land. The king himself supported the chiefs' claims. Yet, Mann observes, the Lagosian kingship had established its jurisdiction over land at least by the first half of the nineteenth century and no longer needed the approval of the chieftaincy families to grant land to outsiders. While the Lagosians invented a customary law to challenge the forced cession, the British reacted by creating a legal argument superseding that law, and ultimately validating the cession. They claimed that the king had nonetheless a "national proprietary right" over Lagos that enabled him to alienate it.

Colonial History Reconsidered

The existence of indigenous legal claims raises some significant questions for our understanding of colonial and global history. First is the question of violence. Historians have focused on indigenous peoples' physical resistance and presented frontier violence as their main form of resistance. While partially correct, this account has failed to reveal how violence worked with law in contests over dispossession. Violence was an important part of indigenous resistance, but it was also used to back up claims. Studies in this volume of the Powhatan and Wabanaki claims show that both northeastern North American peoples used force to compel the English and the French to recognize their claims. The capacity to support claims with the use of force underlined the strength of indigenous positions. It also shows that Europeans and natives shared an understanding of what a sovereign claim was, that is, "a blend of legitimacy and efficacy, legality and force."[31]

Second is the question of the nature of a legal argument. Before reading the following essays, one has to bear in mind that law was not something that just happened in courts. Indigenous peoples sometimes made legal representations before European tribunals (claims tended then to focus upon questions of property rather than disputing sovereignty). The bulk of the recovered indigenous claims show, however, that claims were often not made to any formal institution whatsoever. Indigenous peoples were independent, self-governing political groups living on a defined territory, and they entered into negotiation with Europeans as nation to nation. They made representations orally and in writing, through letters, petitions, and statements recorded by colonial authorities and by colonial rivals. Claims were made to a wide range of colonial representatives, including governors, military officers, administrators, and priests. The Iroquois, for example, officially declared their sovereignty in 1686 before the French colonial authorities, who called for a notary to record that statement. As a French witness then observed:

> We have to assume that the Iroquois do not accept any master, And that although the French carried the arms of France in their territory before and after the English carried those of England, yet they [the Iroquois] recognise no domination; It is what they repeated and wanted to establish twice in two meetings they held in Montreal the summer of this year one thousand six hundred eighty six in the presence of Monseigneur de Laval, ex-bishop of Quebec, Monsieur the governor, and Monsieur the intendant; to perpetually leave marks of their independence from the English and the French, they have established a proper act and written down their savage numbers and hieroglyphs.[32]

A third matter raised by the existence of these legal claims is the question of the audience: what was the forum or judge to which these indigenous peoples appealed? The extraordinary conclusion must be that they were recognizing a system of conventions outside civil society, which contemporary Europeans described as the law of nations and later as international law. Speaking of these indigenous peoples employing the law of nations or international law would, of course, be wildly anachronistic given that those concepts were closely tied to the development of the modern European state system. We could more appropriately understand the tribunal to which these peoples were appealing by the terms that have been used by non-English-speaking European peoples to describe law outside of civil society, for example, the ancient Roman *ius gentium*, the French *droit des gens*, or what we might translate as the "law of peoples." It is a moot point whether such conventions exist as laws given that they lack the sanction of sovereign authority. The more important point is that various peoples, including Europeans, have felt the need to employ the concept of laws that apply between peoples. Given that these peoples were completely separated in time and space, we must ask the question as to whether all human societies have felt the need for a concept of laws that apply between different peoples just as all human societies have developed different concepts of law.

Since the 1990s, a series of studies has represented international law as profoundly Eurocentric, a product of Western political thought that is biased by its history toward the interests of the West.[33] There is unquestionably some truth in this critique if we frame the question in terms of "international law" (although we might object that it takes an unnecessarily pessimistic view of the malleability of cultural tools). We need, however, to look at the larger sense of the *droit des gens*, or the law of peoples, which has been employed in relations between European and non-European peoples over the past five centuries of European expansion. We then discover that the conventions or laws employed outside sovereignty could only be understood to be biased toward Europeans if we systematically exclude the voices of colonized peoples when *they* engaged with a law of peoples, when they made their own representations to this larger tribunal. The studies that have sought to reveal the bias of international law have, ironically, only been able to develop their argument by repeating precisely the exclusion of non-European peoples they decry. Our book will expand our concept of what might constitute a law of peoples, and it will do so by bringing the understandings of indigenous peoples into that concept as well as by recovering the history of how those understandings were employed.

Significance for Indigenous Rights

The significance of our study for indigenous rights claims cannot be underestimated. Frontier histories and anthropological studies have been unable to bring the extent of indigenous resistance to dispossession to light. Indigenous legal arguments are believed to be a phenomenon of contemporary rights claims.[34] Our book shows that colonization was opposed not only by force but also by ideas, often by ideas that were easily translated into European discourse, ideas that drew from European discourse, or ideas that were generated precisely from cross-cultural contacts. The histories written here will change our understanding of the legal character of indigenous rights claims. These claims, we suggest, are not simply a contemporary response to political exigencies making prudential use of the conventions of the colonial state. Rather, contemporary rights arguments have a foundation in native legal understandings that date from before colonization itself. In debates over indigenous rights, many scholars and activists have questioned whether the Western legal instruments that were employed so effectively to dispossess indigenous peoples are not tainted. Can those same legal conventions be used now to deliberate objectively over the future of indigenous rights?[35] Our study reveals the terrible mistake that could be made in assuming that legal debate at the time of conquest was conducted in exclusively Western terms. Indeed, as we have shown, the content of colonial justifications can be seen as, at least in part, a response to indigenous legal claims. We have shown that when indigenous peoples address questions of dispossession, they are drawing upon indigenous legal traditions that were used for the same purpose from the moment colonization began.

In the history of legal argument regarding indigenous rights, the people most concerned by the debate have been kept offstage. Our study uses history to transform our understanding of the nature of the legal conflict regarding indigenous peoples. It shows that the struggle for reconciling indigenous peoples with settler societies can only be met through the inclusion of a legal voice that has often been present but not heard. Importantly, we have placed that struggle over indigenous rights in a global context showing that the moral force of indigenous legal arguments is stronger for having been shared by a wide spectrum of colonized peoples from the inception of European conquests. The fact that there is an extensive and profound history of such claims has great bearing on contemporary rights claims and changes the kind of evidence that can be presented to the courts of former settler societies.

NOTES

1. James Tully, *A Discourse on Property: John Locke and His Adversaries* (Cambridge: Cambridge University Press, 1980); Anthony Pagden, *The Fall of Natural Man: The American Indian and the Origins of Comparative Ethnology* (Cambridge: Cambridge University Press, 1982); Henry Reynolds, *The Law of the Land* (Ringwood, Vic.: Penguin, 1987); Robert A. Williams, *The American Indian in Western Legal Thought: The Discourses of Conquest* (New York: Oxford University Press, 1990); Barbara Arneil, *John Locke and America: The Defence of English Colonialism* (New York: Oxford University Press, 1996); P. G. McHugh, *Aboriginal Societies and the Common Law* (Oxford: Oxford University Press, 2004); Ken MacMillan, *Sovereignty and Possession in the English New World* (New York: Cambridge University Press, 2006); Andrew Fitzmaurice, "A genealogy of terra nullius," *Australian Historical Studies* 129 (2007): 1–15. Indigenous scholars Robert J. Miller, Jacinta Ruru, Larissa Behrendt, and Tracey Lindberg have similarly focused on European legal discourses and ignored indigenous claims notwithstanding that they provide a contemporary indigenous perspective on the study of European arguments: see their *Discovering Indigenous Lands: The Doctrine of Discovery in the English Colonies* (New York: Oxford University Press, 2010).
2. See, for example, McHugh, *Aboriginal Societies and the Common Law.*
3. See William Wicken, *Mi'kmaq Treaties on Trial: History, Land, and Donald Marshall Junior* (Toronto: University of Toronto Press, 2002); Bain Attwood, *Rights for Aborigines* (Sydney: Allen & Unwin, 2003); Rolena Adorno, *The Polemics of Possession in Spanish American Narrative* (New Haven, Conn.: Yale University Press, 2007); Kristin Mann, *Slavery and the Birth of an African City: Lagos, 1760–1900* (Bloomington: University of Indiana Press, 2007); and Brian Owensby, *Empire of Law and Indian Justice in Colonial Mexico* (Stanford: Stanford University Press, 2008).
4. Katherine Hermes, "Law of Native Americans, to 1815," in Christopher Tomlins and Michael Grossberg, eds., *Cambridge History of Law in America* (New York: Cambridge University Press, 2008), 33.
5. On the significance of dialogue in colonial relations, see the seminal work of Eugene F. Irschick, *Dialogue and History: Constructing South India, 1795–1895* (Berkeley: University of California Press, 1994); on the translation of political ideas between European and non-European peoples, see Anthony Parel and Ronald C. Keith, *Comparative Political Philosophy: Studies under the Upas Tree* (New Delhi–Newbury Park, Calif.: Sage, 1992); Fred Reinhard Dallmayr, *Dialogue among Civilizations: Some Exemplary Voices* (New York: Palgrave Macmillan, 2002); and Takashi Shogimen and Cary J. Nederman, eds., *Western Political Thought in Dialogue with Asia* (Lanham, MD: Lexington Books, c2009).
6. Thomas Morton, *New English Canaan* (1639; reprinted, New York: American Library Association, 1963), 17, cited in Peter S. Leavenworth, "'The Best Title That Indians Can Claime': Native Agency and Consent in the Transferal of Penacook-Pawtucket Land in the Seventeenth Century," *The New England Quarterly* 72, 2 (June 1999), 285.

7. Brian Slattery, "The hidden constitution: Aboriginal rights in Canada," *The American Journal of Comparative Law* 32, no. 2 (Spring 1984), 363.

8. Bain Attwood, "The Law of the Land or the Law of the Land?: History, law and narrative in a settler society," *History Compass* 2 (2004): 1–30; Damen Ward, "A means and measure of civilisation: Colonial authorities and indigenous law in Australasia," *History Compass* 1 (2003); McHugh, *Aboriginal Societies and the Common Law*; Alan Lester, "Review of Merete Falck Borch. Conciliation-Compulsion-Conversion (Amsterdam and New York: Rodopi, 2004)," *H-HistGeog, H-Net Reviews in the Humanities and Social Sciences*, 2005, http://www.h-net.org/reviews/showrev.php?id=10924

9. The exceptions include Brian Slattery's *The Land Rights of Indigenous Canadian Peoples* (Saskatoon: University of Saskatchewan Native Law Centre, 1979), Christopher Vecsey and William A. Starna's *Iroquois Land Claims* (Syracuse, NY: Syracuse University Press, 1988), Kent McNeil's *Common Law Aboriginal Title* (Oxford: Clarendon Press, 1989), and Paul Tennant's *Aboriginal Peoples and Politics* (Vancouver: University of British Columbia Press, 1990).

10. On the Mohegans, see Mark Walters, "Mohegan Indians v. Connecticut (1705–1773) and the legal status of Aboriginal customary laws and government in British North America," *Osgoode Hall Law Journal* 33 (1995); and Craig Yirush, *Settlers, Liberty, and Empire: The Roots of Early American Political Theory, 1675–1775* (Cambridge, Mass.: Cambridge University Press, 2011), chapter 4.

11. James C. Scott, *Domination and the Arts of Resistance: Hidden Transcripts* (New Haven, Conn.: Yale University Press, 1992)—not all the indigenous peoples considered here are weak groups: the Powhatans, for example, were much stronger than the English.

12. A catalogue of treaties can be found in M.F. Lindley, *The Acquisition and Government of Backward Territory in International Law* (London: Longmans, 1926).

13. Ann Curthoys and Jessie Mitchell, "Bring this paper to the good governor."

14. Andrew Fitzmaurice, "Powhatan Legal Claims."

15. Mark Hickford, "Framing and Reframing the Agōn: Contesting Narratives and Counter-Narratives on Māori Property Rights and Political Constitutionalism, 1840–1861" and Christopher Hilliard, "The Native Land Court: Making Property in Nineteenth-Century New Zealand."

16. Kristin Mann, "African and European Initiatives in the Development of Land Tenure in Colonial Lagos (West Africa), 1840–1920."

17. R. Jovita Baber, "Law, Land and Legal Rhetoric in Colonial New Spain: A Look at The Changing Rhetoric of Indigenous Americans in the Sixteenth Century."

18. Saxe Bannister, *Humane policy; or Justice to the Aborigines of New Settlements (London, 1830)*, 72–73.

19. James Sheehan, "The problem of sovereignty in European history," *American Historical Review* 111, no. 1 (Feb. 2006), 3–4.

20. Lauren Benton, "Possessing Empire: Iberian Claims and Interpolity Law."

21. Saliha Belmessous, "Wabanaki versus French and English claims in north-eastern North America c. 1715."

22. Rolena Adorno, "Court and Chronicle: A Native Andean's Engagement with Spanish Colonial Law."

23. Anthony Pagden, "Law, colonization, legitimation, and the European background" in Michael Grossberg and Christopher Tomlins, eds., *The Cambridge History of Law in America, vol. 1: Early America (1580–1815)* (New York: Cambridge University Press, 2008), 24.

24. Charles Salomon, *L' Occupation des territoires sans maître: Étude de droit international* (Paris: A. Giard, 1889), 47, 76–78.

25. See Benton, "Possessing Empire: Iberian Claims and Interpolity Law."

26. Nancy Shoemaker, *A Strange Likeness: Becoming Red and White in Eighteenth-Century North America* (New York: Oxford University Press, 2004, 2006), 26.

27. Shoemaker, *Strange Likeness*, 22.

28. Benton, "Possessing Empire."

29. See Mark Hickford, " 'Decidedly the most interesting savages on the globe': An approach to the intellectual history of Māori property rights, 1837–53," *History of Political Thought* 27, no. 1 (spring 2006): 122–167.

30. See, for example, the deed of cession of the Fiji islands to the British Crown in October 1874 in http://www.vanuatu.usp.ac.fj/library/Paclaw/Fiji/DEED%20OF%20CESSION%20%20 FIJI.htm; and the deed of cession of the Rotuma island in November 1879 in http://www.paclii.org/fj/legis/fj-uk_act/docor1879211/

31. Sheehan, "The problem of sovereignty in European history," 4, 6.

32. Archives Nationales (Paris), Archives des Colonies, C^{11E}, vol. 11, fol. 15 (my translation). This letter was written in 1688 by an anonymous churchman, probably a Jesuit, and it was later signed in 1712 by Governor General Philippe de Rigaud de Vaudreuil and Intendant Michel Bégon. See also Francis Jennings, ed., *The History and Culture of Iroquois Diplomacy* (Syracuse: Syracuse University Press, 1985), 161.

33. Martti Koskenniemi, *The Gentle Civilizer of Nations: The Rise and Fall of International Law, 1870–1960* (Cambridge: Cambridge University Press, 2001); Anthony Anghie, *Imperialism, Sovereignty, and the Making of International Law* (Cambridge: Cambridge University Press, 2004).

34. See, for example, McHugh, *Aboriginal Societies and the Common Law*, 8–15.

35. Mick Dodson, "From 'Lore' to 'Law': Indigenous Rights and Australian Legal Systems," *Aboriginal Law Bulletin* 3, 72 (Feb. 1995): 2; Attwood, "The Law of the Land or the Law of the Land."

1

POSSESSING EMPIRE
IBERIAN CLAIMS AND INTERPOLITY LAW

Lauren Benton

Historians have recently taken up with renewed interest the question of the influence of Roman texts, comparisons, and law on the strategies of European powers in asserting, describing, and defending overseas claims in the early centuries of European expansion. This project includes analysis of Europeans' creative efforts to identify parallels between the Roman Empire and European overseas empires.[1] It encompasses debates about the degree to which Europeans applied Roman legal concepts in asserting rights to control colonial territories.[2] And it comprises study of an early-modern turn toward classical writings as sources of "international" law—replacing references to papal authority—in legal frameworks for interimperial relations.[3] The project of tracing Roman legal references in discourse about empire has helped to correct some earlier misconceptions, such as the notion that European powers established claims in idiosyncratic ways that were unintelligible across polities.[4] And the perspective helpfully calls attention to the ways in which addressing the problem of empire prompted European writers to regard sovereignty as divisible.[5]

This multistranded project should be extended to encompass the fluid legal politics of empire. Like other kinds of law, Roman law represented a resource rather than a script for European imperial agents, who constructed legal arguments creatively and flexibly, responding to particular conditions of intraimperial politics, patterns of interimperial rivalry, and perceptions of indigenous people's strategies.[6] An investigation of the legal understandings that informed this process can be combined with study of the dynamics of particular contexts, disputes, and encounters. The approach reveals a field of interpolity law that was both broader than and different from early "international" law as represented in metropolitan legal tracts.[7]

This chapter examines discourses and practices of imperial claims making in the long sixteenth and seventeenth centuries. It explores in particular the importance of both direct and indirect references to possession as a concept of Roman law. Possession has received less attention from scholars of empire than has the Roman legal concept of occupation, a mode of acquiring *res nullius* (things without owners).[8]

Because possession was a doctrine with Roman roots that had special appeal to imperial agents engaged in bilateral competition over the acquisition of empires, it featured
prominently in both diplomatic exchanges and impromptu actions by imperial agents
seeking to lay the foundation for claims. Such actions responded to indigenous strategies and other local conditions while also giving shape to loose conventions for establishing the legality of imperial rule. Indigenous actors sometimes opposed European
claims but also manipulated the symbolic acts associated with possession to pursue
their own goals.

This perspective suggests a particular revision to standard narratives of early "international" law: a reconsideration of the nature and influence of Iberian legal pronouncements and practices. At the same time that historians have exaggerated the precision of
references to Roman law in imperial claims, they have tended to agree that reliance on
Roman law formed part of a broader strategy for other powers wishing to challenge
Iberian hegemony by questioning the role of papal authority within early "international" law. Yet as Iberians supplemented references to papal authority with claims to
possession deeply influenced by Roman civil law, their actions had the effect of urging
European and non-European rivals to adopt a similar mix of strategies. The result was
a striking continuity in arguments about possession over several centuries, alongside
variations defined by different political contexts.

Possession in Law

Much of the debate about the influence of Roman law on early European imperial
strategies has focused on assessments of the degree to which European claims making
referenced the Roman doctrine of *res nullius* (things without owners). One group of
historians has argued that the concept was a central and even routine element of imperial claims, particularly in the context of English and French challenges to Iberian
hegemony. Other scholars assert that Europeans relied more often on different rationales for empire and that evidence of the marginal importance of *res nullius* and occupation can be found in actions and pronouncements showing the explicit recognition
by Europeans of the sovereignty of indigenous polities and peoples. In much of this
debate, the term *res nullius* stands in for something more diffuse and flexible: a legal
orientation and the combination, not always systematic, of a diverse set of practices.
That is, while *res nullius* is a concept clearly found in the Roman law, imperial agents in
making claims did not begin by referencing (or not) a doctrine of *res nullius*; they
began by amassing evidence, some of which might be used to support a narrative about
the acquisition of empire through occupation—a mode of acquisition for things without owners in the Roman law of property—and some of which might be put to other,
equally valuable, legal purposes.[9]

This formulation makes it possible to see that Europeans were often not seeking to establish occupation but instead aiming simply to argue persuasively for *possession*, which in Roman law was based on fact rather than entitlement, potentially leading to ownership (*dominium*) by way of *usucapio*.[10] In this mode of acquisition, a thing had to have been in uninterrupted possession by the claimant for some time, and it had to have been acquired in good faith. Possession had certain features that made it especially attractive in interimperial conflicts. In seeking to support a claim to possession rather than title through occupation, imperial powers were able to focus on presenting *better* evidence in support of title than that offered by another. This feature made the claim especially useful to imperial agents in situations in which they faced specific imperial rivals: for example, Spanish and Portuguese agents in competition with one another, or French, Dutch, or English agents refuting the claims of an Iberian power.

Possession also appealed to imperial agents because it was a claim that could be more easily evaluated than a claim to title. A party argued for possession in response to a counterclaim by another party, and the merits of an argument for possession could be assessed without investigating the nature of the way something had been acquired. The legitimacy of acquisition was relevant only when a specific rival was arguing that a thing had been taken by force or stealth *from that rival* rather than from some third party. In the case of imperial territories, their seizure from indigenous peoples would have been irrelevant to a contest over possession by competing empires.

At the same time, however, it was possible to imagine a European and a non-European polity as rivals in a dispute over possession. There is evidence that in some cases European agents paid close attention to competing claims to possession by indigenous peoples.[11] To do so would not have precluded them from comparing their case for possession to claims by a European rival in another context. Making arguments about possession also did not prevent European agents from asserting that a voluntary transfer of sovereignty had already taken place. Whereas close adherence to Roman law would have led to the conclusion that a formal cession of sovereignty trumped a claim based on possession, the arguments were frequently combined as a matter of strategy.

Juxtaposing the two arguments—possession and the cession of sovereignty—also flowed logically from actions on the ground. Many such acts, especially those designed to demonstrate the political subordination of local inhabitants, were symbolically elastic. As European agents exercised jurisdiction—for example, by treating individual indigenous inhabitants as criminal defendants—they established locals' status as vassals. The same acts demonstrated that local institutions had been constituted, indicating the foundation of settlements that in turn could serve as markers of possession. The creative attachment of different legal significance to the same acts explains, for example, the royal instructions carried by Juan Díaz de Solís on an expedition of reconnaissance and settlement in the Rio de la Plata region in the early sixteenth century. Solís was ordered to take possession of new lands by making a show of legal authority: "[Y]ou shall make a gallows there, and have somebody bring a complaint before you, and as our captain and judge you shall pronounce upon and determine it, so that, in all you shall take the said possession."[12]

Such versatility, combined with a persistent referencing of signs of possession, cut across European empires. Placing markers, founding rudimentary forts or settlements, making maps, raising standards, staging trials or executions, awarding grants, recording displays of authority, or enacting "turf and twig" rituals—these and other ceremonies have been recorded for agents in all the early-modern overseas European empires. It becomes possible to see European strategies in a new light by relaxing the assumption that claims were presented in ways that closely followed Roman legal sources and instead recognizing the widespread influence of imprecise understandings of Roman law. Possession in addition to occupation emerges as an important focus of interimperial discourse; acts of possession, together with accounts of those acts, appear as elements shaping practices of interpolity law. The approach challenges the view that Iberian claims were mainly defined by their relation to papal authority.

Possession and the Treaty of Tordesillas

The 1494 Treaty of Tordesillas, which defined Portuguese and Spanish spheres on either side of a line running between the poles at a distance of 370 leagues from the Cape Verde Islands, followed a series of papal bulls on the division of territories between the Iberian crowns. The document did not mark a high point of the workings of Christendom as a transnational legal order presided over by the pope; instead, it helped to prepare the way for the end of universal papal authority. The treaty represented a peace pact and not a ruling over Iberian powers.[13] It specifically asked that in future the pope "order his bulls in regard to it" and that he align future interventions with "the tenor of this agreement."[14]

Despite its intent of settling questions of Iberian rivalry over overseas possessions, references to the treaty framed a continuation of jockeying over claims. Its indeterminacy flowed from two conditions. The first was legal. The accord strengthened the prerogatives of sovereigns to act unilaterally by legitimizing actions taken without papal approval to oppose a threat by infidels.[15] At the same time, the treaty awarded something short of full title to both Iberian powers in their respective spheres. The treaty announced that "both islands and mainlands, found and discovered already, or to be found and discovered hereafter, by the said King of [Portugal or Spain], and by his vessels on this side of the said line . . . shall belong to, and remain in the possession of, and pertain forever to, the said King [of Portugal or Spain] and his successors." Such language opened the door to future wrangling by recognizing that ownership was attached only to lands that had been or would be "discovered" by the crown's agents and by indicating that such lands would "remain in the possession" of the relevant power. That is, the right bestowed was a right to the fruits of discovery and possession, or, as the 1506 bull confirming the treaty outlined, "the right to navigate the said sea within certain specified limits and seek out and take possession of newly discovered lands."[16] In addition, the treaty stipulated that if agents of the other power took possession of lands within the other's sphere, then the possessors would be obliged to turn the territory over to the crown that held sway on that side of the line.

Together, these provisions, while intended to strengthen the agreement, called on sponsors to show that their agents had performed ceremonies and other symbolic acts to claim discovery and establish possession. They also allowed for at least the possibility that lands outside the demarcated zones might be claimed in the same way and held for some time, though not indefinitely. Read carefully, the terms of the treaty awarded the Iberian powers spheres of influence in which they could acquire empires to the exclusion of others, and this set of rights was different in subtle but important ways from the recognition of sovereignty.[17] The push and pull over early claims necessarily focused on what one historian has called a "politics of facts on the ground."[18] It was a politics in which symbolic acts clearly mattered and in which it was both possible and desirable to mix arguments about locals' consent to a transfer of sovereignty; conquest based on evangelical aims and papal authorization; and occupation or possession, based on a range of evidence including maps, markers, navigational knowledge, fortification, and settlement.

The Treaty of Tordesillas did not alter—but in fact was written to accommodate— long-standing practices of marking possession. The Portuguese routinely had laid the groundwork for claims in the Atlantic by erecting *padrões*, vertical markers usually made of stone, at strategic points such as in estuaries or at prominent points along rivers. Both Spaniards and Portuguese recorded acts and pronouncements interpreted to show that locals had declared themselves as vassals of the distant crowns. The Spanish *Requerimiento*, the document read before often uncomprehending Indian audiences in the sixteenth century New World to present them with an ultimatum to bow to the authority of Christian Spaniards or be subject to attack and servitude, belonged to a wider array of practices designed to signal locals' acceptance of their new status as subjects of Catholic sovereigns. In part because the ability to locate discoveries on maps was viewed as fundamental to completing claims of discovery and possession,

Spanish and Portuguese crowns competed for the service of skilled pilots.[19] Both governments also regularly recorded acts designed to indicate that locals had recognized crown authority. The founding of municipalities, a routine and important early step in establishing dominion in the Spanish empire, often served to support claims to possession and was always potentially more than a move to consolidate authority and patronage.

Iberians built on their experience with elements of the Roman law of private property embedded in peninsular sources and practices. Unlike English legal culture, in which influences of Roman law were sustained through disparate and sometimes indirect means, including university training, canon law, and shrinking civil law jurisdictions, key elements of Roman law were written into the core documents of Iberian jurisprudence and, perhaps more importantly, in locally enforced land law.[20] In Portugal, the *Ordenações Afonsinas* in 1446 completed the reception of Roman law; mixing Roman with other legal sources, the *Ordenações* adopted the classical Roman category of the law of things as the basis for one of its books.[21] This move followed the incorporation of Roman law in the 1375 *lei das sesmarias,* which was intended to encourage agricultural production. Based on the Roman law contracts of emphyteusis, *sesmarias* were grants to land for three lifetimes. They required demonstration that the land was being cultivated. The institution moved with the Portuguese into the Atlantic islands and later to Brazil, where it became less associated with small cultivators, as in Portugal, and more with large holdings.[22] The requirement of cultivation would have helped to spread familiarity with the notion that rights to land depended on a demonstration of settlement or use. Similarly, Spaniards were very familiar with a private law doctrine of possession through the *Siete Partidas*, the thirteenth-century law code adopted in Castile, which relied heavily on Roman law sources. Both the *Siete Partidas* and the *Ordenações Afonsinas* established Roman law as a secondary source of law to be consulted if and when these codes or other royal sources were silent on legal questions. Through the *Siete Partidas,* elements of the Roman law of the acquisition of private property moved directly into the land law of the empire. Ritual *actos de posesión* (acts of possession) were routinely used by both Spaniards and Indians to announce claims in land that might then be further supported or challenged through documentation and evidence of continuous occupation and productive use.[23]

Familiarity with the Roman law of private property did not, of course, translate into a uniform application of public law procedures constructed by analogy. But this direct experience of practices based on Roman law informed flexible strategies for marking and defending broader claims based on possession. Particularly before the threat of incursions by English, French, and Dutch rivals in Iberian imperial spheres gathered strength, the situation of two powers vying for control of trade and territory was conducive to disputes centered around the question of which power could present better evidence in support of claims. This strategy did not negate arguments based on the peaceful acquisition of sovereignty, the right of conquest deriving from religious authorization, or ownership according to treaty provisions. Rather than characterize Iberian strategies of possession as privileging one or another set of arguments, historical analysis should clarify the combination of rationales that arose in response to different local conditions. The relative strength of indigenous communities was one important factor in shaping claims since at times it ruptured the illusion of a peaceful transfer of sovereignty or encouraged a reliance on physical markers of possession. The stakes of Portuguese and Spanish sponsors in contested regions, and the tensions among intraimperial agents, also mattered. In all cases, actors learned quickly to advance their own interests by repeating elements from a widely recognized symbolic vocabulary with a loose relation to Roman legal doctrine.

Possessing the Moluccas "by Common Sense or Common Law"

From their earliest incursions into the Indian Ocean, Iberians adapted strategies for claiming possession to local conditions and the strategies of indigenous people. On Vasco da Gama's voyage, a transition occurred from the usual ritual construction of *padrões* on the southern African coast to an unsystematic toggling between militarism and diplomacy in the cosmopolitan trading ports of East Africa and India. At one stopping place in southeastern Africa, locals seem to arrive on cue to challenge the significance that the Portuguese might want to assign to the recently erected *padrão*:

> Whilst taking in water in this bay of Sam Brás, on a Wednesday, we erected a cross and a pillar. The cross was made out of a mizzen-mast, and very high. On the following Thursday, when about to set sail, we saw about ten or twelve Negroes, who demolished both the cross and the pillar.[24]

As the Portuguese voyaged up the East African coast, the captains grew increasingly wary of encounters; far from setting out for shore to raise *padrões,* they waited for ships to approach them and insisted on taking hostages before landing. In Calicut, where the Portuguese found the ruler disdainful of their mission to "discover," Gama was reduced to asking local notables who had come aboard his ship to carry a *padrão* on shore and place it there for him.[25]

    The Portuguese willingness to recognize and adapt to the power of local sovereigns did not end their attachment to the discourse of discovery and possession. Vasco da

Gama's plea with the Calicut men to erect a *padrão* for him was not a mere afterthought or, because performed without the proper ceremony and local attention, an empty gesture. The act was not directed at locals; it would be described to an audience at home. Discovery and possession were not claims to be abandoned lightly. They retained their significance in diplomacy with other empires and, as a consequence, preserved a high value in communicating the achievements of imperial agents to sponsors at home. Characterizations of Iberian tactics of establishing empire through claims to the control of people overstate the typicality of those strategies.[26] In both diplomatic circles and imperial practice, legal pronouncements referred routinely to possession.

The Spanish and Portuguese dispute over the Moluccas in the early sixteenth century shows both the importance of possession in diplomatic exchanges and the difficulties of tying claims to the facts on the ground. The Portuguese reached the Moluccas, the islands that were the main source of cloves and nutmeg entering the spice trade, in 1512. Spanish interest in the Moluccas was the driving force behind Magellan's voyage of 1518. In dispute was whether the islands fell to the east or west of the line indicated in the Treaty of Tordesillas if extended to the other hemisphere. The Spanish claim that the Moluccas fell within the Spanish sphere was resisted by the Portuguese, leading to a meeting in 1524 at sites alternating between the Spanish town of Badajoz and the Portuguese town of Elvas.

As other historians have noted, the Badajoz-Elvas meeting provides a window through which to observe the political power of collecting and manipulating geographic information.[27] Leading up to the Moluccas dispute, the Portuguese had been concerned with using and even misrepresenting geographic knowledge to protect their rights under the Treaty of Tordesillas to control trade and settlement in the South Atlantic and Arabian Seas. The Portuguese exaggerated the distance from the Cape of Good Hope to India in order to secure its place within their sphere. The Portuguese crown insisted, too, that the starting point for measuring the 370 leagues indicated in the Treaty of Tordesillas into the Atlantic should be the westernmost island in the Cape Verde archipelago, thus pushing the Portuguese sphere further to the west to encompass more of Brazil. The Portuguese drew on a larger group of experienced pilots and expert cosmographers, though the Spanish crown had for some time been engaged in luring such men into its service. Spain prepared to yield to the earlier Portuguese position on the starting place for determining the location of the Treaty of Tordesillas demarcation line in order to improve the chances that the Moluccas would fall within the Spanish sphere. Neither side had accurate information about—or the ability to measure—where the line would fall in the Indian Ocean. The meeting is often recorded as a deadlock, with a slight tactical advantage falling to the Spaniards, who were seeking to halt the momentum of a more organized and longer-operating Portuguese empire in the east.[28]

It is important not to miss the legal dimensions of the meeting. In the agreement to hold the conference at Badajoz and Elvas, the two sides stipulated that each crown would appoint three cosmographers, three pilots, and three mariners to determine the location of the line of demarcation. It was also made clear that the law would serve as the medium for evaluating geographic arguments, with a ruling "rendered as a judgment by competent judges." Appointees with cartographic and geographic expertise would take "a solemn oath . . . in the form prescribed by law and before two notaries." Each side would appoint three lawyers (*letrados*) to "inquire into the possession of Molucca," and the lawyers would review "proofs, documents, treaties, witnesses . . . doing everything that seems necessary for making the said declaration, just as they would do in court."[29]

Given the inability of either side to fix the location of the line of demarcation, the negotiations focused more on the question of possession. Since meeting with Portuguese representatives in Valladolid in 1523, the Spanish had been claiming possession based on the recognition by island locals of Spanish overlordship. The position was laid out in the king's instructions to his ambassadors in the negotiations:

> [The King of Portugal] is aware that I am received and obeyed as king and lord of those Maluco Islands, and that those who, until the present, held possession of those regions, have rendered me obedience as a king and rightful seignor, and have been, in my name, appointed as my governors and lieutenants over the said regions. He knows, too, that my subjects, with much of the merchandise carried by my fleet, are at the present time in these regions. . . . [The Portuguese] King has never held possession, past or present, of any of the said Maluco Islands, or of any others discovered by me up to the present; nor has his fleet touched at or anchored therein.[30]

This presentation recognized local polities as having been in possession of the islands before voluntarily ceding sovereignty. The Spanish claims were bolstered by the sworn statements of mariners who had participated in the Magellan voyage and reported witnessing the king of Tidore declaring himself a vassal of the king of Spain and, with expressions of "pleasure," offering his kingdom to the Spaniards.[31]

The Spaniards' claim of first discovery, however dubious, supported an additional argument that Portuguese activity in the Moluccas would fall outside the terms of the treaty, which had provided for transfers of land falling within the sphere of one power only when it was discovered or possessed by the other. If the islands fell in the Portuguese sphere but Spain had discovered and now possessed them, then Portugal was obliged to petition Spain for possession. If the islands fell in the Spanish sphere, the Portuguese had no basis for a claim if the Spaniards held possession. The Spaniards insisted, too, on a distinction between discovery and possession, noting that even if the Portuguese had sighted the islands, "that which was not taken or possessed could not be said to be found, although seen or discovered."[32]

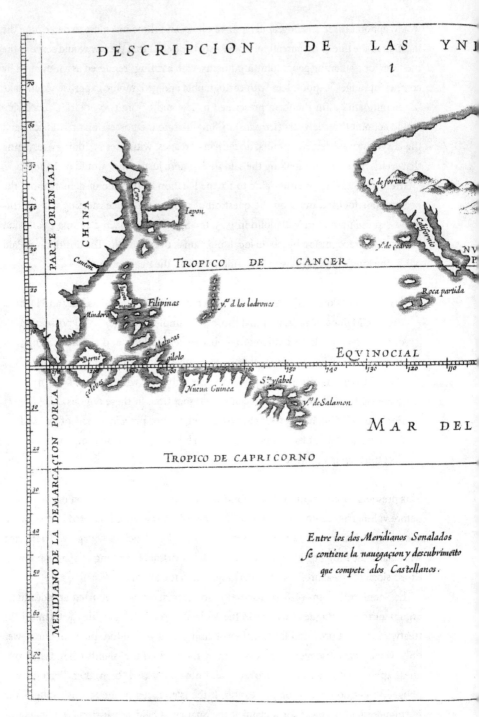

Descripción de las Yndias Ocidentales by Antonio de Herrera y Tordesillas depicts the demarcation line
the antimeridian is shown as lying to the west of the Moluccas rather than to the east, as specified in the
Courtesy of the John Carter Brown Library at Brown University

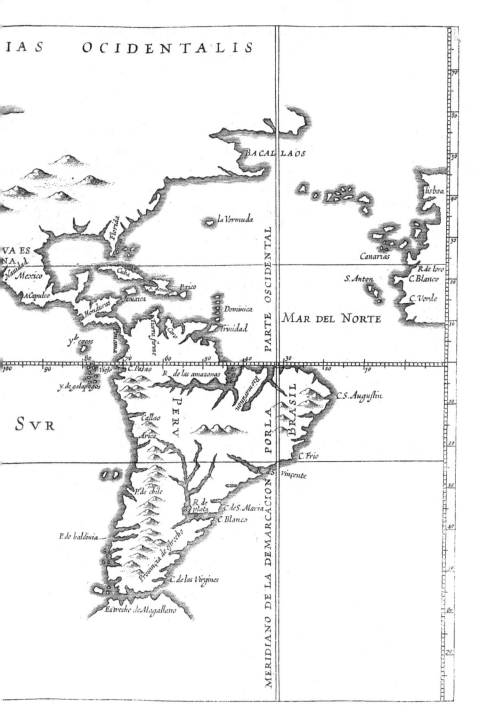

IAS   OCIDENTALIS

BACALLAOS

lisboa

la Vermuda

Canarias

VA ES
NA.
Natidad
Mexico   Cuba   S.Anton   R.de loro
                                                                                 C.Blanco
A.Capulco   Jamaica   P.rico   C.Verde
          Honduras   Dominica   MAR DEL NORTE
                                           Trinidad
y.t cacos
      80   70   60   50   40   30
100   90   20   10
              P.Viejo   C.Pasao   R. de las amazonas
y. de galapagos   C.S.Augustin
                              PERV
        Callao
SVR   BRASIL
        Arica

                                           C.Frio

                                    S.Viçente
                    P.de chile
                              R.de
                              plata   C.deS.Maria
                                   C.Blanco
P.de baldivia
              Prouinçia de estrecho
                    C. de las Virgines

       Es'treche deMagallano

of the Treaty of Tordesillas as well as the antimeridian. In an interpretation favoring Spanish interests,
Treaty of Zaragoza.

29

These positions informed the refusal of either side to act as plaintiff. The Spaniards pointed out that if they had possession as they claimed, then they had no "desire to assume the duties of the plaintiff" and nothing to gain from doing so. And, the crown asserted, if Portugal was claiming that Spain had disturbed Portugal's possession of a territory within the Portuguese sphere of influence, then this claim was "unprovided for by the treaty," which established only a procedure for acting to secure a territory discovered and then held by the other power. Bringing such a claim would in any case have required Portuguese recognition of Spanish possession, so the Portuguese, too, were not interested in acting as plaintiffs.[33]

Given the inability of the two sides to decide the question of ownership, the treaty could not be relied on even to regulate, as the Spanish crown put it, "the restitution of what is well known to be stolen." Instead, the dispute had to be resolved "by common sense or common law [*ius commune*]." The choice of these terms pointed to possession and implied the recognition of a shared European law that overlapped in imprecisely defined ways with the law of nations. Having dispensed with islanders' claims by asserting that they had recognized Spanish overlordship, Spanish diplomats had only to challenge evidence of a continuing Portuguese presence and assert proof of permanent Spanish settlement. The main Spanish objective was to demonstrate that they "possessed these lands more completely than any other."[34]

The goal proved elusive. As a direct result of the Badajoz-Elvas treaty, the Spanish crown mounted a large expedition of seven ships and 450 men to travel to the Moluccas across the Pacific. A much smaller force arrived in the Moluccas in 1527. Here again, at a very long distance from the courts, the existing Portuguese garrison at Ternate and the Spanish challengers acted to establish possession. The Portuguese captain sent letters to the Spanish indicating that "all these Molucca islands and neighboring islands were of the King of Portugal."[35] The Spanish rebuilt a fortification at Tidore and formed alliances with several local polities against the Portuguese. A series of skirmishes between the groups ended with a Portuguese victory over the small Spanish outpost in October, 1529. The Spaniards might have surrendered more quickly had they known that six months earlier, Charles had sold the rights to the Moluccas to the Portuguese.[36] The islands' remoteness, and the difficulties in occupying them, probably aided him in making this decision; three expeditions comprising a total of 15 ships had made voyages to the islands and only one had returned.[37] Spain's emphasis on effective possession had indirectly contributed to pressures to abandon its claim.

The Persistence of Possession

The emphasis on possession persisted for centuries, both in diplomatic circles and in local practices that included indigenous actors. The theme and practice were picked up by other Europeans challenging Iberian hegemony. Disputes over the control of fortified trading posts in West Africa provide a rich example of the strategic use of claims to possession in the much more crowded field of imperial competition in the long seventeenth century. Spanish and Portuguese wrangling over which power exercised legitimate control over the eastern bank of the Rio de la Plata shows the focus on possession at work in a different and distant setting in the same period. Indigenous strategies in the two regions also helped to shape the way arguments about possession were combined with other rationales.

The West African example is perhaps especially significant because the discourse of possession continued to exert influence in a context in which the limitations to European sovereignty were strikingly clear. Beginning with the Portuguese in the fifteenth century, European agents had negotiated for the highly circumscribed control of enclaves in the region. African host polities ceded the right to construct trading posts and, following long-standing practices in dealing with merchants of other trade diasporas, allowed European groups limited jurisdiction over the inhabitants of enclaves and their dependents.[38] No one in West Africa, including European agents, confused these arrangements with evidence of a voluntary transfer of sovereignty. Further complicating negotiations was the layered nature of sovereignty on the European side. By the seventeenth century, most agents in search of sites on which to found forts were not crown appointees but employees of trading companies. These corporate entities were acting as states in the sense that they were authorized by charters to make war and peace, acquire territory, and exercise legal authority over subordinates and subjects of the crown.

Despite these conditions—or in part because of them—possession featured prominently in European claims and counterclaims as well as in European–indigenous relations. The negotiations between the Portuguese and locals surrounding the foundation of São Jorge da Mina in 1482 followed familiar patterns. The Portuguese selected a peninsular site at the mouth of the Benya River, where they conducted a ceremony of possession with the usual elements: performance of a mass and the raising of a royal banner. The local ruler, Caramansa, arrived with a ceremonial entourage and, after a speech by the Portuguese commander, Azambuja, about the benefits in trade that the fort would bring, gave permission for the fort to be built. An unspoken threat of military coercion accompanied the ceremony as the Portuguese were well armed. The ceremony was typical in its symbolic plasticity. Azambuja could represent it to the Portuguese crown as an act of possession marking an inchoate claim to a larger slice of the region—imagined perhaps as the river's watershed—and as evidence of locals' political subordination to the Portuguese. Caramansa, meanwhile, had ceded nothing more than the right to construct the fort, Portuguese control within its walls, and a commitment to trade exclusively with the Portuguese.[39]

The Portuguese soon founded a second fortified trading post at Axim, but most interactions between African polities and Portuguese agents continued to depend on diplomacy and negotiations over rights to trade. Reporting on a series of late sixteenth–century voyages and writing in 1625 to urge a program of settlement in Sierra Leone, André Donelha warned that establishing a greater Portuguese presence in the region "would have to be done lovingly, giving presents and in peace."[40] He recommended a strategy of exhorting locals about the benefits of extending permission to trade, just as Azambuja had done. Such rhetoric continued alongside occasionally more pointed claims to the extension of Portuguese sovereignty, particularly through the conversion of locals to Christianity and recognition of their status as vassals of the Portuguese king. Such moves not only resulted from Portuguese proselytizing but also sometimes reflected strategic alliances with the Portuguese initiated by local rulers, who might themselves urge the Portuguese to conduct ceremonies to mark the occasion. Donelha reports, for example, the invitation by a leader in Sierra Leone to plant the Portuguese flag and to "make him and all his people Christians."[41]

When French and English agents began entering into competition for West African trade in the mid–sixteenth century, they found a local population well versed in symbolic acts of possession and apparently also familiar with the multiple possible meanings of such acts. Africans indicated that they understood that the European commitment to forts was partly practical and focused on trade, and partly directed at a broader regional geopolitics. Eighty years after the founding of São Jorge da Mina and Axim, Africans along the Mina coast "did not need to be introduced to the concept of a 'fort' as imagined by Europeans."[42] Nor did English and French merchants fail to understand that the limited holdings of the Portuguese were intended by them to signal a broader claim to the region. English merchants who financed a voyage to Guinea in 1554–1555 were careful to record that their ships had avoided any Portuguese "fortresse, towne, garrison, or governance" and had traded with Africans only if "informed by them that they were not subjects to the king of Portugal." The English agents also followed the pattern of requesting permission from locals to build forts. Sponsors noted that "the inhabitants of that country offered us and our said factors ground to build upon."[43]

As European competition for trade in the region intensified with the entry of the Dutch in the 1590s and in the seventeenth century with the activity of Swedish and Danish companies, ceremonies of possession were more explicitly combined with statements that locals were ceding a bundle of prerogatives, the most important of which was their right to trade with other Europeans. There is evidence of considerable sophistication on both sides about what was being negotiated in connection with the founding of forts. Africans did not simply oppose the forts—though there were certainly places where violent opposition prevented forts from being established or caused them to be abandoned, as at Kommenda in 1691, where the British flag was taken down by locals soon after it was hoisted by the agent of the Royal African Company (RAC).[44] Polities of various sizes often invited Europeans to found forts and even demanded ceremonies of possession in order to solidify military alliances and trading relationships. At Dixcove factory in 1692, the local host placed gold under the foundation stone of the fort and commemorated the start of construction by slaughtering a sheep.[45] At Winneba in 1693, Queen Tituba specifically requested that the RAC build a fort. When construction was proceeding slowly, the queen reportedly "began to suspect that [the Company] only kept a white man here to keep the possession." To ensure the RAC commitment to establish active trading relations, she again insisted that the agent secure and hoist a flag.[46]

Queen Tituba's intuition that settlements and forts both solidified trading relationships and figured in interimperial diplomacy as markers of possession was exactly right. Diplomatic discourse continued to combine references to possession and arguments about the peaceful cession of sovereignty. A Dutch West India Company letter of 1694 displays the continuing tendency to layer arguments about the nature and basis of claims in the region. The first assertion is that the Dutch had received the forts it controlled through just conquest from the Portuguese. But greater emphasis falls on the argument that the region was "granted by the natives, or bought from the same for a sum of gold." Reflecting understandings in the region, the Dutch letter observes that what was purchased or ceded in such transactions was locals' agreement to refrain from making similar cessions to any other European power. Implicitly referring to a hierarchy of proofs of the acquisition of private property in Roman law, the Dutch agents note that the consent of locals would effectively trump any English claim to rights established on the coast through long possession. And, finally, in a striking illustration of the multilayered and scattershot style of the genre, the letter ends with a simple claim to "full ownership" over the region.[47] Such layered arguments were directed at the many competing companies operating along the Mina Coast. They carried over, too, the approach of Iberian rivals from an earlier era, with its emphasis on possession as a secondary but important rationale for claims.

The Iberian powers also continued to cite proofs of possession in diplomatic exchanges in the long seventeenth century. The similarities to sixteenth-century diplomatic jockeying are striking. Consider the wrangling over Portuguese and Spanish claims in the South Atlantic. Here, as in the Indian Ocean, the location of the line of demarcation of the Treaty of Tordesillas was a matter of uncertainty, and the line's point of origination remained in dispute. As they had in the conflict over the Moluccas, Portuguese and Spanish diplomats supplemented attention to the treaty line with arguments based on possession. An anonymous tract written in support of the Portuguese claim to Colonia do Sacramento, on the east side of the Rio de la Plata estuary, provides a mirror image to the diplomatic letters of the Spanish a century and a half before.[48] The author first examines at length the question of whether Colonia do Sacramento fell on the Portuguese or Spanish side of the Treaty of Tordesillas line.[49] Though he asserts that the evidence was strong that the entire eastern bank of the Rio de la Plata lay in the Portuguese sphere and that no other evidence was therefore needed, the author continues with a detailed defense of Portugal's rights to the territory based on possession. Cabral is said to have taken possession for Portugal of the entire territory between the Marañon River and the Rio de la Plata: "And this act of possession alone, even if it had been the only one and not followed by many more, would have been sufficient" to claim the whole region between the rivers.[50] Subsequently, Amerigo Vespucci, Martim Afonso de Sousa, and Pero Lopes de Sousa strengthened this claim by erecting markers and founding settlements, while unnamed Portuguese agents also furthered the claim by navigating freely on the river, evangelizing, and, in the name of the Portuguese crown, awarding grants within the territory.

The small matter of the Spanish counterclaims pronounced by Juan Díaz de Solís and Sebastião Cabot had to be dealt with. The argument here was that the acts of possession possibly performed by Solís on the island of San Gabriel in 1515 on behalf of the Spanish crown were later repudiated by the Catholic kings in recognition of the prior Portuguese claim.[51] And Cabot, the author notes, had chosen to erect a marker and fort on the opposite bank of the river, an implicit acknowledgment of the Portuguese claim to the eastern bank. The tract goes on to argue that the Spaniards could not base a claim on prescription because they had not had long-standing settlements on the eastern bank and in fact had been expelled on occasion by the Portuguese.[52] It seemed especially significant that there had been no concerted effort to send Spanish settlers to the region and no records of grants to land made during the decades when the crowns had been united. Finally, a legal politics of facts on the ground supported a claim for Portuguese dominion. Two Portuguese subjects had filed a claim for restitution in Buenos Aires after a shipwreck in the estuary forced them to go there for supplies and aid. The author notes that the judgment implicitly recognized the jurisdiction of the Portuguese over the eastern bank by challenging only the right of the ship owners to trade across the estuary, not their right to navigate in the waters off Montevideo.[53]

Later famous for their violence against settlers, the Indians of the region would seem to have little to do with this diplomatic dispute.[54] But Indian opposition accounted for the absence of claims that a voluntary cession of sovereignty had taken place. Indians entered indirectly, too, into the broader discourse about legitimate possession. Portuguese writers accused the Spaniards on the eastern bank of having adopted Indian methods of warfare and of forming military alliances with the Indians against the Portuguese.[55] Tainting Spaniards by their association with "barbarous" Indians was intended to help sustain arguments about the tenuousness of Spanish possession. Little is known about the Charrúas' view of these disputes; it is clear only that their strategies of avoiding or attacking settlers colored the case for possession and robbed both Spaniards and Portuguese of the claim of settled Indian vassalage.

Seventeenth-century discourses about rival claims in West Africa and in the Río de la Plata reveal striking continuities with earlier methods of fashioning claims. At the same time, the juxtaposition shows that context mattered. Possession was combined differently with other arguments to reflect the nature of imperial rivalries and European-indigenous relations. On the Mina coast, locals entering into exclusive trade relationships understood such agreements mainly as providing control over limited enclaves while also recognizing that the forts would receive a broader interpretation in the context of European rivalries. Both locals and European agents sometimes encouraged the confusion between economic interests and political loyalties, and both sides manipulated the signs and symbols of possession. On the eastern bank of the Río de la Plata, Iberian agents regarded Indians as lacking civility. They used this angle not to define the land as unowned but to challenge evidence of settled European political communities. In this context, acts of possession performed centuries before, in temporary encampments, retained their currency.

Conclusion

The late seventeenth-century examples suggest that historians have exaggerated the idiosyncratic nature of Iberian legal rationales for the acquisition of empire as centering on arguments about papal authority, a preoccupation with rights to people, or assertions about a right to trade based on natural law. Similarly, English and French challenges to Iberian claims appear less innovative in emphasizing discovery, prescription, the cultivation of land, and occupation. A discourse of possession in which claims did not depend on specific modes of acquisition pervaded practices of claims making across European empires and through several centuries of intensifying European imperial competition.

The invocation of Roman law still left open important questions about the array of acts and utterances that could signal and support claims. Some acts, such as erecting settlements or exercising legal authority, were themselves symbolically elastic, serving to reinforce arguments for conquest, occupation, or possession. And the widespread importance of possession did not produce uniformity in claims; different combinations of acts and arguments arose in particular contexts. The vagaries of treaty terms led the Spanish and Portuguese to emphasize possession more than other arguments in disputes over the Moluccas and the Rio de la Plata. References to possession were combined inconsistently with evidence of the voluntary cession of sovereignty; in the Moluccas, the Spanish made a confident if dubious assertion that well-established polities had recognized them as lords, while in the Rio de la Plata Indian violence and over a century's delay in settlement moved this claim deep into the background. In citing possession, Europeans targeted the claims of specific rivals. In the western Indian Ocean, the Portuguese enthusiasm for *padrões* diminished in a dense trading network controlled by powerful land polities, while proof of discovery and possession retained its significance for transmittal back to sponsors engaged in discrediting Spanish counterclaims. In seventeenth century West Africa, Dutch legal agents addressed English rivals even though agents of both powers were operating in the context of a crowded field of European companies and African polities with varying military and political capacities.

Although it is important to resist the temptation to represent indigenous groups as driving the preoccupation with possession, their strategies clearly influenced the formation and circulation of norms for negotiating and recognizing claims. Some of this influence flowed from oppositional acts. Locals often blocked ceremonies of possession; think of coastal inhabitants of southeastern Africa dismantling the cross erected by the Portuguese or West African attacks on forts. Just as often, indigenous strategies made use of a European focus on possession and, sometimes simultaneously, formally recognized European authority without equating that authority with sovereignty. As with the recognition of internally inconsistent approaches by Europeans drawing on Roman law to construct claims, indigenous actors negotiated about claims in ways that revealed multiple goals and an unsystematic but not unsophisticated understanding of interpolity legal practices and symbols. And even where engagement was minimal and sporadically violent, as in the Rio de la Plata, Europeans wrote indigenous actions into scripts about possession intended to bolster the legitimacy of claims or challenge claims advanced by other European powers.

With its roots in an unstable analogy to the Roman law of private property, its prominent place in Iberian diplomacy and imperial strategy, and its frequent combination with other legal arguments, possession made cross-imperial and cross-cultural sense over several centuries of global interactions. Unsystematic references to possession appeared in a wide range of writings and acts, even as Roman legal influences structured striking continuities in the content and strategies of claims. A focus on proof of possession accompanied bilateral contests, perhaps even encouraging multisided disputes to be represented as between two parties. At times this logic applied to contests for control between European agents and indigenous polities; at times Europeans sought to preempt or sweep aside indigenous claims by juxtaposing the discourse of possession with assertions that locals had recognized Europeans' authority. Because possession was discussed little by European writers usually regarded as the founders of international law, its influence has sometimes been missed. A search for doctrinally pristine applications of Roman law concepts by some imperial historians has also shifted attention away from possession and toward other rationales for the acquisition of empire. The history of conflicts over claims clearly reveals, instead, a flexible and pervasive discourse of possession with a profound influence on globally circulating interpolity law.

NOTES

1. D. A. Lupher, *Romans in a New World: Classical Models in Sixteenth-Century Spanish America* (Ann Arbor: University of Michigan Press, 2003); Sabine MacCormack, *On the Wings of Time: Rome, the Incas, Spain, and Peru* (Princeton: Princeton University Press, 2007).

2. Ken MacMillan, *Sovereignty and Possession in the English New World: The Legal Foundations of Empire, 1576-1640* (Cambridge: Cambridge University Press, 2006); Anthony Pagden, "Law, Colonization, Legitimation, and the European Background," in Michael Grossberg and Christopher Tomlins, *The Cambridge History of Law in America, vol. I* (Cambridge and New York: Cambridge University Press, 2008), 1–31.

3. E.g., Benjamin Straumann, "Ancient Caesarian Lawyers' in a State of Nature. Roman Tradition and Natural Rights in Hugo Grotius' De Iure Praedae," *Political Theory* 34:3 (2006): 328–350.

4. The account of sharp differences in European styles of claims making is developed most fully in Patricia Seed, *Ceremonies of Possession in Europe's Conquest of the New World, 1492-1640* (Cambridge: Cambridge University Press, 1997). Cf. MacMillan, *Sovereignty and Possession in the English New World*; Lauren Benton and Benjamin Straumann, "Acquiring Empire by Law: From Roman Doctrine to Early Modern European Practice," *Law and History Review* 28:1 (2010) 1–38.

5. See Antony Anghie, *Imperialism, Sovereignty, and the Making of International Law* (Cambridge: Cambridge University Press, 2007); Edward Keene, *Beyond the Anarchical Society: Grotius, Colonialism and Order in World Politics* (Cambridge: Cambridge University Press, 2002); Lauren Benton, *A Search for Sovereignty: Law and Geography in European Empires, 1400-1900* (New York: Cambridge University Press, 2010).

6. See Benton, *A Search for Sovereignty*, chap. 1 and 2.

7. Writing in the 1950s, Voegelin used the term "interpolity law" but divided it into two kinds of law: "interstate law" involving European polities and "intercivilizational law" regulating the relations of European and non-European states. This formulation is faithful to Vitoria, as Voegelin intended, but it is limiting as an analytic framework for early modern global interactions spanning European and non-European polities. Eric Voegelin, *Collected Works of Eric Voegelin, vol. 23, History of Political Ideas, vol. V: Religion and the Rise of Modernity*, ed. by James L. Wiser (Columbia: University of Missouri Press, 1998), chap. 4. I use the term "interpolity law" more broadly, to refer to regulatory practices encompassing European and non-European polities of all varieties, including empires and small states.

8. Possession has received greater attention as a cultural script in colonial society. See Rolena Adorno, *The Polemics of Possession in Spanish American Narrative* (New Haven, CT: Yale University Press, 2007).

9. For more detailed discussion of these points, see Benton and Straumann, "Acquiring Empire by Law." On the place of *res nullius* in Roman law, compare Andrew Fitzmaurice, "A genealogy of terra nullius," *Australian Historical Studies* 129 (2007), 1–15.

10. The discussion here of possession in Roman law follows closely Benton and Straumann, "Acquiring Empire by Law."

11. See the article by Andrew Fitzmaurice in this volume.

12. Arthur Schopenhauer Keller, Oliver James Lissitzyn, and Frederick Justin Mann, *Creation of Rights of Sovereignty through Symbolic Acts, 1400–1800* (New York: Columbia University Press, 1939), 39; and see Benton, *A Search for Sovereignty*, 56–59.

13. Bernal Olmedo, *El dominio del Atlántico en la baja Edad Media: Los títulos jurídicos de la expansión peninsular hasta el Tratado de Tordesillas.* (Valladolid [Spain], Sociedad V Centenario del Tratado de Tordesillas, 1995).

14. "Treaty between Spain and Portugal concluded at Tordesillas, June 7, 1494," Document 9 in Frances Davenport and C. O. Paullin, eds., *European Treaties Bearing on the History of the United States and Its Dependencies* (Washington, DC: Carnegie Institution of Washington, 1917), 99.

15. James Muldoon, *Popes, Lawyers, and Infidels: The Church and the Non-Christian World, 1250–1550* (Philadelphia: University of Pennsylvania Press, 1979), 134–139.

16. Davenport, *European Treaties*, 99.

17. In this respect, the treaty followed the spirit of the series of 1493 bulls that had awarded "jurisdictional zones" within which each crown exercised ecclesiastical responsibility; Muldoon, *Popes, Lawyers, and Infidels*, 136. A similar point is made by Steinberg, who notes that the treaty assigned the Iberian powers not sovereignty but "stewardship" over the seas; Philip Steinberg, "Lines of Division, Lines of Connection: Stewardship in the World Ocean," *The Geographical Review* 89 (1999), 254–264.

18. Olmedo's phrase is "la política de hechos consumados," which might also be translated as "the politics of faits accomplis." Olmedo, *El dominio del Atlantico*, 428.

19. María M. Portuondo, *Secret Science: Spanish Cosmography and the New World* (Chicago and London: The University of Chicago Press, 2009)

20. Some English legal practices also reinforced an emphasis on possession. The need for written records to establish possession of property in sixteenth-century England influenced understandings of rights and privileges as defined by charter. And familiarity with canon law encouraged use of language mimicking papal (and Iberian) claims. James Muldoon, "Discovery, Charter, Conquest, or Purchase: John Adams on the Legal Basis for English Possession in North America," in Christopher Tomlins and Bruce Mann, eds., *The Many Legalities of Early America* (Chapel Hill and London: University of North Carolina Press, 2001), 25–46.

21. Linda Lewin, *Surprise Heirs* (Stanford: Stanford University Press, 2003), 8–10.

22. Carmen Oliveira Alveal, "Converting Land into Property in the Portuguese Atlantic World, 16th–18th Centuries," doctoral dissertation, Johns Hopkins University, 2007.

23. Brian Owensby, *Empire of Law and Indian Justice in Colonial Mexico* (Stanford: Stanford University Press, 2008), chap. 4.

24. Alvaro Velho, Vasco da Gama, João de Sá (trans., Ernest George Ravenstein), *A Journal of the First Voyage of Vasco Da Gama, 1497–1499* (New Delhi: Asian Educational Services, 1995), 13.

25. Sanjay Subrahmanyam, *The Career and Legend of Vasco Da Gama* (Cambridge: Cambridge University Press, 1998), 144.

26. Cortés, Pizarro, and other conquistadors used the founding of towns and other rituals, including raising banners, as acts of possession, often in response to threats by other Spanish officials seeking to position themselves as having first laid claim to particular regions in the name of the king. Examples include Cortés's founding of Segura de la

Frontera as he eyed the approach of a rival force off the coast of New Spain, and the many references to ceremonies of possession under similar circumstances in the conquest of Peru. See Pedro de Cieza de León, ed., *The Discovery and Conquest of Peru: Chronicles of the New World Encounter* (Durham, NC: Duke University Press, 1998), 13, 125, 295, 298, 319, 351. Cf. Seed, *Ceremonies of Possession*, chap. 4.

27. See especially Jerry Brotton, *Trading Territories: Mapping the Early Modern World* (London: Reaktion Books, 1997), 122–159.

28. Ibid., and also Charles E. Nowell, "The Loaisa Expedition and the Ownership of the Moluccas," *The Pacific Historical Review*, 5:4 (1936): 325–336.

29. "Treaty between Spain and Portugal, concluded at Vitoria, February 19, 1524," Document 13 in Davenport, *European Treaties*, 127.

30. "Instructions from the King of Spain to His Ambassadors, in the Negotiations with Portugal," in E. H. Blair, J. A. Robertson, et al. (1903), *The Philippine Islands, 1493–1803: Explorations by Early Navigators, Descriptions of the Islands and Their Peoples, Their History and Records of the Catholic Missions, as Related in Contemporaneous Books and Manuscripts, Showing the Political, Economic, Commercial and Religious Conditions of Those Islands from Their Earliest Relations with European Nations to the Beginning of the Nineteenth Century* (Cleveland, Ohio: A.H. Clark Co., 1903), 83.

31. A sworn statement by three witnesses was not recorded until 1527, but these accounts would have been known in Spain before then. "Probanza sobre el derecho real a las islas Molucas," ES.41091.AGI/1.16416.2.24.16//PATRONATO,49,R.4 accessed at http://pares.mcu.es

32. "Letter of Carlos I of Spain to Juan de Zuñisa, Pamplona, December, 1523," in Blair, *The Philippine Islands*, 88.

33. Ibid., 89

34. Ibid., 90. The Portuguese shared the view that possession was the crux of the matter. The crown proposed that the two sides agree to suspend voyages to the Moluccas while the question of ownership and possession was under consideration. But the Portuguese also allowed that if the lawyers should determine possession before issuing "a final sentence" on the question of ownership, then whoever was recognized as holding possession ought to be allowed to undertake voyages. ("Draft of an unconcluded treaty between Spain and Portugal, 1526," Document 14, Davenport, *European Treaties*, 140–141).

35. Martín Fernández de Navarrete, ed. *Colección de los viages y descubrimientos que hicieron por mar los españoles desde fines del siglo XV: Con varios documentos inéditos concernientes á la historia de la marina castellana y de los establecimientos españoles en Indias* (Madrid: Imprenta Real, 1825), 284.

36. The settlement was part of the 1529 Treaty of Zaragoza, which fixed the antimeridian of the Treaty of Tordesillas demarcation line at 297.5 leagues to the east of the Moluccas. The Spanish crown reserved the right to repay the Portuguese and revisit the agreement if new geographic information surfaced. Brotton notes that the treaty stipulated the joint creation of a map by a team of cosmographers under oath, with the map serving as "a type of visual contract." Brotton, *Trading Territories*, 136.

37. Spain had not yet found a safe route eastward across the Pacific. Two of the ships leaving the Moluccas had been forced to return. Nowell, "The Loaisa Expedition," 335–336.

38. On this point, see Lauren Benton, *Law and Colonial Cultures: Legal Regimes in World History* (Cambridge: Cambridge University Press, 2002), chap. 2.

39. John Vogt, *Portuguese Rule on the Gold Coast 1469–1682* (Athens, GA: University of Georgia Press, 1979), 20–27.

40. André Donelha, *Descrição da Serra Leoa e dos rios de Guiné do Cabo Verde* (1625) (Lisbon: Junta de Investigações Científicas de Ultramar, 1977), 115.

41. Donelha, *Descrição da Serra Leoa*, 351.

42. Avelino Teixeira da Mota and P. E. H. Hair, *East of Mina: Afro-European Relations on the Gold Coast in the 1550s and 1560s*; Issue 3 of *Studies in African Sources* (Madison, WI: African Studies Program, University of Wisconsin-Madison, 1989), 23.

43. Quoted in Teixeira da Mota and Hair, *East of Mina*, 10, 21.

44. Robin Law, ed., *The English in West Africa, 1691–1699: The Local Correspondence of the Royal African Company of England 1681–1699*, Part 3 (Oxford: Oxford University Press, 2006), 136.

45. Ibid., 136.

46. Ibid., 429.

47. Ibid., 629–631, 631.

48. The tract is printed in W. Rela, *Portugal en las exploraciones del Río de la Plata* (Montevideo, Uruguay: Academia Uruguaya de Historia Marítima y Fluvial, 2002), 139–168. The territory, which later became the República Oriental del Uruguay, lay on the northeastern bank of the Rio de la Plata and the eastern bank of the Uruguay River.

49. The case for its being in the Portuguese sphere turns mainly on the familiar argument about the starting point for measuring the distance west from the Cape Verde Islands. Ibid., 152.

50. Ibid., 158.

51. Here the Portuguese were reacting to a Spanish story about the Solís voyage that merged accounts from chronicles, subsequent altered versions, and hearsay into a more definite narrative about Solís's acts of possession. See Gustavo Verdesio, *Forgotten Conquests: Rereading New World History from the Margins* (Philadelphia: Temple University Press), chap. 1.

52. The Buenos Aires cabildo (municipal council) argued that the Portuguese were disturbing Spaniards' "pacific possession of the land, which our king and his predecessors have possessed since the moment of conquest." Quoted in Ibid., 74.

53. A few pages later, the author reverses this argument to say that just because Spanish ships sail in Portuguese waters in the estuary does not signify an act of possession "because otherwise it would be considered an act of possession" any time a ship entered a harbor for supplies or to take shelter from a storm. The Dutch, French, and English, under this logic, would also be able to claim possession in the Rio de la Plata. Rela, *Portugal* p. 165.

54. Accounts of the death of Solís mention cannibalism, and Verdesio *Forgotten Conquests*, chap. 1 points out that this part of the story rested on little evidence and repeated a formulaic exaggeration of Indian violence. Although the Charrúas were later credited with the attack resulting in the death of Solís, Acosta y Lara argues that the attackers were probably Guaraní Indians. The earliest reports that identify Charrúas show them mainly avoiding contact with Spaniards (behavior that also made it difficult to argue that they had ceded sovereignty). Later attacks established Charrúas' reputation for violence, which was then read back into the historical record. Eduardo F. Acosta y Lara, *La Guerra de los Charrúas en la Banda Oriental vol. 1* (Montevideo: Talleres de Loreto Editores, 1998), chap. 1.

55. Verdesio. *Forgotten Conquests*, 80.

2

LAW, LAND, AND LEGAL RHETORIC IN COLONIAL NEW SPAIN
A LOOK AT THE CHANGING RHETORIC OF INDIGENOUS AMERICANS IN THE SIXTEENTH CENTURY

R. Jovita Baber

This chapter examines the changing legal rhetoric of an indigenous community as it sought to assert land claims during the sixteenth century in the colonial Spanish courts. The community, Tlaxcala, was located in New Spain (today, Mexico) at an important nexus for transportation. Halfway between the Gulf of Mexico and the Valley of Mexico, Tlaxcala served as a hub of trading activity throughout most of the postclassical period (ca. 900–1500 A.D.). Traders passed through the region with goods moving from the central valley to the coast and down to the Yucatan. Far from being a closed community, Tlaxcalans were accustomed to welcoming outsiders and continued to do so during the colonial period. The region remained an important thoroughfare for merchants, travelers, and royal officials during the colonial period. A few decades after the arrival of Spaniards to Mesoamerica, however, the Tlaxcalan nobles became frustrated by the behavior of a handful of Spanish settlers and sued to evict them from their province. Concurrent with their court case, the native leaders petitioned the Crown to issue royal mandates on their behalf. Effectively to assert their legal and political agenda, Tlaxcalans accessed Castilian rhetoric. They adopted it to their own purposes and adjusted their arguments to the changing political milieu of the empire.

The Tlaxcalans' case reveals something important about Spanish imperial rule. The legal and political success of the Tlaxcalans was due to their ability to recognize shifts in the political culture, and to fashion their legal rhetoric and strategies accordingly. In this, they were extraordinary but not unique or exceptional. Indeed, the archives are filled with petitions and court cases brought by native people who attempted to reframe their story in order to influence the decisions of royal authorities. Not all of these efforts were successful. Nonetheless, examining this group that was frequently successful provides insight into the effectiveness of particular legal strategies and uncovers a more complex story about how the Crown and its royal officials responded to native claims and counterclaims to land.

Although one cannot neatly fit the legal rhetoric of the Tlaxcalans into rigid stages or boxes, three identifiable strategies are evident in their petitions and court cases. First, immediately following the conquest, the native elite relied on the rhetoric of loyal service and noble subjects. While this rhetoric never fully disappeared, it became less effective by mid-century when the Crown was moving imperial governance away from private individuals (i.e., *encomenderos*) to a royal bureaucracy. During that transition, the authorities became less generous with royal favors. Accordingly, the rhetoric of loyal service gave way to a second rhetoric that appealed to Castilian notions of good government or *buen gobierno*. In this mode, Tlaxcalans supported their claims by appealing to the obligation of the prince to maintain peace and harmony within his kingdoms. Because the strengthening of the bureaucracy coincided with the increase in Castilian settlers and the consequent rise in intercommunal conflict, Tlaxcalans used this rhetoric to elicit royal intervention. Finally, toward the end of the sixteenth century, arguments of *buen gobierno* were replaced by arguments regarding the misery and suffering of the common native population. This third rhetoric, referred to here as *indios miserables*, grew out of the medieval Castilian custom, which obligated elites to protect and provide for the vulnerable members of society—called *miserables*. In Iberia, *miserables* were traditionally widows, orphans, the poor, and students. In using this rhetoric, native people tapped into the widespread Castilian perception that indigenous Americans were inherently vulnerable and needed the guidance and protection of Castilian clergy and royal officials. This last rhetoric proved to be quite effective for native people. It allowed them to paint a picture that was convincing to their audience.

Scholars often erroneously interpret native rhetorical strategies as reality. To be clear, the rhetoric of the Tlaxcalans reflects their ability to fashion legal arguments and strategies to influence legal outcomes; it does not necessarily communicate a lived experience or "a native reality." This discrepancy between rhetoric and reality is quite evident in the court cases and petitions examined in this chapter. Consistently, throughout the sixteenth century, for example, Tlaxcalans argued for complete exclusion of Castilians.[1] While their rhetoric asserted their opposition to all Spaniards, their actions were inclusive. In reality, they accepted Castilians as neighbors, community members, and even as family members.[2] In their lived experience, one can conclude, some Spaniards respected local traditions and customs, and others did not. Tlaxcalans wanted to remove those who did not conform to native authority. However, they also understood that arguing for full exclusion was a more effective legal strategy in the nascent colonial legal system than pursuing a legal means to remove individuals. The interpretation and enforcement of royal mandates remained far too flexible to entrust royal officials with deciding which Spaniards could stay and which should leave. By securing a royal mandate that excluded all Castilians, Tlaxcalans retained the power to determine when to exercise their legal rights. Throughout this chapter, such discrepancy between rhetoric and reality is highlighted in order to reveal native people's conscious use of Castilian rhetoric and their clever legal strategies.

Loyal Service and Noble Subjects

When the Aztec Empire began to rise, the Tlaxcalans initially allied with them to overthrow the existing dominant regional power, the city-state of Azcapotzalco. Tlaxcalans, however, grew tired of their subordinate role within the alliance and ended the relationship. As the native empire continued to expand, it extended its sovereignty over the communities surrounding the Tlaxcalans. Tlaxcalans resisted. Although they retained their autonomy, the Aztecs cut Tlaxcala off from trade in an attempt to force the community to capitulate. With limited access to essential imports, including salt, Tlaxcalans' resentment grew. When Cortés arrived, the Tlaxcalan nobles readily allied with him to overthrow the Aztec empire.

In 1528, seven years after they participated in the toppling of the Aztec capital of Tenochtitlan, the Tlaxcalan elite sent a delegation of native nobles across the Atlantic to petition the Spanish Crown. In their petition, they asked the king to ensure that they never be designated as an *encomienda* and to exempt them from royal tribute. They wanted to retain authority over their subjects, land, and labor. In approaching the Crown for these favors, they reframed their participation in the conquest: rather than mention their antipathy toward the Aztecs, they asserted that they had aided in the conquest of Tenochtitlan and the rest of Mesoamerica as a service to God and the king. This rhetorical strategy—of requesting remuneration for loyalty and services rendered to the Catholic Crown—was standard practice for Castilians seeking royal privileges.

While their early petitions are lost, their language can be glimpsed in the Crown's responses. For example, in 1529, the Crown paraphrased the words of the native leaders in its response to their petition: the king explained that the Tlaxcalans were deserving of privileges because they had provided aid to the Crown and to God in the conquest of the city of Mexico and afterward.[3] This rhetoric of loyal service proved successful. The Crown prohibited its successors and all Spanish officials from granting the Tlaxcalans as an *encomienda* and it limited their annual tribute to a few *cahiz* of corn—a negligible royal tribute, indeed.[4]

A few remaining petitions from mid-century continued to use the rhetoric of loyal service. By examining one from 1562—shortly after Philip II ascended the throne—a sense of how such petitions were crafted is revealed. Appropriately, the petition began by paying homage to the "royal person, as a powerful and Catholic king," and asserting obedience to "our lord." The Tlaxcalan nobles wrote:

> . . . always we have served and desire to serve your majesty. Considering the great need that we have to come before your royal person, as a powerful and Catholic king and as our lord, we have agreed to send don Pablo de Galizia, who is presently the governor, and don Lucas Garcia, don Antonio de la Pederosa and don Alonso Gomez, the leaders of the four divisions of this province so that in the name of all we kiss your royal hands and ask a few things that are extremely important."[5]

In writing the opening salutation to honor the king, the Tlaxcalan nobles were careful to note their own noble status. Each was identified as a "don"—a Spanish title for nobility. Moreover, they established the basis for the nobility by stating that they were the leaders of the four divisions—the foremost leaders of Tlaxcala. On one hand, in asserting their elite status, the petitioners established their right to represent the corporate group of Tlaxcala; and, on the other hand, they clarify their relationship to the Crown and their position within the emerging imperial hierarchy. By asserting their nobility and writing that they "kiss your royal hands and ask a few things," their rhetoric alluded to a contractual relationship between Crown and subject. In medieval Iberian political philosophy, the king was bound by mutual need, respect, and loyalty to those who submitted to his authority. In this contract, the prince was obligated to maintain peace and harmony in this kingdom, and his subjects were obligated to serve with faith and loyalty. The internal governance of each corporate group, however, remained in the hands of the leaders of the community. By evoking the contract between Crown and subjects, the Tlaxcalan nobles concurrently affirmed their authority over their community and their interdependent relationship with the king.

After paying homage to the king's authority, predecessors, and godliness, the petition reminded the incoming king of the services that they had rendered to the Crown during the conquest of Mesoamerica:

> It serves you to remember the faithfulness and great loyalty with which our fathers and forefathers served the royal crown and with which we have served and continue to serve, especially and decidedly when don Hernando Cortés, Marques del Valle, came to this land with other Spaniards.

With this, Tlaxcalans began to lay a solid foundation for their claim that they had upheld their obligations to the prince: they served and continued to serve loyally. Moreover, Tlaxcalans asserted that their ancestors "voluntarily gave obedience to your royal name and placed themselves under the dominion and rule of the emperor, our lord of glorious memory." They were leaders who recognized the king as the leader of leaders and submitted voluntarily to his sovereignty—as the numerous Christian nobles and corporate groups in the peninsula had done during the late Middle Ages.

Despite the similarity to petitions submitted by Castilians, the petition written by the Tlaxcalans was not formulaic. It reflected the distinct legal relationship between the Crown and its native American subjects. In the midst of the debates in the peninsula regarding the legitimacy of Castilian sovereignty (*imperium*) in the Americas, and the rights of infidels to possess property rights (*dominium*) and jurisdiction, the petitions from the Tlaxcalans implicitly took the position that native people were rational, were capable of self-government, and lawfully possessed property rights and jurisdiction. More directly, the Tlaxcalan nobles wrote that their ancestors "were the first who came into the knowledge of our holy Catholic faith." They recognized that Spaniards equated political community with Christian community, and the expansion of Castilian sovereignty with the expansion of Christendom. Beyond simply asserting their confessional status, this declaration asserted their full membership in the Castilian political body and dispelled any doubts about whether Tlaxcalans could lawfully possess *dominium*: Tlaxcalans were NOT infidels; they were Christian converts.

The Tlaxcalans' argument went to the heart of the peninsular debates: Could the Crown lawfully assert Castilian sovereignty in the Americas? Whether the Crown possessed a legal right to assert sovereignty in the Americas rested on jurists' interpretation of papal powers and the nature of the Bulls of Donation—namely the 1493 papal bull of Alexander VI, *Inter Caetera*, which infamously divided the world and granted the Crowns of Spain and Portugal authorities over the newly "discovered" people. Castilians debated whether the pope could transfer his authority to a secular prince, whether the pope possessed temporal authority or solely spiritual authority, and whether the pope held authority over the whole world or only over Christians. At the Junta de Burgos, in 1512, the leading jurists, theologians, and philosophers in Iberia agreed that Castile could assert sovereignty in the Americas in order to convert the native population. Out of this gathering of the leading thinkers in Castile came the Laws of Burgos—which established standardized rules to regulate interactions between colonists and the native population—especially regarding the procedures of evangelization. Within this political climate, Tlaxcalans asserted that they "voluntarily gave obedience" to the Crown and were the first to convert to Christianity. Their argument circumvented questions regarding the nature of papal authority and the Bulls of Donation and asserted that Tlaxcalans were subjects of the Crown because they consented to its authority.

In debating the Bulls of Donation, Castilians also asked whether native people could be forcibly brought into the folds of Christendom, the criteria for which Christians could wage a Just War against infidels, and whether the conquest was a Just War or an illegal war. At the Junta de Burgos, it was concluded that war could be waged against native people if they did not concede to having Catholic fathers preach to them. The *Requirimiento*—the infamous document that Spaniards were required to read (in Spanish to non–Spanish speaking native people) before waging war against native populations—explained that all humanity was one under God, and that God endowed his authorities in the pope, and the pope donated the Americas to the king of Spain. Accordingly, the conquistadors were ordered to treat the native population with love and charity, and as subjects and vassals of the king—insofar as the native people permitted the fathers to evangelize. Tlaxcalans undermined the legal grounds for a Just War against them when they claimed to have converted freely to Christianity. They took this argument a step further in more radical documents, such as the now lost history by Tlaxcalan noble Tadeo de Niza, in which they claimed that a cross appeared to them before Cortés arrived.[6] With the apparition, they recognized the true God and converted. According to these histories, the Castilians did not bring them Christianity. God did.

In conceding to Castilian sovereignty and challenging the basis of a Just War, Tlaxcalans made the argument that they were not a subjugated people. Rather, as they consistently argued, their relationship with the Crown was contractual. To make certain that the basis of their legal relationship with the Crown was clear, Tlaxcalans wrote, "in peace and love, our ancestors received [the Crown's representatives] in the conquest and pacification." While other native Americans might have been incorporated into the Crown and Christendom through a Just War of conquest, Tlaxcalans allied with the Christians and voluntarily recognized the Crown and God. Continuing the petition, they wrote:

> . . . treating Cortés and his companions very well, they give them many presents: a great quantity of gold, precious gems and other necessities of great value, including all the food that they should need. In effect, Tlaxcalans treated them and loved them as our own brothers. . . .

In asserting their brotherly bond and love, the Tlaxcalans asserted their equality with the Crown representative, Cortés, with whom they had allied as equals, and now petitioned the Crown as leader of equals.

With their legal relationship to the Crown clearly articulated, the Tlaxcalans continued their petition with a detailed recounting of the services rendered by their ancestors during the conquest and pacification of Mesoamerica:

> Afterward, our ancestors . . . aided in the conquest of the provinces of Cholula, Tepeyaca, Quauhquiohulla, the city of México, Guatemala, Culhaucan and

others, so much so that they were at war with all the people. They provided all the necessary supplies until the land had been conquered, pacified and reduced to obedience and vassalage of your majesty. In the wars and pacification of this land . . . many lords and highly achieved and skilled persons of the province of Tlaxcala died in your royal service. Additionally . . . when the Marques retreated from Mexico routed and with the majority of his Spanish company dead . . . our ancestors received him in the province of Tlaxcala with love. They voluntarily walked alongside him so that he never felt pain and offered him new assistance and help. The people and all the provisions were provided for the conquest at the expense of the province of Tlaxcala until the city of Mexico and its subjects were subjugated . . . the city and province of Tlaxcala spent and consumed the majority of our rents.[7]

In sum, according to the petition, Tlaxcalans fought for the king and for the glory of God at extraordinary personal and communal expense. By stressing the sacrifices of their ancestors in serving king and God, and in subjugating other native people who did not voluntarily submit, they underscored their shared commitment to the Crown's mission to expand Christendom. In the decades immediately following the conquest, the Tlaxcalans used this rhetoric to secure rights and privileges that provided them relative autonomy (the right to retain their dominion and to self-govern) and status within the emerging imperial world.

Were the Tlaxcalans' arguments a direct response to the debates? While it is impossible to know, the Tlaxcalan nobles were at court in 1529, when the Crown gathered the leading scholars and thinkers of Iberia in Barcelona to discuss Spanish sovereignty and native people in the Americas. Indeed, they spent a year at court in this first visit. Considering the political astuteness of the Tlaxcalans, it seems fair to conclude that they knew about the debates and framed their argument accordingly. When the Tlaxcalans sent a second delegation in 1535, headed by the newly elected governor don Diego de Maxixcatzin, the governor returned to New Spain on the same ship as incoming Viceroy Mendoza.[8] Making use of the opportunity, don Diego Maxixcatzin became acquainted with the incoming viceroy. In reflecting on this first meeting, Viceroy Mendoza wrote that the Tlaxcalans were "honorable people, good Christians and friends of the Spanish."[9] Finally, it is interesting to note that the famous jurist, theologian, and philosopher Francisco de Vitoria (c. 1492 –August 12, 1546) concluded in his famous relection, De Indis (On the American Indians) from 1537–1538, that Just War could be waged for the sake of allies and friends. Vitoria explained, "This is what is said to have happened when the Tlaxcaltecs were fighting the Mexicans; they made a treaty with the Spaniards that they should help them to defeat the Mexicans, and promised them to return whatever they might win by the laws of war."[10] Clearly, the

Tlaxcalans nurtured a powerful network and paid attention to the political discourse in the empire.

In the 1562 petition, the Tlacxalans ultimately asked the king to uphold his end of the contract and to affirm the privileges granted by his father, Charles V, as well as to continue to favor and honor the City of Tlaxcala in all that they requested. To secure the continuity of this political and legal relationship, the Tlaxcalan nobles requested that their privilege and preeminence be granted to the sons, grandsons, and descendents of the lords of Tlaxcala. Among other rights and privileges, Tlaxcalans also requested that Spaniards not be granted lands within the territories of the City and Province of Tlaxcala and that free-ranging livestock not be permitted to graze in Tlaxcala (a law that came back to haunt the nobles when they began to pasture livestock).[11] In remuneration for serving the Crown, they wanted their lands protected.

This rhetoric of loyal service was not limited to petitions; it was a sophisticated campaign to promote an image of Tlaxcalans as loyal servants of the Crown. In 1545 the Tlaxcalans undertook the construction of *casas reales* to house the viceroy and other dignitaries when they stayed in Tlaxcala during their ritualized reenactment of the route taken by Cortes from Veracruz to Mexico City. Upon finishing the buildings, the Tlaxcalans illustrated scenes of the conquest and baptism of the nobles on the walls of the main sitting room to remind the royal officials of their loyal service to the Crown.[12] To reinforce this message, the Tlaxcalans often also staged dramatizations of the conquest for their honored guests. Similarly, in 1548, a Tlaxcalan patriot and member of the *cabildo*, Tadeo de Niza, wrote a Tlaxcalan version of the conquest in Roman script, which probably accompanied a series of petitions that they sent to the Crown mid-century;[13] in 1550, Tlaxcalans commissioned a pictorial history, the *Lienzo de Tlaxcala*, to illustrate Tlaxcalan acceptance of Castilian sovereignty and Catholicism, and their service during the conquest in 76 picture plates. They sent one copy to the king and one to the viceroy, and one stayed in the community archive. In essence, Tlaxcalans never missed an opportunity to articulate their loyalty and service to royal officials and to assert their deserved honored place within colonial society—and the obligation of royal authorities to preserve their authority over the land and labor of their community.

Indeed, this rhetoric garnered Tlaxcalans numerous rights and privileges. In addition to the right to never be assigned status as an *encomienda* and to remain free subjects of the Crown, the community was also granted an exemption from royal tribute and were never required to pay the royal collectors more than eight fanegas—a truly nominal sum. Individual native nobles also secured the trappings of nobility typical to Spanish hidalgos (minor nobles)—including noble titles, coats of arms, the right to bear arms, the right to dress as Spaniards, and the right to ride a horse. Each right and privilege bolstered their status, which was leveraged to their advantage in legal claims and counterclaims.

The Tlaxcalans depicted their alliance with Cortés in the *Lienzo de Tlaxcala* (Paintings of Tlaxcala). Painted in the mid–sixteenth century, the images tell the story of the conquest from a native perspective. This illustration shows the embrace and cross that cemented their relationship with the Spanish. *Source:* Próspero Cahuantzi, ed., *Lienzo de Tlaxcala* (1560, facsimile, n.p., ca. 1890). *Courtesy of The Bancroft Library, University of California, Berkeley*

Despite their early success in the courts, they needed to continue to innovate to succeed in the changing political reality. Within a decade of the conquest, the Crown began to rein in the *encomenderos* and ruling military elite, and to assert the supremacy of a royal authority through an imperial bureaucracy. When the Tlaxcalans observed this shift, they sent a second delegation to Iberia in 1534. Building on the royal promise that they would never be designated as an *encomienda*, they petitioned for a mandate that they never be removed from the Crown and the title "the Loyal and Noble City of Tlaxcala." As in the previous petition, their request was prefaced with a discussion of the invaluable services rendered during the conquest and their continued loyalty to the Crown. However, responding to the changing political environment, the Tlaxcalan nobles also presented themselves as administrators of a city, rather than as conquistadors and lords. They had formed a *cabildo* and sent their new *Gobernador de Indios*, don Diego Maxixcatzin Tliquiyahuatzin, who, not by coincidence, was the highest ranked noble in Tlaxcala.[14] Aligning themselves with the emerging royal bureaucracy, they distanced themselves from their *former* ally, Hernando Cortés, who had become embattled in lawsuits with the *audiencia* and Crown to preserve his *encomiendas* and authority. Instead, they associated themselves with the royal bureaucracy by traveling with the *audiencia* judge Juan de Salmerón.[15] It was in response to this shift in strategy that they received the invaluable privilege on March 13, 1535, that placed the community and its territory perpetually under royal authority.[16] This placed their lands in a legal category that provided them with extraordinary legal leverage to protect their land claims in perpetuity.

In response to the same petition, Tlaxcalans secured a coat of arms and the title "The Loyal City of Tlaxcala" in April 1535.[17] Later, they successfully upgraded their title to "the very noble and very loyal city of Tlaxcala." Although symbolic, the title affirmed the status of their province as a city—the highest municipal status available in Castile. This afforded them the legal grounds to establish the boundaries for their municipality (villages or *pueblos* could not establish boundaries). Indeed, their successful campaign secured them numerous rights and privileges and established their reputation as loyal servants of the Crown. While this perception of Tlaxcalans persists today with less fortunate implications, in the sixteenth century it provided them with important legal means to protect their natural resources.

Why were the Tlaxcalans successful? Other native communities could and did frame their requests to the Crown with the rhetoric of loyal service. In fact, some stated that they wanted rights and privileges similar to those of the Tlaxcalans, and a few asserted that they had provided greater service to the Crown than the Tlaxcalans and therefore deserved greater rewards than the privileged Indian community.[18] Nonetheless, a couple of factors separated these petitioners from the Tlaxcalans. The Tlaxcalans pursued royal favors immediately following the conquest, while most native petitioners sought royal favors several decades after the conquest. When their requests were being brought to the king, the sense of abundance had dissipated: booty had been allocated, and the real cost of maintaining an empire had begun to weigh heavily on the Crown. Why did the Tlaxcalans understand the imperial system so quickly? Although it is difficult to provide the figurative smoking gun of historical evidence, the Tlaxcalans' swift and effective response to Spanish imperialism appears to have rested on their ability to retain their sovereignty in the face of Aztec imperial aggression. In addition to developing sophisticated diplomatic skills, they were skilled warriors who doggedly pursued autonomy. Many native communities and individuals ultimately acquired similar symbolic rights and privileges, but few secured the level acquired by the Tlaxcalans and fewer secured the limited royal tribute obligation enjoyed by the Tlaxcalans.

Furthermore, the Tlaxcalan nobility's inclination to defend their authority and territories coincided with the Iberian political tradition of governing through the local elite. Throughout the late medieval period, the Castilian Crown had ruled through contractual relationships and had expanded and consolidated royal authority by negotiating with aristocrats, urban patricians, Church officials, and other corporate authorities. Remaining rooted in this late-medieval world, early sixteenth-century imperial governance relied on the cooperation of local elites to rule its kingdoms. Accordingly, its primary means for asserting royal authority and control was to ally itself strategically with local and corporate constituents in their quotidian struggles. In rewarding individuals and communities for loyal service, the system strengthened contractual obligations while providing relative autonomy.

The early requests of the Tlaxcalans arrived when the Crown was still building the empire with loyalty and contractual obligations. The petitions of other native people often coincided with the Crown's efforts to rein in the *encomenderos* and ruling elite in order to assert the supremacy of the royal bureaucracy. Although this language of loyal service never entirely disappears, in the changing political culture of the empire it became increasingly obsolete. Despite the efforts of many to secure rights, few petitions based on services rendered during the conquest received rewards after the midcentury.

Buen Gobierno

The rhetoric of loyal service gave way to rhetoric of good government (*buen gobierno*) in the mid–sixteenth century. In their petitions, the Tlaxcalans asserted that the Crown was obligated to maintain peace and tranquility within its realm, and to remedy the injustices and wrongdoings that created social discord. This rhetoric echoed the description of kingship in the second book of the *Siete Partidas*—the thirteenth-century legal compilation of Alfonso X.[19] In describing the duties of the king, Alfonso the Learned drew from the theories of secular authority in Roman, the Visigothic, and the Church traditions. In the *Siete Partidas*, the discussion of kingship is followed by a discussion of the relationship between king and subject, and their mutual obligation. The laws and policies of the Crown needed to accord with the existing legal traditions, canon law and natural law. Whereas these ideals informed the contractual relations between the Crown and its subjects in the Middle Ages, in the fifteenth century they began to form the ideological foundation of the emerging royal bureaucracy in Iberia.

Although not all Castilians agreed that the conquest was just or Castilian sovereignty in the Americas was legal, Castilian *imperium* was a foregone conclusion by mid-century. With the establishment of bureaucratic institutions in the Americas, the peninsular debates shifted to whether native people were rational and how to govern native subjects. Castilians asked: did native people have the capacity to understand civil society (*civitus*) and the rationality to self-govern? While some theologians such as Juan Ginés de Sepúlveda argued that native people fit the Aristotelian category of natural slaves and therefore needed to be ruled, most agreed that native people needed

Spanish tutelage to reach their full potential.[20] They needed to be civilized, and Castilians were obligated to guide native people to live according to canon law and natural law. Attuned to the changes, the Tlaxcalans demonstrated their rationality and adjusted their legal strategies. They had elected municipal officials and a native governor and began to present themselves as a native municipality—rather than a confederacy of noble houses—by the 1530s. By midcentury, they framed their interests in the rhetoric of good government and explained how current circumstances fell short of the Castilians ideals of *buen gobierno*.

The Tlaxcalans' skillful use of Spanish political theory is evident in a petition from 1561. They wrote (see appendix, Document II, for a full Spanish version of the petition):

> Peaceful prince you teach us many things . . . such as that kings compel and force, remove and add laws and statues for the good government of his kingdoms, the peace and tranquility of them.

As before, Tlaxcalans recognized the distinct nature of their relationship to the Crown. Going beyond merely reminding the Crown of its obligation to maintain peace and tranquility in its kingdoms, the Tlaxcalan nobles wrote that the Crown had taught them many things, notably the precepts of good governance. In so doing, the Tlaxcalans remind the Crown of its heightened responsibility to "civilize" its native subjects and to provide an exemplary model of good governance—the fundamental justification for its presence in the Americas. They continued:

> Not only this, but more, you teach your subordinates and your vassals that, when these laws are not kept by your governors and justices, your subjects can humbly approach the royal *audiencias* and *chancillerias* and ask for favor and intervention. When this is not enough, then [we can go] to the feet of the same person in which divine, civil and natural law lies. You are obligated as *señor*, king and father to hear your [vassals], protect them and sustain them in justice. . . .

With this, the Tlaxcalan nobles demonstrated that they understood the procedures for seeking justice within the imperial bureaucracy, and asserted that these were established for their well-being. Again, as always, they demonstrated their rationality and undermined arguments to the contrary. They continued—strongly insinuating that the royal officials in New Spain did not always uphold the ideal of Castilian notions of good governance.

> We, the people and province of Tlaxcala, . . . [know the] cost when these laws, given by your majesty for peace and governance, . . . are not upheld.

> Particularly . . . [the mandates issued] from the Christian heart, perpetual
> and glorious memory of Carlos I, your father who gave and mandated that
> his laws would be preserved perpetually for the great service that we gave for
> your royal Crown.

Finally, they lauded the king for correcting such wrongs—as a good Christian king and head of the royal bureaucracy was obligated to do. With the requisite humility, they informed the Crown that it must honor their requests for laws to protect them from Spanish incursions in order to justify its continued rule in the Americas. In it, they asked the Crown for several new laws, including a law that prohibited the awarding of Spanish ranches within the region.

> We appear with this petition and humbly present ourselves and prostrate
> ourselves at the royal feet of your majesty asking that you . . . not award ranches
> to Spaniards within the limits of our lands and province. . . .[21]

The Tlaxcalan elite's sophisticated use of Castilian political philosophy obligated the Crown to prohibit Iberian settlers from their region.

Responding to similar petitions, the Crown promulgated numerous mandates on their behalf. For example, using the rhetoric of *buen gobierno*, the Tlaxcalans had solicited the Crown in 1550 for a mandate to prohibit royal officials from granting land near native villages in New Spain. In this mandate, the Crown ordered its royal officials to assign land to both large- and small-livestock ranches in uninhabited areas away from native villages, where the livestock could graze without harming native crops. Furthermore, it required that herdsmen accompany all herds and keep the livestock from entering native fields. Finally, when damages occurred, the guilty party was to be punished severely and was to pay for the damages caused by his livestock. For accountability purposes, the Crown required royal officials to report on how such situations were resolved. The Crown admonished its officials to consider this an important matter and to remedy it immediately.[22] Shortly thereafter, this royal mandate was promulgated for all of the American kingdoms and ultimately was included in the 1680 compilation of current laws governing the Americas—the *Recopilación de Leyes*.[23] Tlaxcalan legal rhetoric reflected a chorus of native voices demanding that their land and resources be protected.

It should be noted that despite most historians' assertions that theologians, such as Francisco de Vitoria and Bartolomé de las Casas, or royal officials, such as Vasco de Quiroga or Bishop Sebastian Ramírez de Fuenleal, humanized Crown policy,[24] native people influenced royal policies in concrete and legally significant ways through their skillful use of legal rhetoric.

Indios Miserables

As the policies and enforcement of the imperial bureaucracy developed, its primary purpose was to mediate between communities. Responding to the petitions and lawsuits that asked royal officials to intervene on behalf of native people, the Crown increasingly promulgated imperial laws that addressed widespread grievances. In identifying the population to whom these laws applied, the Crown consistently and conveniently used the legal category "*indios*." Accordingly, the rhetorical strategy of the Tlaxcalans shifted from obligating the Crown to protect the natives (*naturales*) of Tlaxcala—a legal category that signaled one's membership to a particular community based on birth—to requesting that it promulgate and enforce imperial laws that protected the *indios* in Tlaxcala. With these later petitions, they adopted a new political rhetoric, namely, the language of *miserables,* which would dominate their petitions during the last quarter of the sixteenth century.

By the end of the sixteenth century, the Crown's policies of protection had made the category of "*indios*" interchangeable with the legal categories of minors and *miserables*. Similar to *miserables*, persons who identified as *indios* could demand protection, favor, and defense with the royal courts based on their inherent status. As the Crown wrote in 1580:

> It is our wish to charge the Viceroys, Presidents and *audiencias* with the responsibility of looking after the Indians. We order that they protect, favor and care [for the Indians], for we desire, that the harms and sufferings be remedied, and that they live without harassment or vexation . . . that they be favored, protected and defended against whatever harm . . . and that you punish transgressors . . . with rigor. . . .[25]

Accordingly, the viceroy of New Spain, don Luis de Velasco the son, one of the principal proponents of reforming the royal bureaucracy, wrote to Phillip II in 1592, stating that, "the protection and conservation of the miserable natives is one of the most important businesses of this kingdom."[26] He continued by arguing that in addition to favoring Indians when they were defendants—a long-standing Crown policy—native people should also be favored when they were plaintiffs. He wrote, ". . . when they bring a case against a Spaniard, their lands and miserable possessions have already been harmed; it is in these cases, that they most need to be favored."[27] As the imperial bureaucracy matured, one of the primary commissions entrusted to royal officials was the protection and conservation of the native population.

Indeed, Spanish paternalism toward native people persisted. For example, in 1632, when Viceroy don Rodrigo Pacheco sent Licenciado don Alonso de Uria y Tovar to inspect the *obrajes* (sweatshops) in Los Angeles, Tlaxcala, Cholula, and Huejotzingo, he directed the *licenciado* to "be particularly careful and vigilant in executing [his] commission, and in protecting and conserving these miserable people."[28] Likewise, when Pacheco instructed Doctor Diego Barrientos de Rivera to inspect the land titles of the Spaniards living in Tlaxcala, he reminded him that, "the natives of this kingdom—miserable people and of little talent—are defrauded and tricked by Spaniards and other people in the buying of their land and possessions."[29] As Woodrow Borah argues, in his classic book on the *Juzgado General de Indios*, having categorized native people as *miserables*, the Spanish Crown insured them justice.[30]

Concurrently, the legal and political arguments of the Tlaxcalans shifted from emphasizing their services and loyalty to focusing on the suffering of the common Indians. Recognizing the usefulness of the protections offered by the identity of *miserable*, Tlaxcalan nobles increasingly asserted that native commoners needed to be favored and protected by Spaniards. They wrote, for instance:

> [Spaniards] have been introducing . . . small and large livestock that cause many notable damages and problems in the commoners fields of cochineal and corn of the natives, they continue doing such because [the natives] are not favored by the justices, because the sympathy they have is for the Spaniards . . . such that the many native people flee and leave their houses and lands unprotected because of the cattle . . .[31]

Continuing in the petition, they described the various abuses and problems perpetrated by the Spaniards.

Similarly, in the 1562 petition discussed earlier, their rhetoric clearly shifts from asserting loyal service to asserting the status of *miserables*. In addition to asserting that they should not be obligated to pay any royal tribute, they pleaded with the Crown to grant them jurisdiction over several neighboring Indian villages that Cortés had promised them in remuneration for their aide during the conquest. To emphasize the justness of this request and establish the injustice they had endured, they explained how they recently had provided men and supplies, twice, at the request of President Nuño Guzman as well as Viceroy don Antonio de Mendoza, in order to conquer and pacify the kingdom of Nueva Galicia. But, despite their continued loyalty and service, they had never been remunerated for the extraordinary deeds and services of their ancestors, despite the great cost in Tlaxcalan lives and to their treasury. Instead of receiving authority over Tepeyaca, Tecamachalco, Cuauhquehulla, Yctzohcan, and other native communities, as they had been promised, they had suffered poor treatment and vexatious demands for tribute and personal services. Even though the Crown had not properly reciprocated, they asserted to the king that the Tlaxcalans had always served the Crown with the "zeal and loyalty that we always have in serving your majesty." While claims of loyal service persisted, they were framed in rhetoric of transgressions and wrongdoings. This petition illustrates well the shift toward claims to the status of *miserables*.

Similar to the rhetoric of loyalty and service to the Crown, this new rhetoric of *miserables* was creatively deployed and provided a language that obligated royal officials to intervene on behalf of native people. Undoubtedly, many of their claims to misery were justified. Indeed, by the end of the century, disease had decimated much of the native population and had caused economic and political catastrophe. It was this element of truth that made their arguments effective. Nonetheless, misery did not entirely characterize their lived experience. The Tlaxcalan elite continued to pursue and receive privileges for themselves, while using the rhetoric of *indios miserables*. In addition to receiving coats of arms and other rights of nobility, they secured a tribute exemption for the Tlaxcalan families who settled the northern frontier of New Spain and a promise that all the privileges awarded to one Tlaxcalan settlement would be applied to all settlements. The Tlaxcalans used the legal rhetoric that best served their needs and the legal-political situation: sometimes, they used the rhetoric of loyalty and service, asserting their existing privileges and rights; at other times, they claimed misery, and they obligated the Crown to protect the *indios miserables*. Importantly, the elite very seldom used the rhetoric of *indios miserables* to reference themselves.

Tlaxcalans were attuned to the world around them and were astute participants in it. Often scholars have read legal documents as reflecting native reality. Legal documents, however, reveal the legal strategies of native people more than they articulate native reality. Native people understood the political milieu in which they were operating, and they articulated their concerns in language that would bring success for their legal and political pursuits. It reveals their agency in that it shows how they acted in and on the emerging imperial system.

In distinguishing between rhetoric and reality, and in revealing native people's conscious and strategic use of Castilian rhetoric, this chapter attempts to draw a fine but crucial line between asserting that their arguments were dictated by the power relations of the empire, and that their legal arguments reflected an authentic native voice. Implicitly, the Tlaxcalan elite's decision to adopt Castilian traditions and practices acknowledged and legitimated the developing power relations in the empire. They inherently acknowledged the authority of the Crown when they pursued justice in the imperial courts, and, to be effective in their legal arguments, they necessarily told a story that spoke to the Crown and its royal officials and moved the authorities to act on behalf of the Indian community. Conceding the influence of such instances of royal power, it is argued here that they constructed their arguments creatively and consciously as agents and historical actors. Their lived experience and Castilian law influenced but did not determine their story or legal strategy.

In addition, in asserting that their legal arguments were creative stories that were influenced by the rhetorical norms and political culture of Castile, this chapter concedes that legal arguments contain elements of truth and recognizable descriptions of reality but concurrently asserts that they are artifacts of human creativity, first and foremost. It is a fine line between truth and creativity that a successful legal argument must maintain. Thus, rather than being evidence of native people's reality, legal documents reveal native people's ingenuity and agency. Native people were not solely responding to a changing imperial culture, but, as petitioners and litigants, they were part of the legal dialogue that contributed to the shifts in the legal culture of the empire and informed their claims and counterclaims to land.

Appendix: Petitions from Tlaxcalans

I. 1562 Petition from Tlaxcalans to Philip II

Continuando esta ciudad y provincia de Tlascalla en el deseo y voluntad con q siempre hemos servido y deseamos servir a v.m. y considerando la necesidad grande q tenemos de ocurrir a vra rreal persona como a tan poderoso y chatholico rrey y señor nro hemos acordado de ymbiar a don pablo de galizia a q al presente es governador y a don lucas Garcia y a don antonio de la pedrosa y a don alonso gomez principales de las quatro cabeceras desta provincia para q en nombre de todos besen a vm sus rreales manos y supliquen algunas cosas q mucho ymportan al descargo de su rreal conciencia y bien nro comos se entendera por esta y la ynstrucion q les hemos dado suplicamos humillmentea vm sea senido mandar los oys y hazernos merced de que un brevedad sean despachados concediendonos lo, q ellos en nro nombre suplicaron, q en sustancia sera lo mismo, q en esta se dira lo primero suplicamos a vm sea servido tener memoria de la fidelidad y lealtad grande con q nros padres y antepasados sirvieron a la corona rreal y la con q nosotros hemos servido y servimos special y señaladamente, q quando a estas partes vino don hernando cortes marques del valle con la gente española, q en su compania truxo para la conquista y pacificacion dellas le salieron a rrescebir de paz y le rrescibieron con todo amor y paz y voluntad dandole la obediencia en vro rreal nombre y poniendose debaxo del dominio y señorio del emperador nro señor de gloriosa memoria y fueron los q primero vinieron en conoscimiento de nra sancta fe catholica ofresciendo toda la ayuda y socorro para la dicha conquista y hizieron a el y a sus companeros muy bien tratamiento dandoles muchos presentes en mucha cantidad de oro y piedras preciosos y otras cosas necesarias de mucho valor y toda la comida q ovieron menester y en efeto los trataron y amaron como a propios hermanos y despues que se rreformaron en la dicha probincia el dicho marques y sus companeros de las trabajos q avian pashados por el mar y por el camino les socorrieron parar la conquista de las provincias de Cholullan, tepeyacaq cuauhqueohullan y la ciudad de Mexico, y cuauhtemalla y culhuacan y otras q estavan de guerra con toda la gente y bastimentos necessarios hasta q con la dicha ayuda y socorro las conquisto y pacifico y reduxo a la obediençia y vasallaxe de vm y en las dhas guerras y pacificaciones y otras q despues se ofreçieron morieron en su real servicio muchos principales de la dicha provincia de Tlascalla personas muy senaladas y calificadas demas y aliende de otra gente infinita yspecialmente quando el dho marques se rretiro de mexico desbaratado y muerta la mayor parte de la gente española q tenia en su compania q se la mataron los mexicanos le rrescibieron en la dha probincia de tlaxcallan con el amor y voluntad q siempre caminandole para q no tuviese pena y ofreciendole nuevo socorro y ayuda de gente y todo lo demas necesario a costa propia de la dha probincia de Tlaxcallan hasta q ganase la dha ciudad de Mexico y sus subjetos como en efeto le socorrieron y fue mucha gente con el y la ganaron en lo qual todo y en otras cosas muy senaladas q en el servicyo de v.m. hizo la dha ciudad y probincia de tlascala se gastaron y consumjeron la mayor parte de las rrentas y haziendas de nros antepasados y aunque el dho marques rreconociendo los servicyos notables y a vm hexzimos en esto y otras cosas y las perdidas de la hazienda q a esta causa se nos rrecreciero ofrescio y dio palabra en vro rreal nombre de dar a la dha provincia de tlascallan en paga de los dhos trabajos y costas los pueblos de tepeyacac y tecamachalco, y cuauhquehullan y yctzohcan y otros demas q seriamos libres y no obligados a tributar cosa alguna a v.m. hasta agora no se nos andando mi hecho mrd paga ni otra rremuneracion alguna antes rrescibio la dicha probincia despues la dicha conquista muchos malos tratamientos y bexaciones asi en tributos como en servicios personales y aunque asimesmo despues al tiempo q el presidente Niño de Guzman fue a la conquista del nuevo Reino de Galizia y quando sea [] lo de nuevo algunos años despues de conquistada al tiempo que el visorrey don Antonio de Mendoça fue a pacificar la con el zelo y lealtad q siempre hemos tenido al servicyo de vm fuymos ambas vezes con mucha gente y a nra propia consta y servimos en la guerra hasta q se pacifico y allano el dho nuevo rreyno de galizia no se nos hecho merced alguna antes los ofiçiales de la hazienda de v.m. nos haze pagar de tributo en cada un ano lo dho mill fanegas de mahiz sin embargo de lo q asi el dho marques nos ofrescio en la palabra que dio

II. 1561 Petition from Tlaxcalans to Philip II

Ansí como la variedad de los tiempos serenísimo príncipe enseña muchas cosas ansí esa misma trae y acarrea muchas, tantas y tales que a los rreyes compelen y fuerzan a hacer y quitar y añadir leyes y estatutos para el buen govierno de sus rreynos, paz y tranquilidad dellos y no solo esto, más a un a los súbditos y vasallos compele y enseña a que, quando las tales no son guardadas por sus governadores y justicias, acudan humildemente por saludable favor y remedio a los estrados rreales de las audiencias y chançillerias rreales y quando esto no bastare a los pies de esa misma persona rreal el qual en ley divina, çevil y natural esta obligado como señor rey y padre a oyrlos ampararlos y sustentarlos en justiçia por lo qual nos el pueblo y provincia de tascallan por lo qual el pueblo visto y considerado y muy a nuestra costa quan poco algunas leyes dadas por vuestra magestad para la paz y govierno destos rreynos son guardadas y particularmente para esta nuestra rrepublica y provincia mandadas del christianisimo pecho de perpetua y gloriosa memoria don carlos vuestro padre por las quales dio y mando que perpetuamente fueren guardadas atento los grandes servicios por nos hechos a la corona rreal pareçemos y con esta petiçion humilmente presentamos y postrándonos a los reales pies de vuestra magestad suplicamos mande nuestros privilegios sean guardados los quales son que ninguna estancia se pueda dar a españoles en todo el termino de nuestras tierras y provincia mandado se quiten las que contra nuestros privilegios agora a dado vuestro governador pues presupuesto que algun día hemos dejar más que fueron nuestros antepasados hemos menester nuestras tierras y mucho mas.

Otros si suplicamos pues la real corona nos hizo libres y francos de pecho y tributo ateno la mucha sangre que en conquistar y entregar la tierra gastamos mande vuestrra magestad no paguemos ocho mill hanegas de mayz que vuestros officiales nos hazen pagar como pecheros, y porque en todo esperamos y confiamos en todo seremos faborescidos somos leales vasallos que siempre hemos sido, cesamos de proceder y ser más largos y molestos con nuestro tosco y grosero modo de hablar a lo qual nos compele el no a ver ya en esta tierra escrivano que quiera dar nos por testimonio los agravios que nos son hechos por temor de no desagradar a vuestras justicias lo qual visto rrogamos al padre fray Alonso de Maldonado que la presente lleva y hable por nos, visto el amor que nos tiene y el fabor que de sus prelados lleva el qual lleva nuestras firmas y poder y la en que siempre hemos servido a vuestra magestad he dha en esta vuestra muy leal ciudad de Tlaxcala y veinte y tres días del mes de julio año del santo nacimiento de nro salvador jesu cristo de mill y quinientos y sesenta y un año

CRM

muy leales vasallos q como da sujeccion besan sus rreales pies y manos

Pablo de Galizia, D. Blas Osorio, Felipe Mejía, Don Juan Xicoténcatl, Don Juan Maxiscotzin, Don Francisco de Medoça, Don Antonio de Luna, Lucas Garcia, Thadeo de nava, Calixto Portugual, Pedro Diaz, Francisco Vazques, Pedro de San Lazaro.

Detras: Resolucion- q sigan su justicia sonde vieren q les conviene

NOTES

1. *Documentos inéditos del siglo XVI para la historia de México*, ed. by Cuevas, Mariano and Genaro García (Mexico City: Talleres del Museo Nacional de Arqueología, Historia y Etnología, 1914), 183–218; and AGI, México, 94, N. 2.

2. AGI, México, 94, N. 2.

3. "... presidentes et oydores de la nra audiencia y chancelleria Real de la nueva españa yo soy ynformada q los yndios de la provincia de tlaxcala son los q mejor nos han servido en la conquista e pacificacion de esa tierra comidimente en la tomada de la ciudad de México y despues quando se bino a recobrar la dicha ciudad yendo solo de mas e / / en esa tierra y nos fue suplicado y pedido por md q en Remuneracion de sus servicios los mandasemos libertad d estuviesen encomendados a nos ni a otras personas algunas pues por su causa se gano la tierra de q dios nro senior a sido y es tan servydo complidamente que diz que no sierven salvo con ciertos cahizes de mayz y era cosa tan justa que fuesen gratificados como la nra md fuese por ende yo vos mando q/el negozes informmeys de sepays como lo suso dicha et cada cosa e parte de ella a pasado y pasa e q por ninguna es la suso dicha y de los yndios de ella e de su calidad y en q nos han servido y con q contribuyen y aquin y quien los tiene Encomendados e si sera bien libertallos para q no esten encomendados a nadie et de todo de demas de q cerca de esto vieredeis que debemos saber para ser mejor informados de la dicha ynformacion debida con vro parecer de lo q en ello se debe proveer la enbias Ante nos al no consejo de las yndias para que yo la mandever e por verlo q mas convenga a nos servyo fecha en toledo a diez dias del mes de agosto de mil e quinto e beynte et nuebe Años yo la Reyna por mandado de su maj. Juan valezquez senlo lada del conde ed del dottor Beltran e de licenciado de la Corte. La Reyna. AGI, México, 1088, 1, F. 38r–39r; Charles Gibson wrote that no privilege came from this first visit to Spain. However, he did not travel to Spain for his research on Tlaxcala and, therefore, would not have seen this document. Charles Gibson, *Tlaxcala in the Sixteenth Century* (New Haven, CT: Yale University Press, 1952), 164.

4. A *cahiz* is a dry measure equal to 12 *fanegas*, a *fenagas* is equal to about an English bushel, or about a hundredweight of grain; unit of area originally equal to as much tilled ground as was necessary to sow a *fanega* of wheat, but usually standardized as 12 *celemines* or 576 square *estadales*, equal to about 1.59 acres. David E. Vassberg, Glossary in *Land and Society in Golden Age of Castile* (Cambridge: Cambridge University Press, 1984).

5. See this chapter's appendix, Document I, for a full Spanish version of the petition.

6. While the original work no longer exists, Alva de Ixtlilxochitl included excerpts in his Sumaria. These excerpts indicate that it was a cooperative effort of the thirty cabildo members and Niza who wanted to record accurately their memories of the Spanish conquest for the benefit of the king. Fernando de Alva Ixtlilxóchitl, *Obras históricas: incluyen el texto completo de las llamadas Relaciones e Historia de la nación chichimeca en una nueva versión establecida con el cotejo de los manuscritos más antiguos que se conocen.* ed. by E. O'Gorman. 3. ed. (Mexico City [México, D.F.]: Universidad Nacional Autónoma de México, Instituto de Investigaciones Históricas. 1975).

7. AGI, México, 94, N. 2.

8. Gibson, *Tlaxcala in the Sixteenth Century*, 165.

9. "Fragmento de la visita hecha Á Antonio De Mendoza," in *Colección de documentos para la historia de México*, ed. Joaquín García Icazbalceta, 2 vols., (México, D.F.: Antigua Librería, 1866), 2:87.

10. Fray Francisco de Vitoria, "De Indis," in *Political Writings*, ed. by Anthony Pagden and Jeremy Lawrence (Cambridge: Cambridge University Press, 1991), 289.

11. AGI, México, 94, N. 2.

12. Gibson, *Tlaxcala in the Sixteenth Century*, 125; Elisa Vargas Lugo, "*El Bautizo de los Señores de Tlaxcala*," Archivo Español de Arte [Spain] 63 (1990): 621–632.

13. See note 5.

14. James Lockhart has argued that the Tlaxcalans experienced the cabildo as a native institution in Spanish guise; see James Lockhart, "Some Nahua Concepts in Postconquest Guise," *History of European Ideas [Great Britain]* 6, no. 4 (1985). Indeed, within Spanish tradition, the cabildo collected the taxes, allocated the lands of the community, regulated agriculture and markets, and served as the first instance in legal conflicts, which were essentially the same responsibilities the elite exercised during the pre-Hispanic period. While the adaptation of the cabildo did not transform dramatically local governance, as I argue elsewhere, it did allow the four noble houses in the center of the region to centralize political power. See R. Jovita Baber, "Empire, Indians and the Negotiation for Status in the City of Tlaxcala, 1521–1550," in *Negotiation with Domination: Colonial New Spain's Indian Pueblos Confront the Spanish State*, ed. by Ethelia Ruíz Medrano and Susan Kellogg. (Denver: University Press of Colorado, 2010).

15. Juan Buenaventura Zapata y Mendoza, *Historia cronológica de la noble ciudad de Tlaxcala* (Tlaxcala, Mexico: Universidad Autónoma de Tlaxcala); Mexico City (México, D.F.): Centro de Investigaciones y Estudios Superiores en Antropología Social, 1995 [1689]), 141; and Carlos V, *Documentos Y Reales Cédulas De La Ciudad De Tlaxcala*, ed. Mercedes Meade de Angulo (Tlaxcala, Mexico: Gobierno del Estado de Tlaxcala a través del Instituto Tlaxcalteca de la Cultura, 1984), unnumbered.

16. AGI, Patronato, 275, R. 20, AHET, 1533, caja 1, exp. 6, AHET, 1535, caja 1, exp. 7, AHET, 1530, caja 1, exp. 5, ff. 2v–9v.

17. AHET, 1539, caja 1, exp. 10 and Carlos V, *Documentos Y Reales Cédulas De La Ciudad De Tlaxcala*.

18. See for example, Ixtlilxóchitl, Fernando de Alva, "Relación De La Venida De Los Españoles Y Principio De La Ley Evangélica," in *Historia General De Las Cosas De Nueva España*, ed. by Bernardino de Sahagún, (Mexico City [México, D.F.]: Porrúa, 1981).

19. Alfonso X. *Las siete partidas*, ed. by S. P. Scott and R. I. Burns (Philadelphia: University of Pennsylvania Press, 2001).

20. Juan Ginés de Sepúlveda, 1490–1573 *Demócrates Segundo O De Las Justas Causas De La Guerra Contra Los Indios*, ed. by Angel Losada. (Madrid: Consejo Superior de Investigaciones Científicas, 1984).

21. AGI, México, 94, N. 2.

22. Published in Puga, Vasco de, *Provisiones Cédulas Instrucciones De Su Magestad, Ordenanzas De Difuntos Y audiencia, Para La Buena Expedición De Los Negocios Y Administración De Justicia Y Gobernación De Esta Nueva España, Y Para El Buen Tratamiento Y Conservación De Los Indios, Desde El Año 1525 Hasta El Presente De 63*. (Mexico City [México, D.F.]: Pedro de Ocharte,1563), 173.

23. Spain. *Recopilación de leyes de los reynos de las Indias, mandada imprimir y publicar por la Magestad Católica del Rey Don Carlos II, nuestro Señor*. 4 vols. (Madrid: Julián de Paredes, 1681), Ley 12, Titulo XII, Libro IV; full text of royal mandated published in *Disposiciones Complementarias De Las Leyes De Indias*, ed. by Manuel José de Ayala (Madrid: Imprenta Saez hermanos, 1930), 297–298.

24. Regarding the influence of Las Casas, see for example, Lewis Hanke, *All Mankind Is One. A Study of the Disputation between Bartolomé De Las Casas and Juan Ginés De Sepúlveda in 1550 on the Intellectual and Religious Capacity of the American Indians* (DeKalb, IL: Northern Illinois University Press, 1974); and for an argument regarding the role of administrators, see, for example, Simpson, Lesley Byrd, *The Encomienda in New Spain: The Beginnings of Spanish Mexico*. (Berkeley and Los Angeles: University of California Press, 1982 [1950]).

25. "Haviendo de tratar en este libro la materia de Indios, su libertad, aumento, y alivio, como se contiene en los titulos de que se ha formado. Es nuestra voluntad encargar á los Virreys, Presidentes, y Audiencias el cuidado de mirar por ellos, y dar las ordenes convenientes, para que sean amparados, favorecidos, y sobrellevados, por lo que deseamos, que se remedien los daños, que padecen, y vivan sin molestia, ni vejacion, quendando esto de una ves assentado, y teniendo muy presentes las leyes de esta Recopilacion, que les favorecen, amparan, y defienden de qualesquier agravios, y que las guarden, y hagan guardar muy puntualmente, castigando con particular, y rigurosa demostracion á los transgressores. Y rogamos y encargamos á los Prelados Eclesiásticos, que por su parte lo procuren como verdaderos padres espirituales de eta nueva Christiandad, y todos los conserven en sus privilegios, y prerrogativas, y tengan en su proteccion." *Recopilacíon de Leyes de los Reynos de las Indias*, Ley 1, Titulo I, Libro V.

26. ". . . este negocio por uno de los más importantes deste reino y del bien y conservación y amparo destos miserables naturales. . . ." Velasco [el hijo] (1590–1595), Virrey Luis de. 1592. Carta de D. Luis de Velasco el Segundo a Felipe II.—Mexico, 6 de Marzo de 1592, in *Documentos Inéditos Del Siglo Xvi Para La Historia De México*, ed. Mariano Cuevas and Genaro García (Mexico City (México, D.F.): Talleres del Museo Nacional de Arqueología, Historia y Etnología, 1914), 435.

27. ". . . cuando el indio llega a ser actor contra el español es que ya viene agraviado en sus tierras y miserable hacienda, y en este caso es cuando el pobre ha menester más el favor . . .", Ibid., 435.

28. ". . . tener particular cuidado y vigilancia en su ejecución y en el amparo y conservación de gente tan miserable. . . ." AGN, General de Parte, vol. 7, exp. 366, fols. 260v.

29. "los naturales deste reyno como gente miserable y de poco talento son defraudados y engañados de ordinario por españoles y otras personas en comprarles sus tierras y posessiones. . . ." AGN, General de Parte, vol. 7, exp. 67, fols. 49v.

30. Woodrow Borah, *Justice by Insurance: The General Indian Court of Colonial Mexico and the Legal Aides of the Half-Real* (Berkeley: University of California Press, 1983).

31. . . . sean ido introduciendo . . . ganados mayores y menores con que hacen notables daños y agravios con ellos en las sementeras de granas y maíces de los naturales continuándolo de [fuerte] que por esta causa y por no ser favorecidos de las justicias, por la simpática que tienen con los españoles como sus naturales se an ido y cuidado se van huyendo mucho cantidad y numero de Indios dejando y desamparando sus tierras y casas. . . . AGI, México, 274.

3

COURT AND CHRONICLE
A NATIVE ANDEAN'S ENGAGEMENT WITH
SPANISH COLONIAL LAW

Rolena Adorno

By the end of the sixteenth century, Spanish colonial rule was well established in the New World; the major, mainland conquests had toppled the Aztec federation in Mexico in the 1520s and the Inca Empire in Peru in the 1530s. The *encomienda* system of trusteeship, by which private Spanish settlers held grants to the labor and agricultural tribute of native populations, was powerful, and the system of civil governance of the natives in local municipal districts (*corregimiento*) and the ordering of native society by the church, with its ecclesiastical jurisdictions, religious orders, and extirpation-of-idolatries campaigns, were taking the shape that would be recognizable in subsequent centuries. Amerindian cultures with their traditional political loyalties and rivalries survived but were transformed by the demands of Spanish colonialism. Natives assimilated to European language and custom occupied a tenuous middle ground, or "contact zone," between Spanish colonial society and native communities.[1] Such individuals, who served local civil and ecclesiastical institutions as interpreters, frequently used their Spanish language skills to defend their claims to lands and other possessions in the Spanish colonial justice system.

A Quechua- and Spanish-speaking Andean, Felipe Guaman Poma de Ayala, supported his land claims through legal petitioning in the Spanish colonial court system, from the local tribunal in the provincial city of Huamanga all the way to the Real Audiencia, the highest civil and criminal court of the Peruvian viceroyalty, located in Lima, the City of Kings.

When his decade-long legal efforts ultimately failed, Guaman Poma took the extraordinary step of devoting at least as many years to writing a twelve-hundred-page chronicle of ancient Andean history and treatise on colonial reform. He dedicated it to the king of Spain, Philip III, and entitled it *El primer nueva corónica y buen gobierno* [*The First New Chronicle and Good Government*] (1615).[2]

Felipe Guaman Poma de Ayala, a native-born writer and activist in early colonial Peru, depicts in this drawing, entitled *Nueva corónica y buen gobierno*, his recommendation as to how to support the legal claims of native Andeans through the offices of native lords literate in Spanish.
Courtesy of The Royal Library, Copenhagen, Denmark

Guaman Poma's legal and literary activities span the period from the mid-1590s through 1615. In addition to the *Nueva corónica y buen gobierno* in Copenhagen, two sets of related testimony in Peru document Guaman Poma's experience with the Spanish colonial justice system. One, that will be referred to here as the "Compulsa Ayacucho," is preserved in the Archivo Departamental de Ayacucho, and the other, held in a private collection, is commonly called the "Expediente Prado Tello" to reference its owners and editors.[3] The Expediente Prado Tello and the Compulsa Ayacucho, which records the criminal sentence handed down against Guaman Poma in 1600, are mutually illuminating, and both are reflected in the *Nueva corónica y buen gobierno*. This chapter brings together these three bodies of pertinent "data" and assembles them into a single account: Guaman Poma's legal petitions (known since the 1950s but made available only in 1991), the separate court record of Guaman Poma's trial and conviction (discovered and published in 1977), and the *Nueva corónica y buen gobierno* itself (written after, and in part as an implicit response to, the events revealed by the other documents).[4] In his chronicle, Guaman Poma's bitter puns about judicial advocates being thieves ("los proculadores son más proculadrones") and the petitions they wrote for him producing only losses ("más hacía por mí perdiciones que peticiones") point directly back to his failed property claims.[5]

By his own account, Guaman Poma was born "after the time of the Incas," and he declared himself to be eighty years of age at the time he finished writing his book.[6] Although his calculations are unlikely to be precise, it is clear that he was born between the mid-1530s and the mid-1550s and that his death occurred after the year 1615. While Guaman Poma claimed Huánuco as his ancestral home, Huamanga (today's Ayacucho), the colonial city in the Andes of today's south-central Peru, was the site of his recollections of events from the period of his youth as well as the focal point of his legal efforts to support claims to hereditary properties. The province of Lucanas, located in the southern Andean region of present-day Peru about a hundred miles to the south-southeast of Huamanga, was another major site of his activities. He traveled through Lucanas as a church inspector's assistant in the late 1560s, worked there as an assistant to Spanish colonial administrators in the late 1590s, and settled there after his expulsion from Huamanga in 1600.[7]

As a native Andean assimilated to Spanish language and religion, Guaman Poma would have been known as an *indio ladino*, that is, as someone who was presumably proficient in Castilian, Christian in belief, and Hispanicized in custom. Besides denoting ostensible assimilation to Hispanic language and religion, the term *ladino* connoted negative values of craftiness, cunning, and untrustworthiness. Because of the effective erasure of elite status that its use commonly connoted, the term "*indio ladino*" was never used by Guaman Poma to refer to himself (although he used it to refer to others). He must have felt the sting of its negative connotations when he mentioned that he and others were scorned as *ladinejos* or *santicos ladinejos*, that is, as great and impertinent talkers, overzealous converts, and busybodies.[8] In his writings, Guaman Poma presented himself as a devout Christian, and his strident insistence on this point is a measure of the suspicion with which ethnic Andeans' conversion to Christianity was held. With respect to his literacy, Guaman Poma wrote in his chronicle that he learned reading and writing from a mestizo priest, Martín de Ayala, whom he identified as his half-brother and whose piety he celebrated.[9] Despite his expressed admiration for Padre Martín, Guaman Poma condemned *mestizaje* (racial mixture) and the growing numbers of *mestizos* (persons of mixed race) in Spanish colonial society that threatened, in his view, the survival of the Andean race. He later brings this charge to bear against the Chachapoyas, his opponents in his legal battles over lands in Huamanga.

Making Land Claims before Provincial and Royal Courts of Justice

To understand the plight of the Guaman Pomas of the early seventeenth century, it is necessary to examine the relevant background of Spanish colonial practice and its transformation of imperial Inca policy. In the 1570s, the viceroy Francisco de Toledo (1569–1581) revamped the ethnic Andean power structure, institutionalizing state control over the succession of *kurakas* (Andean ethnic lords), converting them into agents of the state for the purpose of overseeing the directed activities of the local community. Toledo had dismissed Inca rule as illegitimate and tyrannical, and he fused the local hereditary leadership with colonial governmental functions. The Toledan legacy is crucial for interpreting Guaman Poma's position and claims because he was descended from fifteenth-century *mitmaqkuna* (members of an ethnic community sent with special privileges by the Inca to settle a newly conquered area), who originated in Huánuco and eventually settled in Huamanga.

In the fifteenth-century Inca state, the *mitmaqkuna* typically staffed military garrisons along the vulnerable eastern borders of the kingdom or populated potentially productive but uncultivated and vacant lands. While they obeyed local administrative rule in their new place of residence, they maintained the dress and symbols of their ethnic homeland. Their duties were to teach the ways of Inca culture, primarily its solar religion and imperial language (Quechua). After the arrival of the Spanish in 1532, the Inca's ambassadorial settlers were viewed by the Spanish colonial regime as mere newcomers or outsiders (*forasteros*) to the communities they inhabited. In the 1570s, the viceroy Toledo fixed permanent residences for the *mitmaqkuna* ("mitimaes," as they were called in Spanish), assigning them to the places where they were residing at the time. They and their descendants were thus separated from the basic kin unit of native

Andean society (the *ayllu*), which held title to lands, organized cooperative labor teams, and performed other collective functions.

Also pertinent to Guaman Poma's legal fate was the Toledo administration's further division of indigenous communities into two clearly defined categories: *originarios*, native-born members of traditional, organized Andean settlements, and *yanaconas*, Andeans detached from their *ayllu* affiliations and living in the service of Europeans. "*Forastero*" and "*yanacona*" were terms used to refer to outsiders or "migrants to the community from elsewhere." The label "*forastero*," designating such transplanted settlers, was also typically employed for their descendants. Removed from the life ways of indigenous society, "*yanaconas*" constituted a more heterogeneous and transitional social group. Despite Toledo's provisions seeking to order and fix the populations of *forasteros*, the very act of doing so brought to the fore the question of migrant status and resulted in considerable social chaos. In the last decades of Guaman Poma's life, colonial officials attempted to distinguish between "*forasteros revisitados*, those 'who live in their respective *ayllus* because their ancestors were born here and were integrated into these communities,'" and "'*forasteros advenedizos* and other recent arrivals who at present are found within the *ayllus* but leave at will.'"[10]

In general, Guaman Poma's experience reflects the attitudes and actions of Andean provincial elites from the mid–sixteenth century onward. They responded eagerly to the chance to seek offices and privileges in the Spanish colonial system, and they continued to compete for positions in the Spanish colonial bureaucracy even after the reorganization of native society under viceroy Toledo. When in the 1590s Guaman Poma set out to defend his interests in lands he claimed as his rightful inheritance in the area of Huamanga, he identified himself as both a member of the local native elite (*cacique principal*) and as an appointee of the Spanish colonial government (*gobernador de los indios y administrador de la provincia de los Lucanas*). Years later, in the *Nueva corónica y buen gobierno*, Guaman Poma used a similar title, "administrator, Indians' advocate, deputy of the administrator of the colonial district" (*administrador, protetor, tiniente general de corregidor*) and, in the final corrections to his finished manuscript, he substituted for the title *cacique principal* (principal lord) that of *capac ques prencipe*, (*qhapaq*, which means prince). By changing his term of self-identification from local lord to dynastic prince, he undoubtedly did so for the purpose of claiming higher status within the colonial hierarchy.

From 1594 to 1600, Guaman Poma served as an interpreter and official witness in proceedings in Huamanga that confirmed new colonial titles to lands and implemented the policies resulting from Toledo's forced resettlements of native communities (*reducciones*), which aimed to bring Andean labor closer to the colonial sites (mercury and silver mines) where it was needed. At the same time, Guaman Poma was busy in legal pursuits, defending in the courts his and his kin's claims to lands in the valley of Chupas, just a few leagues from the colonial city of Huamanga. Guaman Poma's case illuminates the situation of Andeans designated as *forasteros*. Moreover, it illustrates, as Ann Wightman has proven, that increasing land values and shrinking assets of indigenous communities provoked bitter disputes, the debates over which were complicated by migration, with the result that throughout the seventeenth century "land-tenure cases were among the most hotly contested within the colonial judicial system."[11]

Guaman Poma's adversaries in the legal disputes that culminated in the year 1600 were the Chachapoyas, an ethnic group originating in the eastern highlands and western Amazonian slopes of today's northern Peru. They had been assigned by the Inca state to the Quito area, where they were living at the time of the Spanish invasion.[12] The Chachapoyas had not been conquered by the Incas until the period of the last Inca to live out a full reign, Huayna Capac (c. 1493–1525), but when the empire fell to the Spanish in 1532 the Chachapoyas quickly assimilated themselves into the Spanish royal forces as "modern soldiers," continuing the role they had played in late Inca times. In mid-1538 the powerful Chachapoyas became allies of the Spanish in the campaign that eventually defeated the rebellion of Diego de Almagro the Younger in one of the most important battles between the Spanish Crown and rebellious conquistadores. The battle took place at Chupas in September 1542. After the royal victory, the Spanish governor settled the Chachapoyas nearby at Santa Lucía de Chiara in the valley of Chupas in the jurisdiction of Huamanga and exempted them in perpetuity from tribute payment in recognition of their loyalty and military prowess. They were identified as being in service to the "justice officials of this city [Huamanga] and the royal crown."[13]

The struggle between the Chachapoyas and Guaman Poma's interests (the Tingo-Guaman clan) over the lands of Chiara, located some two leagues from the city of Huamanga, began in 1586. At that time, the viceroy Fernando de Torres y Portugal granted the presumably vacant lands to the Chachapoyas under the leadership of their lord, Don Baltazar Solsol. Reasons given were their status as *mitmaqkuna* as well as their ongoing service to the Crown in law enforcement in Huamanga. The lands are described in the decree as being vacant "for more than fifty years, since they had been the lands of the Inca."[14] But just two months after the lands of Chiara were surveyed in February 1587 and the Chachapoyas settled there, a member of the Tingo-Guaman families claimed and received title to the same lands from the same corregidor's deputy, Juan Pérez de Gamboa. The next recorded legal action occurred seven years later in September of 1594, when the rights of the Chachapoyas were confirmed. Again, just a few months later, the Tingo-Guaman families' claim to Chiara of April 1587 was also upheld. Notwithstanding the protests of the Chachapoyas, local colonial authorities honored the renewed Tingo-Guaman claims.

In subsequent years, both parties filed petitions and counterpetitions, each side accusing the other of being recent immigrants (*advenedizos*) to contradict their claims as longtime residents and landholders. For a while, it seemed that Guaman Poma and the Guaman-Tingo families would prevail. On September 5, 1597, the high court (Real Audiencia) in Lima ruled in their favor, and Guaman Poma carried the disposition with him from Lima back to Huamanga. However, the summons that was directed to the Chachapoyas by Guaman Poma's family and the Tingo heirs only a week later, on September 14, suggests a weakness to those claims that the Chachapoya leader Domingo Jauli would exploit against Guaman Poma subsequent to the dispositions of 1598 and 1599 that had favored him.

On that September 1597 occasion, the Spanish legal advocate representing Guaman Poma made a reference to one of his relatives, Martín de Ayala (undoubtedly not the mestizo priest mentioned above), as a *yanacona*, that is, as someone detached from his ethnic community. This simple characterization of a single individual cast a long shadow over Guaman Poma's entire clan as potential outsiders to the Huamanga area. Although earlier Guaman Poma, no doubt recalling their 1540s settlement in the area, had made a similar claim against the Chachapoyas, accusing them of being runaway Indians (*indios cimarrones*) and recent immigrants to the region, the tide of events on this explosive issue now would turn against him.

On March 23, 1600, in Huamanga and before the corregidor's deputy and justice official, Pedro de Rivera, the Chachapoya leaders Domingo Jauli and Juan Sota accused Guaman Poma of falsely presenting himself as a cacique who called himself Don Felipe; they claimed that he was instead a humble Indian named Lázaro. They charged that this "don Felipe/Lázaro" had secured a royal order to have the Chachapoyas' lands surveyed under false pretenses and that he had then failed to appear on the designated date at the Chiara site where the survey was to have taken place. The municipal notary accompanying the survey team affirmed the Chachapoyas' claim. On December 18, 1600, the Chachapoyas' right to the lands of Chiara was upheld.

On that same date, a criminal sentence was imposed on Guaman Poma. As condemned in the verdict, he was accused of being a "common Indian who, through deceit and trickery, called himself a cacique and was neither a cacique nor a *principal,* yet he subordinated Indians so that they respected him as such."[15] Guaman Poma consequently was sentenced to two hundred lashes to be administered publicly, and he was condemned to two years of exile from the city of Huamanga and its six-league radius. If he violated the conditions of the sentence, his exile was to be doubled to four years, and the costs of the suit were to be borne by him. On December 19, 1600, Guaman Poma's sentence was proclaimed publicly in Huamanga.

Domingo Jauli probably had singled out Guaman Poma for criminal charges because he was the most persistent (and the most effective) of Jauli's adversaries. Twice Guaman Poma had traveled to Lima and appeared before the Real Audiencia, on September 10, 1597, and again on March 6, 1599. In both instances, he returned to Huamanga armed with certified documents upholding his claims against the Chachapoyas and confirming his title to the disputed Chiara lands. Under such circumstances, Jauli evidently was able to triumph over him only by successfully convincing the authorities that Guaman Poma was an interloper—a fraudulent representative of the clan whose legal claims had been wrongly upheld by the viceroyalty's highest court. Denying Guaman Poma's credibility by nailing him as an imposter was tantamount to nullifying his successfully upheld claims to the lands in the valley of Chupas and forcing him into exile. He went to the province of Lucanas.[16]

Chupas and the Chachapoyas in the
Nueva corónica y buen gobierno

Guaman Poma makes only one reference to the fateful year of 1600 in his chronicle ("en el año que andamos de 160[o]").[17] It is embedded in a statement employing one of his most persistent literary motifs taken from European tradition, the "world-upside-down." The objects of his ire are low-born Andeans living as kings, or as drunkards and scoundrels, dressing like Spaniards wearing ruffs and carrying swords; he intimates that this social chaos drove him to write his chronicle of Andean history and treatise against injustice.[18] He simultaneously laments that the legitimate lords of inherited rank and noble blood were cast out with the conquest and dispossessed. This latter statement can be read to allude, respectively, to the imposition of Chachapoya privileges in Huamanga in the 1540s and his own personal losses to them in 1600.[19] When he puns that legal representation by licentiates (*licenciados*) is so incompetent that they should be called licentiate-asses ("*lesenciasno*"), his bitterness is evident.[20]

The most direct link between his criminal conviction of 1600 and the episodes he recounts in the chronicle appears in his reference to the battle of Chupas and his mention of the corregidor's deputy Pedro de Rivera, before whom Domingo Jauli successfully had made his accusations against Guaman Poma's integrity.[21] Guaman Poma frames this single admission of his failed suit with an assertion that he makes repeatedly about having taken up a life of poverty in order to "see and understand the injustices of the world" that had not been revealed to him in his life as a lord.[22] The allusively referenced Chupas litigation becomes the main argument for his assertion that the pursuit of justice ends up (literally) as "nothing more than a cudgeling" ("la justicia que más son que palos") when having a suit in defense of some lands that had come to me legitimately by legal title and possession from the time of the Creation, reaffirmed in the time of the Incas and the conquest, and having [my titles] examined and confirmed by the lord viceroys and also having the said land and valley of Santa Catalina de Chupas, where the battle of Don Diego de Almagro took place against the royal crown, examined and confirmed to me.[23]

Guaman Poma goes on to explain that his land titles had been confirmed by "the judge, licentiate Montalvo," who observed all the boundary markers (mojones, "saywa" in Quechua) established by the Inca Tupac Yupanqui and now upheld Guaman Poma's family's title to all the lands, woodlands, and fields that lay within the markers. The list of sites he enumerates in the chronicle is identical to the one he had given to the high court in the 1597 Expediente petition.[24]

Guaman Poma's account of Pedro de Rivera's refusal to obey the order identifies the latter, as does the Expediente Prado Tello as shown previously, as the teniente de corregidor of Huamanga. In the chronicle, Guaman Poma describes Rivera as a "resident of Huamanga and a man who understands nothing of letters and does not even know how to write." Regarding the land survey at which he was accused of failing to appear, Guaman Poma says only that Rivera sent out adjuncts, two notaries, to verify the land claim when it had been Rivera's own responsibility to perform the task. "If this has been done to me," laments Guaman Poma, "what will they do to poor people who don't know any better?"[25] He lets his indignation show but predictably reveals nothing about the humiliating sentence that resulted.

Although Guaman Poma does not tell the full story of his humiliating legal defeat at the hands of the Chachapoyas in the Nueva corónica y buen gobierno, he accomplishes the task by indirection, insisting on the reasons why those lands had rightfully belonged to his clan. Among these factors, he claims his father's service to the Spanish governor, Cristóbal Vaca de Castro, in the defense against Diego de Almagro in the battle of Chupas. Guaman Poma mentions the battle of Chupas on various occasions. In two of these instances, he makes the point that his father, Don Martín de Ayala, and Don Juan Tingo had served the royal forces under Vaca de Castro and that, at that time, they were already in possession of "houses and fields, properties in Santa Catalina de Chupas."[26] By means of this assertion, Guaman Poma implicitly argues that his people (not the Chachapoyas) had championed the royal cause with great success and that when they had done so (again, unlike the Chachapoyas) they had been long and permanently established in the area of Chupas where later the Chachapoyas were unjustly granted lands. All this is significant, but more importantly he claims that his own people were originarios, living as natural lords of the area that belonged to them from "the time that God created the earth" through the most recent, state-mandated surveys and inspections.

His other strategy in the chronicle is an anti-Chachapoya campaign that might be called "collective character assassination." His disparaging remarks about the Chachapoyas are legion. Historically, he makes them responsible for the doom of the Incas. After being conquered by Huayna Capac, he asserts, the Chachapoyas sowed the seeds of the Incas' fall. One of their women, Rava Ocllo, "mother of many bastard princes" ("*auquiconas uastardos*"), gave birth to the "bastard prince" Atahualpa.[27] As immigrants to Huamanga, Guaman Poma accuses the Chachapoyas of practicing idolatry and performing sacrifices of "children and gold and silver and clothing, food and objects made of precious metals."[28] He characterizes them as having been "rebellious Indians and thieves, imposters," for which reason, he claims, the Inca "never gave them any important posts." On the contrary, he claims, they had been subjects of his Chinchaysuyo forebear, the lord Guaman Chaua, whom the Inca honored with "many posts and offices, privileges throughout the kingdom."[29]

Guaman Poma also accuses the Chachapoyas of having been responsible for the death of the legitimate Inca prince Huascar ("they did everything to destroy Huascar Inca and all his progeny so that the legitimate Incas would rule no more") and then becoming outlaws, roaming free, assaulting and terrorizing people on public roads. They were incorrigible rebels and tricksters and thieves—an earned reputation, he says, that continued into the present.[30] His repeated insistence that they pay tribute, serve in the mines, and perform all the personal services to the colonists demanded of other ethnic groups is an aggrieved reference to the official privileges still enjoyed by them in Huamanga.[31] Most significantly, Guaman Poma makes the Chachapoyas responsible for contributing to the proliferation of the mestizo population. He describes the "city of the Chachapoyas, where many mestizos and mestizas multiply and the Indians of these provinces languish and disappear and there is no remedy. . . . And thus the [race of the] Indians is coming to an end."[32]

Writing and Illustrating the
Nueva corónica y buen gobierno

How did Guaman Poma come to write and illustrate this extraordinary and unique testimony of colonial Peru? With its elaborate calligraphy and 399 full-page line drawings, the 1190-page manuscript suggests, first of all, an artistic apprenticeship. This was carried out under the supervision of the Mercedarian friar Martín de Murúa, the first of whose two manuscript chronicles contains approximately one hundred drawings created by Guaman Poma, three of which Murúa later pasted into his second manuscript history.[33] Murúa was working as a parish priest in the province of Aymaraes (in today's Department of Apurimac), nearly due east from the clustered pueblos of San Cristóbal de Suntunto, Concepción de Huayllapampa de Apcara, and Santiago

(San Pedro) de Chipao that Guaman Poma describes as having frequented in the province of Lucanas after his 1600 expulsion from Huamanga. Guaman Poma must have created the drawings in the period between 1604 and 1606, when Murúa was a parish priest in Aymaraes.[34] Guaman Poma's detailed account of Murúa's conflicts with the local native community reveals his sustained contact with the friar. Guaman Poma's discussion of local Andean governance in Yanaca, the native settlement where Murúa lived, and his mention of a score of traditional customs that were practiced there but prohibited by the church, also point to his considerable acquaintance with that community. Because of Murúa's manuscript's references to historical events that were subsequently illustrated by Guaman Poma, it is known that Guaman Poma could not have worked with Murúa before 1596 and that his period of collaboration necessarily extended beyond 1600.[35]

In his chronicle, Guaman Poma fashioned himself in his work as a trustworthy advisor to the king, the importance of which is demonstrated by his portrait of a hypothetical royal interview, visualized as a face-to-face meeting with King Philip for which the presentation of his chronicle is the written surrogate.[36] As his credentials, he claimed that he was the heir to the Yarovilca dynasty that had preceded the Incas and that his grandfather and father, their merits having been recognized by the Incas, had served the lords of Tawantinsuyu in important posts. He described having "disciples" whom he taught to advocate for their rights by filing petitions and making legal claims to the colonial government, and he urged the king to extend literacy in Spanish to the upper echelons of Andean society. He visualized this hoped-for result with the drawing of an Andean lord writing up the complaints of an Indian commoner.[37]

The eight hundred pages of Guaman Poma's prose reveal that his "library" was impressive: he quoted (most often without attribution) Spanish chronicles of the conquest of Peru, didactic and devotional guides produced by Franciscan and Dominican missionary friars, and Spanish classics like the religious writings of Fray Luis de Granada; he knew as well the fifteenth-century Castilian tradition of the exemplary biography and mastered the rhetoric of the Christian sermon.[38] The *Nueva corónica y buen gobierno* provides a bold and scathing look at Spain's actions in "The Indies of Peru" while making literally hundreds of recommendations for colonial reform. Guaman Poma based his recommendations on a platform of juridical principles that came from Roman and canon law, Scripture, and the Christian principle of penitential restitution. On these matters, his most important source was a late treatise by the Dominican friar Bartolomé de las Casas (1484–1566), the *Tratado de las Doce dudas* [*Treatise of the Twelve Doubts*] (1564).

Remarkably, Guaman Poma closely paraphrased *Doce dudas* a half century after the death of its author. Not published in its day, the treatise circulated in manuscript among the Dominicans in the Peruvian viceroyalty. It is likely that Guaman Poma became acquainted with it in his dealings with the local missionary clergy, although he never identified it by title and he may not have known the name of its author.[39] Guaman Poma thus engaged Spanish colonial law in two successive fora: in its practice in the courts and, ultimately, in its theory as articulated by one of Castile's premier political thinkers.

Reclaiming Andean Sovereignty and Rewriting Andean History

Using the scholastic method of argumentation in *Doce dudas*, Las Casas begins by posing the question about what the policy and conduct, by the monarchs of Castile and the Spaniards living in the Indies, should be concerning the just governance and well-being of the Indians. Next, he sets forth the "twelve doubts," that is, the reasons favoring the judgment or solution that oppose the one he considers most worthy. Subsequently, he suggests the principles pertinent to the resolution of the question, supporting them with sources that include Scripture, Patristics, papal bulls, and Roman and canon law. Finally, he proposes his resolution of the twelve doubts, presenting these conclusions: Restitution must be made to the Andeans for the sins committed against them, and this restitution should consist of the restoration of the Inca prince Titu Cusi Yupanqui as rightful and sovereign lord of Peru.[40]

The principles subtending Las Casas's proposal can be summed up as follows:[41] By natural, divine, and human law, the native inhabitants of the Americas, who never harmed, or had been subject to, any Christian prince, are free and sovereign in their own lands; the papal Bulls of Donation gave the church the right to evangelize but not to dispossess the native peoples of their lands or to abrogate their right to rule them. Spain's invasion and rule of the Indies is illegitimate and tyrannical; the only means by which Spain can rule legitimately is at the invitation, and with the free and willing consent, of the Indies' native peoples.[42] The logical conclusion was to restore sovereignty to the native lords of Peru; in doing so, they were to recognize, in Las Casas's words, "His Majesty and his successors, the kings of Castile and León, as supreme lords or protectors, but retaining in all else their complete liberty and hence the peaceful possession of those kingdoms."[43] The last Inca princes, Titu Cusi Yupanqui and Tupac Amaru, were alive at the time; hence, though visionary and quixotic, Las Casas's proposal for the Inca restoration was not illogical.

By the time Guaman Poma was completing his work in the second decade of the seventeenth century, Titu Cussi and Tupac Amaru had been gone for more than forty years.[44] Guaman Poma nevertheless reiterated Las Casas's propositions, adapting them in a chapter that emulates the style and content of the moralistic reflections known as "considerations" (*conzederaciones*). Addressing himself to his princely reader, Guaman Poma writes,

> You must consider that the whole world belongs to God, and thus Castile belongs to the Spaniards and the Indies belongs to the Indians, and Guinea, to the blacks . . . each one of these is a legitimate proprietor, . . . according to the law, just as St. Paul, who for ten years resided [in Rome], called himself a Roman.[45]

This passage refers to the first principle (*Principio I*) of Las Casas's (486) treatise: All pagans have sovereign jurisdiction over their own territories and possessions; this right to jurisdiction is mandated not only by human legislation, but also by natural and divine law. Las Casas cites St. Augustine's reference to Paul's epistle to the Romans (Rom. 13:1), in which the apostle insists that the Christian community obey the monarch under whose jurisdiction that community lives, even though the ruler be a pagan. Thus, says Guaman Poma, Saint Paul "called himself a Roman." In the same manner, Guaman Poma implies, the Spaniards and all other foreigners should obey the Andean authorities while in the sovereign kingdom of Peru.

In the passage that follows, Guaman Poma points out that native-born inhabitants of Castile, whether Jews or Muslims, are subject to the laws of that land. It follows, he argues, that those Spaniards living in Peru are considered foreigners or outsiders. Guaman Poma relates this concept to that of the *mitmaqkuna* of the Inca era (see Section II, above). As foreigners living in a sovereign Andean land, Guaman Poma writes, the Spaniards are duty bound to obey Andean, not Spanish, law.[46] In this instance, Guaman Poma reiterates Las Casas's second principle (*Principio II*), in which the Dominican designates four classes of non-Christians and their respective rights and jurisdictions.[47] Pertinent to Guaman Poma is Las Casas's first class, consisting of those, among whom he names the Jews and Muslims, who, by living in Castile, are subject to the rule of the Christian king by right and by deed ("*de jure y de facto*") and are thus obligated to obey the just laws of the Spanish realm.

Guaman Poma concludes his argument, again relying on Las Casas's *Principio II*:

> Each one in his own kingdom is a legitimate proprietor, owner, not because of the king but by God and through God's justice: He made the world and the earth and established in them every foundation, the Spaniard in Castile, the Indian in the Indies, the black in Guinea . . . . And thus, although [the Spanish king] grants a favor to the priest or to the Spaniard in the lands that are settled under the king's authority, they are not landowners. And thus there must be obedience to the principal lords and magistrates, the legitimate owners of the land, male or female.[48]

Here Guaman Poma classifies the Andeans as belonging to Las Casas's fourth category of nonbelievers, that is, those who have never been and are not at present subject to a Christian ruler, either by right or by deed.

The reasons Guaman Poma gives are those that Las Casas had articulated:[49] namely, that the Andeans had neither usurped Christian lands nor done Christians any harm nor intended to do so; they had never been subjugated by any Christian prince nor by any other member-state of the church. By emphasizing their rights as legitimate possessors and declaring that such rights are mandated by God, not by the king, Guaman Poma appeals to one of the basic precepts of natural law, the Scholastic concept of the right of all peoples to jurisdiction over their own lands, followed since Thomas Aquinas.[50] Las Casas had made it explicit in *Principio II*:

> All these [nations] have their kingdoms, their dominions, their kings, their jurisdictions high and low, their judges and magistrates and their territories, within which they exercise legitimately, and can use freely, their power; and within them, it is not lawful for any king in the world, without breaking natural law, to enter without the permission of their kings or their republics, and much less should they use or exercise any authority or power whatsoever.[51]

Furthermore, Guaman Poma cites the first chapter of the book of Genesis ("*Dios hizo el mundo y la tierra y plantó en ellas cada cimiente*"), reiterating Las Casas's[52] own citation of Genesis 1, presented in *Principio I* as proof of all people's right to sovereignty in their own lands under the precepts of natural law.

In addition to Guaman Poma's reelaboration of Las Casas's arguments favoring the rights of all peoples to their own sovereignty (Principles I and II), the remaining six principles expounded in *Doce dudas* present two additional clusters of ideas of importance in Guaman Poma's thinking. First, the only right granted to the Catholic kings by the pope had been to evangelize, not to conquer, subdue, or rule the native populations. Second, the conquests had been illegal.[53] They had not conformed to generally accepted principles of Just War, namely, the right of a sovereign realm to defend its sovereignty when threatened, to recover that which had been unjustly taken, or to punish an enemy for harm received.[54] According to these criteria, for Las Casas there existed no just title of war in the Indies, but by the same criteria he did recognize as legitimate and just the war of Spain (and Europe) against the Ottoman Turks.[55] Through these eight principles, Las Casas argued in *Doce dudas* that the only way by which the Castilian king could save his soul was to make restitution to the remaining Inca princes and their descendants and to restore the Incas as legitimate lords in their own lands.[56]

Guaman Poma follows up, arguing not that the conquest of Peru had been illegal, but that it simply had not occurred: there had been no war of conquest because the Inca's ambassadors (in Guaman Poma's account, his own forebears) had accepted Spanish rule peacefully, and later attempts at Inca resistance had been quelled by miraculous visions of Santiago (Saint James the Major) and Saint Mary. He makes two claims on the basis of his "historical" account: first, the *encomienda* system was illegal because the Inca Empire had not been conquered in a Just War: "there was no conquest" [*no ubo conquista*], writes Guaman Poma.[57] Second, because the gratuitous aggression of the foreign invasion had violated natural, divine, and human law, the Spanish were bound by their religion to make restitution for lands and wealth taken and were required to relinquish the dominion they exercised.[58]

On the basis of these arguments, Guaman Poma makes a not-too-modest proposal: the king of Spain would preside ceremonially over all the world, which would be divided into four great autonomous monarchies, representing Europe, Africa ["Guinea"], the world of the Ottoman Turk ["*el Gran Turco*"], and the Indies. Each crowned head would be a sovereign lord: Philip III would occupy the role of universal monarch ["*monarca del mundo*"], whose prerogatives would be restricted to serving as protector of the faith over the Christian kingdoms while lacking political jurisdiction over all of these duly sovereign realms.[59] Guaman Poma offered his son as the appropriate candidate for the post of sovereign "king of the Indies."

Outlandish as it seems, this proposal is, in effect, a repetition, but with a twist, of Las Casas's bid for the Inca restoration presented a half-century earlier in *Doce dudas*. First, Guaman Poma's presentation of a new candidate effectively replaces the departed Inca princes. Second, this new prince, Guaman Poma's son, represents both the Inca dynasty and a more ancient one: he identifies his son not only as a great-grandson of Tupac Inca Yupanqui but also as an heir of the pre-Inca Yarovilca dynasty of Allauca Huánuco. Guaman Poma's grand scheme of 1615 for the creation of the universal monarchy, with the Spanish king reigning over the sovereign and autonomous kingdoms of the "four parts of the world," and with the Indies being ruled by a prince who combined both Inca and pre-Inca lineages, thus updates Las Casas's earlier proposal and takes into account Toledo's judgment of the Incas as illegitimate rulers. Guaman Poma presents the only reasonable alternative to prior proposals: a replacement for Las Casas's last Incas and one that fulfills the viceroy Toledo's criteria for legitimate rule in the Andes that did not rely on Inca "tyranny." Because by 1615 the era of Toledo with its attacks on Inca legitimacy was long gone, and the last direct descendants of the Inca Huayna Capac had perished, the presentation of a candidate who could be seen either as an Inca descendant or as the heir of an older, presumably legitimate dynasty was logical, making up in boldness what it suffered in impracticality.

The particular urgency of Toledo's efforts to prove the illegitimacy of Inca rule decades earlier had originated from what he saw as the dangerous influence of Las Casas's followers, Dominicans and others, for whom Las Casas's ideas and books were "the heart of most of the friars of Peru."[60] Toledo, therefore, had ordered that Las Casas's printed pamphlets and treatises of 1552–1553 be suppressed in line with a royal mandate that all books published without prior royal sanction were to be withdrawn from circulation. King Philip was willing to have excommunicated anyone who owned Las Casas's books, but Toledo wanted additional harsh punishments for those who were guilty of possessing them because he considered the ordinary prohibitions to be insufficient.[61] Toledo definitively solved the problem of a potential Inca restoration when he executed the fifteen-year-old prince Tupac Amaru on September 24, 1572.

Guaman Poma's proposal for a neo- (or non-) Inca restoration takes these historical factors into account. His chronicle shows that he was well acquainted with Toledo's tenure as viceroy: he describes Toledo's arrival in Cuzco and demonstrates an intimate knowledge of (indeed, expresses high praise for) many of the laws Toledo promulgated; at the same time he condemns the viceroy's execution of Tupac Amaru and his forced resettlement program for native communities.[62] Signaling his vivid recollection of Toledo's times, these accounts also reveal his awareness of the conditions that would potentially satisfy the living Toledan legacy still evident in Spanish colonial governance.

Because Guaman Poma proposed the restoration of Andean sovereignty as an act of Christian restitution, he had to rewrite the history of the Spanish conquest of Peru to deny to the Spanish any rights that would be theirs as victors in a Just War. His argument for full restitution of "life, honor, and wealth" to the Andeans and the restoration of Andean autonomy ultimately rested on his claims, briefly mentioned above, about the peaceful and voluntary acceptance of Spanish rule by the Andeans that required him to rewrite key chapters of Spanish conquest history. Here again, Guaman Poma gives a startling twist to Las Casas's earlier arguments. Las Casas had argued that the conquests had been illegal (the general argument of Las Casas's "*Avisos y reglas para confesores*" and of Principles VII and VIII of *Doce dudas*) and that the only hypothetical alternative to justify Spanish rule would have been the peaceful and voluntary submission of the natives. Guaman Poma turns the two around, arguing that his father, along with the three other lords of the four divisions of the empire (*suyus*), had welcomed the arrival of the Spanish emissaries of Charles V (the Pizarro invading party). Therefore, there had been no war, just or unjust, and the *encomienda* system's rewards of the vanquished to the victors had been imposed entirely without justification.[63]

Ironically, Guaman Poma's dramatization of events to effectively deny the violent military conquest of Peru followed what was generally known about the Spanish conquest of Peru at the time. Many of the early published accounts of the war conveyed the idea that the Incas had succumbed without a struggle.[64] Guaman Poma echoed it. On the other hand, he argued that a Just War was indeed waged in Peru in the 1530s when Manco Inca (c. 1516–1545), the fourth son of Huayna Capac, carried out a Just War of self-defense against the Spaniards, laying siege to Cuzco for the offenses suffered at their hands. Guaman Poma portrayed the actions of Manco Inca and, after him, Quis Quis Inca, as legitimate acts of self-defense that occurred after the peaceful Inca submission to Spanish rule.[65] Defeated not by arms but by a miraculous vision of a mounted Santiago, Guaman Poma asserts, Manco Inca retired to Vilcabamba, abandoning the kingdom and leaving "the crown and royal fringe [*masca paycha*] and weapons to the lord king and emperor, our lord don Carlos of glorious memory, who is in heaven, and his son, don Felipe II, who is in heaven and his son don Felipe III, our lord and king."[66]

Thus, Guaman Poma's erasure of the Spanish war of conquest was based not on one event but two: the hypothetical diplomatic submission of the four *suyus* to Pizarro at Tumbes and Manco Inca's historical relinquishment of royal command as he fled to Vilcabamba. Both events make the executions of Atahualpa and of Manco Inca's son, Tupac Amaru, illegal in exactly the same manner, that is, as gratuitous crimes committed against the already acquiescent and submissive Andeans. According to Guaman Poma's argument, the peaceful submission at Tumbes in 1532 and its reiteration by Manco Inca in 1539 left open to the Spanish king only one course of action: the restoration of Andean sovereignty. With these assertions, Guaman Poma's recommendations for a universal monarchy and the creation or recognition of four princely, autonomous realms are fully rationalized.

Did King Philip III ever receive and read Guaman Poma's book? Probably not, although its ultimate and present location is the Royal Library of Denmark suggests that the manuscript almost certainly arrived at the Castilian court. The manuscript book has been part of the Danish royal collections since the mid-1660s, a gift, probably, to his king from a Danish diplomat in grateful acknowledgment for the title of nobility just received.[67] Because of their intrinsic interest, the chronicle's nearly four hundred pen-and-ink drawings no doubt assured the work's survival. The ideological interests of the Protestants of Northern Europe in their enmity toward the princes of the Catholic south must have found Guaman Poma's sensational account of Spanish arrogance and cruelty appealing for its contribution to the Black Legend of Spanish history.

Did Guaman Poma truly, ultimately have hope for an Andean restoration with his own son as its anointed and crowned Andean prince? Probably not. Guaman Poma's despairing lament about the hopelessness of the Andean situation, to the effect that "there is no hope or recourse in this world" ["*y no ay rremedio en este mundo*"], overwhelms the reader with each iteration as it must have overwhelmed its author. The words he wrote in conclusion, "There is no god and there is no king. They are in Rome and Castile," betray his ultimate lack of confidence in the possibility of colonial reform.[68] It is likely that, in the course of his writing, Guaman Poma realized the futility of his earlier, hopeful goals and decided instead he was writing "for the record." Writing for the record was clearly Guaman Poma's aim when he asked the Spanish king to preserve his chronicle "in the archive of heaven as in that of earth," that is, in eternity, and in Rome and in Castile. It was to stand as testimony and record (*"para memoria"*) and to serve the cause of justice, both in this life and the next (*"en el archibo del mundo como del cielo . . . para uer la justicia"*).[69]

Guaman Poma's "rewriting of history" shows that vibrant legal principles, more than empirical past events, were best capable of telling his version of the Andean story. From Guaman Poma's early occupation as a church inspector's assistant to his failed legal disputes in claiming ancestral lands to his years-long research and writing of the work he sent to the king of Spain, his experience reveals the precariousness of native Andean life under colonial rule. When the law as practiced disfavored and punished him, betraying his faith in the judicial court system, he turned to political theory and the writing of his chronicle. In that account, he ordered historical and hypothetical events of the past according to juridical principles that could show why the "world was upside-down," even if they could not right it. His failed property claims stand at the heart of his disillusionment with the world he inhabited, and the intricate, subtle construction of his chronicle reveals the passion he invested in pursuing legal justice. Although there are in Spanish colonial Peru no other native works of the magnitude of Guaman Poma's, his repeated journeys to the seat of power in the City of Kings must have been reiterated countless times by other hopeful Andeans. Guaman Poma's case suggests the tenacity with which Andean efforts to be recognized and rewarded by the Spanish colonial legal system were undertaken.

NOTES

1. "Zona de contacto" was the term I coined in 1987 to describe the space occupied by cultural intermediaries like Guaman Poma; it was taken up in English as "contact zone" by Mary Pratt in her 1992 book. See Rolena Adorno, "Waman Puma: el autor y su obra," in Felipe Guaman Poma de Ayala, *Nueva corónica y buen gobierno*, edited by John V. Murra, Rolena Adorno, and Jorge L. Urioste (Madrid: Historia 16, 1987), 1: xvii–xviii; Mary Louise Pratt, *Imperial Eyes: Travel Writing and Transculturation* (New York: Routledge, 1991), 6–7.

2. Housed in the Royal Library of Denmark in Copenhagen since the 1660s, the Director of the Library of the University of Göttingen, Dr. Richard Pietschmann, brought Guaman Poma's holograph manuscript to international attention in 1908.

3. The complete, digitized *Nueva corónica y buen gobierno* manuscript, its transcription as a searchable data base, and the Expediente Prado Tello consisting of Guaman Poma's legal petitions, are available on the Royal Library of Denmark's Guaman Poma website: http://www.kb.dk/permalink/2006/poma/info/en/frontpage.htm. Print editions: Felipe Guaman Poma de Ayala, *El primer nueva corónica y buen gobierno*, ed. John V. Murra and Rolena Adorno, Quechua translations by Jorge L. Urioste (Mexico City: Siglo Veintiuno, 1980) (see also note 1), *Y no ay rremedio . . .* , ed. Elías Prado Tello and Alberto Prado Prado (Lima: Centro de Investigaciones y Promoción Amazónica, 1991), and Juan A. Zorrilla, "La posesión de Chiara por los indios Chachapoyas," *Wari* 1 (1977): 49–64. All citations of Guaman

Poma's chronicle correspond to the consecutive pagination of the autograph manuscript used on the website and in the Murra/Adorno 1980 and 1987 print editions.

4. The chronicle's elliptical account of the Compulsa's events confirms that the Felipe Guaman Poma of the chronicle and the one criminally charged and sentenced in the Compulsa Ayacucho are the same person. Moreover, the Expediente Prado Tello lays to rest any notion that Guaman Poma might have used a fraudulent identity as charged in the Compulsa.

5. Guaman Poma, *Nueva corónica*, 309, 918.

6. This brief overview of Guaman Poma's life and legal battles summarizes Rolena Adorno, *Guaman Poma and His Illustrated Chronicle from Colonial Peru: Guaman Poma y su crónica ilustrada del Perú colonial* (Copenhagen: Museum Tusculanum Press, University of Copenhagen, and the Royal Library, 2001), 27–29, 36–38, with grateful acknowledgement to the publisher for permission to reprint. Documentation of the legal proceedings are found in Rolena Adorno, "Introduction to the Second Edition," *Guaman Poma: Writing and Resistance in Colonial Peru* (Austin: University of Texas Press, 2000), xxiii–xxxviii.

7. Guaman Poma writes of having served the ecclesiastical inspector (*visitador*) Cristóbal de Albornoz in identifying for punishment the practitioners of traditional Andean religion; he was probably recruited in Huamanga for Albornoz's 1568–1570 campaign to the provinces of Soras, Lucanas Laramati, and Lucanas Andamarca.

8. Guaman Poma, *Nueva corónica*, 796, 838.

9. Guaman Poma, *Nueva corónica*, 15–20.

10. Ann Wightman, *Indigenous Migration and Social Change: The Forasteros of Cuzco, 1570–1720* (Durham, NC: Duke University Press, 1990), 54.

11. Wightman, *Indigenous migration*, 135.

12. Frank Salomon, *Native Lords of Quito in the Age of the Incas: The Political Economy of North Andean Chiefdoms* (Cambridge: Cambridge University Press, 1986), 160, characterizes the Chacha groups as "small homogeneous enclaves forming a far-flung net of small mitmaq operations" found in the environs of former aboriginal sites converted into Inca centers, possibly with "responsibility for controlling the interaction of aborigines with the privileged population of the new citadels."

13. Zorrilla, "La posesión de Chiara," 59.

14. Zorrilla, "La posesión de Chiara," 51, 57.

15. Zorrilla, "La posesión de Chiara," 63.

16. Guaman Poma's chronicle references to activities after 1600 are confined to the Lucanas region. He wrote about local events spanning the years from 1608 to 1615; noteworthy occurrences of the years 1611, 1612, and 1613 are especially plentiful. References to some twenty-odd native settlements and colonial officials of Lucanas are found in the *Nueva corónica y buen gobierno* as well as in his February 14, 1615, letter to Philip III; the letter is transcribed and translated into English in Adorno, *Guaman Poma and His Illustrated Chronicle*, 79–86.

17. Guaman Poma, *Nueva corónica*, 886. This section summarizes and updates the section of the same title in Adorno, *Guaman Poma*, 2nd ed. (Austin: University of Texas Press, 2000), xxxviii–xli.

18. Guaman Poma, *Nueva corónica*, 886, 1138. He makes this accusation about social pretensions against low-born, tribute-paying Andeans, mestizos, Catholic priests, Jewish merchants, and Muslim tradesmen (Guaman Poma, *Nueva corónica*, 222, 411, 450, 544, 618, 776, 1136, 1138).

19. Guaman Poma, *Nueva corónica*, 618, 776.

20. Guaman Poma, *Nueva corónica*, 411.

21 Zorrilla, "La posesión de Chiara," 59.

22. Guaman Poma, *Nueva corónica*, 916, 1106.

23. Guaman Poma, *Nueva corónica*, 918.

24. Guaman Poma, *Nueva corónica*, 918. His family's lawful rights to the designated areas had been confirmed on August 10, 1597, and officially entered into the Audiencia's records in Lima on August 7, 1598 (Prado Tello and Prado Prado, eds., 332, 337–339).

25. Guaman Poma, *Nueva corónica*, 918–919.

26. Guaman Poma, *Nueva corónica*, 415, 563, 750, 918, 1058; see especially 415, 1058.

27. Guaman Poma, *Nueva corónica*, 113–114, 140, 163–164, 168, 174, 334–335.

28. Guaman Poma, *Nueva corónica*, 269.

29. Guaman Poma, *Nueva corónica*, 347.

30. Guaman Poma, *Nueva corónica*, 347, 391, 397.

31. Guaman Poma, *Nueva corónica*, 857, 871, 994.

32. Guaman Poma, *Nueva corónica*, 1026.

33. Facsimile editions of Murúa's manuscript histories are: Fray Martín de Murúa, *Historia del origen y genealogía real de los reyes Ingas del Pirú, de sus hechos, costumbres, trajes, y manera de gobierno, Códice Murúa. Facsímil* (Madrid: Testimonio Compañía Editorial, 2004); idem, *Historia general del Pirú: Facsimile of J. Paul Getty Museum Ms. Ludwig XIII 16* (Los Angeles: Getty Research Institute, 2008). Rolena Adorno and Ivan Boserup, "Guaman Poma and the Manuscripts of Fray Martín de Murúa: Prolegomena to a Critical Edition of the *Historia del Perú*," *Fund og forskning I Det Kongelige Biblioteks samlinger* (Copenhagen) 44 (2005): 107–258, analyze the relationship between Murúa's and Guaman Poma's manuscripts.

34. Ossio, "Introducción," in *Códice Murúa: Estudio*, by Juan M. Ossio (Madrid: Testimonio Compañía Editorial, 2004), 18, 50, 191n175.

35. Adorno and Boserup, "Guaman Poma," 191–198; idem, "The Making of Murúa's *Historia general del Piru*," in *The Getty Murúa: Essays on the Making of Martín de Murúa's "Historia general del Piru*," J. Paul Getty Museum Ms. Ludwig XIII 16 (Los Angeles: Getty Research Institute, 2008), 42–43.

36. Guaman Poma, *Nueva corónica*, 975.

37. Guaman Poma, *Nueva corónica*, 784, reproduced here.

38. See Adorno, *Guaman Poma*, chaps. 1–3.

39. Several surviving manuscript versions of the work survive, and Las Casa's role in them varies. See J. Denglos, "Estudio preliminar," in Bartolomé de las Casas, *Obras completas de Fray Bartolomé de las Casas 11.2*, ed. J. B. Lassegue, estudio preliminar, índices y bibliografía de J. Denglos (Madrid: Alianza Editorial, 1988), iii–xlviii.

40. Denglos, "Estudio preliminar," vii, xliv.

41. This section V is taken from Rolena Adorno, *The Polemics of Possession in Spanish American Narrative* (New Haven and London: Yale University Press, 2007), 41–60, to which I hold the copyright.

42. Henry R. Wagner and Helen Rand Parish, *The Life and Writings of Bartolomé de las Casas* (Albuquerque: University of New Mexico Press, 1967), 234.

43. Bartolomé de las Casas, *Tratado de las doce dudas*, in *Obras escogidas de Fray Bartolomé de las Casas V*, ed. Juan Pérez de Tudela Bueso, Biblioteca de Autores Españoles 110 (Madrid: Atlas, 1958), 535: "Harán ciertos actos jurídicos por los cuales protesten recibir a Su Majestad por superior monarca o protector, y a los sucesores de Castilla y León, quedando ellos en lo demás en su entera libertad, y de aquello le den pacífica posesión en aquellos reinos."

44. Titu Cussi was deceased in 1571, and Tupac Amaru was executed by the viceroy Francisco de Toledo in 1572.

45. Guaman Poma, *Nueva corónica*, 929: "Que aués de conzedearar que todo el mundo es de Dios y ancí Castilla es de los españoles y las Yndias es de los yndios y Guenea es de los negros. Que cada déstos son lexítimos propetarios, no tan solamente por la ley, como lo escriuió San Pablo, que de dies años estaua de posición y se llamaua romano."

46. Guaman Poma, *Nueva corónica*, 929: "Que uien puede ser esta ley porque un español al otro español, aunque sea judío o moro, son españoles, que no se entremete a otra nación sino que son españoles de Castilla. La ley de Castilla, que no es de otra generación que a razón de los yndios que se qüenta y le dize por la ley y la de llamar estrangeros, y en la lengua de los yndios, *mitmac*, Castilla*manta samoc*, que uiniera de Castilla."

47. Casas, *Doce dudas*, 487–488.

48. Guaman Poma, *Nueva corónica*, 929: "Cada uno en su rreyno son propetarios lexítimos, poseedores, no por el rrey cino por Dios y por justicia de Dios: Hizo el mundo y la tierra y plantó en ellas cada cimiente, el español en Castilla, el yndio en las Yndias, el negro en Guynea . . . Y ancí, aunque (el rey español) le haga merced al padre, al español en las tierras que se componga con el rrey, no es propetario. Y ací a de tener obedencia al señor [*sic*] principales y justicias, propetarios legítimos de las tierras, que sea señor o señora."

49. Las Casas, *Doce dudas*, p. 489.

50. Joseph Höffner, *La ética colonial española del Siglo de Oro: Cristianismo y dignidad humana*, introd. Antonio Truyol Serra, trans. Francisco de Asís Caballero (Madrid: Ediciones Cultura Hispánica, 1957), 331–343.

51. Casas, *Doce dudas*, 489: "Tienen todas éstas (repúblicas) sus reinos, sus señoríos, sus reyes, sus jurisdicciones, altas y bajas, sus jueces y magistrados y sus territorios, dentro de los cuales usan legítimamente y pueden libremente usar de su potestad, y dentro dellos a ningún rey del mundo, sin quebrantar el Derecho natural, es lícito sin licencia de sus reyes o de sus repúblicas entrar, y menos usar ni ejercitar jurisdicción ni potestad alguna."

52. Casas, *Doce dudas*, 486.

53. Wagner and Parish, *Life and Writings*, 234.

54. Casas, *Doce dudas*, 505.

55. Casas, "Memorial-sumario a Felipe II," in Casas, *Obras escogidas . . .* V, 459.

56. Casas, *Doce dudas*, 531.

57. Guaman Poma, *Nueva corónica*, 564.

58. Guaman Poma, *Nueva corónica*, 572, 573, 741.

59. Guaman Poma, *Nueva corónica*, 963: "A de ser monarca el rrey don Phelipe el terzero que Dios le acresente su uida, estado para el gobierno del mundo y defensa de nuestra santa fe católica, servicio de Dios. El primero: Ofresco un hijo mío, príncipe deste rreyno, nieto y bisnieto de Topa Ynga Yupanqui, el décimo rrey, gran sauio, el que puso ordenansas; a de tener en esa corte el príncipe para memoria y grandesa del mundo. El segundo, un príncipe del rrey de Guinea, negro; el terzero, del rrey de los cristianos de Roma o de otro rrey del mundo; el quarto, el rrey de los moros de Gran Turco, los quatro coronados con su septro y tuzones. En medio destos quatro partes del mundo estará la magestad y monarca del mundo rrey don Phelipe que Dios le guarde de la alta corona. Representa monarca del mundo y los dichos quatro rreys, sus coronas bajas yguales. . . . Porque el rrey es rrey de su juridición, el enperador es enperador de su juridición, monarca no tiene juridición; tiene debajo de su mano mundo estos rreys coronados."

60. Toledo insisted: "Los de Chiapa era el coraçón de los más frailes de este reino"; see Roberto Levillier, *Gobernantes del Perú: cartas y papeles, siglo XVI*, 14 vols. (Madrid: Juan Pueyo, 1921–1926), vol. 4, 442, 462; idem, vol. 5, 312, 405.

61. Herein lies part of the reason of Guaman Poma's silence, deliberate or de facto, regarding Las Casa's name. See Arthur Franklin Zimmerman, *Francisco de Toledo: Fifth Viceroy of Peru, 1569–1581* (Caldwell, ID: Caxton Printers, 1938), p. 105; Levillier, *Gobernantes*, vol. 4, 462.

62. These recollections are registered in Guaman Poma in the *Nueva corónica* as follows: Tole-do's arrival in Cuzco (447), the laws promulgated by the viceroy (287, 302, 448, 449, 598, 951, 966, 967, 989), his execution of Tupac Amaru (452, 461, 950, 951), and the forced reset-tlements (*reducciones*) of native communities (p. 965); see also 450, 1044, 1056, 1058, 1076.

63. Guaman Poma, *Nueva corónica*, 377, 378, 564.

64. The full extent of Inca aggression against the Spanish invasion has been revealed relatively recently. The second rebellion of 1538–1539, which was the "last effort on a national scale to dislodge the invaders," was not recorded by any single chronicler at the time; just a few decades ago, John Hemming (*Conquest of the Incas* [San Diego: Harcourt Brace Jovanov-ich, 1970], 255, 584) reconstructed the events of this insurrection on the basis of dispersed public records.

65. Guaman Poma, *Nueva corónica*, 401, 408.

66. Guaman Poma, *Nueva corónica*, 408.

67. The manuscript had been obtained by a former Danish diplomat in Madrid, as Sir Clem-ents Markham announced in his introduction of Richard Pietschmann at the 1912 Interna-tional Congress of Americanists in London, in *Proceedings of the XVIII International Congress of Americanists* (London: Harrison and Sons, 1913), xxx. Danish research librarian Harald Ilsøe has estimated that the manuscript entered the royal collections by 1663 and that the probable donor, as also mentioned by Peruvian historian Raúl Porras Barrenechea in *El cronista indio Felipe Huamán Poma de Ayala* (Lima: Editorial Numen), 79, was Cornelius Pedersen Lerche (1615–1681). Lerche served as Danish ambassador to Spain (1650–1655, 1658 to 1662). Owning manuscripts acquired from the library of Don Gaspar de Guzmán (1587–1645), the Count-Duke of Olivares, his Spanish collection was unparal-leled in the Denmark of his day. Knighted by Frederick III in 1660, he likely presented the manuscript to the monarch upon his return to Copenhagen from Madrid in 1662. See Rolena Adorno, "A Witness unto Itself: The Integrity of the Autograph Manuscript of Felipe Guaman Poma de Ayala's 'El primer nueva corónica y buen gobierno' (1615/1616)," *Fund og forskning I Det Kongelige Biblioteks samlinger* (Copenhagen) 41 (2002): 16–23.

68. Guaman Poma, *Nueva corónica*, 1136.

69. Guaman Poma, *Nueva corónica*, 751, 991: "Lo tendrá en el archibo del mundo como del cielo, en el catretral de Roma para memoria y en la cauesa de nuestra cristiandad de nues-tra España, adonde rrecide Sacra Católica Real Magestad, que Dios le guarde en España, cauesa del mundo:" "ací escribo esta historia para que sea memoria y que se ponga en el archibo para uer la justicia."

4

POWHATAN LEGAL CLAIMS

Andrew Fitzmaurice

After more than twenty years of colonial failure in America, the English began to establish what would become a permanent colony in the Chesapeake region in 1607. The people who inhabited the Chesapeake area were the Powhatans and their tributaries. Their territories covered an area of approximately one hundred miles from east to west and one hundred forty miles from north to south, populated by approximately 30,000 people. The English did not reel in shock and wonder at the radical difference between themselves and the Powhatans. Rather, as in all encounters between alien peoples, they sought common points of understanding. One of the most important languages they found in common was the language of war. As Inga Clendinnen showed twenty years ago, war provides a means of mutual engagement. When understanding completely broke down between the Spaniards and Aztecs, the continuation of war became impossible.[1]

The Powhatans and English engaged each other through intermittent warfare between 1607 and 1614 and then again after 1622. War provided a "permeable barrier" through which the two martial cultures could come to understand each other.[2] Aspects of the technology of war were strikingly familiar. For example, when the English crossed the Atlantic they found people for whom, as for themselves, the main weapon of war was the bow and arrow. Not only did the native Americans use bows and arrows, but, to the surprise of the English, their bows and arrows were also remarkably similar to those used by the English. It was not uncommon for each side to pick up the arrows shot by the other and to shoot them back. Recent archaeological discoveries at the site of the Jamestown fort have revealed numerous Indian arrowheads buried with European artifacts from the 1607–1610 period. Even more surprisingly, evidence of stone flakes matching the arrowheads suggests the presence of a Virginian Indian manufacturing arrowheads within the fort itself during this period.[3] Through the technology of the bow and arrow, as Joyce Chaplin has argued, the English perceived a people who were in important respects similar to themselves.[4] Karen Kupperman has also shown that the understanding of social relations more generally provided a permeable point in the barrier between English and Powhatans.[5]

I will explore another point in the permeable barrier between English and Powhatans: namely, law. Points of comparison between early-modern English and Algonquian cultures extended beyond technology and social hierarchy into the legal realm. Just as the two cultures were able to communicate through war they could also engage through their understanding of law, for example the laws of war, which for Europeans was the basis for the law of nations, and through laws concerning territory. Contemporary English observers were able to identify a sophisticated set of Algonquian legal arguments that concerned title over the contested territory, and they also felt provoked to respond to those claims. The Powhatans used three arguments to make claims to their land, which were comparable to European understandings of title and property and were perhaps for that reason reported: they were reported, that is, because they were permeable points in the cultural barrier. The first of these three legal arguments was custom, or attachment to the land since time immemorial. This was the argument of precedent, which the English perceived through their own systems of legal humanism, the common law, and the ancient constitution.[6] The second argument used by the Powhatans was use and occupation. This was the argument that they had already taken possession of the land and established property in it and thus it was rightly theirs. A comparable argument was also central to the understanding of property in the European heritage of Roman law, natural law, and the law of nations.[7] Finally, the Powhatans justified their claim to territory through the right of conquest. They had established control over much of the Chesapeake territories through their conquest of neighboring peoples and they claimed just title on that basis. For Europeans this argument was resonant of the Roman law and the law of nations.

Our sources for these claims are mainly from the contemporary reports of English settlers. The problem in assessing the claims given that they come from European reports is whether they are merely projections of European ideas: that is, whether they are examples of ethnological ventriloquism. Ventriloquism would certainly account for the points of comparison. There are a number of reasons, however, why *not* taking these legal arguments seriously as Virginian Algonquian claims, rather than English projections, would be more fraught than taking them seriously. First among these reasons is the fact that the Powhatans' claims can be triangulated in contemporary reports: that is, more than one report makes reference to the same genre of argument. Second, the textual evidence is supported by limited anthropological and archaeological evidence. Third, similar claims can be identified among Algonquian peoples later in the century when they were in a position to publicize their own arguments directly.

This chapter does not aim to demonstrate what is both obvious and well documented: namely, that the native Americans had concepts of government and property.[8] The purpose, rather, is to identify how the native Americans articulated their understanding of control over territory in the face of the English incursions. The concern is

not, therefore, about English arguments that the native Americans had property or
sovereignty, although such arguments were frequently made. Rather, it is with trying to
identify American Indian claims to title made in opposition to the English, albeit the
historical evidence for them is difficult to bring to the surface. Having established that
such claims were made and having outlined their nature, the next step is to show that
the English defense of their right to property and sovereignty in America was precisely
that: a defense, a reaction against another set of arguments.

Evidence

The two main anthropological sources for the first years of settlement in Virginia are
John Smith's writings, particularly his *Map of Virginia* published in 1613, and William
Strachey's *Historie of travell into Virginia Britania*, which was written as a manuscript
in 1612.[9] Indeed, these are virtually the only two sources for the first several years of the
colony, although they were supplemented by Henry Spelman's observations and
George Percy's *Relation*, both of which are used here. Smith's role in the early colony is
well known. He has been the central figure in histories of the colony's first years. In
those first fragile years, Smith was the leader of the colony who had most experience in
dealing with the Powhatans and their tributary tribes in the Chesapeake. His time was
cut short in 1609 when "a matchlock dropped into his lap and ignited the gunpowder
bag dangling from his belt."[10] The explosion "destroyed Smith's genitals." Miraculously,
he did not die. He spent much of the rest of his life, as David Shields has argued, claiming his posterity through his writing rather than, as he had originally hoped, through
his American offspring.

As the colony's secretary living in Jamestown fort, William Strachey was far less ad-
venturous than Smith. But he was, arguably, more careful in recording all that he heard
from his sources (who included Smith) as well as his own observations. Strachey was a
trained lawyer—he was a member of Gray's Inn, one of the Inns of Court—but he was
also a shareholder in the Children of the Queen's Revels, which controlled the Blackfri-
ars Theatre in which Shakespeare's plays were performed. Strachey was apparently
acquainted with Shakespeare, who used his account of the wreck of Gates' expedition
upon the Bermudas while writing *The Tempest*. Strachey was also a friend to the dra-
matist Ben Jonson. He had moved, that is, in sophisticated legal and literary circles in
London before he became a resident amid the human misery that was Jamestown fort.[11]

While this essay is concerned with identifying the Powhatans' use of legal arguments
to contest English encroachments, that purpose requires at the same time consideration of the depth of legal understanding within early-modern English culture. If the
traces of Powhatan legal argument are to be found in English treatises, then those
traces can only exist there because the English colonizers on their side were able to

identify certain legal arguments through a permeable barrier. The English middling sort must themselves have had some kind of grasp of law if the permeable barrier was going to function.

It may be difficult to imagine how a legal and literary man like Strachey, or even a military man like Smith, could find meaningful ways in which to engage with a culture as alien to him as that of the Powhatans. It is perhaps even more difficult to imagine how he could have made such an engagement on a legal level, rather than merely in terms of material culture. One barrier to the ability to grasp this possibility is the image, shared by many historians, of early-modern Europeans engaged in colonization being largely divided between those people who sat in European libraries and wrote about the New World and those who actually did things. This latter group boarded boats and traveled to America, and their understanding was shaped by being "on the ground." At the same time, they lacked the same intellectual tools possessed by their countrymen sitting in libraries.

The distinction made here is between intellectuals immersed in high culture, who do not do much, and ordinary people engaged with popular culture, who are men and women of action. The assumptions behind these distinctions are false. Early-modern European culture was not characterized by a distinction between elite and popular culture to the same degree that became common from the eighteenth century.[12] Indeed, the distinction was largely a creation of the late seventeenth and the eighteenth centuries. The distinction excludes the "middling sort," but it also obscures Peter Burke's observation that "popular culture was everyone's culture".[13] Moreover, popular culture was fractured and diverse. It has also been observed that "elite culture" was itself very diverse.[14] Indeed, to go further, many of the legal, political, and philosophical ideas that are associated with "elite culture" permeated through early-modern European society and could not be said to belong to any particular group. Elite culture was everyone's culture. It was not particularly elite.

Many of the voyagers to the New World had an education that provided a good working knowledge of law and of the law of nations. Such knowledge was particularly useful for ships' captains and their crews, who knew that disputes at sea often ended up in the courts of England and other European nations. Soldiers, too, were familiar with the laws of occupation and conquest and plunder. The law of occupation in war was, of course, the same Roman law–based argument of occupation that was employed in thinking about rights of colonization. A soldier such as Captain John Smith was not university educated, but his grammar school education equipped him with a very good knowledge of the humanist curriculum, based upon Greek and Roman texts. In his spare time from soldiering, he spent his days reading Marcus Aurelius and Machiavelli.[15] His reading would have provided Smith with an understanding of the laws of war and a working knowledge of law more generally. That knowledge is apparent in his writings.

Strachey, on the other hand, as a trained lawyer, and a well-educated man, was clearly perceived to be a very useful colonist. Humanism was the dominant influence upon early-modern culture, and for humanists the most important value to be placed on knowledge was its usefulness. Indeed, an insistence that knowledge should be useful drove the humanist reform of education from the fourteenth century through to the end of the seventeenth. That insistence was closely tied to the reform of religion in which there was a similar desire that the word of God should be available to all. Smith and Strachey's educational profiles underline the fact that the template of elite and popular culture is anachronistic when imposed upon an understanding of early-modern colonization.

A further reason to assume that engagement between the English and Powhatans would be particularly difficult on a legal and political level is that the contact between the cultures was limited, and language barriers hindered the exchange of complex legal views. It is clear, however, that there was a very great degree of interaction between the Powhatans and the English. That interaction is reflected in the textual accounts left by Smith and Strachey in particular, but recent archaeological evidence points to an even greater degree of mixing than has previously been understood.[16] In light, however, of the mere language differences, surely the exchange of complex legal views would have been particularly unlikely? There were many well-documented exchanges of people between English and Powhatans as well as goods. These exchanges reflected a deliberate effort on both sides to learn more about the culture and language of the other, in other words, to gather intelligence. The exchanges began immediately when the colony was established and, in some instances, predated it.[17]

Indians recorded as visiting or living in James Fort include a man the English called "Kemps." Kemps was captured by Smith, who described him as an "exact villain."[18] Strachey described him as a good Christian but, more importantly, noted that he lived in the fort for a year before he died of scurvy and could "speake a pretty deale of English."[19] While Kemps was initially a prisoner, he played the role of broker between the Powhatans and the colony. "Machumps" was another Powhatan who mixed with the English. He had visited England and, Strachey reported, "comes to and fro amongst us."[20] Namontack was a Powhatan who came to live with the English as part of the exchange whereby Thomas Savage, an English boy of 13, went to live with the Powhatans' chief, Wahunsonacock (commonly referred to as "Powhatan"). Namontack's voyage to England was intended to facilitate better access to the prestige goods that helped sustain Wahunsonacock's rule.[21] James Fort may have accommodated an Indian arrow maker and hosted frequent visits from neighboring Powhatans, including more than one girl called Pocahontas. A number of Englishmen were sent to live with the Powhatans and other Chesapeake Indians, notably Thomas Savage, who was a gift from Captain Newport to Wahunsonacock, and Henry Spelman.

Spelman's experience and background are instructive because he was one of Strachey's most important sources and he also wrote a short account of his experiences. "Beinge in displeasuer of my frendes, and desirous to see other cuntryes," Spelman traveled as a fourteen-year-old boy to Virginia with the Gates and Summers expedition of 1609 (although his was not one of the ships wrecked on the Bermudas).[22] Shortly after arriving, John Smith left him with Parahunt, one of Wahunsonacock's tributary werowances, for the purpose of learning the Indians' ways and keeping peace between the Parahunt and the colony. Spelman remained a short time and was allowed to return to the colony, but, upon finding a starving fort, he elected to return with Thomas Savage to live with Wahunsonacock. Savage had come to the fort with venison from Wahunsonacock, and he was seemingly expected to return with another Englishman in exchange: "he was loith to goe with out sum of his cuntrymen went with him, wher uppon I was apoynted to goe, which I the more willinglie did, by Reason *that* vitals were scarse with us".[23] Spelman then spent approximately six further months with Wahunsonacock until March 1610, at which point he began to fear that the chief had begun to tire of him. At that moment, the Patawomeck werowance came to visit Powhatan, and he invited Spelman, Savage, and a Dutchman known only as Samuel to come and live with him.

The Patawomecks were the only nation on the south side of the Potomac who did not pay tribute to Wahunsonacock, although their diplomacy was loosely controlled by him.[24] They saw the English as possible allies who could help establish their complete independence. The escape of Savage, Spelman, and Samuel the Dutchman to their own territory was part of that plan.[25] The plot was undone when Savage decided in mid-flight that he would return and betray Spelman and Samuel to Wahunsonacock. Samuel the Dutchman was killed by an axe from one of Wahunsonacock's pursuers, but Spelman managed to arrive in Patawomeck territory and spent the next year there living among them. Samuel Argall finally purchased Spelman's liberty with some copper in 1611 after having learned of his presence with the Patawomecks. Spelman returned to England with Argall and Lord De La Warr on March 28, 1611, but came back to the Chesapeake region in 1616 and rose to the rank of captain. Among other duties, he acted as an interpreter for the colony. According to contemporary reports, he "spake their Languages very understandingly," and the colonist Peter Arundel wrote after his death that he was "the best linguist of the Indian Tongue of this Country".[26] He probably helped Strachey compose his *Dictionary of the Indian Language*, which was the most comprehensive vocabulary produced in the first decades of the colony, being seven times more extensive than a similar effort by John Smith.[27] Spelman's writing, and perhaps his own verbal account, was also used by Samuel Purchas in the composition of *Purchas his Pilgrimage*.[28]

Upon his return to the Chesapeake area, Spelman took a prominent role acting as a broker between the English, the Powhatans, and the Patawomecks, eventually rising to the rank of captain. As a broker, he was engaged in facilitating some intellectually complex and demanding exchanges across the permeable barrier. Strachey recounts one instance from 1610 in which Spelman explained Captain Argall's metaphysical beliefs in great detail to Iopassus, the Patawomeck chief's brother. Spelman used an illustrated copy of the Bible in order to convey this account. In response, Iopassus used Spelman to explain to Argall the Patawomecks' understanding of the origin of life, "the nature of certayne spirritts," and gods and the nature of life after death.[29] Spelman showed a remarkable degree of prudence in this exchange, refusing Argall's request to press Iopassus further on the foundation of some of his beliefs "lest he should offend him."[30] Indeed, Spelman would later fall more on the Algonquian side of this balancing act. In 1619 he was degraded from the rank of captain for having been found guilty of criticizing Governor Yeardley to Opechancanough.[31] The exchange between Iopassus, Spelman, and Argall points to the capacity to explain complex metaphysical beliefs across the permeable barrier, and it also underlines the degree to which two cultures engaged in such an exchange had the means as well as the motive to discuss the nature of their legal claims to the territory that they contested. The matter of whether cultural brokers such as Spelman had any ability to converse in the language of law follows.

While Spelman's role as a broker has often attracted historians' interest, his family links deserve passing comment. He was the nephew of Sir Henry Spelman,[32] who was, with William Camden and Sir Robert Cotton, among the most eminent antiquarian scholars of his generation, and with those friends he established the Elizabethan College of Antiquaries.[33] Sir Henry Spelman helped bring about a revolution in English thinking about the common law and the ancient constitution.[34] Contemporaries such as Edward Coke and John Selden argued that the English common law had roots stretching beyond the Norman conquest and beyond the Anglo-Saxons into time immemorial. Spelman put the English common law in a European context. He showed that it had its origin in Germanic law, and importantly, he also showed that it had been greatly influenced by civil and canon law.[35] Certainly, Roman and civil law, and the law of nations, were alive and well in England at the time Spelman conducted his research, and that fact was reflected in justifications of the Virginia colony. Strachey, while a common lawyer trained in Gray's Inn, employed Roman and civil law in his discussion of English title in the Chesapeake region.

Prior to his role as Strachey's informant, Sir Henry's nephew may not have had much opportunity to absorb his uncle's thoughts on the law, although fourteen was the age at which Spelman's cousin, John Spelman, Sir Henry's first son, was admitted to Gray's Inn in 1608.[36] But his background points again to the fact that Englishmen "on the ground" in Virginia were equally exposed to what can be anachronistically described as "elite" culture as they were to popular culture. Sir Henry Spelman also had a great interest in American colonization, which may be linked to his nephew's placement among the Virginian adventurers. Sir Henry was heavily involved, with Sir Ferdinando Gorges, in the frustrated New England Council from 1620. He acted as the Council's chief legal authority and, strikingly, given his antiquarian concerns, advised them to move to a more feudal form of colonial government. He also became treasurer of the Guiana Company in 1627.[37] Unfortunately, Spelman (the nephew) never had the opportunity to reflect on his time in the Chesapeake area other than to provide his very short account of his first years and to inform Strachey. He finally proved to be incapable of sustaining the diplomatic balancing act. He was last seen on March 27, 1623, when his head was thrown over the bank of the Potomac.[38] In the wake of the Powhatan "rebellion," he had fallen victim to the Patawomecks' enemies, the Nacotchtanks.

Historical anthropologists have contrasted the political structure of Eastern Algon-quian societies at the time of first contact with that which prevailed in Europe. Exam-ining the political relations between the Powhatans and the English colonists, historians such as Daniel Richter and James Rice have largely followed the anthropological rank-ings of political systems into bands, tribes, chiefdoms, and states.[39] On the one hand, the hierarchical and profoundly inegalitarian chiefdom political system of the Pow-hatans is contrasted with egalitarian tribal political systems. On the other hand, it is contrasted with the modern state from which the English came. Following Elman R. Service and Morton R. Fried, Richter describes chiefdoms as "redistributional societies with a permanent central agency of redistribution".[40] They are focused on exalted he-reditary leaders. Those leaders consolidate their power through the distribution of goods in a prestige-goods economy. Because the resources on which chiefs rely for their power are scarce, chiefdoms are inherently unstable. Chiefs lack a monopoly over force to defend their privileges.

States, according to this anthropological analysis, are stable societies in which the central authority has a monopoly on force and is territorially competent. According to James Rice, "chiefdoms were also fundamentally unlike a modern nation-state; they lacked bureaucracies, centralised record keeping, police, courts, standing armies, and other trappings of modern nation-states".[41] There is a fundamental problem with this contrast between the chiefdom of the Powhatans and the modern state from which the English voyaged. The anthropological description of the modern state is certainly consistent with how historians and political theorists understand modern states. The description of chiefdoms and the fact that Powhatan political organization was cha-racteristic of chiefdoms are not in question. What is questionable is the degree to which the understanding of the modern state can be applied to sixteenth- and early seventeenth-century English society. The contrasts between the Powhatans and the English tend to make rather flattering assumptions about the nature of politics in early-modern England (flattering, that is, from a progressive point of view).

In England, as in much of Europe, the various elements that would constitute the modern state were beginning to coalesce in the sixteenth century. The modern state is a political body combining territorial competence with an impersonal holder of sovereignty separate from *both* the ruler and the ruled. This understanding of the state was first apparent in 1576 in Jean Bodin's *Les six livres de la république*. [42] But the full implications of that coalescence of ideas were not fully explored before Thomas Hobbes published *Leviathan* in 1651.[43] The period in which the English confronted the Powhatans was thus one of flux in the understanding of politics. The state had not yet arrived, not even conceptually. When it did arrive, it would remain permanently enmeshed in ideological disputes over its nature.[44] Moreover, the newly forming conceptions of the state often fell short of political practice.

Many of the features that were supposedly characteristic of chiefdoms could also describe Jacobean England. The English, like the Powhatans, focused their political system on an "exalted hereditary leader." That leader, like Wahunsonacock, was obliged to consolidate his power through the redistribution of goods among his powerful subjects. To the degree that a state existed as a form of established authority, it maintained authority through the support of local elites (in precisely the way Wahunsonacock maintained authority), who in turn maintained order through a shared culture of civic virtue.[45] James I, like Wahunsonacock, faced scarce resources with which to pursue the process of redistribution. James, too, lacked a monopoly over force. Control over local elites was tenuous. As would later become apparent from the execution of Charles I, James I's son, the scarcity of those resources made rule in Europe highly unstable, perhaps more unstable than it was for Wahunsonacock. Like Wahunsonacock, James did not possess a large bureaucracy, centralized record keeping, police, or a standing army. While in retrospect the outlines of the modern state can be understood to emerge through the course of the seventeenth century in England, the century cannot, as Phil Withington has commented, be perceived in terms of a "remorseless centralisation of power".[46]

In order to underline how fragile James I's realm was, an example is presented here of his relations with one of his most important subjects: namely, Henry Percy, the Wizard Earl of Northumberland. The Wizard Earl merits attention for two reasons. Firstly, Strachey had dedicated his *Historie* to the earl. And, secondly, in his dedication, Strachey praised Henry's brother, George Percy, who was one of the leaders of the James Fort colony and who had been, Strachey claimed, one of the main informants for his history. Since medieval times, the earls of Northumberland had controlled a chiefdom based on the massive fortress of Alnwick Castle on the northern border of England with Scotland. The Northumberlands had been since that time more often in rebellion against the English Crown than not. Or, to put it from the Northumberlands' perspective, the English crown had been attempting to expand its dominions north with varying degrees of success over the course of the thirteenth, fourteenth, and fifteenth centuries.

The rebellions of the Percy family of Northumberland were immortalized by Strachey's theatrical colleague, William Shakespeare, in the figure of Harry Hotspur in *Henry IV, Part 2*. The fortunes of the Percy family in the sixteenth century remained consistent with their past. The Wizard Earl's father, Henry Percy, the eighth earl of Northumberland, met his death in the Tower of London in 1585 for suspected complicity in a plot to rescue Mary Queen of Scots (in which he was aided by the Duc de Guise). Henry's cousin, Thomas Percy, met his death as one of the five conspirators in the Gunpowder Plot. And Henry himself was imprisoned in the Tower of London in 1605 and remained there for the next sixteen years because of suspicions that he, too, was a conspirator in the Gunpowder Plot. It was in the Tower of London, therefore, that Henry the Wizard Earl would have received the manuscript of William Strachey's *Historie of travell into Virginia Britania*. Certainly, anyone from the Percy family would have found Wahunsonacock's troubled relations with his tributary werowances strikingly familiar. Neither James I, nor his European counterparts, possessed a monopoly of force. That they were not territorially competent had been amply demonstrated by the wars of religion in the sixteenth century. The failure of territorial competence would again be evident in the Thirty Years' War, which ignited just ten years after the English arrived in the Chesapeake and would tear apart the many principalities and city-states of Europe.

Powhatan Claims

It should come as no surprise, therefore, that Smith and Strachey found much in the Powhatan political system that was familiar or even superior to the instability that characterized European polities. As John Smith observed: "they have amongst them such governement, as that their Magistrats for good commanding, and their people for du subjection, and obeying, excell many places that would be counted very civill. The form of the Common wealth is a monarchical government."[47] Similarly, Alexander Whitaker, another inhabitant of James Fort, and one of the more negative writers on the Powhatans, conceded that Indians must be regarded as living in civil society (which was, for the Jacobean English, a more significant political category than the state): "There is civill governement amongst them which they strictly observe, and shew thereby that the law of Nature dwelleth in them: for they have a rude kinde of Commonwealth, and rough governement, wherein they both honour and obey their Kings, Parents, and Governours . . . they observe the limits of their owne possessions, and incroach not upon their neighbours dwellings."[48]

Henry Spelman knew Algonquian society as well as any other Englishman in the first years of the colony and also wrote a report on the nature of Indian society and government. Fulfilling his role as an intelligence gatherer, Spelman commented on "*The Justis and government*" of the Algonquians. He remarked that he had assumed that infidels have no laws or rights: "Concerninge ther lawes my years and understandinge, made me the less to looke after bycause I thought that Infidels wear lawless."[49] Karen Kupperman has commented that Spelman made a "childish assumption" in concluding that infidels were lawless.[50] But one might equally conclude that he made a rather medieval assumption (not inconsistent with his uncle's absorption with all things medieval). It had been Spelman's medieval countryman, the canon lawyer Alanus Anglicus, who had argued, in justification of the crusades, that infidel peoples held no rights and that their laws effectively counted for nothing.[51] Just one year before Spelman left for James Fort, Edward Coke had argued similarly in Calvin's Case that the laws of infidels are "not only against Christianity, but against the Law of God and of Nature".[52] Laws that were against the law of nature were no laws at all (although some of Coke's contemporaries, including Whitaker and Strachey, concluded that the law of nature thrived among the Indians). Spelman's initial assumption was consistent, therefore, with Alanus and Coke's positions. But he then proceeded to show how his expectations were confounded by the discovery that law did rule the Powhatans, and he recounted examples in which offences were punished by death.

According to William Strachey, it was not only natural law but also divine law that could be discovered operating in the Powhatan political system. Strachey noticed that the "forme and ostentation of such majesty" expressed by Wahunsonacock "oftentimes strykes awe and sufficient wonder into our people." He was left needing to explain why Englishmen should be awestruck by a barbarous prince. His conclusion was that all rule was based upon a supernatural force granted by God: that is, Strachey managed to detect divine right upholding the rule of Wahunsonacock just as it maintained James I. He explained that what had struck the English was "the Impression of divine nature". Even though the Powhatans were "heathens forsaken by the true light, [and] have not that portion of the knowing blessed Christian-spirit, yet I am persuaded there is an infused kind of divineness, and extraordinary (appointed that it shalbe so by [the] king of kings) to such who are his ymediate Instruments on earth."[53] Thus, for Strachey, rule was maintained by God's instruments on earth, not by the instruments of the modern state. Far from perceiving sovereignty to be separate from the ruler, Strachey believed that sovereignty was embodied by the ruler, whether he be Wahunsonacock or James I. His perception of "divine nature" in the person of the sovereign, and of majesty which strikes awe, reflects an understanding of political authority performed not through the abstract instruments of the state but through display, splendor, and blazon.

This personal and performative understanding of politics was not a screen for disguising interests and relations of social domination (as ceremony might be understood in Western cultures since the seventeenth century).[54] It constituted the object of politics in itself. The gulf between this premodern understanding of political authority and the conception of the modern state was great. It was so great that it could be easier to translate between the mentality of blazon and the Powhatan chiefdom, or the nineteenth-century Balinese *Negara*, than it is for historians to translate between early-modern and modern European culture (although historians presume to do so because, like the English colonists in the Chesapeake, they have no alternative).

It was in the context of the English and Powhatan political systems being perceived to be analogous that law became a common language in the permeable barrier between the two cultures. In writing about Virginia in 1609, several London-based pamphleteers declared the Indians had a right to their territory based upon "inheritance." Inheritance was the foundation that English common lawyers, such as Coke and Selden, and antiquarians such as Cotton and Spelman, believed to be the source of their rights. The preacher Robert Gray, one of the most damning critics of native American culture, declared that, "there is no intendment to take away from them by force that rightful inheritance they have in that Countrey."[55] For Gray, therefore, the Powhatans' right to territory lay in their prior occupation, but he did not say that the Powhatans had made this claim themselves. Indeed, he did not say what his source for this claim was. The London preacher William Symonds came closer to putting this claim in the mouths of the native Americans or at least in the mouths of first-hand observers: "the countrey, they say, is possessed by owners, that rule and governe it in their owne right: then with what conscience, and equitie can we offer to thrust them, by violence out of their inheritances?"[56] Again, the acknowledgment of the Powhatans' rights was based upon inheritance as well as the recognition of a civil society that possesses a legal system of rule, but still the source for the claim was not stated other than to declare, "they say." It is unclear who "they" are. Gray and Symonds could be dismissed as making assumptions on behalf of the Powhatans if it were not for the fact that the same claim was attributed to the Powhatans themselves in the writings of John Smith and William Strachey.

Turning to John Smith's *Map of Virginia*, first-hand reports of the time represented the Powhatans themselves to be making this claim to title through inheritance and custom, and they were making it, moreover, to the English observers. Speaking of the chief, Wahunsonacock, Smith observed that: "Some Countries hee hath which have beene his Ancestors, and came unto him by Inheritance, as the Countrie called Powhatan, Arronhatek, Appamatuke, Pamavuke, Youghtanud, and Mattapanient. All the rest of his Territories expressed in the Map, they report have beene his severall conquests. In all his ancient Inheritances, hee hath houses built after their manner like arbours."[57] It is striking that Smith twice repeated that Wahunsonacock possessed these countries by "inheritance," and that they were therefore his by custom.

Importantly, Smith also states that these understandings of the Powhatans' claims to land were based upon the Indians' "report" and refers to "his [that is, Wahunsonacock's] Territories expressed in the Map". In other words, according to Smith, the Powhatans did have a concept of territory that must be respected by other peoples, but which could also be transferred by various means, such as conquest and inheritance. Katherine Hermes has observed that Eastern Algonquians did not have a concept of territorial jurisdiction—jurisdiction was over persons and things—but they did, as Hermes acknowledges, have a concept of territory nevertheless.[58] Similarly, for Europeans prior to the seventeenth century, sovereignty was largely concerned with persons and subject matter. Although medieval Europeans possessed a concept of territorial sovereignty, the continued legal powers of the church and feudal barons greatly limited the jurisdiction that was exercised over those territories.

William Strachey echoed Smith's emphasis upon the Powhatans' right to land deriving in part from inheritance. Using sources that were independent of Smith, including Spelman, Strachey declared: "Ten or 12. miles lower on the south-syde of this River is *Kiskiack*, these (as also *Appamatuck*, *Orapaks*, *Arrohatack*, and *Powhatan*) are their great kings Inheritance, chief Alliance, and Inhabitance. Upon *Youghtamund* is the seat of Powhatans [ie., Wahunsonacock's] 3. bretheren, whom we learn are successively to governe after Powhatan, in the same dominions which Powhatan by right of Birth, as the elder brother now holdes, the rest of the Countryes under his Commaund are (as they report) his conquests".[59] For Strachey, therefore, the Powhatans inherited "dominion." In early modern English, the term "dominion," from the Latin "*dominium*," denoted property in land as well as sovereignty. Again there is an indication of territory here because this property in land was not private; it was held by the sovereign. It is also important that Strachey distinguishes between lands that were held by "inhabitance" and those held by "conquest," which were tributary (this second category will be discussed shortly). In other words, inhabitance, or occupation, formed another basis to title by inheritance for the Powhatans. Crucially, Strachey, like Smith, included in recounting these understandings the fact that they were from the Powhatans' own "report." These forms of title were not, that is, understandings that he had surmised but claims that had been "reported" to him by the Powhatans.

In addition to custom, inheritance, and occupation, the other form of title claimed by the Powhatans, and also familiar to Europeans, was conquest. Both Smith and Strachey reported that the Powhatans made claims to particular territories on the basis of conquest. After listing Wahunsonacock's inheritances, Smith, as previously shown, declared that: "All the rest of his Territories expressed in the Map, they report have beene his severall conquests." Similarly, Strachey stated that: "the rest of the Countryes under his Commaund are (as they report) his conquests." Again, it was the Powhatans who *reported* that they held title by virtue of their conquests: this was their

POWHATAN
Held this state & fashion when Capt. Smith
was deliuered to him prisoner
1607
MONACANS
POWHATAN
MANGOAGS
CHAWONS
MANNAHO
KUSKARA
Iames towne
Powhatan
Povnt comfort
Cape Henry
Cape Charles
Smyths Iles
Washeborne
Russels Iles
THE
VIRGINIAN SEA
Scale of Leagues

According to John Smith, this map, published in 1612 as *A map of Virginia vvith a description of the countrey,*
Courtesy of the John Carter Brown Library at Brown University

the commodities, people, government and religion, represented the Powhatans' claims to territory.

claim, not, a projection by the English. Moreover, it would appear that this claim was made by Wahunsonacock himself because the context in which it appears in Strachey's narrative is as part of a lengthy description in which Wahunsonacock recounted one of his particular conquests. By telling the story of that conquest, Wahunsonacock demonstrated that certain territories more generally were held by right of conquest and implicitly warned against encroachment on those territories. Indeed, Strachey noted that Wahunsonacock related this story while displaying the heads of the conquered men with their skin scraped off as well as the scalps of the women and children.

The Powhatans' claim to the right of conquest is again evident in John Rolfe's writings. Rolfe was of one of the most important colonists in the early years in the Chesapeake region. He had an important role in bringing the 1607 to 1614 war to an end through his diplomatic marriage to Pocahontas. Pocahontas was, of course, Wahunsonacock's daughter, whom the English had kidnapped in 1613. In addition to his peacemaking role, Rolfe also initiated the eventual prosperity of the colony through the introduction of tobacco as a crop. On returning to England in 1616 with Pocahontas, where she was presented at court, Rolfe wrote to Queen Anne, James I's consort, justifying his marriage to a savage heathen. Such marriages had been expressly forbidden by the Virginia Council.

Rolfe also addressed the question more largely of the justice of the colony. He stated: "Now that your highnes may with the more ease understand in what condition the colony standeth, I have briefly set downe the manner of all men's severall imployments, the number of them, and the several places of their aboad, which places or seates are all our owne ground, not so much by conquest, which the Indians hold a just and lawful title, but purchased off them freely, and they very willingly selling it."[60] The claim to right by cession, or purchase, was, of course, spurious. But the reference to the Powhatans' understanding that conquest was a just form of title was all the more revealing because of the offhanded way in which it was made and by the fact that it did little to further Rolfe's cause. Rolfe appeared to be in little doubt about the justice of the colony, and it is for this reason that he easily revealed his knowledge of native legal claims. As one half of a mixed diplomatic marriage, Rolfe was in a better position than most colonists to have access to the Powhatans' understanding of law. Like Smith and Strachey, Rolfe noted that it was the Powhatans themselves who report, or "hold," that conquest is a just basis to title.

The English Response to Powhatan Legal Claims

It is important to remember the context in which the Powhatan understanding of title arising from inheritance, occupation, and conquest was communicated to Smith, Strachey, and Rolfe. Neither Smith, Strachey, nor Rolfe was a neutral anthropological observer. Nor were the Powhatans disinterested subjects of observation. The conversations with the Powhatans about the nature of dominion were made in the context of conflict and war over precisely the territories to which the Powhatans were explaining the nature of their title. The Powhatans' representations of the legal status of their territories were being made in the face of invasion. Indeed, Strachey reported that Wahunsonacock feared that the English would harm him "by taking away his land from him . . . which we never yet ymagined nor attempted, and yet albeit the Conceipt of as much strongly possesseth him."[61] Given this context, it is difficult to understand the Powhatans' representations as anything other than legal contests with the English. This was the Powhatans' legal compliment to the military opposition that they pursued with the bow and arrow.

Once it is understood that the Powhatans were making these legal claims against the English and that the English recognized the claims from their own legal vocabulary, then the understanding of what the English were doing in turn when they launched their legal offensive against the Powhatans can be reexamined.

In 1607 the Virginia Council met in London at the time they sent their ships to the Chesapeake area and before they had any news of the events of the first settlement there. They decided in this meeting that it would *not* be necessary to publish legal claims to the territory they were engaged in colonizing. The minutes to that meeting show that they acknowledged that they would be "hard put" to establish legal title against the "naturals" and it was therefore better to say nothing at all.[62] Two years later, they reversed this decision. Between 1609 and 1612, the Virginia Company and its supporters published a battery of pamphlets. Historians have been rather baffled about why the company changed its decision not to promote its aims. It has been widely assumed that the pamphlets were published with the purpose of attracting investment and personnel to a faltering enterprise. This understanding of their motivation is undoubtedly correct. But large sections of the pamphlets were devoted to addressing concerns about the justice of colonizing in Virginia, and those concerns were only tangentially related to the problems of investment and personnel.

The authors of these pamphlets claimed title to Virginia by appealing to the rights of custom, occupation, and conquest. It has usually been supposed that in addressing the question of justice the pamphlets were primarily responding to competition from rival European colonial powers including the Spanish, French, and Dutch. And yet, those rivalries did not change substantially between 1607, when the decision was taken not to publish, and 1609 when the promotional campaign started. Moreover, the greatest attention by far in making these arguments to title was devoted to the question of "the naturals," that is, to the Indians, and not rival European powers.

What did change dramatically between 1607 and 1609 was that the colonizers found themselves face to face with an indigenous people who were making powerful and recognizable legal claims to their land backed by force. It is perhaps for this reason that the promotional tracts unleashed after 1609 repeatedly refer in an oblique and euphemistic way to the "objectors to the enterprise" on the grounds of justice. Clearly, there were a number of English who were skeptical about the Virginia enterprise and who raised objections, including objections about the justice of supplanting the native Americans. But it would also appear that these objections were being made by the native Americans themselves, and they were being made, furthermore, in terms which were recognizable, or translatable, for the English. The incoherent claims made by the English to title based on custom, occupation, and conquest mirrored the claims that the Algonquins were reported to have made at the same time. This was a dialogue.

In the law of nations, it was usual to make a claim in response to the claim made by another nation. The law of nations was necessarily a dialogue conducted between nations. When the English launched their claims to territory in North America, they did so through explicit appeals to the law of nations. This means that they perceived themselves to be in dialogue with some other nation or nations. Some of their claims were directed against other European states. But others were also explicitly aimed at the Powhatans. It is necessary now to understand that these claims, too, were part of a dialogue and that they were launched against the Powhatans' own arguments. The English tracts that responded to the Powhatan legal claims would not, of course, have been read by the Powhatans (although it is notable that Henry Spelman read to the Indians from at least one book: namely, the Bible). Rather, those tracts should be understood merely as the only trace of a legal debate that was being conducted *in* the Chesapeake area. They provide a trace, that is, not only of the Powhatans' legal arguments but also of the kinds of claims that the English were clearly making in return. A dialogue was being conducted through the languages of inheritance, occupation, and conquest.

It was no more remarkable for the English that the Powhatans should launch these legal arguments than that they employed bows and arrows. It was these Algonquian claims that forced the English reversal regarding the need to justify the colony. What the English began to do in 1609 was not to initiate a legal claim to their North American territory but to launch a *counterlegal* claim for title. To a large degree, that legal contest had been initiated not by the English but by the native Americans. The native Americans' formal legal resistance to the invasion of Europeans began at the same time as their armed resistance. The Powhatans and English exchanged claims about rights of conquest, occupation, and inheritance in the same way that they picked up each other's arrows and shot them back.

NOTES

1. Inga Clendinnen, "Fierce and unnatural cruelty," *Representations* 33 (Winter 1991), 65–100.
2. For the term "permeable barrier," see Joyce Chaplin, "No magic bullets: Archery, ethnography, and military intelligence," in Chaplin, *Subject Matter: Technology, the Body, and*

Science on the Anglo-American Frontier, 1500–1676 (Cambridge, MA, Harvard University Press, 2001), 85.

3. William M. Kelso, *Jamestown, the Buried Truth* (Charlottesville: University of Virginia Press, 2006), 111–112.

4. Chaplin, *Subject Matter*, 79–115.

5. Karen Kupperman, *Indians and English: Facing off in Early America* (Ithaca, NY: Cornell University Press, 2000). Richard White has shown that social relations formed a "middle ground" between European colonizers and Native Americans, a violent and unstable forum in which knowledge was exchanged; see White, *The Middle Ground: Indians, Empires, and Republics in the Great Lakes Region, 1650–1815* (Cambridge: Cambridge University Press, 1991). See also Nancy Shoemaker, *A Strange Likeness: Becoming Red and White in Eighteenth Century North America* (Oxford: Oxford University Press, 2004): Shoemaker examines the similarities between settler and Indian cultures in a later period.

6. On legal humanism, see: Julian H. Franklin, *Jean Bodin and the Sixteenth-Century Revolution in the Methodology of Law and History* (New York: Columbia University Press, 1963); Donald Kelley, *The Foundations of Modern Historical Scholarship* (New York: Columbia University Press, 1970). On the ancient constitution and the common law in England, the standard work remains J.G.A Pocock, *The Ancient Constitution and the Feudal Law: A Study of English Historical Thought in The Seventeenth Century: A Reissue with a Retrospect* (Cambridge: Cambridge University Press, 1987); see also Alan Cromartie, *The Constitutionalist Revolution* (Cambridge: Cambridge University Press, 2006). For the use of legal humanism and the ancient constitution to legitimize the colonization of America, see Andrew Fitzmaurice, *Humanism and America: An Intellectual History of English Colonisation 1500–1625* (Cambridge: Cambridge University Press, 2003), 148–157.

7. On the natural law tradition and the justification of European colonization, see Anthony Pagden, *The Fall of Natural Man: The American Indian and the Origin of Comparative Ethnology* (Cambridge: Cambridge University Press, 1982); James Tully, *An Approach to Political Philosophy: Locke in Contexts* (Cambridge: Cambridge University Press, 1993); and Andrew Fitzmaurice, "Moral uncertainty in the dispossession of Native Americans," in Peter Mancall, ed., *The Atlantic World and Virginia, 1550–1624* (Chapel Hill: University of North Carolina Press, 2007), 383–409.

8. On Native American concepts of political organization and property, see for example: Helen C. Rountree, *The Powhatan Indians of Virginia: Their Traditional Culture* (Norman: University of Oklahoma Press, 1989); Daniel K. Richter, *Facing East from Indian Country: A Native History of Early America* (Cambridge, MA: Harvard University Press, 2001); Katherine A. Hermes, "The law of Native Americans to 1815," in *Cambridge History of Law in America. Volume 1 Early America (1580–1815)*, eds. Michael Grossberg and Christopher Tomlins (Cambridge: Cambridge University Press, 2008), 32–62.

9. I will use the edition of Smith's *Map of Virginia* (Oxford, 1612) in Philip L. Barbour, ed., *The Jamestown Voyages under the First Charter 1607–1609*, 2 vols., (Cambridge: The Hakluyt Society, 1969), vol. 2, 327–374. For Strachey, see: William Strachey, *Historie of Travell into Virginia Britania* (1612), eds. Louis B. Wright and Virginia Freund, (London: The Hakluyt Society, 1953).

10. David S. Shields, "The genius of ancient Britain," in Mancall, ed., *Atlantic World and Virginia*, 493.

11. For Strachey's biography and his connections to London literary circles, see: Wright and Freund, "Introduction," to Strachey, *Historie of Travell into Virginia Britania*, xiii–xxxii.

12. Tim Harris "Problematising popular culture," in Tim Harris, ed., *Popular Culture in England, c.1500–1800* (Basingstoke: Palgrave, 1995); Peter Burke, *Popular Culture in Early Modern Europe* (London: Temple Smith, 1978); Keith Wrightson, *English Society 1580–1680* (London: Routledge 1980).

13. Harris "Problematising popular culture," 1.

14. Harris "Problematising popular culture," 4. See also Jonathan Barry, "Literacy and literature in popular culture: Reading and writing in historical perspective," in Harris, ed., *Popular Culture in England*, 69–94.

15. Fitzmaurice, *Humanism and America*, 183.

16. See Kelso, *Jamestown, the Buried Truth.*

17. For the exchanges, see: Daniel K. Richter, "Tsenacommacah and the Atlantic World," in Mancall, ed., *The Atlantic World and Virginia*, 29–65; Kupperman, *Indians and English*; Frederick Fausz, "Middlemen in peace and war: Virginia's earliest Indian interpreters, 1608–1632," *Virginia Magazine of History and Biography* 95 (1987), 41–64.

18. Smith, "Map," in *Jamestown Voyages*, vol. 2, 443.

19. Strachey, *Historie of Travell into Virginia Britania*, 61. See also Kupperman, *Indians and English*, 195–196.

20. Strachey, *Historie of Travell into Virginia Britania*, 61–62. See also Rountree, *Powhatan Indians of Virginia*, 4.

21. For Namontack, see Richter, "Tsenacommacah," 59.

22. For Spelman's time in Virginia, see Henry Spelman, *Relation of Virginea*, in Edward Arber, ed., *Travels and Works of Captain John Smith* (Edinburgh: J. Grant, 1910), ci–cxiv; Fausz, "Middlemen in peace and war"; Kupperman, *Indians and English*, 77–78, 206–211; Kupperman, *Jamestown*, 232–237; Rice, "Escape from Tsenacommacah," 132–134; Rountree, *Powhatan Indians*, 4.

23. Spelman, *Relation of Virginea*, ciii.

24. James D. Rice, "Escape from Tsenacommacah: Chesapeake Algonquians and the Powhatan Menace," in Mancall, ed., *The Atlantic World and Virginia*, 131.

25. Rice, "Escape from Tsenacommacah," 132.

26. Alexander Brown, *Genesis of the United States*, 2 vols. (Boston: Houghton, Mifflin and Co., 1890), vol. 2, 1020–1021. Arundel cited in Kupperman, *Indians and English*, 211.

27. *Jamestown voyages*, vol. 2, 325.

28. *Jamestown voyages*, vol. 1, 5.

29. Strachey, *Historie of Travell into Virginia Britania*, 101–103.

30. Strachey, *Historie of Travell into Virginia Britania*, 102.

31. Strachey, *Historie of Travell into Virginia Britania*, 46–47, n.4. Kupperman, *Indians and English*, 209–211.

32. On Spelman as Sir Henry Spelman's nephew, see the will of Francis Saunder (1613) in Philip Alexander Bruce, "Virginia gleanings in England," in *Virginia Magazine of History and Biography* XV (1907/8), 304–306. Saunder left money and goods to all of Henry Spelman's brothers, sisters, and cousins (the children of Sir Henry), and yet he "exempted" Henry, who apparently had not yet been forgiven for the sin that drove him to Virginia. See also: *Jamestown Voyages*, vol.1, 5; Strachey, *Historie of Travell into Virginia Britania*, 46.n.4; and Kupperman, *Jamestown*, 232. Brown, *Genesis of the United States*, vol. 2, 1020–1021; and Edward Arber, *Works of Captain John Smith*, vol. 1, ci, mistakenly recorded Spelman as the third son of the antiquary.

33. Linda Van Norden, "Sir Henry Spelman and the chronology of the Elizabethan College of Antiquaries," *Huntington Library Quarterly* 13, 2 (Feb. 1950): 131–160.

34. Pocock, *The Ancient Constitution and the Feudal Law,* 91–123.

35. Pocock, *The Ancient Constitution,* 104.

36. See "Sir John Spelman" in the *Oxford Dictionary of National Biography.* John Aubrey knew Spelman's grandson and claimed that Sir Henry informally discussed his antiquarian ideas with his family; see *Aubrey's Brief Lives,* ed. Oliver Lawson Dick (London: Secker & Warburg, 1992), 281.

37. On Spelman and the New England Council; see Charles M. Andrews, *The Colonial Period of American History. The Settlements, Volume 1* (New Haven: Yale University Press, 1934), 400–405; and "Sir Henry Spelman" in the *Oxford Dictionary of National Biography.*

38. Rice, "Escape from Tsenacommacah," 136.

39. Richter, "Tsenacommacah and the Atlantic World," Rice, "Escape from Tsenacommacah," 97–140. See also Elman R. Service, *Primitive Social Organisation: An Evolutionary Perspective* (New York: Random House, 1962); Morton H. Fried, *The Evolution of Political Society: An Essay in Political Anthropology* (New York: Random House, 1967).

40. Richter, "Tsenacommacah and the Atlantic World," 31.

41. Rice, "Escape from Tsenacommacah," 111.

42. On the development of the idea of the modern state, see Quentin Skinner, "From the state of princes to the person of the state," in Skinner, *Visions of Politics. Volume 2: Renaissance Virtues* (Cambridge: Cambridge University Press, 2002), 368–413; and Quentin Skinner, "A genealogy of the modern state," *Proceedings of the British Academy* 162, 2009, 325–370.

43. Hobbes was a participant in the Virginian colonizing enterprise, attending 37 meetings of the company in the 1620s in his capacity as secretary to William Cavendish (3rd earl of Devonshire), and he also did some work for the company; see Noel Malcolm, "Hobbes, Sandys and the Virginia Company," *Historical Journal* 24 (1981); Noel Malcolm, *Reason of State, Propaganda and the Thirty Years War* (Oxford: Oxford University Press, 2007), 8.

44. Skinner, "A genealogy of the modern state," 326.

45. Michael J. Braddick, *State Formation in Early Modern England 1550–1700* (Cambridge: Cambirdge University Press, 2001); Phil Withington, *The Politics of Commonwealth* (Cambridge: Cambridge University Press, 2005).

46. Withington, *The Politics of Commonwealth,* 53.

47. Smith, *A Map of Virginia,* 369.

48. Alexander Whitaker, *Good Newes from Virginia* (London, 1613), 26–27.

49. Henry Spelman, *Relation of Virginea,* cx–cxi.

50. Kupperman, *Indians and English,* 78.

51. For Alanus, see James Muldoon, *Popes, Lawyers and Infidels: The Church and the Non-Christian World 1250–1550* (Philadelphia: University of Pennsylvania Press, 1979); Robert A. Williams, *The American Indian in Western Legal Thought* (Oxford: Oxford University Press, 1990), 40–41. On the widespread acceptance of Alanus' doctrine by the end of the twelfth century, see Richard Tuck, *The Rights of War and Peace* (Oxford: Oxford University Press, 1999), 59.

52. Edward Coke, "Calvin's Case, or the Case of the Postnati," in *The Selected Writings and Speeches of Sir Edward Coke,* ed. Steve Sheppard (Indianapolis, IL: Liberty Fund, 2003), vol. 1, 207.

53. Strachey, *Historie of Travell into Virginia Britania,* 60–61.

54. Clifford Geertz, *Negara. The Theatre State in Nineteenth Century Bali* (Princeton: Princeton University Press, 1980), 121–123.

55. Robert Gray, *A Good Speed to Virginia* (London, 1610), sig.[C4]r.

56. William Symonds, *Virginia* (London, 1609), 10.

57. Smith, *Map of Virginia*, 369.

58. Hermes, "The law of Native Americans to 1815," 43. See also Rountree, *Powhatan Indians*, 17 and 114–115, who points to a Powhatan sense of territory.

59. Strachey, *Historie of Travell into Virginia Britania*, 44.

60. John Rolfe, *Relation of the state of Virginia* [1616] in *Virginia: Four Personal Narratives* (New York: Arno Press, 1972), 106.

61. Strachey, *Historie of Travell into Virginia Britania*, 58.

62. "A justification for planting in Virginia" in S. M. Kingsbury, ed., *The Records of the Virginia Company of London*, 4 vols., (Washington: Library of Congress, 1906–1935), vol. 3, 1–3, printed from Tanner Manuscripts, XCIII, folio 200, Bodleian Library, Oxford.

5

WABANAKI VERSUS FRENCH AND ENGLISH CLAIMS IN NORTHEASTERN NORTH AMERICA, C. 1715

Saliha Belmessous

This chapter will focus on the dispute over territory between the Wabanaki, otherwise known as the Dawn Land people, the French of Canada, and the English of New England at the turn of the eighteenth century. The Wabanaki confederacy included Abenaki, Mi'kmaq, Maliseet, Passamaquoddy, and Penobscot peoples. These northeastern Algonquian peoples were culturally closely related, and the Europeans found it hard to distinguish one tribe from another. For this reason, the French called them "Abénaquis" while the English generally referred to them as "Eastern Indians." Their ancestral country covered modern Newfoundland, Nova Scotia, and part of New Brunswick in Canada, the states of Maine, New Hampshire, and Vermont in the USA. Wabanaki claims were made in the context of a long imperial struggle between the French, the English, and other native American peoples. Wabanaki claims reveal that indigenous peoples could position themselves in the contests between other nations as much through legal as military means. They also illustrate the extraordinary degree to which European legal claims could be, in fact, a response to indigenous claims.

In the seventeenth century, the French had settled in Wabanaki territory on uninhabited lands and with the approval of the native neighboring tribes whom they had Christianized and with whom they concluded long-term alliances that encompassed commercial, political and military matters. The Wabanaki had also allowed the English to settle on their lands and build posts where they could trade pelts for European goods at favorable rates. The English were welcomed provided that their settlements were requested according to native rules and approved by Wabanaki councils. The Wabanaki resented English violations of these reservations and constantly reminded the English that they had no title to settlements that remained Wabanaki property. Eventually, they backed up their claims with the use of force, and English colonists were forced to leave Wabanaki lands. By the treaty of 1678, which calmed down the hostilities, the Wabanaki imposed the payment of a tribute to English settlers requesting authorization to resettle. Colonists' refusal to comply with the treaty articles provoked the use of force once again.[1] Although new peace treaties were signed in 1693 and 1699, land encroachments did not stop, and, in August 1699, the Commandant of Sacoa Fort, John Hill, reported to the Council of Massachusetts and to Earl of Bellomont that the Wabanaki leader Bombazeen [Bomoseen] claimed that "all those Lands belonged to his uncle Moxis the Chief Sachamor of that place, and [John Hill] saith that those Eastern Indians carry themselves verry surly and insolently and do say, that the English shall not repossess and enjoy ye Lands in ye province of Maine otherwise than by agreement wth them."[2] In other words, according to the Wabanaki leader, the English were allowed to stay as long as his people agreed.

Constant British encroachments on Wabanaki territory created much tension between the two peoples, which fed a continuing cycle of diplomatic negotiations and violent clashes.[3] These encroachments also created tension among Wabanaki peoples themselves as some Wabanaki supported the French alliance whereas others favored the English and a third faction promoted neutrality.[4]

Between 1702 and 1713, France, Spain, and Bavaria on one side, and Austria, Prussia, Great Britain, Holland, Denmark, and Portugal on the other, fought a war that is known as the War of the Spanish Succession in Europe, and as Queen Anne's War in America. This war ended in 1713 with the signature of a series of treaties between the participating countries. The Treaty of Utrecht is the general name given to these treaties. European wars frequently ended with gain or loss of territories. Colonies and dependencies were not spared by these exchanges. By the Treaty of Utrecht, France ceded to Great Britain her claims on Newfoundland, the Hudson Bay territories, and Acadia. This cession would generate endless disputes between France and Great Britain as the borders of Hudson Bay were not delimited and those of Acadia were also contested. Although the French gave away Acadia according to "its ancient boundaries," these limits had never been defined and displayed. The English claimed that these boundaries included what, at the time, were exclusively Wabanaki lands whereas the French restricted Acadia to its peninsula.

France was able to cede Acadia because it had claimed, according to European rules, sovereignty upon that Wabanaki territory by right of discovery (that is, French settlers were the first Europeans to reach and settle on that territory). Following the Treaty of Utrecht, the English based their claim on Acadia by right of cession—albeit their understanding of the territory ceded was not the same.

When they first heard of the treaty, the Wabanaki thought that the English, who had broken the news of the cession before the French officials were able to do so, were lying to them. The enormity of what they were told was such that disbelief was their immediate reaction. When the English offered to show them the treaty and have it translated by the Jesuit missionaries, the Wabanaki understood that the French had wronged them: "Then the Abenakis lost their temper and asked on which right the French could give away a country which they did not own. Their fit of anger would even have gone further had the missionaries not calmed them by saying that they were misled by an equivocation and that their country was not included in what the King of France had ceded to the English.[5]" Reassurances were not enough, and the Wabanaki took the matter further. In a letter written to the King of France in 1715, they rejected French rule over their territory as well as the French ability to cede a land they had never owned.[6] The Wabanaki acknowledged a French right to cede an area that the English had conquered but warned the French that they could not dispose of their land: "is not my land different from the land where Port Royal is which the English has taken? My land is entirely different; and to give to the English the entire land where the fort he has taken is, is not giving him the country in which I live." Although the Wabanaki claimed that they "would be happy to see the French settle and fortify themselves in [their] rivers," they also frankly asserted their ownership on those lands and asked the king to deny his supposed cession of their lands to the English.[7] They similarly denied the British Crown any right to their land, warning the governor: "But thou sayest that the Frenchman has given Plaisance and Portrail [Port Royal], which are in my neighborhood, with all the adjacent country; he may give thee all that he will. As for me, I have my own land, that the Great Spirit has given me on which to live; as long as there shall be a child of my tribe, he will fight to retain it."[8]

To understand why and how the remarkable dispute opposing the Wabanaki to the Europeans in 1721 appeared in the colonial correspondence, it is necessary to understand the importance of Wabanaki lands for the French and the English. The treaty of Utrecht marked the end of French expansion while it gave a legal impulse to British progression. The French rejected the English claim that Acadia extended to New England, and to protect New France from possible English encirclement, they erected the fortress of Louisbourg, on the island of Cape Breton, thus menacing Acadia. The French also supported Wabanaki land claims, as those lands would constitute a buffer zone between French and English settlements.

The English, on the other hand, wanted Wabanaki lands not only in order to settle their people but also to take control over the large forests that covered those lands and that would strengthen their navy by providing wood for ships; finally, the English coveted Wabanaki lands for geopolitical reasons, and the military conquest of Canada was always on their agenda.

English encroachments generally followed the same pattern: the English would get native approval to establish stores where they would sell European goods at very favorable prices compared with French rates, then they would establish hundreds of families nearby and construct military forts to protect them.[9] The containment of English settlements was crucial for the Wabanaki, who used both diplomacy and force (especially cattle killing) to oppose English violations of their territory. Following the signature of

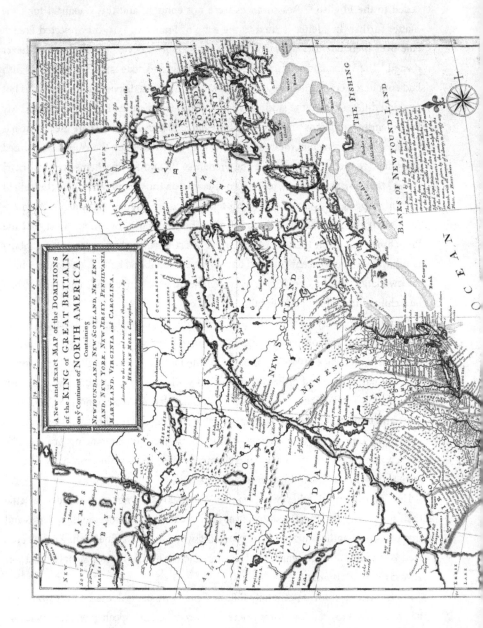

A New and Exact MAP of the DOMINIONS of the KING of GREAT BRITAIN on y Continent of NORTH AMERICA. Containing NEWFOUNDLAND, NEW SCOTLAND, NEW ENG: LAND, NEW YORK, NEW JERSEY, PENSILVANIA MARYLAND, VIRGINIA and CAROLINA. According to the Newest and most Exact Observations By HERMAN MOLL Geographer.

A new and exact map of the dominions of the king of Great Britain on ye continent of North America . . . by the geographer Herman Moll, 1715, records British claims on North America following the treaty of Utrecht. Wabanaki lands have been included in British possessions under new names (see Newfoundland, New Scotland, and the northeastern part of New England) despite French and native rejection of this claim. In doing so, the map sought to legitimize British claims and create grounds for future ambitions.
Courtesy of the John Carter Brown Library at Brown University

the Treaty of Utrecht, they made formal representations to the governors of New England against British usurpation of their lands. A group of New England merchants, known as the Pejepscot Proprietors, had bought out a title to a large portion of Wabanaki territory, on the lower Androscoggin and Kennebec Rivers, and they had started settling part of that area: the town of Brunswick was founded and forts were built. The Proprietors' claim relied on a 1632 land grant that two merchants obtained from the Council for New England and various deeds supposedly acquired from Wabanaki sellers.[10] Other Englishmen (both settlers and people living in England) contested that title, and the Crown received conflicting petitions asking for royal confirmation of previous purchases from native sellers or royal grants: in 1714, Baronnet Sir Bibye Lake and Edward Hutchinson asked the Queen to grant them patent letters for their right on the surroundings of the Kennebec River, which they inherited from their relatives Captain Lake and Major Clarke—both of whom had supposedly purchased the region between 1639 and 1654—and which they had improved and settled prior to the war with the Wabanaki.[11] A Robert West thought about challenging Bibye's right on the basis that the island of Arrowsick had been granted by the Governor of New York to his relative John West, but he quickly withdrew his claim, having realized that Bibye's ancestor had purchased the region "from the naturall Landlords and Propriet[rs] the Indian Natives" many years earlier.[12] Another petition, in the name of the Duke of Hamilton, asked for the confirmation of the ten thousand acres of land he had been previously granted in the region.[13] While colonial agent for Massachusetts and Connecticut Jeremiah Dummer petitioned the Crown, arguing that those lands belonged to the Province of Massachusetts Bay by virtue of the royal charter given to the province, other petitioners argued that it belonged to the Crown by right of conquest, having won it from the French.[14]

The multiplicity of these claims over Wabanaki lands shows that the English were themselves struggling in trying to take control over native land even though Governor Samuel Shute of Massachusetts chose to defend the rights of the Pejepscot Proprietors against their English challengers.

At Georgetown on Arrowsick Island in 1717, the Norridgewock leader and spokesman Wiwurna contested any English right to settle in those regions and claimed Wabanaki sovereignty over the whole country. Wiwurna claimed first that "we are under no other Government than our own"; he then firmly reminded Governor Shute that "This place was formerly settled and is now settling at our request: and we now return thanks that the English are come to settle here, and will imbrace them in our bosoms that come to settle in our lands."[15] In other words, the English did not have valid title on Wabanaki land on which they had settled as guests. Despite the Governor's interruption that "they must not call it their land, for the English have bought it of[f] them and their ancestors," Wiwurna warned him that, "We desire there may be no further settlements made. We shan't be able to hold them all in our bosoms, and to take care to shelter them, if it be like to be bad weather, and mischief be threatned."

English reactions to Wabanaki claims were confused, not to say inconsistent. On the one hand, they claimed that their recent settlements had "been promoted partly on their [Wabanaki] accounts," that is, with the approval of the native owners. The English also claimed that the Wabanaki "must be sensible and satisfied that the English own his land, and have deeds that shew, and set forth their purchase from their ancestors."

Disingenuousness apart, there is some degree of cultural misunderstanding here: while the Wabanaki claimed that they could give some portions of their land without losing their rights of ownership, the English claimed that the Wabanaki had ceded their lands to them. The Governor of New France, Philippe de Rigaud de Vaudreuil, understood well the distinction when he said that the Wabanakis had lent ("prester") some land to the English and not given it to them.[16]

The Wabanaki were ready to compromise and establish a formal boundary to their territory, thus confirming existing English establishments, and Wiwurna offered "to cut off our lands as far as the mills, and the coast of Pemaquid." Shute declined this proposition on the basis that "we desire only what is our own, and that we will have. We will not wrong them, but what is our own we will be masters of," leaving open the Proprietors' prospects to extend their settlements.[17]

Every time the English gave goods or money for Wabanaki lands, they claimed that they had purchased them whereas the Wabanaki considered those goods and money as presents for allowing strangers to settle on their lands. This explained why Wiwurna replied to Governor Shute, "We can't understand how our lands have been purchased, what has been alienated was by our gift." The Wabanaki were astonished by the English claim that their lands had been sold and by the translation of the contents of the deeds of sale of land that were exhibited to them. In search of peaceful relations with the English, the Wabanaki were ready to acknowledge the reality of existing English settlements, if not the reality of those transactions, but they reaffirmed their superior right over their land. They claimed that the English neither should settle on their lands without negotiating with them, nor should they build forts that would undoubtedly threaten their lives rather than protect them as the English argued.

Wabanaki opposition to English forts suggests also that they were aware that the founding of forts was intended as marking possession.[18] The founding of trading posts was often requested by native communities who sought to establish or strengthen existing trading and, sometimes, military relations with the Europeans. Europeans founded forts for strategic reasons: interimperial competition for the lucrative indigenous trade demanded organizing the exchanges at the source to repel other European rivals. Trading alliances sometimes, but not always, came with invaluable military alliances. Europeans also used forts as a privileged way to take possession of native lands on which they had no valid title. In allowing these establishments to be built, indigenous peoples did not seek to relinquish their claims over the land upon which the forts stood, as the Europeans were aware. But, in the interimperial interplay, forts represented, for Europeans, the physical evidence of their presence. Forts were not merely trading posts. They were fortified posts, "and such (. . .) Fortifications cannot be made by any subject, without the Royal Authority."[19] Forts were built with the assent of the Crown, and they carried royal authority among indigenous peoples. As Governor Shute explained to Wiwurna, "King George builds what forts he pleases in his own Dominions, and has given me power to do it here, and they are for their [the Wabana-ki's] security as well as our's, and the French do the like, They build what forts they please, and all kings have that power, and the Governours they appoint do the same."[20] As a marker of possession and a symbol of royal authority, forts were a powerful in-strument in extending colonial influence among the natives and in validating claims in interimperial politics. The natives responded diversely to these claims: some nations destroyed the forts; others played colonial competition to invalidate European claims— in the 1720s, for instance, the Senecas reacted to the unauthorized fortification of the French blockhouse in Niagara by allowing the English to build Fort Oswego; other nations contested verbally the building of the forts or simply ignored them.

Between 1717 and 1721, the British continued encroaching on Wabanaki territory in the Kennebec and Androscoggin valleys. In November 1720, a Wabanaki delegation, led by Wiwurna and Mog, met four commissioners of the Massachusetts government at Georgetown to protest against English settlement at Merrymeeting Bay (Swan Island).[21] The Wabanaki asked "that the People that are upon our land at Merry meeting may be removed." The English answer was disingenuous. The commis-sioners claimed that they were "directed by the Government to tell you that the Eng-lish have no design to take your Country or any of your lands from you, or to deprive you of any of your Just rights or Privileges." At the same time, they asserted that, "The claims of the English to those lands in Kenebeck River have been examined and we are fully satisfied that the English have a good title thereunto as appears by their Deeds and Conveyances from Indians above 70 years since and the government is resolved to defend the Proprietors in those their just rights. It's therefore in vain for you to expect that ever those inhabitants will be removed." They threatened the Wabanaki that they would "draw the sword" to force them to respect the supposed rights of the English over the lands. Although the pro-English faction of the Wabanaki delegation eventually prevailed during the conference and accepted English settle-ments (but not their claims) on Wabanaki lands, the issue was far from being resolved. Factions disagreed upon the extent of British settlements, but there was a consensus on Wabanaki ownership of the land.

To avoid open hostilities, the Wabanaki Confederacy made new representations at Georgetown in July 1721. More than 250 natives, mainly Wabanaki but also Christian Mohawks, Hurons of Lorette, and Algonquins, assembled to meet the Governor of Massachusetts, who did not turn up, although they waited for him for more than a month. The natives were accompanied by two Jesuit missionaries, Father Pierre de La Chasse and Father Sébastien Rale, both of whom had been working among the Wabanaki for at least twenty years. As a result of Shute's absence, they signed a formal letter addressed to Shute, which Wiwurna read in his language; a copy was read in English by the Wabanaki Pehouaret, then Father La Chasse read it in Latin and explained it to the English.[22] Finally, a copy in French was handed to an English official to be forwarded to Governor Shute.[23]

Why did the Wabanaki write a letter, thus breaking with the practice of making verbal representations? According to the French Governor Vaudreuil, the Wabanaki sent their speech to Shute in writing so that he could neither contradict them nor change the content of their speech.[24] Their insistence in their letter being written and read in four different languages was also meant to make clear that, despite earlier English claims that the Jesuits controlled their speeches, they were the true authors of their letter.[25] The original letter was in Wabanaki while the French, Latin, and English copies were translations.

Why did the Wabanaki write a letter and not a petition? After all, neighboring native peoples wrote petitions to the British Crown at the same period to complain of colonial encroachments.[26] The reason lies in the nature of the Wabanaki claim. Petitions were requests meant to get the support of the British Crown whereas the Wabanaki were not requesting or pleading for assistance: they were asserting their territorial rights and appealing to some kind of superior law that governed nations. To give more power to their claim, they brought with them their witnesses, native and French.[27]

As shown previously, the political context is crucial for understanding how the Wabanaki claim to territory came to appear in colonial archives. The English kept this letter for several reasons. The danger of the event was the first reason. After receiving news of the meeting, Governor Shute wrote to the House of Representatives that:

the Indians to the number of two hundred have marched in Hostile manner, under French colours, accompanied by two Jesuits, into the town of Arowsick, where they had a conference with the inhabitants of that Place, and afterwards delivered an Insolent & menacing Letter directed to me your Governour [sic], which Papers I shall order to be laid before you. Whereupon with the advice of the Council I immediately sent a sufficient number of forces to the assistance of our alarmed Eastern settlements as also some Gentlemen of the Council, who are to demand of the Indians the Reason of this notorious Insult upon His Majestys Territories and Liege Subjects. I Expect the Gentlemen of the Council

in a few days to make a report of their Proceedings in this affair, which I believe
will require your serious attention.[28]

The content of the Wabanaki letter, which will be examined shortly, was the second
reason for keeping it.

The French also recorded this letter, although their version was modified.[29] The argument was the same, but the writer improved its articulation, converting it to a more
powerful and legally recognizable document. For the French, the letter was a priceless
document worth recording and preserving to contest English claims.

The Wabanaki letter was meant to achieve two goals: the release of Wabanaki hostages and the removal of British settlers from Wabanaki lands. The letter establishes
Wabanaki rights on their land in two ways: first, the Wabanaki claimed that they
owned their land by divine right: "my land which I have received from God only, my
land which no King or foreign power could have or can dispose of."[30] In the English
translation kept in the Colonial Archives, that claim has disappeared. It had been
purely and simply deleted from the Wabanaki letter. Although concern with divine
right was weaker in Great Britain since the Glorious Revolution, it was regarded as a
dangerous political doctrine in the early eighteenth century, particularly in the context
of Jacobism. The explosive nature of such a doctrine might be the reason for the dele-
tion of the Wabanaki claim.

The Wabanaki then rejected all possible claims the French and especially the English
could put forward: "my land dont belong to the, neither by right of Conquest nor by
Donation, not by purchase." All three arguments were central to European claims in
America, and the Wabanaki then explained why the English could not use those arguments to justify their encroachments.

The English could not use the right of conquest as they had not conquered the
Wabanaki: "It's not thine by right of Conquest? when didst thou drive me from thence?
and have not I driven the away thence? every time we have had a war together, which
proves it is mine by several titles." During King Philip's War, which the English and
their Mohawk allies won over the decimated Narragansetts and other tribes of southern New England, the Wabanaki, for the large part, tried not to get directly involved
even though they suffered from the great dispersals that shook northeastern North
America at the end of the war. During Queen Anne's War, the English failed to bring
the Wabanaki to their knees, and their strikes against Wabanaki villages were often
unsuccessful, the latter fleeing before the arrival of their attackers. The Wabanaki
would then return when the English were gone. In contrast, the Wabanaki multiplied
devastating raids against Massachusetts and New Hampshire villages (they spared New
York with which they were trading). Conquest was therefore not an argument appropriate to the circumstances.

The Wabanaki cited three problems with the English claim to a right by donation. First, the King of France could not have given what did not belong to him. The Wabanaki mentioned this possibility, only to dismiss it in two sentences: "the King of France thou sayest has given it to the, but could he give it to the? Am I his subject?" That question was only rhetorical, and the Wabanaki then rejected the argument that some of their kinsmen had given land to the English: "The Indians have given it to thee; some few Indians which thou didst surprize by causing them to drink, could they give it thee, to the prejudice of their whole nation, who very far from ratifying that donation which would be necessary to give the right to it, declare it to be vain and deceitful." According to the Wabanaki, property was collective. Individuals had no special rights on the land and could not, consequently, give it or sell it to foreigners. The most they could have done was to allow English settlers to establish themselves on their territory: "Some ones have lent the some places, but know thou that all the nation revokes the lending, because of the abuse which thou hast done me. When did they permit the to build forts, & to advance as far as thou hast done in their River?" The Wabanaki were careful to explain that by lending some land to the settlers, they did not alienate their right to it. They could accordingly revoke that lending for whatever reason they thought was appropriate. In this case, constant English encroachments were a powerful reason for taking back what they had allowed earlier.

Finally, the English could not use the right of purchase: "It's none of thine by reason of purchase; and I am told a thing which my grand fathers, & fathers never told me, that they had sold my land." Here the Wabanaki rejected the English claim that they had acquired Wabanaki lands properly, that is, with respect to their property rights and therefore through purchase. The Wabanaki, first, claimed that their ancestors had not sold their land: if those transactions had taken place, they argued, their history would have recorded them. Yet, it had not. Why should they trust the English deeds of those supposed transactions while they were aware that their words were sometimes misrepresented and even altered in English transcripts of diplomatic meetings? As one Wabanaki leader later said, "I know not what I am made to say in another language, but I know well what I say in my own."[31] Let us consider, the Wabanaki continued, for the sake of the argument, that the English did buy some piece of land: "when some one may have sold some place, which is not so, since you cant not say that thou hast sufficiently paid for the least of the islands which thou seizest on." Although native sellers no longer accepted trade goods as payment, British settlers were still not paying enough for the large tracts of land they were buying: in 1686, for example, a settler of New Hampshire bought a large tract of land for £7.[32]

The English fortified their existing villages and extended their settlements without the approval of the Wabanaki; they also used treachery, intimidation, and alcohol to silence the local natives. As Boston minister Thomas Bannister once reported to the

Board of Trade: "Their Injuries have been verry great; as divesting them of their Lands by Force or Fraud; makeing them drunk & then sign they know not what."[33] The Wabanaki similarly condemned the English for their "treacheries" and claimed that the supposed transactions the English were justifying their rights with were "An effect of the drink which thou givest in abundance to the Indians, after which they promise thee whatever thou will have; and effect of the violence which thou hast exercised towards them in several re-encounters."

The Wabanaki also argued that even though their ancestors could have sold some portions of their land, they could revoke those sales as their ancestors were not entitled to sell their patrimony: "I have right to reuse in an Estate, which they could not alienate to my prejudice, and which I have so many times reconquered." This argument has to be read alongside the earlier claim that the Wabanaki owned their land from time immemorial ("Know that we have been on this land which you override and upon which you are walking, even before those trees that you see have come through it. This land is ours and nothing could ever take it over from us or oblige us to abandon it").[34] For the Europeans, this argument was familiar as allodial right. Land held in allodium was inalienable. Such a title would invalidate all English claims to Wabanaki lands. To make things worse, the Wabanaki even added that they had secured their inheritance by conquest.[35]

The Wabanaki ended their letter by discarding all previous agreements made between the English and certain individuals for the reason that these agreements were not approved by the whole nation: "Know furthermore Great Captain that the whole Abnaquise nation protest that all the acts that thou hast past hitherto with the Indians are null; & because they have not been acknowledged nor received by the whole nation." Yet consensus was necessary in Wabanaki politics. The English could not argue that a few Wabanaki, whom they either made drunk or they intimidated, could speak on behalf of their whole nation as they were not entrusted by their people. Accordingly, the Wabanaki dealt their last legal blow against the English by insisting that their letter had been endorsed by the whole nation: "these are not the words of four of five Indians; who by the presents, lyes & crafts thou thinkest to cause easily to fall into thy sentiments: It's the word of the whole nation of Abnaquise spread out on this continent & in Canada; and of all the Christian Indians their allies."

Their territorial rights on the region asserted, the Wabanaki then made an injunction to the English to retire from their land up to a specific boundary, which they defined in terms of river drainages: the nation "summons thee to retire from off the land of the Abnaquis, which thou will usurp unjustly, & which had for its boundaries the river of Kounibigou, which separates it from the land of the Mohawks. I have right to demand of the all that space, which lyes from the River as far as I am, since thou possessest nothing of it but by surprize, but I am willing to leave the in that space in condition that absolutely there shall not one English man lodge within a league near my River of Pigounvakki, nor from that boundary all along the seasisde, which answers to the whole extent of my land, nor at the bottom of my River, nor in any of the Islands that answer to my Land which are at large & where my canno may pass." In establishing boundaries, the Wabanaki were not only marking the limits of their territory. They were also claiming how far their sovereignty extended and where English claim to sovereignty stopped.[36]

The English reacted strongly to this letter. First, Governor Samuel Shute "immediately sent a sufficient number of forces to the assistance of our alarmed Eastern settlements as also some Gentlemen of the Council, who are to demand of the Indians the Reason of this notorious Insult upon His Majestys Territories and Liege Subjects." He also forwarded what he qualified as an "Insolent & menacing Letter" to the House of Representatives.[37] In its reply to the Governor, the House regretted that English kindness toward the Wabanaki had been rewarded with "Repeated Injuries and wrongs."[38] The House flayed the "unparralled Impudence of those Indians Rebels" who not only came bearing the French flag but also "sent your Excellency that imperious Letter (. . .) full of the most scornful expressions and audacious menaces and threats to the people there."

The English refused to address directly Wabanaki claims by claiming that the French were behind their representations. According to the English, there were several elements that made obvious the French responsibility in what they described as a rebellion: the French flag, plus the presence of two Jesuit missionaries and a French officer, and an exchange of letters between those Jesuit missionaries and the Government of Canada that discussed the matter. Strong French support of Wabanaki claims meant, for the English, that the French, at the forefront of which was Governor Vaudreuil, instigated those claims.[39] The accusation of ventriloquism was therefore used to delegitimize Wabanaki claims. The English in good faith could have suspected the French of having manipulated the Wabanaki letter as they had consistently employed similar practices since the 1690s. Governor William Phips had, indeed, introduced the practice of altering, in their written forms, the content of the treaties that were verbally read to the Wabanaki leaders and to which they subsequently agreed. In the written treaties, Phips included Wabanaki supposed acceptance of submission to the British Crown. His successor, Joseph Dudley, even "refined this tactic into a full-blown system of parallel diplomacies."[40]

English suspicions of ventriloquism gained further force from the fact that the French also thought that they instigated Wabanaki claims. Although the King's plan, after the signature of the Treaty of Utrecht, was to migrate all the Wabanaki to the newly established colony of Isle Royale where French settlers of Acadia and Newfoundland were also encouraged to move, it soon appeared that making such a proposal to the Wabanaki would be politically suicidal.[41] Following Father de La Chasse's advice, the French authorities decided to defend Wabanaki interests and assist them in their dealings with the English, whether diplomatic or military.[42] From then on, Governor Vaudreuil prompted the Wabanaki to stand for their rights and resist English encroachments whereas the Jesuits La Chasse and Rale encouraged the Wabanaki of different regions to join and form a united front to oppose the usurpers.

French efforts to excite Wabanaki anger against the English did not mean that they succeeded in manipulating Wabanaki minds. The Wabanaki had opposed French and English land transactions from the moment they heard of the Treaty of Utrecht, and it was they who reminded the French Governor of the terms of their alliance: the French had to assist them, whether they liked it or not. They also reminded him that all the native nations of the continent might one day "reunite to chase away from the continent all the strangers, whoever they were."[43] Similarly, constant Jesuit efforts to promote French interests among the Wabanaki and their real influence among certain groups did not mean that the Fathers could ventiloquize for their flock, as they were themselves aware.[44]

Governor Shute could not yet believe that ventriloquism was not the cause of the claims, and he decided to kill Father Sébastien Rale, the supposed ventriloquist (the reason why La Chasse was spared remained unknown). Rale was in charge of the Norridgewock village, which he had founded in 1694. He had already attracted English anger, and in July 1720 the Massachusetts Council had offered a reward of £100 for his arrest. Shute also kept asking Vaudreuil to recall Rale for the reason that English and colonial laws did not allow Catholic priests to live and preach in British territory. In January 1722, an English party looking for Rale attacked Norridgewock, but the Jesuit managed to escape in the woods. Other attempts to capture Rale failed until the English eventually shot him in August 1724 during a large-scale attack on Norridgewock.[45]

Rejecting Wabanaki claims in the name of ventriloquism and even getting rid of the supposed ventriloquist were nonetheless not enough to strengthen the grounds of English titles over Wabanaki land. In a series of letters first to the Board of Plantations and then to the Governor of Canada, the colonial governor dismissed native title, and in doing so, he made the colony's own counterclaims to Wabanaki territory. The English first argued that they owned the lands contested by right of purchase:

> Your Lordships will observe that the French Government (in the inclosed letters) advise the Indians to drive the English off from their lands; from which I must remarke to Your Lordships that those lands which the French Government call the Indians land, are lands which the English have long since purchased off the Indians, and have good deeds to produce for the same: & have also erected some Forts thereupon. And that the said lands have been at several

general meetings of the Indians and English confirmed to them; and once since my being Governour of these Provinces; as will appear by the inclosed Treaty of the 19th August 1717.[46]

Shute was untruthful because, as previously shown, the Wabanaki had clearly objected to recent English settlements at the Arrowsic Conference in 1717. The split between Wabanaki delegates during that conference, and the willingness of the Anglophile leaders not to alienate the English, allowed Shute to have the treaty approved, but to what the Wabanaki really agreed is not really known.

In his letters to the Governor of Canada, Vaudreuil, Governor Shute claimed that the English owned Nova Scotia, formerly known as Acadia, by right of cession as the French had given it to them. Instead of speaking of native land, Vaudreuil had to understand that the territories upon which the Wabanaki had settled "fall within the English Pale or Territory, inasmuch as the Crown of Great Britain have now the Right & Dominion of Nova Scotia formerly called L Acadie with all its Dependencies." These lands were English lands and not native lands. Shute also reversed the chronology of settlement by arguing that the English were the first inhabitants of those lands and it was the natives who then "setled upon one of the principal Rivers of New England, that live in the Neighbourhood of Our English Towns & Garrisons, & until very lately have Constantly conversed and traded with them, and pass by the English settlements every time they come to the sea for their fishery."[47]

Second, and more importantly, Shute argued that the Wabanaki had ceded their sovereignty to the English Crown a long time before: "But above all, and what I very much insist on, This Tribe of the Indians, as well as that of Penobscot, have for a great number of years last past, by frequent and solemn Treaties, willingly and Joyfully put themselves under the Protection of the Crown of Great Britain & the Governmt of New England & on these occasions have had Tokens of His Majesties kindness & Friendship presented to them; And you may depend upon it His Majesty will never quit His right and Interest with respect to those Indian Tribes, but Insist upon it to the last."[48] Once again, Shute was untruthful. Whereas earlier he had recalled the 1717 conference where the Wabanaki had supposedly approved the extent of the land transactions, he forgot to mention that the meeting started with the leader Wiwurna rejecting the English claim that they had submitted to Great Britain. As Wiwurna replied to Shute: "We have had the same discourse from other Governours, as from your Excellency: and we have said the same to them; (. . .) that we are under no other Government than our own."[49]

The English also argued that they owned the contested lands by right of purchase. The island of Arrowsic, for example, had been bought nearly seventy years before from the natives; the land had then been settled and the purchase confirmed by the British

Crown. Shute then objected that the denial by the natives of those transactions would not cancel English title to the lands: "That the Indians will deny their own Deeds tho never so solemnly Ratified and Justly obtained, I am very apt to Believe, but in the mean time that does not destroy the Title to such Lands."[50] He also contested native claim, relayed by Vaudreuil, that treaties with the Wabanaki had to be negotiated by entrusted leaders and confirmed by the nation to be valid ("neither can I be of your opinion, as to their Treaties, That they are null, because the Body of their nation shall please afterwards to disavow it"). Shute then appealed to the law of nations to contest what he understood as Wabanaki refusal to comply with international practices:

> I am sure it is otherwise by the Law of Nations and usage of all Civillised Gov-
> ernments in the World; All Treaties, Stipulations and Transactions that are
> managed and concluded by Plenipotentiaries or Delegates being obligatory to
> the Nation or Government that Imploy them; Now it is Notorious That at all
> times when this Government accepted the Submission of, or Treated with those
> Eastern Indians, their Delegates, or some of their Chiefs were present, and pro-
> duced their Powers or Credentials from the Tribe; and it is very wrong and
> unjust in them to Insinuate That they were ever Menaced or forced into any of
> their Deeds, Treaties, or Submissions.

The Governor proved the validity of English title by arguing for English sovereignty, established both by native submission to the Crown of Great Britain and the cession of Acadia by the King of France, and he established English dominium by claiming to have deeds which proved that land sales had taken place.

Discussions of property and sovereignty were, as expected, not conducted as clearly in the debate surrounding Wabanaki claim to their land. Confronted by Wabanaki claims that the French King had no right whatsoever to their land and could not, con- sequently, cede it to the British Crown, the French argued that Wabanaki lands were not included in the donation. Therefore, the Treaty of Utrecht did not threaten Wabanaki title. In other negotiations with the English, the governor of Canada argued that, as long-time allies of the Wabanaki, the French held sovereignty over Wabanaki lands, which remained, nonetheless, the property of the Wabanaki. The French ac- cused the English of clinging to official statements to European sovereignty over native lands while ignoring the reality of relations between Europeans and natives:

> I know not what you think of the war with the Abenakys which you have drawn
> upon your selves in taking and possessing against all right their land; you may
> see that it is not so easily a thing as you thought at first to reduce those Indians;
> I can likewise assure you that you will find more difficulty in the pursuit that

ever; for besides their resolution of defending their country as long as any of them remains & not to hearken to any accommodation until you entirely abandon all their Rivers and that things be set on the same foot as they were before the Treaty of Utrecht.[51]

Vaudreuil continued: "What new right have you acquired upon the Abenakis & their lands. I know not of any." To this, the English repeatedly replied that they precisely had a new right, which was dominium. The British Crown was, so they argued, ceded the property of the whole of Acadia, and it was, consequently, their right to take possession of those lands, establish their settlers, improve the lands, and so on. While the French government, for various reasons due mainly to the small number of French settlers in America, was content with the appearance of power over native peoples, the English wanted true power. They could not, as the new Governor of New England wrote to the King, accept the Wabanaki demand that "this government should quit and abandon all the forts and towns for the space of thirty leagues on the sea coasts within the grant of this province from your Majesty's royal predecessors which has been settled and peopled more than seventy years."[52]

The English thought the Wabanaki were being unreasonable while the Wabanaki argued they were claiming what was theirs. When the English commissioners, sent by the government of Massachusetts in 1725, asked them from which land they wanted them to retreat, the Wabanaki delegates replied:

that their land commenced at the River Gounitogon, otherwise called the long river which lies to the west beyond Boston; that this river was formerly the boundary which separated the lands of the Iroquois from those of the Abenakis, that according to these undisputable boundaries, Boston and the greater part of the English settlements east of it are in Abenaki lands; that they would be justified in telling them to retreat from there; but that they had considered that their settlements were established and that they were still inclined to tolerate them; but they demanded as an express condition of peace that the English should retreat from the country from one league beyond Saco River to Port Royal, which was the line separating the lands of the Abenakis from those of the Micmaks.[53]

When an astounded English delegate asked them ironically if they wanted Port Royal (Annapolis Royal for the English), the Wabanaki replied that, "they only wanted the lands which belonged to them; that they had heard that the English boasted that they had submitted to them, that this was an imposture and they defied them to prove it." The English commissioners conceded that they did not have any valid claim beyond the west bank of the Kennebec River, and that the fort at St. George was built not by them, but by the government of Port Royal. As for the lands of the Kennebec region down to Boston, the Wabanaki denied having ever sold them to the English and declared that the deeds produced were mere forgeries. They had, among them, delegates who were over eighty years old and who had never heard of these land sales. When the English changed tactics and claimed that they had possessed these lands for eighty years and that "even though they had not bought them, this possession gave them a title," the Wabanaki replied: "We were in possession before you, for we have held it from time immemorial."

A bloody war opposing the English to the Wabanaki confederation, traditionally known as Dummer's War, was waged from 1722; it lasted five years and exhausted both parties.[54] The English suffered heavy losses on their eastern frontier and were at great pains in subduing their enemy, who found shelter and assistance in Canada—from 1724, the French Crown granted £4,000 to refugee Wabanaki families who needed support while the men were involved in the war.[55] The Wabanaki, nonetheless, suffered very heavy losses as well and could not get military aid from the French, who were officially at peace with the English. Both parties urged peace and met to settle their old disputes. In those meetings, the English stopped referring to the Treaty of Utrecht, in which the Wabanaki had no part, to justify their claim on Acadia, and concentrated instead on both supposed Wabanaki submission to the British Crown and English purchase of lands.[56] Although English records of the conference proceedings and agreements do not mention any Wabanaki opposition to British sovereignty, other evidence shows that Wabanaki leaders strongly rejected any admission of submission when treaties were translated to them.[57] Loron, the Wabanaki spokesman who negotiated the Boston Treaty—wrongly called "Treaty of Submission" by the English— wrote to Governor Dummer to tell him that "having hear'd the Acts which you have given me I have found the Articles entirely deffering from what we have said in presence of one another, 'tis therefore to disown them that I write this letter unto you." He denied having submitted "in my name or in the name of my nation to you & to King George your king." He also denied to "have acknowledged your king for my king & that I have own'd that my Ancestors have Acknowledged Him for such & have declar'd themselves subjects to the Crown of England." "As for what relates to your King, when you have ask'd me if I acknowledg'd Him for King I answer'd yes butt att the same time have made you take notice that I did not understand to acknowledge Him for my king butt only that I own'd that He was king in His kingdom as the king of France is king in His."[58] Loron cautioned the Governor against what he described as "The disagreement I find between your writtings & what I spoke to you viva voce (. . .)," adding that "I thought to have spoken Justly and according to the Interests of my Nation butt I have had the confusion to see that my words have been taken in a quite contrary sense."[59]

As for English claims to rightful property that was attested by the presentation of deeds bearing native signatures, Loron expressed sotto voce doubts on their authenticity and suggested that "it would be better to come wholly upon a new Footing, for all those former Treaties have been broke because they were not upon a good Footing."[60] No lasting peace could be concluded if the rights of the Wabanaki were not respected. The English, nevertheless, insisted on the authenticity of their deeds, and the Wabanaki eventually ratified a treaty that officialized English encroachments over their ancestral lands. It would be wrong to think that this ratification marked the Wabanaki acceptance of the British claim over their title. The Wabanaki continued to make claims, which they backed up with the use of force. British presence was, nonetheless, even more firmly established than it was before, and this fait accompli would increasingly limit the territory that the Wabanaki could claim and control militarily.

That dispossession did eventually happen did not mean that the Wabanaki and other indigenous peoples passively witnessed the process or opposed it only by using violence. To recover the history of their legal resistance, it is essential to break with a teleological perspective that overlooks historical developments to focus on their eventual outcomes.[61] The history of Wabanaki claims brings to center stage native and European voices. It has shown that the aftermath of the Treaty of Utrecht was a colonial site where natives and Europeans expressed their claims to territory using comparable legal arguments (rights of discovery, cession, purchase, conquest). By looking at how the Wabanaki negotiated this dispute and forced the Europeans to take seriously their claims, this essay has shown that dispossession was not a legally silent process for indigenous peoples. It has also shown that for Europeans, dispossession was a process that had to be legally negotiated.

NOTES

1. John G. Reid, *Essays on Northeastern North America, Seventeenth and Eighteenth Centuries* (Toronto: University of Toronto Press, 2008), 156.
2. Records of the Province of New Hampshire, Portsmouth, August 5, 1699, National Archives, Kew (England), CO 5/787, fols. 503–504 (previously 250).
3. Emerson W. Baker and John G. Reid, "Amerindian power in the early modern Northeast: A reappraisal," *William and Mary Quarterly* 61: 1 (2004): 35 pars. Oct. 20, 2008 http://www.historycooperative.org/journals/wm/61.1/baker.html, pars. 13–14.
4. Reid, *Essays on Northeastern North America*, 144.
5. "Mémoire sur les limites de l'Acadie, envoyé à Monseigneur le Duc d'Orléans par le Père Charlevoix," Quebec, October 29, 1720, in Jean Blanchet, *Collection de manuscrits contenant lettres, mémoires, et autres documents historiques relatifs à la Nouvelle-France* (Quebec, 1884), vol. 3, 51. All translations are mine unless otherwise noted.
6. "Lettre des Abénaquis au roi de France" (a French translation is attached to the original, in Abenaki language), ca. 1715, Archives Nationales de France (hereafter, AN), Archives des Colonies (microforms), Série C¹¹A, vol. 1, fols. 266–267.

7. Ibid., fol. 267–267v.

8. Plaisance is Newfoundland and Port Royal, Nova Scotia. "Letter from Father Sebastien Rasles, Missionary of the Society of Jesus in New France, to Monsieur his Brother," Narantsouak, October, 12, 1723, in Reuben Gold Thwaites, ed., *The Jesuit Relations and Allied Documents*, vol. 67, (Cleveland: Burrow Brothers, 1896–1901), 207.

9. Governor General Philippe de Rigaud de Vaudreuil to the Conseil de Marine, October 31, 1718, AN, C¹¹ᴬ, vol. 39, fol. 159; Thomas Charland, "Rale, (Râle, Rasle, Rasles), Sébastien," *Dictionary of Canadian Biography Online* (University of Toronto/Université Laval, 2000).

10. Reid, *Essays on Northeastern North America*, 155–156.

11. Petition of the Sir Bibye Lake to the Queen to confirm a title to lands near Kenebec River, c. April 1714, CO 5/866, fol. 19 (i) (or 92).

12. Robert West to the Board, May 19, 1714, CO 5/866, fol. 22 (prev. 96).

13. Letter of Duchess of Hamilton in behalf of the Duke, her son, to the Board, May 1717, CO 5/866, fol. 119, previously 346.

14. Dummer's petition to the Board, 1717, CO 5/866, fol. 120 (prev. 342); petitions to the Board, 1717, CO 5/866, fol. 138 (prev. 397); and printed petition to the Board, "On the King's right to the land lying between the province of Maine and Nova Scotia against the Massachusetts Bay," 1718, CO 5/866, 145 (fols. 420–421). More petitions in fol. 143 (i), 144, 144 (i), 144 (ii), 144 (iii).

15. "George Town on Arrowsick Island Aug. 9th 1717, (. . .) A conference of His Excellency the Governour, with the Sachems and Chief Men of the Eastern Indians," CO 5/868, fol. 195–201.

16. Governor Vaudreuil and Intendant Michel Bégon to the Conseil de Marine, October 26, 1719, AN, C¹¹ᴬ, vol. 40, fol. 46; for an earlier example of a similar misunderstanding involving English settlers and Penacook-Pawtuckets, see Peter S. Leavenworth, "'The Best Title That Indians Can Claime': Native Agency and Consent in the Transferal of Penacook-Pawtucket Land in the Seventeenth Century," *The New England Quarterly*, vol. 72, no. 2 (June 1999), 281.

17. "George Town on Arrowsick Island Aug. 9th 1717, (. . .) A conference of His Excellency the Governour, with the Sachems and Chief Men of the Eastern Indians," CO 5/868, fol. 195–201.

18. See the essay by Lauren Benton in this volume.

19. *African Company, An Explanation of the African-Company's Property in the Sole Trade to Africa* (London, 1712), 9.

20. "George Town on Arrowsick Island Aug. 9th 1717, (. . .) A conference of His Excellency the Governour, with the Sachems and Chief Men of the Eastern Indians," CO 5/868, fol. 195–201.

21. Proceedings of the Georgetown conference: "At a conference with the chiefs and some others of the Kenebeck Indians at George Town November the 25th 1720," CO 5/869, fols. 100–104.

22. Governor Vaudreuil and Intendant Bégon to the Minister, Quebec, October 8, 1721, in Blanchet, *Collection de manuscrits*, 59. I have been unfortunately unable to find La Chasse's Latin copy despite the generous assistance of Professor Luca Codignola, Deputy Archivist Cindy Lépine (Archives des Jésuites du Canada) and Jesuit historian Father Jacques Monet.

23. "Letter from several tribes of Indians to the Governor of New England," July 28, 1721, CO 5/869, fols. 106–107 (original in French); and fols. 108–109 for the English translation. Other letters had already been sent to the English to ask them to move off Wabanaki lands: see Reverent John Baxter, *Journal of Several Visits to the Indians on the Kennebec River (1717)* (Boston: David Clapp & Sons, 1867), 16.

24. Report of Vaudreuil and Bégon, Quebec, October 17, 1722, in Blanchet, *Collection de manuscrits*, 85.

25. "Mémoire sur l'entreprise que les Anglois de Baston font sur les terres des Abénakis, sauvages alliés des François," in Blanchet, *Collection de manuscrits*, 69.

26. See the essay by Craig Yirush in this volume.

27. Vaudreuil to Shute, Quebec, June 7, 1722, in Blanchet, *Collection de manuscrits*, 82.

28. Samuel Shute to the House of Representatives, c. August 1721, CO 5/868, fol. 139.

29. "Parole de toute la Nation Abnaquise et de toutes les autres nations sauvages ses alliés au gouverneur de Baston au sujet de la Terre des Abnaquis dont les Anglois s'emparent depuis la Paix," n.d. (July 28, 1721), AN, F³, vol. 2, fols. 413–415.

30. "ma terre que Jais receu de Dieu seul, ma terre de laquelle aucun Roy ni aucun puissance estranger na peut ni ne peut disposer," "Letter from several tribes of Indians to the Governor of New England," July 28, 1721, CO 5/869, fol. 106.

31. Panaouamskeyen, "Indian explanation of the treaty of Casco Bay, 1727," cited in Colin G. Calloway, ed., *Dawnland Encounters: Indians and Europeans in Northern New England* (Hanover, NH: University Press of New England, 1991), 118. A similar concern is expressed in "Proceedings of the ratification of the Boston Treaty, 16 August 1726," CO 5/869, fol. 383–394.

32. Leavenworth, "The Best Title That Indians Can Claime," 278–279; see also Stuart Banner, *How the Indians Lost Their Land: Law and Power on the Frontier* (Cambridge, MA: Harvard University Press, 2005), 62–64.

33. Memorial of Thomas Bannister to the Board of Trade and Plantations, July 17, 1715, CO 5/866, fol. 53 (previously 183–184).

34. "aprands de nous que nous sommes sur cette terre que tu foule aux pieds et sur laquelle tu marche, avant mesme que ses arbres que tu voy, nous sont commancé à en sortir, Elle est a nous et Rien ne pourra jamais nous L'Oter ny nous La faire abandonner," "Discours des Sauvages au sujet des mouvements du gouverneur de la Cadie, et les Reponses que monsieur de St Ovide Leur a faite," 1720, AN, C¹¹ᴬ, vol. 122, fols. 84–85.

35. On the allodial right, see Denman Waldo Ross, *The Early History of Land-Holding among the Germans* (1883, Manchester, NH: Ayer Publishing, 1971), 174.

36. James Sheehan, "The problem of sovereignty in European history," *American Historical Review* 111, no. 1 (Feb. 2006), 3.

37. Governor Shute to the House of Representatives, c. August 1721, CO 5/868, fol. 139.

38. The House of Representatives to the Governor Shute, September 1, 1721, CO 5/868, fol. 140–141.

39. Governor Samuel Shute to the Board of Plantations, Boston, March 13, 1721 (1722), CO 5/868, fol. 188–189; Vaudreuil to Père Rales, Qubec Quebec, September 25, 1721, "A true copy from the original," March 6, 1721 (1722), CO 5/868, fol. 190; English copy of the letter of Intendant Bégon to Father Rale, June 14, 1721, CO 5/869, fols. 110–111.

40. Reid, *Essays on Northeastern North America*, 154–155.

41. After the loss of Acadia and Newfoundland, the French founded the colony of Isle Royale, which included Isle St-Jean (Prince Edward Island) and the Isle Royale, previously known as Cape Breton. Louisbourg was established as the capital of the colony, and it soon became one of New-France's most important economic and, especially, military centers thanks to its extensive fortifications.

42. "Mémoire sur les limites de l'Acadie (. . .) par le Père Charlevoix," 51; the king to Governor Vaudreuil and Intendant Bégon, Versailles, June, 8, 1721, in Blanchet, *Collection de manuscrits*, 54.

43. "Mémoire sur les limites de l'Acadie (. . .) par le Père Charlevoix," 58.

44. See, for example, "Mémoire sur les limites de l'Acadie (. . .) par le Père Charlevoix," 51–2; Vaudreuil and Bégon to the Minister, Quebec, October 8, 1721, in Blanchet, *Collection de manuscrits*, 57.

45. Charland, "Rale (Râle, Rasle, Rasles), Sébastien."

46. Governor Samuel Shute to the Board of Plantations, Boston, March 13, 1721 (1722), CO 5/868, fol. 188–189.

47. Governor Shute to Vaudreuil, March 14, 1722, CO 5/10, fols. 283–284.

48. Ibid.

49. "George Town on Arrowsick Island Aug. 9th 1717, (. . .) A conference of His Excellency the Governour, with the Sachems and Chief Men of the Eastern Indians," CO 5/868, fol. 195–201.

50. Shute to Vaudreuil, Boston, April 23, 1723, CO 5/10, fols. 285–287.

51. Governor Vaudreuil to Governor William Dummer, Quebec, October 28, 1723, CO 5/869, fol. 116.

52. Governor Dummer to the king, Boston, June 25, 1725, CO 5/869, fol. 86–90.

53. Intendant Bégon to the minister, Quebec, April 21, 1725, in Blanchet, *Collection de manuscrits*, 121; Report of Commissioners Samuel Dexter and William Dudley to Governor Dummer, Boston, May 26, 1725, CO 5/869, fol. 196–197.

54. Colin G. Calloway, *The Western Abenakis of Vermont, 1600–1800: War, Migration, and the Survival of an Indian People* (1990, Norman: University of Oklahoma Press, 1993 ppbk.), 113.

55. The king to Governor Vaudreuil and Chazel, Versailles, May 15, 1725, in Blanchet, *Collection de manuscrits*, 123; see also minister to Father La Chasse, Versailles, May 13, 1726, Ibid., 127.

56. On the presentation of English deeds to the Wabanaki, see James Phinney Baxter, ed., *Documentary History of the State of Maine*, vol. XXIII containing the Baxter Manuscripts, *Collections of the Maine Historical Society*, second series (Portland: Fred. L. Tower Company, 1916), 204–207.

57. The Jesuit Father Etienne Lauverjeat and the French officer and Wabanaki chief Baron de Saint-Castin, who attended the peace negotiations, witnessed Wabanaki delegates rejecting articles mentioning their submission to the British Crown when the treaty was being translated to them during the Boston conference (see "Traité de paix entre les Anglois et les Abénakis," Caske Bay, August 1727, in Blanchet, *Collection de manuscrits*, 134–135).

58. Loron Sagouarrab [Laurent Sagouarrat] to Governor Dummer, January 28, 1726, Baxter, *Documentary History*, vol. 23, 208–209.

59. Ibid.

60. Baxter, *Documentary History*, vol. 23, 197.

61. A similar approach can be found in Leavenworth, "The Best Title That Indians Can Claime," 298.

6

"CHIEF PRINCES AND OWNERS OF ALL"
NATIVE AMERICAN APPEALS TO THE CROWN
IN THE EARLY-MODERN BRITISH ATLANTIC

Craig Yirush

In the last twenty years, the history of legal and political ideas has experienced a renaissance as scholars in these fields have discovered important connections between many
of the seminal theorists of the early-modern period and empire.[1] While this new scholarship on the intellectual justifications of European expansion has brought the question of the rights of the indigenous peoples of the Americas to the center of our
understanding of seventeenth- and eighteenth-century political thought, it has, for the
most part, ignored the *ideas* of the indigenous peoples themselves. Yet in these encounters, the native Americans were not merely passive objects of European discourses.
Rather, they responded to European claims with their own conceptions of law, property, and political authority.

This essay uncovers these indigenous norms by looking at a little-studied legal genre:
the appeals made by the native Americans to the British Crown in the seventeenth and
eighteenth centuries.[2] These appeals show that they were aware of (and able to exploit)
the complicated politics of the British Atlantic world for their own ends, turning the
Crown against the settlers in ways they hoped would preserve their rights, and in the
process becoming trans-Atlantic political actors.[3] Focusing on three such appeals—the
Narragansetts' in the mid–seventeenth century; the Mohegans', which spanned the first
three quarters of the eighteenth; and the Mashpee's on the eve of the American Revolution—this essay explores the way that these native peoples in eastern North America
were able to resist the depredations of the settlers by appealing to royal authority, in the
process articulating a powerful conception of their legal status in a world transformed
by the arrival of the English.[4] In doing so, it brings an indigenous voice to the debates
about the legalities of empire in the early-modern Atlantic world.[5]

The Narragansetts' and the Mohegans' appeals were products of the complicated aftermath of the Pequot War in the late 1630s. Both peoples had allied with the English

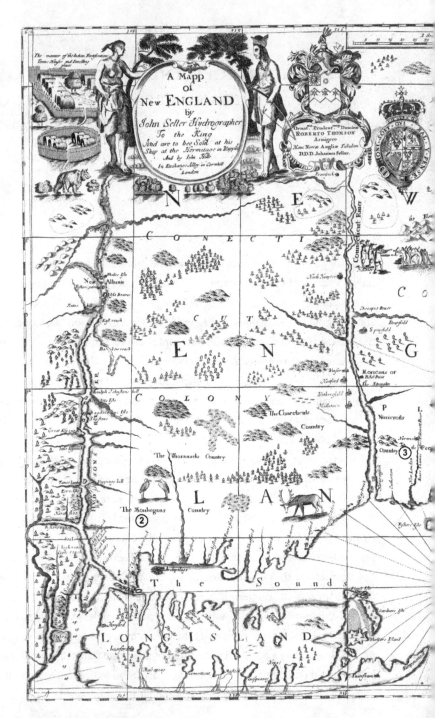

John Seller's 1676 map of New England shows the disputed territory in both the Narragansett is on Narragansett Bay, northeast. The territory that the Mohegans controlled after the Pequot the time their case was heard by the first royal commission in the early 1700s was mainly be-places their territory. The territory the Mashpee occupied during their appeal to the Crown lay

Courtesy of the John Carter Brown Library at Brown University

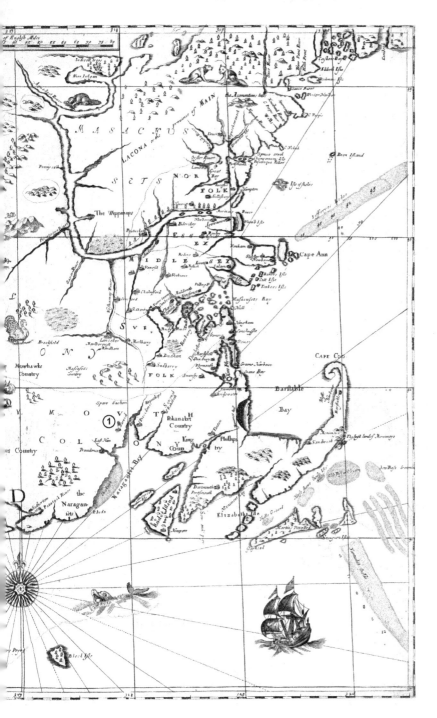

and Mohegan appeals. The town of Warwick (1), which Miantonomo sold to Samuel Gorton, War (2) is on the far west side of the map. But the territory the Mohegans actually inhabited be tween New London and Norwich on the Thames River (3)—that is, to the east of where this map just to the east of Dartmouth and Portsmouth on Cape Cod.

against the Pequots, as they coveted their territories, and the Mohegans in particular desired to get out from under the Pequots' control (they were a tributary of the Pequots).[6] The subsequent defeat of the Pequots created a power vacuum, one that Connecticut, Massachusetts, the Narragansetts, and the Mohegans all sought to fill by controlling the defeated tribe's territory.

The nascent and aggressively expansionist colony of Connecticut beat Massachusetts to the punch by allying (through the offices of Captain John Mason) with Uncas, the leader of the Mohegans, who controlled the former territories of the Pequots. The alliance with Uncas allowed Connecticut (which still lacked a charter) a claim to valuable land to its west. As well, Connecticut, worried that if the Narragansetts got access to the Pequot territory, then their allies, Massachusetts, would benefit, compelled both the Narragansetts and the Mohegans to submit to them in the Treaty of Hartford (1638), even though the Narragansetts had already allied themselves to Massachusetts in 1636.[7]

Miantonomo, the sachem of the Narragansetts, was less than happy about the *status quo post bellum*. He thought that the indiscriminate killing of Pequot women and children at Mystic during the war was unjustified. And he resented the demand (made by both Massachusetts and Connecticut) that the Narrangansetts pay them tribute for each Pequot captive.[8] Miantonomo was also displeased that his rival, Uncas, now allied with Connecticut, controlled land he coveted.[9] To add insult to injury, he was angry about being compelled by Connecticut to sign the treaty at Hartford in 1638, the terms of which violated the agreement that Miantonomo had already made with Massachusetts.[10]

Miantonomo was not alone in his dissatisfaction with the balance of power in New England after the defeat of the Pequots. Massachusetts was jealous of Connecticut's territorial gains in the former Pequot territories. As well, Massachusetts had designs on the land around the Narrangansett Bay. As such, they were particularly angry that Miantonomo, their erstwhile ally, had sold some of this land to a radical sect called the Gortonists, whose leader, Samuel Gorton had, like Roger Williams, been banished from the Bay Colony.[11] Because the sale gave these religious radicals safe haven from the jurisdiction of Massachusetts, the Bay Colony's magistrates made two of Miantonomo's sub-sachems (Pumham and Sacononoco) subject to them and were thus able to claim that Miantonomo's sale to the Gortonists was illegitimate.[12]

The Gortonists resisted Massachusetts' land grab, insisting on the legitimacy of their deed from Miantonomo. For their pains, they were attacked by Massachusettts in the fall of 1643; some of them were killed, and the rest were captured and put on trial. Miantonomo, however, was less concerned by the attack on the Gortonists than he was with the threat from his foe Uncas, who had attacked a kinsman and tributary of his. So he sought permission (by the terms of the 1636 treaty, he had ceded war-making power) from Massachusetts to retaliate, which he received. However, Uncas got the upper hand and took Miantonomo captive, after which the newly formed United Colonies, eager to get rid of a powerful sachem, connived with Uncas to kill Miantonomo.[13]

The murder of their sachem, along with Massachusetts' assertion of its authority over them, led the Narragansetts to join the Gortonists in appealing to the Crown. In the spring of 1644, Samuel Gorton took the Narragansetts' petition to England to be presented to Charles I. For their part, the Gortonists benefited from having the Narragansetts join them, as they could use Massachusetts' abuse of the natives to bolster their own case against the Bay Colony.[14]

The Narragansetts' appeal was a direct challenge to settler authority, and in particular to that of Massachusetts, which insisted that its decisions were not subject to royal oversight. Its authors, Pessicus and Conanicus, informed the king that they were the "chiefe Sachems, Princes or Governors of the Nanhigansets (in that part of America, now called New England)," adding that their petition resulted from "the joynt and unanimous consent of all our people and subjects," who, the sachems held, did "freely, voluntarily, and most humbly (. . .) submit, subject, and give over ourselves, peoples, lands, rights, inheritances, and possessions whatsoever, in ourselves and our heires successively for ever, unto the protection, care and government of that worthy and royal Prince, Charles, King of Great Britaine and Ireland, his heires and successors forever."[15]

In doing so, the sachems insisted that they were to be "governed according to the ancient and honorable lawes and customes, established in that so renowned realme and kingdome of Old England." And they acknowledged themselves "to be the humble, loving and obedient servants and subjects of his Majestie; to be ruled, ordered, and disposed of, in ourselves and ours, according to his princely wisdome, counsel and lawes of that honourable State of Old England (. . .)"[16] But despite this seeming submission, the Narragansett sachems went on to say that they were not "necessitated hereunto"—that is, they maintained that they did not have to submit to the Crown on account of their relationships with any of the "natives in these parts, knowing ourselves sufficient defence." Rather, they were seeking the king's protection because they had "just cause and jealousy of some of His Majesties pretended subjects" (i.e., Massachusetts). And as a result, they desired to "have our matters and causes heard and tried according to his just and equal lawes."[17] Moreover, their appeal to the Crown was intended to put them on an equal footing with Massachusetts, as both peoples would now be subjects of the same king. Or as the sachems put it, "*Nor can we yield over ourselves unto any, that are subjects themselves in any case . . .*" Indeed, the Narragansetts showed they were aware of the fraught politics of empire by informing the king that some of the settlers in New England were but "pretended subjects."[18]

The sachems also insisted that this submission was only *"upon condition of his Majesties' royal protection*, and wrighting (sic) us of what wrong is, or may be done unto us, according to his honourable lawes and customes, exercised among his subjects, in their preservation and safety . . ." In other words, theirs was not an unconditional surrender of authority to the Crown. Rather, the Narragansetts were seeking protection from the king and in return were offering their allegiance. Moreover, this submission to the Crown was not meant as a submission to English authority *tout court*. On the contrary, it was designed to restore what they saw as a relationship of equals with the king's subjects in the New World, a relationship that the settlers had subverted by assuming an unwarranted authority over them, denying them the right to wage war, for example, and demanding tribute, as well as encroaching on their territory. And finally, the Narragansett sachems' appeal to the Crown was predicated on the full sovereignty and rights of property they had exercised precontact. As they reminded the king in their appeal, they had "been the chief Sachems or Princes successively of the country, time out of mind."[19]

Having forged an alliance with the Crown, the Narragansett sachems sent a letter to the General Court of Massachusetts informing that body that they would not be appearing before it, nor submitting to its jurisdiction, for, they argued, "we have subjected ourselves, our lands and possessions, with all the rights and inheritances of us and our people, either by conquest, voluntary subjection or otherwise" to the "government of that Royal King, Charles, and that State of Old England, to be ordered and governed according to the laws and customs thereof." That is, they were "subjects now . . . unto the same King and State" as Massachusetts, a condition they had entered into by "joint and voluntary consent." As a result, they were not legally subordinate to Massachusetts in any way. And, they informed the colony, if there is to be any dispute between the two peoples, both will now have "recourse" to the king and "repair unto that honourable and just Government."[20] By subjecting themselves conditionally to the English king, the Narragansetts intended to protect their land rights and political autonomy from the aggressive extension of the Bay Colony's jurisdiction.

Appealing to the king in 1644–1645 was not the best way to guarantee even a modicum of justice, for as England spiraled into Civil War, Parliament, which was sympathetic to the Puritan colonies, gained the upper hand.[21] Indeed, in 1645, Massachusetts, aware that the balance of power in England was shifting in their favor, was able to extract concessions from the Narragansetts under duress, gaining revenge for the fact that the previous year the tribe had rebuffed their envoys who had come to complain about the appeal, leaving them standing out in the rain for hours. To add insult to injury, the Narragansetts also had to mortgage their territories to a group of colonial land speculators in order to pay a fine to Massachusetts. Unable to do so, they lost some of this territory in 1662.[22]

Following the Restoration, however, the Stuart King, Charles II, intended to reassert royal authority in the face of Puritan intransigence (especially by Massachusetts). The subsequent arrival of a royal commission in 1664 to investigate the recalcitrance of the Puritan colonies gave the Narragansetts another chance to appeal to the Crown.[23] In doing so, they were again aided by Samuel Gorton, who had kept a copy of their original submission to the Crown in 1644. Gorton also published a letter recounting the travails that he and his followers (as well as the Narragansetts) had suffered at the hands of Massachusetts, the agents of which he claimed had acted like "subjects unto themselves."[24] For its part, the Crown, always eager to hear evidence of Puritan malfeasance, instructed the commissioners "to examine any injuries done to" the Narragansetts "by our subjects" and to "doe them justice." The Crown also promised the tribe that "wee will always protect them from any oppression."[25] After meeting with the Narragansetts, the commissioners voided the deeds of those settlers who had taken the tribe's land.[26] The commissioners then visited the Narragansetts, who submitted themselves to the Crown, and the two sides exchanged gifts.[27] So the Narragansetts had once again used their status as equal subjects, and their embrace of English law and jurisdiction, to protect their lands and their autonomy from Massachusetts. According to Francis Jennings, the decision of the royal commission bought the Narragansetts "a decade of reprieve from Puritan conquest."[28] However, when Metacom's war came in the mid-1670s the Narragansett ultimately took the side of the Wampanoags against the English. As a result, they suffered the fate common to many once independent native tribes, subjected to colonial law and placed on reservations.[29]

By contrast, their old enemies the Mohegans fought on the side of the settlers against Metacom (King Philip). However, this did not protect them from Connecticut, which had had designs on their land ever since the end of the Pequot war. Foreseeing this, John Mason, a settler in Connecticut who had forged an alliance with Uncas during the Pequot War, entailed a tract of land (approximately 20,000 acres, the bulk of it near New London) to the tribe in 1671. By doing so, Mason hoped to provide the tribe with a secure land base that could not be sold without their consent. As well, in 1681 Uncas signed a treaty with Connecticut, the terms of which guaranteed that the tribe would be reserved sufficient land to hunt and plant on.[30] But despite these attempts to codify their rights in law, by the early 1700s the Mohegans' vast holdings were reduced to the land that had been entailed to them by John Mason in 1671. And when even this land came under threat, the tribe, with the help of disaffected colonists (including the heirs of John Mason), appealed to the Crown. So began what one eighteenth-century lawyer called "the greatest cause that was ever heard" before the Privy Council.[31]

Pursuant to the appeal, Oweneco published a "Letter to a Gentleman Now in London," which was conveyed to the queen by Nicholas Hallam, a settler from Connecticut with his own grievances against the colony.[32] In it, Oweneco made his case to "the Great Queen Ann, and to her Noble Council" about the "Oppression" that he and his "People" had suffered at the hands of the General Court. In addition, Oweneco warned the queen that should he fail to obtain relief, his "People" might "scatter from Me, and flee to the Eastern Indians," who, he noted, were "the French's Friends, and the English's enemies." In addition to pointing out the strategic significance of the Crown's alliance with the Mohegans, Oweneco argued that his people had a "Hereditary Right to the Soyl and Royalties of our Dominions and Territories, before the English came into our Country." Oweneco also claimed that his authority as sachem was "not confer'd . . . by the English, but by the gods." His letter further bolstered the authority of the sachemship by relaying a story of a pipe that the gods had given his ancestors as "a Token" of "Our happy Reign." He then spoke of gifts—a Bible and a sword—sent by Charles II, which the tribe had kept in the same place as a sacred pipe given them by their "gods."[33] In establishing the divine-origin authority of his family's rule, Oweneco sought to place himself on an equal footing with the English Crown, a status that the exchange of diplomatic gifts with Charles II reinforced.[34] Oweneco's claim of equality with the English monarch was in marked contrast to the case Hallam made before the Board of Trade on the tribe's behalf, where he claimed that the Mohegans had always "acknowledged the Kings and Queens of England as their Sovereigns and have been ever ready to pay all due obedience and to yield subjection to them."[35]

Having established a claim to authority, property, and jurisdiction independent of Connecticut, or indeed of any English authority, Oweneco's letter asked that the tribe's "Hereditary Right to the Soyl and Royalties of our Dominions and Territories, before the English came into our Country" be made known "to the Great Queen Ann, and her Noble Council." The letter went on to say that "Owaneko, and his Ancestors, were formerly Chief Princes, and Owners of All, or great Part of the Country now called Connecticut-Colony in New-England." Furthermore, it claimed that "when the English first came, these Indians received them very kindly, and for a very small and inconsiderable Value, parted with all or most of their Lands to the English, reserving to themselves only a small Quantity of Land to Plant upon, and Hunt in." In addition, Oweneco noted that the Mohegans had also "assisted" the colony "in their wars against the other Indians; and have, until of late, quietly enjoyed their reserved Lands." However, Uncas complained, "about a Year or two ago" the colony annexed "these lands to the Townships of Colchester and New London." As a result, "these poor Indians have been unjustly turn'd out of Possession, and are thereby destitute of all means of Subsistence."[36]

Oweneco's letter met with a favorable response in London. The Board of Trade referred the question to the Crown's legal advisors. On February 29th, 1704, the Attorney General gave his opinion on the merits of the Mohegans' appeal:

> It doth not appear to me that the lands now claimed by the Indians were intended to pass or could pass to the Corporation of the English Colony of Connecticut or that it was intended to dispossess the Indians who before and after the Grant were the owners and possessors of the same, and therefore what ye Corporation hath done by ye Act mentioned is an apparent injury to them, and H.M., notwithstanding the power granted to that Corporation, there not being any words in the Grant to exclude H.M., may lawfully erect a Court within that Colony to doe justice in this matter, and in ye erecting such Court may reserve an Appeal to H.M. in Council, and may command ye Governors of that Corporation not to oppress those Indians or deprive them of their right, but to doe them right notwithstanding the Act made by them to dispossess them, which I am of opinion was illegall and void.[37]

[handwritten margin note: Anglie, Lockean kind of idea that the colonizers had a right to dispossess the Natives of their land]

According to the Attorney General, then, the Mohegans were the original owners of the land in question. Furthermore, the royal charter had not dispossessed them, nor did it stop them from appealing to the Crown for redress. Following this opinion, the Queen authorized a royal commission to hear the dispute, informing the colony that "complaints have been made to us in behalf of the Mohegan Indians, that you have by an Act or Order of your General Court or Assembly taken from the said Indians that small tract of land which they have reserved to themselves." In addition to its concern that the colony's law was "unjust," the Crown also warned the colony that, in the middle of a war with the French, its treatment of the Mohegans "may be of fatall consequence by causing a defection of the Indians to our enemies." As such, the Crown instructed the colony "to pay all due obedience" to its commission, and, if "upon enquiry it be found that the said Indians have been deprived of their lands," to "immediately cause them to be put into possession thereof . . ."[38]

The language the Crown used in establishing the commission indicates that it viewed the Mohegans as allies, who, in addition to being the "chief proprietors of all the land in those parts," had "entertained and cultivated a firm friendship by league, with our said subjects of Connecticut, and have, at times, assisted them when they have been attacked by their enemies."[39] However, if the Mohegans were a separate people governed by their own rulers and capable of entering into treaties with the Crown's subjects, they were also, in the words of the Board of Trade, "under your Majesty's Dominion," a status that gave them a right to appeal to the Crown for redress.[40]

The Crown chose Joseph Dudley, the Governor of Massachusetts, to head the royal commission. For years, Dudley had been hostile to what he saw as the excessive autonomy afforded Connecticut by its charter, which had survived the Dominion of New England, and which still featured an elected governor.[41] Indeed, due to the lobbying of both Dudley and Lord Cornbury, the royal Governor of New York, Connecticut's dispossession of the Mohegans was one of the charges in the 1706 Parliamentary Bill designed to annul the charters of all of the private colonies.[42]

Given the threat to its charter rights, Connecticut refused to appear before the Dudley commission, claiming that the Crown had no legal right "to enquire and judicially determine concerning the matter in controversy."[43] Such royal oversight, its lawyers argued, was "contrary to law and to the letters patent under the great seal." In addition, the colony maintained that the establishment of a juryless royal commission with authority over the private property would violate "the known rights of her majesty's subjects throughout all her dominions . . ."[44]

But Connecticut's resistance was to no avail. On August 24, 1705, the Dudley commission unanimously decided in favor of the Mohegans and the Masons. The commissioners held "That the said Moheagans are a considerable tribe or people . . . and cannot subsist without their lands, of which they have been deprived *and dispossessed. . . ."* Furthermore, they "have at all times served the interests of the crown of England and the colony of Connecticut" and "have *faithfully kept their leagues and treaties* with the said colony."[45] However, the colony, "contrary" to these "reservations, treaties, and settlements," had "*granted away considerable tracts of the planting grounds of the said Moheagans.*"[46] As a result of the colony's encroachments on their lands, the tribe has "been reduced *to great want and necessity,* and, in this time of war, are in great danger of deserting their ancient friendship."[47] Accordingly, the commissioners ruled that the Mohegans "had a very good and undoubted right to a very large tract of land within the colony of Connecticut,"[48] and it ordered the colony to return to them the tract that Mason had entailed in 1671 between New London and Norwich, as well as several smaller tracts of land.[49]

Upon hearing the verdict, Oweneco pledged that he and his sons would be "ever under the allegiance and government of the queen and crown of England . . ." Captain Ben Uncas, his brother, also thanked the court, claiming that its favorable decision prevented him from "staining his hands with the blood of the English, notwithstanding the many and frequent provocations from them . . ." In reply, the commissioners thanked "the said Indians for their zeal and affection to her majesty, the crown, and the government of England, and the interests of the English nation," assuring them that "her majesty would always be ready to take care of them and their people, both in protecting them and preserving of their rights and properties."[50]

The colony then instructed its agent, Henry Ashurst, to appeal the commission's verdict. In doing so, Ashurst laid out a case for the settlers' rights that contrasted sharply with the Mohegans' vision of their place in the empire. According to Ashurst, Connecticut had conquered the land in question from the Pequots; they had then allowed the Mohegans (who were merely tributaries of the Pequots) to possess some of the land (but only enough to make a hunt). Ashurst insisted, however, that this did not mean that Uncas had "any right" to the land, but "only the *permission* of your petitioners, *the conquerors*, to *suffer* him to possess the same."[51] In addition to conquest, Ashurst held that the settlers now had a right to the land in question by labor and improvement as well as by prescription or long usage.

Ashurst's appeal was enough to get the Privy Council to call for the establishment of a commission of review. However, despite its willingness to reconsider Dudley's verdict, the Privy Council upheld the legality of the Crown's jurisdiction over the colony, arguing that because "the Mohegan Indians are a Nation with whom frequent Treatys have been made, the Proper way of Determining the aforesaid Differences, is by her Matys Royall Commission."[52] In his year-end letter to the Board of Trade, Governor Dudley seconded the Privy Council's conclusion: "if H.M. cannot grant commissions to hear so apparent a breach between that Government and a Tribe of independent [Indians]. . . . that Corporation must be beyond all challenge."[53]

The Mohegans' victory before the Dudley commission did not stop the settlers in Connecticut from continuing to encroach on their land. Faced with the colony's ongoing intransigence, the Mohegans resumed their appeals to the Crown. In the spring of 1736, one of Uncas' descendants (Mahomet), along with one of Mason's descendants (also called John), traveled to the seat of empire and was able to obtain a new royal commission to hear the case.[54] In his petition to the king, Mahomet stressed the tribe's assistance to the settlers, noting that they had fought with them against the Pequots, after which Uncas had entered into a "firm League of Alliance and friendship with the English." But faced with ongoing dispossession, as well as the colony's disregard of the terms of the 1681 treaty, the tribe had appealed to Queen Anne for justice. The colony, however, had ignored the Dudley commission, and the tribe was now reduced to a land base so small "that they are not able to Subsist on it." As a consequence, Mahomet was now turning to the king so that "he & his People may be restored to & protected in that part of their Ancestors' Lands which they had reserved to themselves & their Tribe, for their Hunting & Planting." And he was doing so because the Mohegans had been "for the Space of 100 years faithfull friends & Allies to your Colony of Connecticut," and "true to your Matie, & your Royal Predecessors, against all Enemies."[55]

In response to the pleas of the tribe, the Crown authorized a royal commission in 1738. However, the commissioners were drawn from Rhode Island and, as representatives of a colony that was also protective of its charter rights, were sympathetic to Connecticut. In particular, they refused to let the majority of the tribe testify, recognizing instead a rival claimant to the sachemship (Ben Uncas), who was willing to cede the land in question to Connecticut, despite the fact that a majority of the Mohegans insisted that he was not their legitimate sachem.[56]

As a result, the Mohegans appealed again to the Crown in 1739, arguing that they had a right as a people to determine, *via* their own laws, the election of their leaders, a right that the 1738 commission had refused to recognize. As they put it, "We made our Appearance in a Body, and we were denied to be heard." Instead, Connecticut set up an "Impostor as Sachem," who was "made by said Government" to "evade Justice" and "to Deprive is of our Lands . . ." As a result of this injustice, the tribe claimed that they were now "Exposed to the Utmost Limits of Poverty and Want . . ."; and they pleaded with the Crown to "receive us under your Protection" and "Restore us to our Lands and Libertys."[57]

After entertaining these pleas, the Privy Council determined that the case should be heard again on the grounds that the proceedings of the 1738 commission had been "very irregular."[58] In January, 1743, George II set aside its verdict and issued a new commission, this time composed of the Governors and councillors of New York and New Jersey.[59] It was to be the fullest airing of the legal arguments for and against indigenous rights in the eighteenth-century Anglo-American world.

The Mohegans were represented before the 1743 commission by William Bollan, who had been involved on their side in the ill-fated 1738 commission. Although Bollan has been portrayed as working mainly for the Masons, the case he made before the royal commission adopted many of the legal arguments that the tribe had advanced in previous iterations of the dispute—in particular, their inherent rights to the soil, their autonomy as the original inhabitants of the land, and their long-standing alliance with the English.[60]

Bollan began his case by claiming that the Mohegans "were the original only owners of a large tract of land in these parts," and called for the Dudley commission's verdict to be "affirmed by this honourable court." According to Bollan, when the English arrived, the Mohegans, believing them to be "a just and honest people, received and entertained them as friends, and entered into a strict alliance with them." This was an alliance, Bollan insisted, that the Indians had, despite "the severest trials," "at all times observed and kept." Furthermore, "in order to promote the settlement of the English," the Mohegans had "from time to time spared them divers parcels of their lands," save for "the lands in controversy (a small portion compared to what they owned when the English first settled here)." However, having "admitted the English to settle in their country," the Mohegans found some of them to be "full of craft and guile" and so had made an alliance with John Mason and his family "to prevent their being cheated by any fraudulent or unfair purchase." By doing so, they hoped to preserve "a sufficient portion of lands for them to plant and hunt in, which were absolutely necessary for them, in order to their continuance as a people."[61]

The Mohegans' claim to these lands was strengthened, Bollan argued, by the 1681 treaty, which he called a "league of perpetual peace and friendship." According to its terms, "the Moheagans propriety in lands, and their having countries and territories" was "directly acknowledged by the said colony."[62] As such, it would be a great "injustice" if the colony were to now "depart from their treaties with their old and constant friends and allies."[63] In construing the terms of the treaty, Bollan urged the commissioners to understand it from the Mohegans' perspective. According to Bollan, "the Mohegans beg leave to observe, that they are a people unskilled in letters." What's more, "their adversaries have had the penning this treaty, and all the records of their other transactions with the said Indians." Since Connecticut "doubtless took care to express matters favourably to their own interest," Bollan urged the commissioners to put "the most favourable construction for the said Indians . . . upon these writings."[64]

For Bollan, the political autonomy that enabled the Mohegans to sign binding treaties was necessary in order for them to protect their "antient territories."[65] As Bollan reminded the commissioners, the Mohegans were "a free and independent people" who were governed by an "ancient established constitution."[66] Responding to Connecticut's claim that they were better off under its jurisdiction, Bollan insisted that the Mohegans' "policy, customs, and manners differ widely from those of the English (which they neither despise nor can approve) so they, by no means, like to be so mingled with them, which the Indians find, by experience, has a direct tendency to drive them away from their ancient possessions."[67]

Indeed, Bollan contended that when the two peoples first met in the 1630s, it was the settlers and not the Mohegans who lacked a polity. Given that the settlers were effectively stateless until the grant of the charter to Connecticut in 1662, Bollan argued that there could have been no valid land transfers between them and the Mohegans prior to that time. As he told the commissioners, "it is impossible any lands should pass to them by force of any conveyance whatsoever, until they were enabled . . . by the incorporation of their prince."[68]

In making this argument, Bollan once again adopted an indigenous perspective. As he explained to the commissioners: the "Indians say that surely that prince, when he granted a charter to some of his own subjects, never intended thereby to pass to them the lands of his friends and allies." After all, "If the English colonies be permitted" to "depart from their treaties with their old and constant friends and allies, the Moheagans cannot but say, that the English interest must finally suffer among the Indian nations . . ." For Bollan, then, the only effect of the royal charter was "to make such of their lands become part of the English colony as should from time to time be fairly purchased of them."[69]

Despite Bollan's advocacy, the commissioners ruled in favor of Connecticut on the narrow question of whether the colony had set aside a sufficient amount of land for the

Mohegans. But the commissioners held that the Mohegans had every right to appeal to the Privy Council, thus endorsing the tribe's long-standing contention that they were not subordinate to Connecticut but were, rather, a coequal part of the empire with them. And in supporting their right to appeal, one of the commissioners, Daniel Horsmanden, even held that "the Mohgeans," "though living among the king's subjects in these countries, are a separate and distinct people from them." After all, Horsmanden noted, "they have a polity of their own" and "they make peace and war with any nation of Indians when they think fit, *without controul* from the English." Furthermore, according to Horsmanden, the "Crown" in both "Queen Anne's and his present majesty's commission by which we now sit" "looks upon them not as subjects, *but as a distinct people*" who have "the property of the soil of these countries."[70] So despite ultimately losing the case, the Mohegans had, beginning in 1704, succeeded in convincing a number of royal officials (in London and the colonies) of their view of indigenous rights. And in the following decade, influenced in part by the complaints of native groups like the Mohegans, the Crown would embark on a policy of centralizing land distribution in the New World, providing a modicum of protection for the indigenous peoples of North America at the cost of alienating an increasingly expansionist settler population.[71]

The Mohegans continued their struggle in the decades following the 1743 commission ruling, obtaining another hearing before the Privy Council in 1773 as the empire was on the brink of revolution. Although the Mohegans lost their final appeal to the Crown,[72] the Mashpee fared better in the fateful decades before the revolution, successfully appealing to the Crown over repeated attempts by Massachusetts to curtail their political autonomy and interfere with their ability to control the resources on their land. However, their victory proved short lived as in the decades after the revolution, Massachusetts, now a state in a republican union with no Crown oversight, once again undermined their autonomy. The long-simmering discontent of the Mashpee led to a revolt in 1833, and the restoration of a measure of self-government.[73]

The Mashpee were Christian Wampanoags who inhabited resource-rich territory on Cape Cod.[74] Unlike the Narragansetts and the Mohegans, they stayed neutral during Metacom's (or King Philip's) War and were able to remain largely self-governing into the eighteenth century, despite the presence of a minister on their territory and the encroachment of settlers from nearby Barnstable. In response to threats to their lands, they repeatedly petitioned the legislature, reminding the government of Massachusetts that they "chose officers among ourselves and appointed men to oversee our lands and marsh and take care that everyone had his share and no more."[75] But in 1746, this period of self-government ended when Massachusetts enacted a law that placed white guardians in charge of all legal and financial matters, including control over resource allocation and land sales. Although intended to protect natives from unscrupulous settlers, the guardianship law ultimately reduced their collective ability to control the resources—fish, timber, pasturage—necessary to provide subsistence. Unable to get the colony's General Court to remove the guardians, the Mashpee appealed to the Crown, sending Rueben Cogenhew, the schoolteacher at Mashpee, to London in the spring of 1760.

Cogenhew had a harrowing journey across the Atlantic, surviving an attempt to sell him into slavery, a subsequent shipwreck, and impressment. Upon finally arriving in England, however, he was able to present his petition to royal officials. In it, Cogenhew contended that:

> the English Inhabitants of the said province of Massachusetts Bay have of late years unjustly encroached upon the said Lands and have hindered and obstructed the Indians in the Exercise of that just Right they have to fish in the River Mashbee within the said Limits, and though several attempts have been made by the said Indians to obtain redress for these Injuries by a proper application to the General Court of the Massachusetts Bay; Yet such attempts have been constantly frustrated by the Art of Deceit of such Agents[76] as they have been obliged to employ in this affair . . .

Given "this unhappy Situation," Cogenhew maintained that the Mashpee "found themselves under the necessity of laying their Case at the Footsteps of Your Majesty's Sacred Throne, where alone they could hope from Your Majesty's known Justice and Equity, to find that Redress which Your Majesty is at all times so ready to give to the Just Complaints of all that live under Your Royal Patronage and Protection . . ."[77]

As Cogenhew was crossing the Atlantic in the spring of 1760, the colony's House of Representatives, led by its speaker James Otis, defended the guardianship system to the royal governor, Francis Bernard. The House conceded that the guardians did control the Mashpee's land and natural resources, but it argued that this was because the tribe was "at all times of an indolent slothful disposition, and averse to any kind of labour for their support." As such, "from mere compassion towards them and to prevent them from falling into the lowest indigence the General Court many years since by an Act of Government restrained them from making sale of their lands to any English subjects, and upon the same principles by subsequent Acts restrained them from leasing out their lands without the consent of guardians appointed by the Court and made accountable to it." The House also informed the Governor that the only basis for the Mashpee's complaint was "the desire that some of them have of being restored to as full liberty of disposing of their real Estates as His Majesty's English Subjects." But this was a liberty that, the House insisted, "the most sensible part of the

Indians themselves are averse to [,] knowing it must be an occasion of their speedy ruin and destruction."[78]

Despite the protestations of the Massachusetts legislature, the Mashpee's appeal to London was successful. The Board of Trade, desirous of centralizing the empire in the wake of the Seven Years' War, ordered the colony to redress the tribe's grievances.[79] In 1763, the Massachusetts assembly passed an act allowing the Mashpee (at annual meetings) to elect their own overseers, who were then empowered to decide on the allocation of the community's resources.[80] But despite that fact that the Mashpee fought with the colony during the Revolutionary War, this autonomy was not to last long. In 1788, the new state's legislature passed a law overturning the 1763 act and reinstating the system of unelected guardians. This in turn led to decades of conflict as the majority of the tribe, dissatisfied with the conduct of the guardians, repeatedly petitioned the legislature for relief.[81]

The spark that led to revolt came in the spring of 1833 when William Apess, a Pequot preacher, came to live among the Mashpee. The tribe soon adopted him as one of their own, and he in turn encouraged them to once again present their grievances to the General Court.[82] On May 21, 1833, a large majority of the tribe met in an assembly and passed a series of resolutions, the first of which proclaimed that "we as a tribe, will rule ourselves, and have a right to do so; for all men are born free and equal, says the Constitution of the country." The second resolution stated that the tribe would not allow any "white man to come upon our plantation" and "carry off" "wood or hay" or any other "article, without our permission." And the third and final resolution informed authorities in Massachusetts that after July 1 any person found to be in violation of these terms will be forcibly evicted from "the plantation."[83]

The Mashpee then elected a tribal council and discharged their guardians. And on July 1, Apess and a small group of armed Mashpee stopped two settlers from carrying a load of wood off tribal land. Concerned that the Mashpee were in effect nullifying Massachusetts law, local authorities arrested Apess. The revolt and subsequent arrest stirred public debate and put pressure on the legislature to deal with the Mashpee's grievances. William Lloyd Garrison, the abolitionist, was a strong supporter of the tribe, remarking sarcastically in his newspaper The Liberator that Massachusetts, "believing they were incapable of self-government as free citizens," had "placed" the Mashpee "under a servile . . . dependence."[84] The Mashpee cause was also taken up by the Jacksonian Democrat and newspaper editor Benjamin Hallett, who made arguments on their behalf before the legislature.[85] And in early 1834, the Mashpee made their own case to the state government. In their memorial, they accused the people of Massachusetts of being "filled with the fat of our fathers' land" and reminded the legislators that it was the tribe and not the settlers who "were the original proprietors of the soil." They also contended that the "Marshpee government is unconstitutional, and far transcends the Constitution of the country, and of course is extremely defective and injurious to us as a people." On the latter point, they declared that a failure to abolish the guardian system would be akin to "murdering us by inches." As a remedy, they called for "a grant of the liberties of the Constitution, to form a Municipal Code of Laws amongst ourselves, that we may have a government that will be useful to us as a people; for sure we have never had any since our original Sachem fathers fell asleep." They also invoked the memory of the Revolutionary War in which "our fathers fought, bled, and died for the liberties of their now weeping and suffering children." This sacrifice, they insisted, meant that Massachusetts was obliged to "break the chains of oppression, and let our children go free."[86]

In response to the petitions of the Mashpee and the pressure of nonnatives like Garrison and Hallett, the Massachusetts legislature abolished the guardianship system and incorporated the members of the tribe as a township with the ability to elect its own government. The victory of the Mashpee, a small, isolated group surrounded by powerful settlers, was the last successful resistance of these southern New England tribes to the sovereignty of the Anglo-American settlers, a lonely exception to the fate of native Americans in the new republic in the following decades.

How the Indians lost their land is one of the central questions of Anglo-American history.[87] The appeals that the native Americans made to the Crown are an important if understudied part of the answer to this vital historical question, for they demonstrate that natives had a significant degree of political agency in the empire, able to recognize (and leverage) the tensions between colonial and metropolitan authority in a bid to maintain control over their traditional territories. As well, these appeals show that the natives were able to respond to European arguments for dispossession with their own conceptions of law, property, and authority. Indeed, as the three examples discussed in this essay show, the Algonquin peoples of southern New England had a compelling vision of their place in the empire. Faced with the incursions of the settlers, they appealed to the Crown, arguing that they were both the original owners of the land in question as well as its paramount rulers. And it was on this basis that they had voluntarily subjected themselves to the Crown in return for protection from the settlers.

In doing so, they saw themselves as both subjects and allies of the Crown. That is, they were under the dominion of the Crown but were also "friends" and "allies" who had made leagues and treaties with the English. It was, in other words, a conditional subjection in which they ceded some of their original rights in return for being treated as coequal polities in the empire, with autonomy over their own affairs, a claim that the Mashpee carried into the era of American independence.[88] Moreover, these New England native peoples saw a close connection between their claims to property and their collective right to govern themselves, which in turn suggests that the debate over indigenous rights in the eighteenth-century Anglo-American world was about more than just the ownership of land. Rather, property rights and political capacity were intertwined, for whichever group—the settlers or the natives—could successfully assert its status as a polity was also likely to be the one in control of the distribution of land under their jurisdiction.

The sophistication of the natives' legal and political arguments did not, of course, stop their dispossession in the aftermath of the American Revolution and the subsequent removal of royal authority in the thirteen rebellious colonies, the result of which was to transfer power to new governments controlled by the settlers on the ground.[89] Nevertheless, these appeals are a reminder that this process of dispossession did not go unchallenged. Rather, there was an indigenous critique of the claims of the settlers, one which originated in the first decades of contact, and which continues to influence legal arguments about the justice of dispossession in the empire's successor states to the present day.[90]

NOTES

1. For a state-of-the-art summary of this large literature, see Duncan Ivison, "The Nature of Rights and the History of Empire," in David Armitage, ed., *British Political Thought in History, Literature and Theory, 1500–1800* (New York: Cambridge University Press, 2006), 191–211. I have attempted to refine this focus on prominent European political theorists by examining the arguments about empire made by the Anglo-American settlers in the crucial century before the revolution. See Yirush, *Settlers, Liberty, and Empire: The Roots of Early American Political Theory, 1675–1775* (New York: Cambridge University Press, 2011). In this essay, however, I try to uncover the other side of these debates—the arguments of the indigenous peoples of eastern North America who stood in the way of this new Anglo-American empire.

2. In doing so, it builds on the important work of Jenny Pulsipher on native appeals to the Crown in seventeenth-century New England, as well as the related work of Katherine Hermes on native use of colonial courts in New England. See Jenny Pulsipher, *Subjects unto the Same King: Indians, English, and the Contest for Authority in Colonial New England* (Philadelphia: The University of Pennsylvania Press, 2005); Katherine Hermes, "Jurisdiction in the Colonial Northeast: Algonquian, English and French Governance," *The American Journal of Legal History* 43 (1999), 52–73; and "'Justice Will Be Done Us': Algonquian Demands for Reciprocity in the Courts of European Settlers," in *The Many Legalities of Early America*, eds., Christopher Tomlins and Bruce Mann (Chapel Hill: The University of North Carolina Press, 2001), 123–149.

3. On which, see Alden T. Vaughan, *Transatlantic Encounters: American Indians in Britain, 1500–1776* (New York: Cambridge University Press, 2006).

4. A project like this raises a number of methodological difficulties, the most pressing of which is the veracity of the textual materials that form its evidentiary base. Given that they were often recorded by Europeans who might have known little about the indigenous peoples whose views they were taking down (or had interested reasons for distorting the record), these documents may tell us more about the biases of the English

than about the ideas of the natives themselves. In addition to bias, these texts also had to endure what James Merrell calls the "perils" of translation and transcription. James H. Merrell, "'I desire all that I have said . . . may be taken down aright': Revisiting Teedyusung's 1756 Treaty Council Speeches," *William and Mary Quarterly* LXIII (2006), 777–826 (quote at 783). While these are serious concerns, the legal records that this chapter is based on can, if used with care, yield important insights. As Daniel Richter, one of the leading New Indian historians, argues: "the most valuable clues to Iroquois perspectives come from the speeches native leaders made during diplomatic encounters with Euro-Americans." Richter, *Ordeal of the Longhouse: The Peoples of the Iroquois League in the Era of European Colonization* (Chapel Hill: The University of North Carolina Press, 1992), 5–6. And despite his warnings about the perils of these texts, Merrell also contends that some of the difficulties of translation and cultural bias can be rectified by using multiple accounts of the same document, thereby achieving a "quadraphonic" or even "polyphonic" effect, allowing scholars to find "genuine echoes of a long-forgotten native voice and native sensibility." Merrell, " 'I desire all that I have said,' " 819.

5. For one of the few accounts of this indigenous perspective, see Robert A. Williams, Jr., *Linking Arms Together: American Indian Treaty Visions of Law and Peace, 1600–1800* (New York: Routledge, 1999).

6. By contrast, the Narrangansetts were powerful enough that the Pequots appealed for their help against the English. The tributary status of Uncas and the Mohegans is evidence that Algonquin societies recognized hierarchical forms of organization and thus were able to put themselves under a European Crown, though as we will see they did this on their terms. On the Algonquins' precontact conceptions of political authority, see Kathleen J. Bragdon, *Native People of Southern New England, 1500–1650* (Norman: University of Oklahoma Press, 1996), 140–155.

7. On these two treaties, Pulsipher, *Subjects unto the Same King*, 21–24.

8. On this, see Pulsipher, *Subjects unto the Same King*, 25–26.

9. Uncas seized these lands; when Miantonomo appealed to Massachusetts, he received no help.

10. On which, see Francis Jennings, *The Invasion of America: Indians, Colonists and the Cant of Conquest* (New York: W.W. Norton & Co., 1975), 259.

11. There is little modern scholarship on Gorton. For a detailed (albeit somewhat hagiographic) account, see Adelos Gorton, *The Life and Times of Samuel Gorton* (Philadelphia, 1907). On the connections between his rhetoric and his religious beliefs, see Michelle Burnham, "Samuel Gorton's Leveller Aesthetics and the Economics of Colonial Dissent," *William and Mary Quarterly* 67 (2010), 433–458.

12. Pulsipher, *Subjects unto the Same King*, 25–26; and Jennings, *The Invasion of America*, 264.

13. Jennings, *The Invasion of America*, 265–268.

14. For Samuel Gorton's published defence of his actions, along with a detailed critique of the conduct of Massachusetts, see *Simplicities Defence against Seven-Headed Policy* (London: J. Macock, 1646).

15. John Russell Bartlett, ed., *Records of the Colony of Rhode Island and Providence Plantations, Volume I, 1636–1663* (Providence, RI, 1856), 134–136 (hereafter, *RCRP*).

16. *RCRP*, I, 134–136.

17. *RCRP*, I, 134–136. Francis Jennings attributes the tribe's embrace of English law to their surprise that the Gortonists were released from custody by Massachusetts after appealing to common law rights, whereas their own leader was murdered. See Jennings, *The Invasion*

of America: Indians, Colonists and the Cant of Conquest (New York: W.W. Norton & Co., 1975), 272–273.

18. On which, see Pulsipher, *Subjects unto the Same King, passim.*

19. *RCRP*, I, 134–136.

20. *RCRP*, I, 136–138.

21. Though Cromwell was to prove more sympathetic to dissenters and Indians in the 1650s than the Puritans would have liked.

22. On the politics of this speculation, see *Subjects unto the Same King*, 56, and Richard Dunn, "John Winthrop and the Narragansett Country," *William and Mary Quarterly* 13 (1956), 68–86.

23. See Pulsipher, *Subjects unto the Same King*, 54–57.

24. *Samuel Gorton's Letter to Lord Hyde in Behalf of the Narragansett Sachems* (1662; reprinted for the Society of Colonial Wars in Rhode Island and Providence Plantation by E. L. Freeman, 1930).

25. J.R. Brodhead, ed., *Documents Relative to the Colonial History of the State of New-York*, III (Albany: Weed, Parsons & Co., 1853), 56.

26. See *RCRP*, II, 59–60.

27. *Calendar of State Papers, Colonial: America and West Indies*, #1103. Volume 5 (1665–1688), 342 (hereafter *CSPC*).

28. Jennings, *Invasion of America*, 282.

29. According to Yasuhide Kawashima, in the aftermath of Metacom's war "independent tribal government virtually disappeared from southern New England." See his *Puritan Justice and the Indian: White Man's Law in Massachusetts, 1630–1763* (Middletown, CT: Wesleyan University Press, 1986), 234.

30. For the text of the treaty, see *The Governor and Company of Connecticut and Mohegan Indians, by their Guardians. Certified Copy of the Book of Proceedings before the Commissioners of Review, 1743* (London: W. and J. Richardson, 1769), 39–41.

31. Quoted in Joseph H. Smith, *Appeals to the Privy Council from the American Plantations* (New York: Columbia University Press, 1950), 418. Despite its importance, the Mohegan case has not been the subject of extensive scholarly discussion. Paul Grant-Costa's 2008 Yale dissertation (*The Last Indian War in New England: The Mohegan Indians v. The Governour and Company of the Colony of Connecticut, 1703–1774*) is the only book-length modern account. I discuss the legal claims made by both Crown and colony in "Claiming the New World: Empire, Law, and Indigenous Rights in the Mohegan Case," *Law and History Review* 29 (2011), 333–373. Part of my account of the legal arguments in the case is drawn from this article. Copyright © 2011 the American Society for Legal Histroy, Inc. Reprinted with the permission of Cambridge University press. However, no scholar has yet tried to analyze just the arguments made by the Mohegans in the case, although Amy Den Ouden's anthropological account of their internal politics provides important background on their understanding of the dispute. See Den Ouden, *Beyond Conquest: Native Peoples and the Struggle for History in New England* (Lincoln: The University of Nebraska Press, 2005), 91–141. For important treatments of (respectively) the arguments of the Crown and the lawyer for the Mohegans, see Mark D. Walters, "Mohegan Indians v. Connecticut (1705–1773) and the Legal Status of Aboriginal Customary Laws and Government in British North America," *Osgoode Hall Law Journal* 33 (1995), 785–829; and David Conroy, "The Defence of Indian Land Rights: William Bollan and the Mohegan Case in 1743," *Proceedings of the American Antiquarian Society* 103 (1993), 395–424.

32. Hallam and his brother John were challenging the disposition of their stepfather's estate by a Connecticut court. They were joined in their appeal to the Crown by Edward Palmes, the

brother-in-law of Fitz-John Winthrop, who was also contesting the legality of a will. The Privy Council ruled against them, though it upheld their right to appeal to the Crown notwithstanding the charter. See Robert Taylor, *Colonial Connecticut: A History* (New York: KTO Press, 1979), 195–197. On the Crown's inherent right to hear appeals from all of its subjects, see J. M. Sosin, *English America and Imperial Inconstancy: The Rise of Provincial Autonomy, 1696–1715* (Lincoln: University of Nebraska Press, 1985), 179. The private colonies' denial of such a right was a central grievance in the Board of Trade's case against the chartered colonies. On this, see Louise P. Kellogg, *The American Colonial Charter* (Washington, DC: Government Printing Office, 1904), 267–272.

33. *Owaneko, Chief Sachem or Prince of the Moheagan-Indians in New England, HIS Letter to a Gentleman Now in London* (London: Printed for Daniel Brown at the Black Swan without Temple-Bar, 1704), 1–2. The title page claims that Oweneco's letter was "Faithfully Translated from the Original in the Indian Language." It is a verbatim copy of a letter Oweneco wrote to Nicholas Hallam on July 14, 1703, which bore the sachem's mark, as well as a claim that it was "The true Interpretation of Oanhekoe's Grievance & Narration, by me John Stanton Interpreter Gent." Oweneco's letter is reprinted (with an interpretive essay by David Murray) in Katrina Bross and Hilary E. Wyss, eds., *Early Native Literacies in New England: A Documentary and Critical Anthology* (Amherst: University of Massachusetts Press, 2008), 15–27.

34. A point made by David Murray in *Early Native Literacies in New England*, 25–27.

35. *CSPC*, #1353. Volume 21 (1702–1703), 856–857.

36. *Owaneko, Chief Sachem or Prince of the Moheagan-Indians*, 3.

37. *CSPC*, #146. Volume 22 (1704–1705), 60–61.

38. *CSPC*, #181. Volume 22 (1704–1705), 76–77.

39. *The Governor and Company*, 24.

40. *CSPC*, #171. Volume 22 (1704–1705), 72–73.

41. On Dudley's enmity toward the private colonies (which he shared with Hallam and Palmes and the others who supported the Mohegans), see Kellogg, *American Colonial Charter*, 301–302.

42. Kellogg, *American Colonial Charter*, 303. For an example of Dudley's complaints against Connecticut for—among other things—its treatment of the Mohegans, see *CSPC*, #69. Volume 23 (1706–1708), 29–32.

43. The colony also forbade individual colonists from giving testimony before the commission.

44. *The Governor and Company*, 32–33. The colony also accused Dudley and the other commissioners of having an interest in the land in question. On this point, see Richard S. Dunn, *Puritans and Yankees: The Winthrop Dynasty of New England, 1630–1717* (Princeton: Princeton University Press, 1962), 340.

45. *The Governor and Company*, 26–27.

46. *The Governor and Company*, 28.

47. *The Governor and Company*, 29.

48. *The Governor and Company*, 27.

49. *The Governor and Company*, 29.

50. *The Governor and Company*, 66–67.

51. *The Governor and Company*, 154.

52. "Report of the Committee for hearing of Appeals from the Plantations touching ye Mohegan Indians Lands" [21 May 1706]. PC 2/81, pp. 204–205. On the 1706 appeal, see also Smith, *Appeals to the Privy Council*, 427.

53. *CSPC*, #1422. Volume 22 (1704–1705), 659.

54. The Mohegans were assisted by William Shirley, a powerful imperial figure whose protégé, William Bollan, would represent the tribe before the final royal commission in 1743. Shirley was able to get a copy of the Mohegans' complaint to the Duke of Newcastle, then the Secretary of State with responsibility for the American colonies. See Shirley's letter to the Duke of Newcastle in *CSPC*, #259. Volume 42 (1735–1736), 160. On the Mohegans' journey to London, see Alden Vaughan, *Transatlantic Encounters*, 162–163.

55. Mahomet's petition is in Mary K. Talcott, ed., *Collections of the Connecticut Historical Society*, Volume IV (Hartford, 1892), 368–372. For a discussion of Mahomet's memorial at the Privy Council, see W. L. Grant and J. M. Munro, eds., *Acts of the Privy Council of England, Colonial Series*, Volume III (1720–1745), 531 (hereafter, *APCC*).

56. On the conflict over who the legitimate sachem was, see Den Ouden, *Beyond Conquest*, 132–135.

57. For the Mohegans' petition, see *Collections of the Connecticut Historical Society*, V, 159–164.

58. *APCC*, Volume III (1720–1745), 536.

59. For the text of the 1743 commission, see *The Governor and Company*, 5–8.

60. I have been influenced by David Conroy's account of Bollan's role in the case, especially his claim that Bollan adopted an indigenous perspective before the 1743 commission. However, I disagree with his assumption that Bollan was acting for the Masons and not the Mohegans. Although we appear to have no record of who Bollan consulted with (or was paid by), his forceful defense of the Mohegans is closer in substance to the position of the tribe (expressed in Oweneco's 1704 letter, as well as their petitions to the Crown in the 1730s) than the less robust claims of the Masons (which held that the tribes' members were subjects of the Crown rather than allies). See Conroy, "The Defense of Indian Land Rights."

61. *The Governor and Company*, 87.

62. *The Governor and Company*, 91.

63. *The Governor and Company*, 91–92.

64. *The Governor and Company*, 92.

65. *The Governor and Company*, 91.

66. *The Governor and Company*, 94.

67. *The Governor and Company*, 93.

68. *The Governor and Company*, 90.

69. *The Governor and Company*, 91–92.

70. *The Governor and Company*, 126–127.

71. A policy that included the appointment of two Indian commissioners in the mid-1750s, and the announcement of the Royal Proclamation in 1763. On the strength of the settler opposition to the Crown's desire to protect indigenous rights, see Daniel Richter, "Native Americans, the Plan of 1764, and a British Empire that Never Was," in *Cultures and Identities in Colonial British America*, eds., Alan Tully and Robert Olwell (Baltimore: The Johns Hopkins University Press, 2006), 269–292.

72. For the decision, see *APCC*. Volume V (1766–1783), 218. The decision was issued on January 15, 1773, based on a December 19 committee report.

73. As with the other two appeals, little has been written on the Mashpee's struggles with Massachusetts. I have relied on the following: Daniel Mandell, " 'We, as a tribe, will rule ourselves': Mashpee's Struggle for Autonomy, 1746–1840," in Colin G. Calloway and Neal Salisbury, eds., *Reinterpreting New England Indians and the Colonial Experience* (Boston: The Colonial Society of Massachusetts, 2003), 299–340; Jack Campisi, *The Mashpee Indians: Tribe on Trial* (Syracuse: Syracuse University Press, 1991); Donald M. Nielsen, "The

Mashpee Indian Revolt of 1833," *The New England Quarterly* 58 (1985), 400–420; and Kim McQuaid, "William Apes, Pequot: An Indian Reformer in the Jackson Era," *The New England Quarterly* 50 (1977), 605–625.

74. They are often referred to as the Marshpee in these documents, but modern scholars usually refer to them as the Mashpee.

75. Quoted in Campisi, *The Mashpee Indians*, 82, who also remarks on "the vigor with which the Mashpees prosecuted their claims and defended their rights."

76. A reference to the guardians the colony had imposed on them.

77. Cogenhew's petition is in the Colonial Office Papers at the Public Record Office (now the National Archives), C.O.5/890, pp. 31–32. I am indebted to Daniel Mandell for bringing this document to my attention.

78. Letter of the House of Representatives, April 28, 1761, to Governor Francis Bernard [PRO, C.O.5/891, 29–30].

79. On the Board's desire for reform of Indian policy, see Daniel Richter, "Native Americans, the Plan of 1764, and a British Empire That Never Was."

80. For a more detailed discussion, see Mandell, "'We, as a tribe, will rule ourselves,'" 304; and Campisi, *The Mashpee Indians*, 85.

81. On which, see Mandell, "'We, as a tribe, will rule ourselves,'" 309–319.

82. On Apess, see McQuaid, "William Apes, Pequot," 605–625; and Barry O'Connell, ed., *On Our Own Ground: The Complete Writings of William Apess, A Pequot* (Amherst: University of Massachusetts Press, 1992), xiii–lxxvii. On the revolt, see Nielsen, "The Mashpee Indian Revolt of 1833," 400–420.

83. The resolutions are in William Apess, *Indian Nullification of the Unconstitutional Laws of Massachusetts relative to the Marshpee Tribe; or the Pretended Riot Explained* (Boston: Press of Jonathan Howe, No. 39, Merchants Row, 1835), 21.

84. See the issue of January 25, 1834.

85. See Hallett, *Rights of the Marshpee Indians: Argument of Benjamin F. Hallett before a Joint Committee of the Legislature of Massachusetts* (Boston: J. Howe, printer, 1834).

86. "Memorial of the Marshpee Indians," January, 1834. Ayer Manuscripts collection, the Newberry Library (Ayer, #251). It was signed by 78 males and 92 females on the "Plantation"; as well, it stated that there were those "who are absent, and will not return to live under the present laws – in all 287." The Memorial was also reprinted in William Lloyd Garrison's newspaper *The Liberator* on February 1st, 1834.

87. To borrow Stuart Banner's succinct statement of the question. See Banner, *How the Indians Lost Their Land: Law and Power on the Frontier* (Harvard University Press, 2005).

88. Jenny Pulsipher suggests in a recent article that in the early eighteenth century the Wabanakis viewed the English king as a "paramount sachem" who offered protection in return for loyalty, but without interfering in the tribe's "local governance." According to Pulsipher, this was not inconsistent with indigenous claims to be subjects of the Crown. See Pulsipher, " 'Dark Cloud Rising from the East': Indian Sovereignty and the Coming of King William's War in New England," *The New England Quarterly* LXXX (2007), 592.

89. On the rise of settler sovereignty across the Anglo-American world in the early nineteenth century, see Lisa Ford, *Settler Sovereignty: Jurisdiction and Indigenous People in America and Australia, 1788–1836* (Cambridge: Harvard University Press, 2010).

90. On which, see John Burrows, "Sovereignty's Alchemy: An Analysis of Delgamuukw v. British Columbia," *Osgoode Hall Law Journal* 37 (1999), 537–596.

7

FRAMING AND REFRAMING THE *AGŌN*
CONTESTING NARRATIVES AND
COUNTERNARRATIVES ON MĀORI PROPERTY
RIGHTS AND POLITICAL CONSTITUTIONALISM,
1840–1861

Mark Hickford

This chapter's argument is threefold.[1] First, territorial claims speak to more questions than those of "European *versus* indigenous" claims. They speak to issues internal to both indigenous and European politics—the continuation of intra-European and intra-indigenous politics in other guises. Second, territorial claims ought not to be thought of as falling solely or even principally within the province of the courts and litigation. Focusing upon court decisions per se can allow indigenous territorial claims or counterclaims to be interpreted as occurring *within* or *inside* the colonial legal system when such conditions of interiority cannot always be assumed. Third, territorial claims were not denuded of their political or jurisdictional significance insofar as they were also entwined with claims about political authority over territorial space rather than simply being claims to proprietary interests in the land itself. Territorial claims also represented a problem of government, both from the vantage point of indigenous politics and from that of imperial and colonial politics. "Negotiated empire" occurred not only between metropole and colonial bridge-heads;[2] it also characterized the interplay between and within those *arriviste* colonial settlements and diverse indigenous communities. Seeing it in this way broadens the compass of the politics of transoceanic empire.[3] It recalls the well-known injunction of Ann Laura Stoler and Frederick Cooper, to which a number of scholars have responded, to explore the interactions between the metropolitan and colonial within a single "analytic field."[4] Māori, officials, and settlers were intimately involved in negotiating relationships and in refreshing or discomforting those negotiated relationships from time to time. At these points of intersection, the presence of settlers as strangers wrought unmanaged change and instability among indigenous sources of political authority and territorial dominion. Claims and counterclaims concerning Māori property rights demonstrate this negotiated aspect of empire—its *agonistic* qualities. This was not a place of Manichean binaries—of simple distinctions of European and indigenous, colonialism and resistance.[5]

Framing and reframing the *agōn* (a theatre for contest and conversation) suggests a provisional, work-in-progress quality. As used here, the metaphor of the *agōn* comprised a composite of the particular fields for diverse narratives and accounts to be brought to bear and contested regarding the myriad intersections of Māori and settler interaction (as well as intra-Māori and intra-Pākehā interaction) with landscapes.[6] Each interacting aspect exhibited its own conditions and politics of interiority and exteriority—internal and external hinges. New Zealand was marked by polyvalent authority, both among Māori and settlers. The use of the metaphor also assists in explaining what is characterized elsewhere as an "empire of variations" on indigenous property claims rather than one of abstracting monist uniformity.[7] Contesting claims to territorial space—whether they could be seen as proprietary claims or claims to government and political autonomy—led to a thickening of colonial and imperial conceptions of Māori proprietary interests, which began to affect the languages of claiming among Pākehā and Māori.[8]

The framing of these contests need not have been deliberate or intentional. Yet efforts to statutorily set out and circumscribe the fields for interaction and debate through legislation certainly occurred. Key illustrations included the Native Council Bill (versions promoted in the House of Lords and House of Commons at Westminster in 1860 and the colonial legislature in New Zealand in late 1860), the Native Territorial Rights Bill of 1858 (passed in New Zealand but disallowed in London), the Native Districts Regulation Act, 1858, and Native Circuit Courts Act, 1858. In March 1861, Sir Frederic Rogers, Herman Merivale's successor as permanent undersecretary at the Colonial Office characterized the Native Circuit Courts statute as "this interesting & important experiment."[9]

Each of these measures was an experiment in looking for contained points of intersection or convergence with Māori territorial claims. Further, these legislative proposals were tied to attempts to craft portals of legal recognition through which customary property claims would pass. Seen together, they proposed and circumscribed ways in which the terms of litigation—of contest and dispute resolution about territorial claims—might be set. They would not only purport to stamp a level of legal security relevant to the colonial property regime upon perceived indigenous diversity and difference—to adapt and render preexisting or novel Māori claims to natural resources meaningful and legible to the introduced colonial legal system; they were also constitutional experiments, endeavoring to calibrate intersections between indigenous political relations with New Zealand landscapes and the colonial government.[10] From the late 1830s until the 1860s, for example, one sees extensive experimentation as to how to situate and frame property rights in New Zealand. This essay shall focus upon the 1850s and early 1860s in the main. Throughout 1858–1861, a plethora of schemes for incorporating the contested narratives regarding Māori customary property rights and containing them were promoted, scrutinized, accepted, modified, or rejected, in New Zealand and in Britain.

This chapter largely concentrates on anglophone elements attempting to frame ways of claiming territory and to induce Māori to accept such framings. How these deliberate imperial and colonial forays fared, even in failure, reveals the nature of negotiated empire—its grooves and grains—together with the manner in which indigenous communities engaged in it or not. Chichester Fortescue, when Colonial Office parliamentary undersecretary, characterized the issue astutely in an internal memorandum of March 1861, using a metaphor of limited association both temporally bound and geographically bound. "[T]he Government," he said, "conducts its relations with the native tribes by occasional *negociation* [sic], (as to Land buying, surrender of criminals & c) as though it were with foreigners, and performs scarcely any of the functions of a Gov[ernmen]t towards its *subjects*."[11] The experiments might not have received any uptake from Māori polities, as indigenous communities adapted their own alternatives. Fortescue frustratingly referred to the ""Native Districts" & "Native Circuit Courts" Acts of 1858 [as] hav[ing] been dead letters."[12] The period is important because it was a time when Māori polities were not necessarily inside or fully implicated within the introduced colonial legal system. They need not have accepted its strictures or assumptions in defining their relations to territorial spaces and landscapes. Indeed, they need not have conformed to what has been characterized as the "ventriloquism of forms"[13]—to bend their representations of claiming natural resources and spaces to the requirements of recently transposed legal forms or approaches, whether through petitions, in courts, or elsewhere.

Building on a notion of "occasional *nego[t]iation*," colonial New Zealand exhibited a pluralized legal-political situation. A variety of genres and vocabularies operated in practice, not all of which were shared or accessible. A plural situation—a multiplicity of sites of incomplete political autonomy throughout the archipelago and tied to politics and agendas across the seas—required ways of seeking and negotiating points of association and convergence, as well as divergence or difference. Interaction among and between Māori communities—*hapū*[14] or constellations of *hapū*—and imperial or colonial participants in politics contributed to this sense of an *agōn*. Narratives and counternarratives concerning claims to speak meaningfully and authoritatively for using and allocating natural resources and territorial space—and to account for these claims as claims to property rights—occurred in this context.

Using an *agonistic* metaphor also implies the salience of conflict and disagreement, often of a profound sort, as to the ordering of relations of power.[15] No situation is completely open to accommodating other ways of seeing or thinking about human interaction. Political questions, whether expressed in legalistic genres or not, invariably involved decisions that required choices between conflicting alternatives in circumstances where certain constituencies or audiences might not concur.[16] Politicians needed ways of getting things done. Within the colonial legislature, for instance, one politician noted that the "extreme views of no one [on the Native Lands Bill 1862] could have been carried, and a certain amount of compromise had to be made on every side."[17] "As usual any advantage gained by such compromise has been balanced by the imperfections necessarily attending a design worked out by many people."[18] Participants in these disagreements could promulgate their own preferred interpretations, not only concerning the nature of proprietary interests within New Zealand but also the nature of constitutionalism—the relations between political authority and governmentality, on the one hand, and ordering space and how populations might interact with such spaces within New Zealand, on the other.

The Political Significance of Claims to Territorial Space

What can be learned from looking at speechifying about claims and counterclaims to exert authority over natural resources? A variety of interconnected claims and conceptions of seeing and speaking about relations to New Zealand landscapes. A tangled mingling of constitutional politics operated within New Zealand, with multiple sites of Māori and Pākehā political authority operating, and able to muster resources—people and coalitions of opinion—in support. The language of debate concerning territory was filled with claims and counterclaims to an entitlement to government—to meaningful political authority over the allocation of space to strangers—or to proprietorship or both. This observation resonates with Jeremy Webber's comments regarding the outcome of recent native title litigation in Australia in the late twentieth century. Webber spoke of the recognition of indigenous title as necessarily involving the acceptance, if only provisional, of a measure of normative or political autonomy.[19]

Claims to ascertain interests in natural resources, as well as how and to whom they might be allocated and on what terms, also involved debates as to whether the claims to do so were properly characterized as "proprietary" or governmental. Overlapping and conflicting claims (together with the narratives or histories underscoring them) could suggest claims to govern space, as much as assertions of proprietary entitlements to that space vis-à-vis other Māori elements. This very issue swirled around the vexed government purchase at Waitara in Taranaki from Te Teira Manuka in 1859–1860, an event that precipitated a civil war within Te Ātiawa (Ngātiawa) and ignited disputes among imperial and colonial actors within the external and internal hinges of negotiated empire. Pamphlets and papers published in distant London mused on whether the territorial dominion or political authority of Wīremu Kīngi Te Rangitāke (Kīngi or "William King") could be exercised to preclude the acts of Te Teira, who asserted a right to sell the land on the south bank of the Waitara. Waitara spoke to the failure of diplomacy—of negotiation and purchase.

Māori themselves participated in writing campaigns critiquing the performance of the introduced colonial administration, particularly in its failure to keep the peace after the Waitara purchase negotiations. In doing so, they could present themselves as better interpreters of territorial claims and the appropriate constitutional place and conduct of the multidimensional Crown than the governor, his local officials, or settler politicians. In 1861, in denouncing government over its conduct at Waitara, Rēnata Tama-ki-Hikurangi Kawepō of Ngāti Kahungunu rhetorically recalled the metaphors deployed by the Waikato chieftain, Potātau Te Wherowhero, elected king, of the peaceful scripturally mediated community governed by law contrasted with the former god, Uenuku(-kai-tangata), the eater of men. As such, the colonial governor was the innovating inverter of this new order of things. He said, "[T]he Governor, the foundation of Jehovah, [has] risen up and taken Uenuku-kai-tangata to Taranaki, as his god for the extermination of the people!"[20] The colonial governor, Thomas Gore Browne, frustratingly referred to the tendency of "the King's Council [runanga] openly assume the right to decide on the justice of my proceedings, and consider whether or not they will aid a chief in rebellion against Her Majesty's Government" in a report of April 1860 to the secretary of state for colonies, the Duke of Newcastle.[21] The runanga at Ngāruawāhia in the Waikato, aligned with the king-elect, Te Wherowhero, was significant. It positioned itself as able to assess the relative merits of the territorial claims of Te Teira and the colonial government to the Waitara block, on the one hand, and the claims of Kīngi to withhold approval for the transaction. It claimed investigative and adjudicative authority respecting the entwined sets of claims before committing any support for the possible positions in the dispute. This appeared in keeping with the comments attributed by Kawepō to Te Wherowhero in a speech to the governor at Waiuku, south of Auckland. "When I accepted your God," he was alleged to have said, "I thought all wrongs were to be made the subject of investigation, great wrongs as well as little ones."[22] The runanga at Ngāruawāhia was presenting itself as conducting that which the governor had failed to do to its satisfaction: the calm deliberative investigation of the merits of the territorial claims at Waitara. In doing so, the runanga was claiming authority and jurisdiction over such matters, as much as the governor. The subsequent conference of chiefs assembled at Kohimarama in July 1860 at the invitation of the governor could be characterized likewise, at least in the view of certain attending chieftains. The merits of the claims of Kīngi relative to those of Te Teira and the governor were assessed.

The territorial claims of Kīngi were explained in a number of ways. The Māori language evidence suggests comfort with claiming authority over territory in the present tense without any appeals to the historical past or to narratives of past interaction of a tangible sort with the landscape in question (what would later be encapsulated within the concept of *take*—the historical root, cause, or reason of or for anything). Chiefly authority did not sense the need to recite histories to establish entitlements to speak for territorial space. It was enough to utter the names of chieftains and to speak about the dispositions of client *hapū* groupings and what was to be done with the natural resources. The words of Te Wherowhero recorded at Ngāruawāhia in 1860 not long before his death on June 25 of that year testified to a sense of effortless authority over peoples and places. He reputedly said, "W[illia]m King, had been invited by him to return to the land [in Taranaki] owned by his ancestors."[23] Then, according to this account, he said, "W[illia]m King had removed to the south for a short time before the conquest by the Waikato of the Ngatiawa at Pukerangiora, he also stated that immediately previous to W[illia]m King's return the Ngatimaniapoto were occupying the Waitara but abandoned it at his request."[24]

Lengthy historical disquisition to explain or to justify chiefly claims to command space was not required. To present such recitations to Pākehā officials suggested to some a lack of entitlement—a need to prove or to establish one's entitlement to determine or influence outcomes concerning land. This sense may be garnered from the manner in which Māori politicians engaged with colonial government. Thus, Kawepō chastised the superintendent for Hawke's Bay province, Thomas Fitzgerald, for saying Te Teira was a chief entitled to sell Waitara "because his genealogy was published last winter." Kawepō replied: "Sir, what about his [Te Teira's] genealogy? This is the second proof that he has given you (against himself) . . . W[iremu] King[i] would never give his genealogy because it is known throughout this island; it is not recounted." He added that, to recite one's genealogy "is a thing for the common man to do, who never was heard of before, or for an obscure thief."[25] On November 29, 1859 at New Plymouth, Kīngi was recorded as accepting that Te Teira, and "his party" had an interest in the lands at Waitara: "Yes; the land is theirs but I will not let them sell it."[26] When asked to explain the basis for his claim, Kīngi said simply, "I do not wish that the land should be disturbed, and though they have floated it, I will not let it go to sea." Christopher Richmond, writing on behalf of responsible ministers in May 1860, said the "right set up by King[i] is simply the old title of the Maori chief."[27] He internalized Kīngi's claim as a mere assertion without reason or foundation, compounded with aspects of what he characterized as a "manorial right" or "a species of minor sovereignty—over the whole district."[28] Subsequently, in December 1860, Richmond asserted, "the unrestricted right of alienation has in practice accompanied the right of property, whether subsisting in the tribe or in any smaller native community and that no seign[i]orial or tribal right of controlling sales by the native owners has ever been exercised, or in anywise asserted, since the commencement of land purchases in New Zealand."[29] He supposed this so-called "seign[i]orial or tribal right" was a de facto power exercised in practice politically but without any basis in customary law. Importantly, the *loci* for these discussions were not the adjudicative spaces of the introduced colonial courts. Litigating claims and using legalistic genres can occur by other means and did occur in numerous noncurial sites.[30] The Native Land Court appearing in the 1860s can be inappropriately valorized as the main site for contests on property questions of an intra-Māori nature as well as with and among Pākehā or their officials.[31]

The presence of precariously poised bridgehead settlements occupying coastal niches at Port Nicholson, Auckland, New Plymouth, and Nelson required complicated and often halting thought and debate concerning intersections between the preexisting normative orders of Māori polities and introduced ones. The settlements were staging areas for introducing transposed legal norms regarding claims to territorial space. As bridgeheads, to use the terminology elaborated upon by John Darwin, they were the creeping platforms carrying a certain ordering of relationships with the landscape.[32] Through building demographic pressures, incoming settlers could lead to periodic lunges into the hinterlands and along coasts.[33]

Jostling claims and counterclaims regarding property ought not to be confined to court proceedings. Colonial settlements' continued focus on a land market in the period after the assertion of British sovereignty in New Zealand in 1840 proved influential. It encouraged a shift in the systems of references for Māori communities toward noting the centrality of land both to the newcomers and the nascent colonial administration. As Pākehā settlements began on the beaches, political relations between coastal and neighboring hinterland descent groups could be reorientated or exacerbated anew. Coastal indigenous communities that might have suffered from the predations of clusters of powerful hinterland *hapū* in the past (or even the awareness that this might occur) as at the mouth of the Whanganui River were able to benefit from proximity to Pākehā settlements. These European settlements were conduits for exotic commerce. They required the absence of conflict, as well as the occupation of space, if they were to continue to supply access to incoming trading opportunities. Blurred zones between descent groups, previously allowed to remain vague, were allowed to acquire more determinacy, as the presence of the newcomers in instant townships tended to inhibit intra-Māori warfare related to migratory patterns and the pursuit of resources.[34] Indigenous location on land, and claims to possess it, were increasingly equated with the indigenous possession of power—an ability to exert an influence on relationships and outcomes in the context of the incoming settlers. John Hutton and Lyndsay Head see the transition in the 1840s and 1850s as influencing the emergence of novel categories of Māori political leaders—claiming authority premised upon the command of land—prone to challenge the authority of chiefly elites or to be perceived by others that way, where incumbent sources of chiefly authority tended to be predicated on personalized *mana* and political relationships with client *hapū* on territories.[35] Aspiring leaders, or those recasting themselves as such, might present themselves as able to command the transfer of spaces to the settlements—to act as preeminent purveyors of land and natural resources. Te Hāpuku of Ngāti Te Whatuiāpiti, based near Te Mahia, was one significant *rangatira* or chieftain who controversially adopted such an approach, particularly in the 1850s, presenting himself as a purveyor of lands relative to others not so inclined or less inclined than he.[36]

Complications prevailed. Māori polities, as much as imperial and colonial participants, dwelt within conditions of interiority and exteriority, with moments of cooption from the external politics of Pākehā settlers intertwined with periods of disinterest—what, in other contexts, John Pocock refers to as an *aussenpolitik* (histories of relations with others) as opposed to an *innenpolitik* (histories of self-formation).[37] Māori also aired their own fluid musings upon political and legal orders within indigenous communities, not necessarily shared with strangers. Speaking of 1845, Angela Ballara has characterized the foci of chiefly elites as "multi-directional."[38] This situation continued. Silence and political tactics suggesting indifference or displeasure could be evident. Single colonial officials, such as resident magistrates, could be isolated and rendered ineffectual, suggesting the degree to which indigenous politicians might nevertheless exert influence on the theaters of colonial politics external to their direct administration. This was the experience of Francis Fenton, the lone resident magistrate in the Waikato, who became associated with offering opportunities for new or rebranded, aspirational Māori leaders to the irritation or at least concern of those Māori elites tied to recollections of the *status quo ante* or of long-standing lineage. Certain Māori elites could still purport to manage change and novelty. In many areas, the situation had not yet got to the point witnessed later in the nineteenth century with the Native Land Court and pre-court hearing negotiations, where choices to disengage or refrain from engaging with the court lacked political cachet because they exposed the nonparticipants to political disadvantage relative to those Māori opting to participate.

A double game of selective participation and broad disengagement was often in evidence. Indigenous communities could be inside and outside settler politics without inconsistency. Māori could be seen contingently as players in the universe of *ius gentium*, a law of nations, its texts and norms, or as players at British subjecthood, or not.[39] Others, such as Pākehā judges, might not agree.[40] Reflecting on recent warring in the Taranaki in June 1861, the Duke of Newcastle, as secretary of state for colonies, commented that the relevant indigenous participants could "scarcely be looked upon as subjects in rebellion."[41] He referred to "the fictitious uniformity of law" prevailing in colonial New Zealand.[42] The negotiations for the acquisition of the Waitara and the troubled aftermath leading to military action and intense debates crystallized the underlying issues regarding the nature of agonistic politics and law within New Zealand. Territorial claiming at Waitara proved to be one vital twitch on the thread.

An internal hinge or set of hinges within colonial politics was also in play. The transposed Crown within New Zealand and the governmental apparatus was not a mere transcription from those of the United Kingdom. They hosted peculiarities particular to New Zealand. Institutionally the political framework within Pākehā New Zealand was indubitably complicated. New Zealand was spoken of as a place of "six colonies"— more akin to separate municipalities—which convoluted the dimensions of intracolonial politics and the relations between the "localized" or municipal forms of these politics with the governor and the General Assembly for the colony as a whole. Section 71 of the New Zealand Constitution Act, 1852, provided that Her Majesty could by letters patent declare districts within which native laws, customs, or usages should be observed and prevail over English common law. No such districts were formally declared under that statutory power. In practice, however, this situation would arise, a matter that could not be concealed, as the governor, Browne, recognized in 1859. "English law prevails in the English settlements," he said, "but in the native districts the Maoris are not yet willing to accept it."[43] This constitutional architecture has been prone to passing caricature in some recent legalistic and political studies.[44] Often the legal accounts remain descriptive. Yet aspects of the historiographical literature after the Second World War were sensitive to fragmentary albeit interlocking complexities of the constitutional situation obtaining in the colony after the implementation of the Constitution Act.[45] These features have also received recent historiographical attention.[46]

Imperial and colonial officials recognized that local informal economies engaging Māori and Pākehā elements in various entrepôts and in so-called native districts depended on transactions characterized as illicit, such as Māori leasing of lands to European run-holders. This factor is a relatively well-appreciated element of European settlements in parts of the historiographical literature.[47] Political gaming undoubtedly occurred. Māori *rangatira* were keenly aware that admitting strangers into their territories was fraught with potential political risks and possible advantages. Admitting Pākehā could demonstrate the ability of a chieftain relative to others within local indigenous communities to attract a novel range of options tied to a variety of commercial relations suffusing the incoming colonial economies.[48] It could yield an income stream. A number of influential participants in colonial communities paid annuities or rent to Māori lessors, as a "Return of Europeans in the Occupation of Native land" recorded in 1863.[49] George Law, the civil commissioner and resident magistrate for Taupō, had since 1862, by what was described as an "agreement signed by the principal men of the tribe," paid no consideration at all, but the value of the property was said to amount to £35.[50] Chapman and Synott, described as sheep farmers, were paying £330 per annum for a 12,000 acre run in the Hawke's Bay region on the eastern coast of the North Island under a lease with effective occupation from May 1861.[51] As Sorrenson in 1955 and Monin in 2009, as well as others, have observed, considerable pressure for direct dealings between Māori and settlers proved to be a persistent feature.[52]

Yet, as Māori elites were aware, the presence of such strangers also carried risks of political management. Strangers might convey expectations concerning alien norms and practices that were not necessarily within the inviter's system of reference points. They might pull in the officials of the incoming Crown, leading to the setting up of normative orders contrary to those preferred by the host communities or viewed as less congenial than the preceding situation. The economic outcomes of accommodating strangers might not reflect the outcomes initially hoped for, exposing the chiefly hosts to political recriminations within the fluid politics of their own communities. Disappointed economic or political expectations or unwanted outcomes—the presence of too many strangers to manage effectively—might provide leverage for long-standing or ambitious political critics and competitors within the indigenous groupings. Settlers who pursued spaces within areas beyond the scope of bridgehead settlements were warned that their arrangements might not be legally recognized at some point in the future once the institutional apparatus of enforcement caught up and the weight of such interests relative to others were assessed. The withholding of legal recognition could be an important form of leverage. Settlers often took the risk, however. Some failed; others did not. Few prosecutions occurred under the Native Land Purchase Ordinance, 1846, with most districts reporting no prosecutions in resident magistrates' courts under that ordinance in 1862. Taranaki was an exception, where Josiah Flight, the resident magistrate, recorded eight prosecutions under the Native Land Purchase Ordinance from August 1847 through to May 1856.[53]

Property claims were invested with undoubted political significance in several ways, two of which will be discussed from an anglophone perspective. This sort of significance encouraged the view that a political commitment was required to support a specialized statutorily engineered forum to address indigenous claims to territorial space. First, the perceived nonjusticiability of native title in the ordinary courts—the Supreme Court—before the operational advent of the Native Land Court in 1864, initially at "Kaipara, South" and "Kaipara, North" districts,[54] heightened the significance of political, noncurial sites, as well as diplomacy with Māori (whether through purchase or in other engagements). As early as 1845 or early 1846, Henry Chapman, the first puisne (junior or ordinary) judge of the Supreme Court of New Zealand, second only to William Martin, the chief justice, claimed in a series of notes that, "The rights and dominion which native tribes exercise over land are not such as come within the cognizance of the Tribunals."[55] Furthermore, he said, "No grant can be disputed to the subject on the ground that the Crown has not extinguished the native title." On this account, neither writs of *scire facias* nor petitions of right could be used to undermine Crown grants. Martin, engaged in advocacy against emerging proposals to legislate the taking of Māori territories in late 1863, stated that the "case stands thus[:] no native can, in any way, enforce any right of ownership or occupation of land, held by the native tenure, in the courts of the colony."[56] Moreover, he added, the "native is excluded from the political franchise even in cases where there is, in fact, a right of individual occupation, on the ground that his right, whatever it might be, is not in the technical sense a "tenement" [within the meaning of the Constitution Act]."[57] Earlier, in May 1860, Martin had composed a memorandum at the request of the governor addressing the state of "native affairs" and the alleged defects in "our Maori policy," as he characterized it. He advocated the deployment of Crown grants to secure the soil upon which "native communities" would be "sufficiently organized."[58] Once that territorial security had been obtained, he noted, the indigenous communities "would then be under the protection of the courts of law, and on the same footing as their English fellow subjects." Martin contended that in the absence of such accommodation, two regimes of tenure would sit apart, mediated by the diplomacy of purchase.

Martin's position had become less equivocal since 1859, partly due to his reading of the opinion of the law officers in the United Kingdom on the entitlement of Māori to exercise the electoral franchise under the Constitution Act and motivations to do with stressing the legal vulnerability of Māori as erstwhile "British subjects" within the meaning of the third article of the Treaty of Waitangi. The law officers of the imperial Crown, Richard Bethell and Henry Keating, surmised that the proprietary interests of Māori "must be such a holding, habitation and occupancy that English law would take cognizance of and protect."[59] They added, implying the native title, that there, "is nothing to provide for many persons promiscuously using one common habitation." In closing, the law officers posed the following question: "But suppose, in a District of Native Land lying within the limits of an Electoral District, that one Native by consent of the rest is permitted to have exclusive possession of a piece of Land, on which he builds a native hut for his habitation, but is afterwards turned out, or trespassed on by another Native; could he bring an action of ejectment or trespass in the Queen's Court in New Zealand? Does the Queen's Court ever exercise any jurisdiction over real property in a Native District?"[60] In answer, they replied: "We presume these questions must be answered in the negative, and that it must of necessity therefore follow that the subjects of Householding, Occupancy, and Tenements, and their value in Native Districts, are not matters capable of being recognized, ascertained, or regulated by English Law."[61] The very nature of such title continued to be the subject of considerable dispute and bewilderment, as legal commentators contended with translating the quality and incidents of such claims to space in ways explicable to English law. Thus, in 1862, Henry Sewell, as colonial attorney general, observed that it was still argued "whether . . . the lands of the native

[were] properly *lands of the Crown*, subject to the occupational right of the natives, or . . . land over which the natives hold *private proprietary rights* by a kind of allodial tenure."[62]

What might be considered softer or contrary interpretations as to the justiciability of native title certainly existed. For some, Māori title and English concepts of real property were not seen as especially commensurable, either jurisdictionally or conceptually. But in practice, these views of jurisdictional or conceptual incommensurability converged with the ultimate assumptions of nonjusticiability in preferring specialist, statutorily crafted tribunals or bodies to address indigenous property claims. Indeed, given the general trend of discussions among opinion leaders in the session of 1858 in the General Assembly, such as Sewell, and provincial councils in that direction by the early 1860s, the judges could afford to present a softer view. By 1861, Chief Justice George Arney, and the other two justices of the Supreme Court bench, Alexander Johnston and Henry Gresson, considered "the constitution and mode of procedure of the Supreme Court as it exists at present are not well adapted for the investigation and determination of questions relating to Native Title *generally*."[63] Familiar with *Regina v Symonds* in 1847, the judges acknowledged that the procedure and constitution of the Supreme Court might, nevertheless, "be sufficient for the purpose when such questions arise incidentally in the course of other proceedings."[64]

In September 1850, Merivale at the Colonial Office observed in a draft note that a "European marrying a native woman acquires no further rights in such land [subject to native title], whether allotted before or after his marriage, than she possessed herself: consequently that he is under the same restraints as to alienation, and certainly has no claim to a Crown grant of such land."[65] A so-called "code" of *The Laws of England compiled and translated into the Maori language*, prepared by Fenton and presented to the House of Representatives on June 16, 1858, reflected the view that anglophone norms on real property at common law were ill adapted to accommodating indigenous angles of vision regarding territorial space and resources. It did so with brevity in a minor section toward the end of the volume on "civil injuries" or "*hara hiwhiri*." It averred that the "Law of the Pākehā in reference to land, does not apply to land held under the Maori title."[66] Its title used the term "ture" for "law," a neologism that had its etymological roots in an adaptation of the word "torah," but which appeared in the speeches of chieftains from time to time.[67] The document played host to an assumption that the different normative approaches to claims to territorial space, including those as to its distribution and use, could not speak among themselves effectively. "If, however," it continued, "the Maori tenure were made similar to that of the Pākehā, the provisions of the Law of the Pākehā, in reference to land, might be brought into operation for the adjustment of those disputes which now arise among the Maori people, and cause strife between their tribes."[68] Otherwise, Māori tenure and English concepts of real property were seen as incommensurable. "If their lands were divided, and each individual had his own portion, and held it under the same kind of title as the Pākehā holds his land, that is, *under a title that could be recognized by the Law*, the Pākehā Law might then with propriety and advantage be brought to bear upon all cases of disputed ownership."[69] The possibilities of peaceable dispute resolution—the absence of war-ring, of a resort to arms—were vaunted as a reason for preferring English law concern-ing proprietary rights. A subsequent, less ornate and much more functionally expressed summary or abstract of *The Laws of England* or *Ko Nga Ture o Ingarani,* prepared by Martin at the governor's request, was available for circulation by February 1860. Two copies were received at the Colonial Office, although the subsequent copy was referred to as a "draft."[70] Henry Kemp, the district commissioner for the Bay of Islands, correctly ascribed the authorship of this "code of laws" to Martin.[71] Kemp commented that the "new tikanga" was discussed in various Māori *rūnanga.* But, overall, Māori attendees strategically reserved their positions on the code without committing themselves.

Crown grants were seen as transformative. In this sense, the historicity of property rights is of considerable significance—their relations to past and present. Indigenous "territorial rights" certainly had a spatial quality—the extent of space claimed—the exact dimensions of which were subject to disagreement and uncertainty, largely because the preferred theoretical and institutional means to arrive at conclusions on this point were themselves disputed.[72] Yet these communal claims to territory also had a temporal dimension—a particular quality of historicity in two senses. First, they were seen as rights of the past. The transformative processes of converting these titles into Crown-derived grants were seen as vital to bringing these entitlements and other features of Māori lifeways up to date. Such processes were to bring Māori communities within the reaches of settlement—to incorporate their members legally and politically within these settlements, to compromise indigenous sources of jurisdiction and au-thority, and to translate their proprietary claims into interests cognizable in English law. Second, native title was seen as logically prior or anterior to Crown-derived forms of proprietary interest, requiring attention before grants could be issued.

Converting native title into Crown-derived titles in the wake of extinguishment was considered a gateway for admitting Māori into the statutorily defined franchise under the Constitution Act. In drafts of the Constitution Act, toward the conclusion of the third Earl Grey's tenure as Secretary of State for colonies in January and February 1852, incorporating Māori within the embrace of the electoral franchise was anticipated to occur "by degrees" as they "advance[d] in civilization and [acquired] property."[73] Admission to the electoral franchise on account of this imperial statute was certainly anticipated in some parts of the colonial media, including the *Taranaki Herald* and the *Otago Witness.* In an issue of November 1852, the latter extracted an article from the former concerning the "admission by the proposed constitution of the natives to the electoral franchise."[74] Following its enactment and publication in New Zealand, debates persisted in both localized provincial contexts and in politics associated with the General Assembly as to whether Māori were entitled to exercise the electoral franchise. The Church Missionary Society missionary, Taylor, asserted in 1855, with scant attention paid to legal nuance, that "there is nothing in that constitution to hinder the native from being a representative of the people as well as his European neighbour."[75] "Maori enfranchisement," as the *Otago Witness* classed the issue in May 1853, arose where moves were undertaken to register electors, the concern being that large numbers of inappropriate individuals might be recruited as electors. In the South Island, a pressing issue was whether Māori communities dwelling within native reserves set aside under deeds of purchase had a sufficient proprietary interest to qualify for the franchise. Henry Sewell's journal entry for April 4, 1853 set out his view that the reserves could not possibly qualify.[76] He confided in his journal that the "native interest in reserves" was not legal, "for the legal interest [was] vested in the Crown which alone has the *jus possessionis* ["right of possession"], as well as the *jus dispositionis* ["right of disposition"]."[77] Nor was it an equitable interest, he thought, as he doubted a petition of right in a court exercising the equity jurisdiction of Chancery "calling on the Crown to execute the legal estate in favo[u]r of the natives" would succeed.[78] Sewell, educated at Hyde Abbey in Winchester, had joined the legal practice of his family in Newport on the Isle of Wight in England as a solicitor after serving articles. Arriving in the colony in 1853, he was elected a member of the House of Representatives for the "town of Christchurch" seat on August 20 of that year. The point of entitlement under the franchise remained a matter of contention, irrespective of the opinion of the law officers in London in 1859.

This "tendency to self-organization":
Looking for Inroads, Intersections, and Uptake

The "peculiar feature of the time," remarked the colonial premier, Edward Stafford, in May 1857, "is the tendency to self-organization now being exhibited by a large section of the Maori people."[79] Stafford characterized the "numerous meetings in course of being held throughout the country; - the recent attempts at legislation which have taken place at the villages of the Waikato Tribes, and the agitation for the appointment of a Native King" as "the signs of this movement."[80] Claims to localized political authority over natural resources were intertwined with property-based claims to land and other natural resources. These claims to government of people and territory and of sorting out entitlements to proprietary rights to the space itself crystallized most distinctly in the late 1850s on account of the Kīngitanga and the so-called "land league," which was more a loose disposition toward a policy of withholding territories from sale (a "*tikanga pakeke*" or obstinate policy to withhold).[81] Each contained its own fault lines and diverse points of view. Some adherents of Kīngitanga professed a version of coexistence, saying: "The King on his piece; the Queen on her piece, God over both; and Love binding them to each other."[82] The use of scriptural sources to critique the colonial administration and to sustain chiefly political stances was not unconventional.[83] They made an implicit claim to comment on the relative status of the recently admitted Crown—circumscribed, constrained (under scriptural tenets)—and its preferred conduct relative to those Māori placed under the *mana* of the Kīngitanga. The very presence of such confederacies of opinion eventually pressed other Māori polities to choose forms of response, about which there could be much internal and external debate. Some *hapū* of Ngāti Kahungunu adopted *kūpapa* status or military "neutrality," as it was interpreted upon the eastern coast of the North Island (rather than alliance with either the Crown or Kīngitanga). Other reported episodes illustrated what Stafford called indigenous "self-organization." In August 1858, the Māori language newspaper *Te Karere o Poneke*, produced in Wellington under Walter Buller, an official of the native department, recorded the resolution of a land dispute by a local *rūnanga* at Te Hautōtara within Ngāti Kahungunu territories in the Wairarapa.[84]

A variety of theoretical and practical differences of view were in play. Some areas of convergence were also evident, with Māori borrowing and adapting as well as adding distinctive spins to dispute resolution techniques, such as *komiti* (committees) and *rūnanga* (councils). A resident magistrate or missionary might be present at such points of intersection, yet their influence was less than determinative. It was seldom even arbitral, although accounts returned to government in Auckland might suggest otherwise with a view to demonstrating efficacy of a certain sort, specifically, success in inducing Māori to participate and to comply with dispute resolution processes. Rather, among Māori, the presence of resident magistrates was registered more as an advisory and dialogical engagement with various participants, including the "native assessors" or "native magistrates." Fenton, as resident magistrate at Whaingaroa and Rotorua from February 20, 1856, reported on what he referred to as circuit court proceedings at Taupari in the Waikato in July 1857, listing the cases of "*Hapurona v Tamati and John*" (concerning the destruction of fencing and the consumption of the plaintiff's potato crop by pigs belonging to the defendant) and "*Tamihana v Pairama*" (taking of a horse with a claim for damages of £60).[85] In "*Hapurona v Tamati and John*" it was the accompanying person described as the "native magistrate" who issued the decision, none other than Waata Pihikete Kukutai, a leading chieftain of Ngāti Tīpā of Waikato, a *hapū* dwelling along the western coast of Waikato between Kāwhia and Waikato Heads, as well as along the banks of the Waikato River to Onewhero.[86] The plaintiff had gone to Kukutai with his complaint, the gravamen of which concerned the allegedly wrongful consumption of his crop on the part of the defendants' pigs. Kukutai gave judgment for the defendants, concluding that the fence was of doubtful quality, and that the plaintiff could not claim damages if his "fence is a pretence."[87] Whether those participating among the indigenous communities might have thought of these proceedings as those of a "circuit court," to use Fenton's aspirational nomenclature, is not apparent. Clearly, they need not have done so. The recorded volume of intra-Māori matters engaging resident magistrates was slight. Arthur Thomson calculated that in 1854 a mere "thirty-one purely native cases were tried by the resident magistrates' courts in the colony," whereas by "1856 the numbers had risen to sixty-six."[88]

Stafford's ministry appreciated the complexities at work. Intelligence sources identified shades of opinion. Thus, reported Stafford in May 1857, "[w]ith some amongst the natives there is reason to think that social organization is sought chiefly, if not wholly, as a means to the ulterior end of counteracting the growing predominance of the European, preventing the further alienation of territory, and maintaining the national independence."[89] Others, Stafford claimed, pursued the establishment of order in coexistence with a colonial presence, with many strains of opinion coursing between these views. Abrupt transitions could not be sought. Māori politics proved appreciably less permeable and receptive than might have been anticipated by some, but, in general, those engaged in colonial legislative politics displayed little surprise. For settler politicians within Stafford's responsible ministry in mid-1859, the legal architecture for expressing indigenous choices on territorial claims had to be calibrated in such a way as to induce reticent Māori polities to participate. Stafford and his colleagues within the executive council were looking for intersections with Māori.

The diplomacy of purchase—not introduced courts—had been seen as the principal medium for translating space and other natural resources into territory from which Crown-derived titles in the form of Crown grants could ensue. By 1858, in the face of decreasing interest from Māori polities, the preexisting system of purchase predicated on gubernatorial oversight and diplomacy was seen as less reliable than it had been. Official returns for acres purchased suggested an overall decline in the northern island.[90] In October 1859, members of the provincial council of Auckland and certain Auckland members of the General Assembly, in objecting to the London's disallowance of the Native Territorial Rights Act, 1858, proposed a "Scheme for the partition and enfranchisement of lands held under native tenure."[91] In essence, it advocated direct transactions between settlers and Māori. The Auckland memorialists noted their "conviction that the abolition of tribal tenure, effected through the agency of the natives themselves, and the consequent security [of] individual property" were necessary.[92] In addition, they did not "think it desirable that "the line which separates the purchased lands on which European law is to prevail, from the unpurchased lands on which the native usages will continue to subsist," should be "broad". . . ."[93] "[I]f maintained at all," they said, "we certainly desire that it should be 'unequivocal' drawn by law in accordance with the provisions contained in the seventy first section of the

Constitution Act, and not by the tacit or equivocal understanding from which only a temporising system can result, and a continual risk of bringing the Queen's authority into contempt."[94]

Two characteristics are notable. First, to speak of "the enfranchisement of Maori land" was an exemplar of *paradiastole* or "rhetorical redescription"—in this case, to cast something in a less unfavorable light.[95] Second, if not precisely the same as Thomas Hobbes' notorious unmasking of the nature of the asserting sovereign as noted by Skinner and Runciman,[96] the memorial of 1859 represented an inversion of such an approach in that it both unmasked and published the limits of colonial authorities in archived imperial conversations. Admitting the hollowness of British preeminence, unremarkable in itself, engendered various responses both contemporaneously and at a later time. In 1860, against this background, Martin promulgated the efficacy of external dominion, relative to foreign powers external to New Zealand, and internal dominion, relative to all classed as "British subjects," including Māori populations.[97] The fact that he felt compelled to write so in 1860 revealed a desire to riposte the variety of discordant and politically influential interpretations then surging around the issue of political autonomy to speak for natural resources and rights to it. The persistence of native title within the northern island was seen as disciplining the spatial extent of settlement. Imperial authorities were comfortable with this sense of demarcated spaces at least transitionally—native districts in practice (if not formally declared under section 71 of the Constitution Act) were places where native title was not extinguished and where native laws and customs might accordingly prevail.[98] This sense of demarcation resonates with what Salesa has suggested in another vein, namely that territorial space was "racialized" in a concrete form.[99] Charts sketched with the assistance of Māori in the Whanganui in 1863 portrayed a tangible sense of broad difference, setting out boundaries between "Native land" and "European land," acquired via purchase.[100]

Interior anglophone debates within New Zealand and London concerning the Native Territorial Rights Bill and the Native Council Bill from 1858 until 1861 were revealing. There was a degree of comfort with plural or diverse approaches for the time being. But there was also an exploration of ways to converge, to find intersections for relatively contained disputes, which government might construe as litigation or analogous to it. Accessing territorial space for anglophone settlement was a driving theme. Claiming space, therefore, and the authority to allocate it (or not) lay at the heart of spearheading experiments to induce Māori participation in contained litigation about property rights—the socialization of conflict on introduced terms through setting up a council and using magistrates. Colonial and imperial administrations were looking for inroads, intersections, and uptake—for legible access points. The Kīngitanga, a confederated attempt at parallel government from the perspective of some aligned with it, suggested its own preferred areas of convergence and divergence. The Kīngitanga illustrated the competitive political autonomies operating in New Zealand.[101]

Māori groupings remaining neutral and not necessarily aligned with the Kīngitanga did not refrain from criticizing introduced, anglophone versions of framing claims to territory and constitutionalism. A number of Māori chieftains and others within indigenous communities denounced what they saw as misinterpretations of territorial claims and the distribution of political authority on the part of elements within colonial politics. The ecclesiastical sphere afforded opportunities for a range of Māori criticisms to be brought to bear in certain areas where networks with predominantly Anglican mission stations had been established. A petition produced with Archdeacon Octavius Hadfield's assistance at Otaki in 1860 was one such instance. The remonstrance requested the governor's removal for his "unwarrantable proceeding in purchasing Teira's land at Taranaki."[102] Māori and Hadfield were not so much criticizing the Crown's evil counselors, although there were undoubted resonances.[103] Rather, they were criticizing her misguided representative in New Zealand. Browne endeavored to marginalize the petition on account of Hadfield's alleged hand in its gestation and production, a point that was severely contested. The *rūnanga* at Kohimarama in 1860 also supplied a venue for ventilating a variety of elite Māori narratives regarding territorial claiming and the place of the introduced Crown in constitutional settings. Participants were broadly united on the importance of restoring peace to the Taranaki in the wake of Waitara. But disagreements persisted as to whether chiefs ought to mediate territorial disputes or not. Intra-Māori politics and differences were evident. Yet the presence of such voices revealed that there was no monopoly on the interpretation of constitutionalism, the distribution of political authority, or territorial claims within New Zealand.

Constitutional experimentation was involved in addressing the intricate question of claims to territorial space and of staging ways of ensuring communicability between opinion within Māori communities, concepts of native title and the demands of settlement. The voyages of the Native Council Bill are revelatory in this sense. It has received scant attention within the historiographical literature.[104] Yet it represented recourse to a form of imperial intervention—ultimately unsuccessful—to recast the legal portal for the multilogue on property claims and to evade the inertia within the colonial system. A portal for legal recognition was to be set out, admitting certain intersections between indigenous claims to authority regarding territorial space albeit not others. It brought the question of native title, again, within the purview of cabinet and parliamentary discussions in the United Kingdom. The concept of a native council further diversified the political marketplace, proposing to formally add voices of influence to those already aired in the House of Representatives and Legislative Council of the General Assembly in New Zealand, as well as the provincial councils. As imagined by the

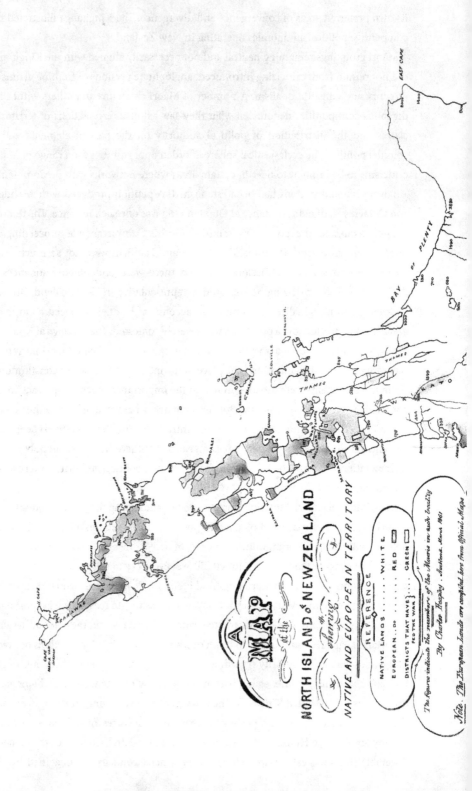

A map of the North Island of New Zealand shewing native and European territory by Charles Heaphy, March 1861, illustrates the tentative bridgehead quality to British coastal settlements in New Zealand and the need for a politics of negotiability—often in the form of negotiated deeds of purchase—to mediate relations between settler and indigenous territorial claims. In color, the Province of Taranaki and surrounding areas are green, for "districts that have fed the war," while scattered shaded areas in the north and southeast are red for European ownership.

Courtesy of the Sir George Grey Special Collections, Auckland City Libraries, Auckland, New Zealand governor, the conciliar body would comprise a selection of those individuals from whom he already sought advice informally in addition to his "responsible advisers." Prominent among these persons were Martin, the former chief justice, William Swainson, the second attorney general, and the Bishop of New Zealand, George Augustus Selwyn. Swainson advocated instituting a "competent tribunal" to ascertain the proprietorship of lands held in common, prior to the partitioning of such territories among the claimants by mutual agreement.[105]

At this juncture, Sewell developed "Heads of a Bill promoting the colonization of lands in New Zealand whereof the native title is at present unextinguished." Forwarded to London in September 1859, this draft hosted a proposal that all powers of the governor were to be "exercised by and with the advice and consent of the [Native] Council" and not otherwise.[106] Under Sewell's suggestions, a resident magistrate and at least two Māori assessors would be appointed for each district proclaimed to be subject to the statute. These officers would assist the governor in implementing the legislative regime. The council was to operate only in those districts where the native title remained unextinguished. Annexed memoranda from Martin, Swainson, and Selwyn supplied individual accounts of how best to reconceptualize policies concerning Māori claims to territory. Martin agreed "in thinking that it is a matter of vital importance to devise some systematic mode of operation for the purpose of obtaining from the natives a cession to the Crown of the large tracts which they still retain, particularly in the central parts of this Island."[107] He thought it vital that "the machinery must be of a permanent kind, not liable to be affected by change of Ministry" and that the "commissioners or native council should consist of members appointed by the Crown and responsible to the Crown, the Governor of course being the President."[108] The governor's "responsible advisers," however, opposed the proposals for a native council, as it appeared "improbable that such a system could work in harmony with the representative institutions of the Colony."[109] In effect, the option of a council would establish an independent board that would not act upon the advice of ministers answerable to the legislature.

The responsible advisers proposed three draft bills of their own, including a "Native Crown Grants Act," and a "Native Districts Colonization Act." The proposal suggested by the governor imagined "*The Governor in (Native) Council . . .* to have larger powers of dealing with native lands than he at present possesse[d]—especially—he was to have power to grant *Crown titles* to natives for land wh[ich] he might render alienable to individual purchasers—to make *reserves* of land & sell them for the purpose of defraying the cost of purchase, or other 'native purposes'—and to *borrow money* for the same purposes—"the same to be a lien upon the land acquired from the natives'".[110] The porous demarcation between areas where native title persisted and the bridgehead settlements, where it was seen as extinguished, was interpreted as

"provisional" albeit very real, nevertheless. In London, on reviewing the native council proposal, the Colonial Land and Emigration Commissioners noted, "Policy and
charity alike require that the existing order of things should be treated with the
utmost tenderness—but those who are entrusted with the authority of the Crown
should never for a moment forget that however long it may be destined to last, it is
by its very nature merely provisional."[111]

The conciliar option aligned a native council, comprising nominees of the imperial
Crown, with the governor who would preside as "president." The acts of the governor
concerning native affairs under the Constitution Act would be classed as acts of the
governor in native council rather than the governor acting in the executive council
consisting of advisers responsible to the colonial legislature. The Native Council Bill
was defended as a conservative measure and not as an innovation—it was characterized as furnishing the means or "machinery" by which the authority already reposed in
the Crown under the Constitution Act could be deployed in relatively detailed terms.
It was not seen as modifying the constitutional membrane. Rather, it was said to elaborate and "finely grain" what was already implicit. Thus, the parliamentary undersecretary argued that the proposed "Bill would not have transferred power from the Colonial
to the Home Government, but would only have furnished a machinery for the exercise
of a power already given."[112]

How to frame indigenous *versus* European territorial claims was negotiated in
London, as much as in colonial settings. These debates had multidimensional hinges in
the form of relations between metropole and colonies, transposed intellectual sources
and vocabularies, and networks of correspondence between participants across these
spaces. Certain settler politicians, such as James Fitzgerald, while present in London,
effectively lobbied opinion within the House of Commons against Colonial Office preferences on managing issues of Māori property rights claims in 1860. Lobbying pressures—an
intrinsic part of politicking at Westminster—were referred to as a reason for rendering
parliamentary support in the House of Commons uncertain or marginal at best for the
proposed Native Council Bill.[113] Fitzgerald resigned his seat in the General Assembly in
New Zealand in 1857 and acted as emigration agent based in England for the province
of Canterbury for three years, refusing offers of the governorship for British Columbia
and Queensland. Becoming embroiled in disputes on the Native Council Bill in the
United Kingdom, he published in July 1860 a pamphlet entitled *Memorandum relating
to the conduct of the native affairs in New Zealand, as affected by a bill now before Parliament*. A second memorandum was issued on July 30, 1860. Fitzgerald dubbed the proposed council a "new irresponsible nominee Parliament" insofar as it would purport to
make or amend "native laws" and regulate the sale of land to settlers.[114]

When the General Assembly in New Zealand produced its competing version of a
Native Council Bill, received at the Colonial Office on February 23, 1861, its measure

reorientated the balance toward the colonial legislature. Fortescue, the parliamentary undersecretary, lamented that it "creates indeed a 'native Council' to be appointed by the Crown, & provides £2350 a year for its support—But it carefully avoids connecting the Council with the *Governor*—it gives the Council no initiative—it subordinates it to the 'Government' i.e. the Ministers of the day in all its action."[115] With reports of war in the Taranaki over Waitara, William Gladstone, as Chancellor of the Exchequer, cautioned Newcastle about the "hopeless & incurable faults of our plan of attempting to manage such controversies whether on paper or in the field from the other end of the world."[116] He concluded that the "doom of that system is written even if its hour be not yet come."[117] In ways that have not been previously identified in the secondary literature, Newcastle suggested a degree of conditionality in the relations between the imperial Crown and Māori polities. Legislative change that might be perceived as modifying the terms of the Treaty of Waitangi of 1840 and any statutory forms of its expression, such as section 71 of the Constitution Act, suggested the political need for seeking the "consent" of Māori. Newcastle elaborated further that "[t]hey have never been consulted as to its provisions, and those provisions deprive them of that which they believe is their best security as given by the Treaty – the direct protection of the Sovereign of England."[118] Newcastle concluded that, "[i]n the face of the Treaty of Waitangi this Ordinance cannot be sanctioned without injustice and bad faith to the natives."[119] Shifting denizens of the multidimensional Crown exerted disciplines upon themselves and their policy preferences.[120] A legalistic genre, internally debated, was one source of internal discipline. But there were others as well, including a sense of the "hono[u]r" residing with the imperial Crown, which had not obtained any actionable effect at law.[121] Confirmation of the colonial measure was withheld.

Extensive musings upon the policy of a "native council" occurred within London as a way of interacting with Māori territorial claims. Yet events overtook the native council option, with Sir George Grey appointed to assume the role of governor a second time in New Zealand.[122] The eruption of disputes concerning negotiations for government's acquisition of the Waitara block within Taranaki in 1859 raised concerns as to the political stability and fiscal impact of a system predicated upon governmentally driven purchase. Directions to Grey in June 1861 addressed this point: "You will direct your earliest attention to this subject,—examining whether the system of nego[t]iation between the agents of the Gov[erno]r, and the native owners, though in conformity with the Treaty of Waitangi & for many years successfully, may not, in the present condition of the natives & settlers, require to be modified or superseded, - and whether, if it should in whole or in part be maintained, some tribunal cannot be established, entitled to the confidence of both parties, for the purpose of adjudicating upon disputed claims, when argued in a legal & peaceable manner."[123]

Reflections

This essay suggests the relevance of *agonistic* politics to seeing the finely grained workings and interactions of indigenous claims to territorial space and those made by incoming colonial administration. Such an approach has been used to illustrate the relevance of contest plus the external and internal politics of those participating in these power relations of claiming. It has also shown that much territorial claiming occurred outside of the courts and occurred externally to the introduced colonial system by means of diplomacy (negotiations for purchase, for instance). By examining attempts to frame the *agōn* and terms of legal recognition within it, even those faltering attempts, the argument has endeavored to show the extent to which disputes about claims to territorial space encouraged, revealed, and exacerbated constitutional debates about the distribution of political authority in colonial New Zealand. The nature of these disputes implied the iterative, provisional nature of the framing and reframing of debates concerning relations within and without Māori polities, the nature of territorial claims, and how they might be represented. In doing so, it suggested the relevance of such contests to attempts to unmask the limits on colonial legal orders and the relative comfort with plural approaches to asserting authority and other claims over territorial space. It also revealed the claims of Māori political elites to adjudicate contested territorial claims in various sites—with the *rūnanga* at Ngāruawāhia and the Kohimarama conference in 1860 purporting to do so concerning the government's putative purchase at Waitara—and from different points of view. In so acting, while they were commenting on and contesting how political authority was distributed, they were also presenting different, indigenous interpretations of constitutionalism within New Zealand.

NOTES

1. Mark Hickford was the 2008 New Zealand Law Foundation International Research Fellow while completing research for this chapter. He is grateful for the comments of Saliha Belmessous, Tack Daniel, John Hutton, and the anonymous reviewers.

2. Robert Travers, *Ideology and Empire in Eighteenth-Century India: The British in Bengal* (Cambridge: Cambridge University Press, 2007), 41; Amy Turner Bushnell, "Gates, Patterns, and Peripheries: The Fields of Frontier Latin America" in Christine Daniels and Michael Kennedy, eds., *Negotiated Empires: Centers and Peripheries in the Americas, 1500–1820* (New York: Routledge, 2002), 17.

3. Mark Hickford, "Making 'Territorial Rights of the Natives': Britain and New Zealand, 1830–1847," D.Phil. thesis, University of Oxford, 1999.

4. Frederick Cooper and Ann Laura Stoler, "Between Metropole and Colony: Rethinking a Research Agenda," in *Tensions of Empire: Colonial Cultures in a Bourgeois World* (Berkeley: University of California Press, 1997), 15.

5. Kerry Howe, "The Politics of Culture: A Personal History of History in New Zealand," in Roger Openshaw and Elizabeth Rata, eds., *The Politics of Conformity in New Zealand* (Auckland, NZ: Pearson, 2009), 22.

6. The relevance of contest was emphasized in Hickford, "Making 'Territorial Rights,'" 19–24.

7. Ibid, 184. Hickford, "'Decidedly the most interesting savages on the globe': An approach to the intellectual history of Māori property rights, 1837–1853," *History of Political Thought*, 27 (2006), 152.

8. Hickford, "Making 'Territorial Rights,' " 19–24.

9. Rogers, March 28, 1861, CO209/157, fol. 397a, The National Archives, Kew, London ("TNA").

10. Following earlier historians like Keith Sinclair and W.P. Morrell, Damen Ward has suggested the importance of such proposals to intra-settler politics concerning the distribution of authority between governor, legislature, and judiciary within colonial New Zealand: "Civil Jurisdiction, Settler Politics, and the Colonial Constitution, circa 1840–1858," *Victoria University of Wellington Law Review*, 39 (2008), 497–532.

11. Fortescue, March 12, 1861, CO209/156, fol. 168a, TNA (emphasis in original).

12. Ibid.

13. Lisa Ford, "The 'Ventriloquism of Forms': Australian Aboriginal Land Claiming in Context," "Indigenous *versus* European property claims" workshop, University of Sydney, August 20–21, 2009.

14. A clan or descent group associated with a distinct territory and settlement or settlements, and which may take collective action for certain purposes.

15. Cf. the contemporary literature upon the subject of agonistic politics, especially the illuminative insights of Paul Muldoon, "'The Very Basis of Civility': On Agonism, Conquest and Reconciliation" in W. Kymlicka and Bashir Bashir, eds., *The Politics of Reconciliation in Multicultural Societies* (New York: Oxford University Press, 2008), 114-135. Also J. G. A. Pocock, "The Politics of Historiography" in *Political Thought and History: Essays on Theory and Method* (Cambridge: Cambridge University Press, 2009), 260–261.

16. Cf. Chantal Mouffe, *On the Political* (London: Routledge, 2005), 10.

17. F. D. Bell, November 5, 1862, CO209/170, fol. 25, TNA.

18. Ibid.

19. Jeremy Webber, "Beyond Regret: *Mabo*'s Implications for Australian Constitutionalism," in Duncan Ivison, Paul Patton, and W. Saunders, eds., *Political Theory and the Rights of Indigenous Peoples* (Cambridge: Cambridge University Press, 2000), 63.

20. Renata Tamakihikurangi, *Ko Te Korero me te Pukapuka a Renata Tamakihikurangi, no te Pa Whakairo; ki a te Kai-whakahaere tikanga o nga Pākehā ki Ahuriri – Renata's speech and letter to the Superintendent of Hawke's Bay on the Taranaki War Question* (Wellington, NZ: The "Spectator" Office, 1861), 14L. The critical analysis here is owed to Head, "Land, Authority and the Forgetting of Being in Early Colonial Maori History," Ph.D. thesis, University of Canterbury, 2006, 256–257.

21. Browne to Newcastle, April 27, 1860, CO209/153, fol. 424a, TNA.

22. Tamakihikurangi, *Ko Te Korero me te Pukapuka a Renata Tamakihikurangi*, 14L.

23. Thomas Smith, CO209/153, fols. 435–435a, TNA.

24. Ibid, fol. 435a.

25. Tamakihikurangi, *Ko Te Korero me te Pukapuka a Renata Tamakihikurangi*, 21L.

26. Parris, District Commissioner, New Plymouth, to Chief Land Purchase Commissioner, December 4, 1859, CO209/153, fol. 473, TNA.

27. Richmond, May 25, 1860, CO209/154, fol. 98a, TNA.

28. Ibid, fol. 99a. Contrary evidence existed to suggest that Kīngi had an interest in the land itself, exhibited by cultivated sites attributable to his *hapū*: Alan Ward, *A Show of Justice: Racial "Amalgamation" in Nineteenth Century New Zealand* (Auckland, NZ: Auckland University Press, 1995), 115–116.

29. Richmond, December 3, 1860, CO209/157, fol. 128, TNA.

30. Hickford, " 'Decidedly the most interesting savages' "; Hickford, "John Salmond and Native Title in New Zealand: Developing a Crown theory on the Treaty of Waitangi, 1910–1920," *Victoria University of Wellington Law Review*, 38 (2008), 853–924; "Strands from the Afterlife of Confiscation: Property rights, constitutional histories and the political incorporation of Māori, 1920s," in Richard Hill and Richard Boast, eds., *Raupatu: The Confiscation of Māori Land* (Wellington, NZ: Victoria University Press, 2009).

31. M. P. K. Sorrenson, "The Purchase of Maori Land," M.A. thesis, University of Auckland, NZ, 1955; Sorrenson, "The Politics of Land," in J. G. A. Pocock, ed., *The Maori and New Zealand Politics* (Auckland, NZ: Blackwood and Janet Paul, 1965), 21–45; Richard Boast, *Buying the Land, Selling the Land: Governments and Maori Land in the North Island, 1865–1921* (Wellington, NZ: Victoria University Press, 2008); Boast, "Recognising Multi-textualism: Rethinking New Zealand's Legal History," *Victoria University of Wellington Law Review*, 37 (2007), 547–582.

32. Darwin, *The Empire Project: The Rise and Fall of the British World System, 1830–1970* (Cambridge: Cambridge University Press, 2009), 49.

33. James Belich, *Replenishing the Earth: The Settler Revolution and the Rise of the Anglo-World, 1783–1939* (Oxford: Oxford University Press, 2009), 85–99.

34. Angela Ballara, *Taua: "Musket Wars," "Land Wars," or tikanga? Warfare in Māori Society in the Early Nineteenth Century* (Auckland, NZ: Penguin, 2003).

35. Head, "Land, Authority and the Forgetting of Being," 168–173; Hutton, ""Troublesome Specimens": A Study of the Relationship between the Crown and the Tangata Whenua of Hauraki 1863–1869," M.A. thesis, University of Auckland, NZ, 1995.

36. Ballara, *Iwi: The Dynamics of Māori Tribal Organisation from c.1769 to c.1945* (Wellington, NZ: Victoria University Press, 1999), 80–81.

37. Pocock, "Hedgehogs, foxes, and lions: The future of sovereignty and history," lecture, November 20, 1997, University of Oxford.

38. Ballara, *Taua*, 457.

39. Hickford, "'Decidedly the most interesting savages'" 164–166; Hickford, "Making 'Territorial Rights,' " 299.

40. P. G. McHugh, *Aboriginal Societies and the Common Law* (Oxford: Oxford University Press, 2004), 177.

41. Newcastle to Grey, June 5, 1861, CO209/156, fol. 244, TNA.

42. Ibid fol. 248a.

43. Browne, CO209/151, fol. 259a, TNA.

44. Jon Johansson, *The Politics of Possibility: Leadership in Changing Times* (Wellington, NZ: Dunmore Press, 2009), 55–56.

45. Keith Sinclair, *The Origins of the Maori Wars* (Wellington, NZ: New Zealand University Press, 1957), 94.

46. Ward, "Civil Jurisdiction."

47. Cf. Peter Karsten, *Between Law and Custom: "High" and "Low" Legal Cultures in the Lands of the British Diaspora - The United States, Canada, Australia, and New Zealand, 1600–1900* (Cambridge: Cambridge University Press, 2002), 122–123.

48. Ann Parsonson, "The Challenge to Mana Māori," in Geoffrey Rice, ed., *The Oxford History of New Zealand* (Auckland, NZ: Oxford University Press, 2nd ed., 1992), 178, 182; Head, "Land, Authority and the Forgetting of Being," 229–250 (concerning Ngāti Kahungunu), 300 (Wiremu Kīngi).

49. "Return of Europeans in the Occupation of Native Land in the Northern Island of New Zealand," *Appendix to the Journals of the House of Representatives ("AJHR")—1863*, E16, 10 *et seq.*

50. Ibid, 9.

51. Ibid, 11.

52. Sorrenson, "The Purchase of Maori Land," 15–16. Paul Monin, "Maori Economies and Colonial Capitalism" in Giselle Byrnes, ed., *The New Oxford History of New Zealand* (Melbourne, Australia: Oxford University Press, 2009), 132.

53. "Return of Europeans in the Occupation of Native Land in the Northern Island of New Zealand," 13.

54. See Donald Loveridge, "The Development and Introduction of Institutions for the Governance of Maori, 1852–1865" (report for the Crown Law Office; September 2007; Wai-903), 216 *et seq.*

55. Chapman, legal notes, undated [1845-1846], Ms-Papers-8670-0417, Alexander Turnbull Library, Wellington, NZ ("ATL").

56. Martin, "Observations on the proposal to take Native Lands under an Act of the Assembly," CO209/178, fol. 163, TNA.

57. Ibid, fols. 163–163a.

58. Martin, May 12, 1860, CO209/154, fols. 44–44a, TNA.

59. Bethell and Keating to Newcastle, December 7, 1859, CO209/152, fol. 290a, TNA. Bethell (1800–1873) would ultimately become Lord Westbury (and would also become a Lord Chancellor). For a brief account of Bethell as Solicitor-General (he was appointed in 1852), refer to J. Edwards, *The Law Officers of the Crown* (London: Sweet and Maxwell, 1964), 48. Henry Keating (1804–1888) was Solicitor-General from May 1857 to February 1858, and again in June 1859, during the two administrations of Viscount Palmerston.

60. Ibid, fols. 290a–291, TNA.

61. Ibid.

62. Sewell, November 22, 1862, CO209/170, fols. 221–221a, TNA (emphasis in original).

63. Arney et al. to Browne, May 9, 1861, *AJHR—1861*, E-3, 13 (emphasis in original). Sidney Stephen had been acting Chief Justice before Arney's appointment.

64. Ibid. On *Symonds*, see Hickford, "'Vague Native Rights to Land': British Imperial Policy on Native Title and Custom in New Zealand, 1837–1853," *Journal of Imperial and Commonwealth History*, 38 (2010), 190–196.

65. Draft, [Merivale—September 28, 1850], Earl Grey to Grey, September 1850, CO209/159, fol. 135, TNA.

66. [Fenton], *The Laws of England compiled and translated into the Maori language by direction of His Excellency Colonel Thomas Gore Browne CB, Governor of New Zealand & c (Ko Nga Ture o Ingarani; He Mea Whakahau Iho e His Excellency Colonel Thomas Gore Browne CB, E Te Kawana o Nui Tirani)* (Auckland, NZ, 1858), 45: version presented to the House of Representatives, LE1/1858/229, Archives New Zealand, Wellington ("ANZ(W)").

67. Buddle, "Notes of Native speeches delivered at Ngaruawahia April 11th 1860 on the arrival of a deputation sent from Taranaki to present the allegiance of the Ngatiruanui and Ngatiawa tribes to Potatau," CO209/153, fol. 451, TNA.

68. *The Laws of England*, 45.
69. Ibid (emphasis added).
70. Martin, "Rules for the proper administration of justice," draft, CO209/153, fols. 361 *et seq* (received at the Colonial Office on August 10, 1860); "Rules for the Proper Administration of Justice, being a translation of the rules put forth in Maori by the Governor in February, 1860," CO209/154, fols. 67–73, TNA, also received at the Colonial Office on August 10, 1860.
71. Kemp, District Commissioner, Bay of Islands, to McLean, October 10, 1860, CO209/157, fol. 401a, TNA. Doubts as to Martin's authorship have been raised in the past, as noted by Guy Lennard in *Sir William Martin: The Life of the First Chief Justice of New Zealand* (Christchurch, NZ: Whitcombe and Tombs Limited, 1961), 121–122, referring to M. W. Hancock's suggestion that Fenton was the author in "Sir William Martin and the Maori People" Victoria College, 1950.
72. Hickford, "'Decidedly the most interesting savages,'" 160–166.
73. Draft, Earl Grey to Grey, January 29, 1852, CO209/159, fol. 335a, TNA.
74. *Otago Witness*, issue 77, November 6, 1852, 3.
75. Taylor, *Te Ika a Maui, or New Zealand and Its Inhabitants* (London: Wertheim and Macintosh, 1855), 275.
76. Sewell, April 4, 1853, *The Journal of Henry Sewell 1853–7*, W. David McIntyre, ed., (2 vols., Christchurch, NZ: Whitcoulls, 1980), I, 229.
77. Ibid.
78. Ibid.
79. Stafford, memorandum, May 6, 1857, LE1/19, 1858/232, ANZ(W).
80. Ibid.
81. Keith Sinclair, "Te Tikanga Pakeke: The Maori Anti-Land-Selling Movement in Taranaki 1849–59," in P. Munz, ed., *The Feel of Truth: Essays in New Zealand and Pacific History* (Wellington, NZ: Reed, 1969), 79–92.
82. "Curiosus," *The New Zealander*, July 3, 1858.
83. Judith Binney, "History and Memory: The Wood of the Whau Tree, 1766–2005," in Giselle Byrnes, ed., *The New Oxford History of New Zealand*, 81.
84. *Te Karere o Poneke*, August 30, 1858, 3–4.
85. Fenton and Kukutai, Native Magistrate, "Specimen of Proceedings in Circuit Courts," CO209/156, fols. 343–367, TNA.
86. Waata Pihikete Kukutai (?–1867): *The People of Many Peaks: The Māori Biographies from The Dictionary of New Zealand Biography, Volume 1: 1769-1869* (Wellington, NZ: Bridget Williams Books, Dept. of Internal Affairs, 1991), 17.
87. CO209/156, fols. 343–367 (page 36 of printed report), TNA.
88. A. Thomson, *The Story of New Zealand, Past and Present – Savage and Civilized* (2 vols., London: John Murray, 1859), II, 272.
89. Stafford, May 6, 1857, LE1/19, 1858/232, ANZ(W).
90. "Approximate return of all lands purchased by the Crown in the northern Island of New Zealand; From the 5th of July 1850 to the 30th of September 1859," CO209/152, fol. 153a, TNA.
91. William Daldy et al., to Newcastle, October 20, 1859, CO209/152, fols. 59–100a, TNA.
92. Ibid, fol. 74.
93. Ibid, fols. 88–88a.
94. Ibid, fol. 88a.

95. Quentin Skinner, "Moral Ambiguity and the Renaissance Art of Eloquence" in *Visions of Politics: Volume II, Renaissance Virtues* (Cambridge: Cambridge University Press, 2002), 276; Runciman, *Political Hypocrisy: The Mask of Power, from Hobbes to Orwell and Beyond* (Princeton: Princeton University Press, 2008), 30.

96. Runciman, *Political Hypocrisy*, 30–35; Runciman, *Pluralism and the Personality of the State* (Cambridge: Cambridge University Press, 1997), 253–256.

97. Martin, "Observations on the proposal to take Native Lands under an Act of the Assembly," enclosed in Martin to Fox, November 16, 1863, CO209/178, fols. 144–144a, TNA.

98. Although substantially accurate, the impression of a stark divide in maps ought not to be overplayed, as colonial legislation in the late 1850s sought to make distinctions (often unsuccessfully) between native title and European areas of occupation or homesteads located within predominantly native title areas.

99. Salesa, "Race Mixing: A Victorian Problem in Britain and New Zealand 1830–1870," D.Phil. thesis, University of Oxford, 2000, 119–120.

100. White to Mantell, May 20, 1863, JC-WG1/4, 86, ANZ(W).

101. Richard Hill, *State Authority, Indigenous Autonomy: Crown-Maori Relations in New Zealand/Aotearoa 1900–1950* (Wellington, NZ: Victoria University Press, 2004), 33–35.

102. Browne to Newcastle, April 28, 1860, CO209/153, fos.483a; "Translation of petition to the Queen," March 30, 1860, CO209/154, fols. 165–166, TNA.

103. Cf. Austin Woolrych, *Britain in Revolution 1625–1660* (Oxford: Oxford University Press, 2002), 200.

104. Donald Loveridge supplies the best chronological account to date in "Origins of the Native Land Acts and Native Land Court in New Zealand" (report for the Crown Law Office; November 3, 2000; Wai 686), 128–155; "The Development and Introduction of Institutions for the Governance of Maori, 1852–1865" (report for the Crown Law Office; September 2007; Wai 903), 113–115.

105. Swainson, memorandum, May 7, 1860, CO209/154, fol. 56, TNA.

106. Section 1 of the "Heads of a Bill promoting the colonization of lands in New Zealand whereof the native title is at present unextinguished by Mr Sewell," CO209/151, fol. 206, in Browne to Newcastle, September 20, 1859, CO209/151, fols. 134–166, TNA. This draft was circulating as early as July 1859: Browne to "responsible advisers," July 2, 1859, CO209/154, fol. 478a, TNA.

107. Martin to Browne, September 7, 1859, CO209/151, fol. 240, TNA.

108. Ibid, fols. 241a–242.

109. Richmond, "Remarks by Ministers on Mr Sewell's draft Bill," August 19, 1859, CO209/151, fol. 214, TNA.

110. Fortescue, March 12, 1861, CO209/156, fol. 167a, TNA (emphasis in original).

111. Rogers and Murdoch to Merivale, January 1, 1860, CO209/158, fols. 200–200a, TNA.

112. Fortescue to Browne, August 27, 1860, CO209/159, fol. 783, TNA.

113. Ibid.

114. Fitzgerald, "Memorandum, No. 2 Relating to the Conduct of Native Affairs in New Zealand, as affected by a Bill now before Parliament," July 30, 1860, 16.

115. Fortescue to Newcastle, February 21, 1861, CO209/156, fols.130–130a, TNA (emphasis in original); Rogers, February 21, 1861, CO209/156, fol. 138, TNA.

116. Gladstone to Newcastle, January 30, 1861, B[ritish] L[ibrary] Add Mss44531, fol. 113.

117. Ibid.

118. Newcastle, February 23, 1861, CO209/156, fol. 135a, TNA.

119. Ibid. Newcastle to Browne, April 26, 1861, NeC10885, 90, University of Nottingham.

120. Hickford, "Strands from the Afterlife of Confiscation."

121. But the phrase has acquired legal significance in the contemporary Canadian context, as is evident from the *Haida Nation* proceedings before the Supreme Court of Canada in 2004: *Haida Nation v British Columbia (Minister of Forests)* [2004] 3 SCR 511.

122. Newcastle to Sir George Grey, June 5, 1861, CO209/156, fols. 243–252, TNA.

123. Ibid, fol. 249.

8

"BRING THIS PAPER TO THE GOOD GOVERNOR"
ABORIGINAL PETITIONING IN BRITAIN'S AUSTRALIAN COLONIES

Ann Curthoys and Jessie Mitchell

Blackfellows now throw away all war-spears. No more fighting but live
    like white man almost.

Blackfellows hear that your first son has married. Very good that! Black-
    fellows send all good to him, and to you, his Great Mother, Victoria.

Blackfellows come from Miam and Willum to bring this paper to the
    Good Governor. He will tell you more.

All Blackfellows round about agree to this.

That is all.

—*Kulin address to Queen Victoria, 1863*[1]

In January 2010, Aboriginal people in Sydney met with Prince William.[2] They presented him with a petition, seeking the return of the skull of Pemulwuy, a Dharug warrior whose resistance to colonists around Sydney had made him an outlaw, shot and beheaded by British forces in 1802. They also passed on to the prince a copy of a letter originally written to King George VI in 1937, protesting against the treatment of Aboriginal people.[3] In making these representations, these Aboriginal people were keeping alive a very long tradition of seeking assistance from the Crown, one that they share with their counterparts in former British colonies worldwide. This chapter focuses on Aboriginal petitioning, interpreted broadly to include written documents and appeals made through gifts and performances.[4] Petitions, which were made to various colonial and imperial authorities, were a crucial means by which Aboriginal people made claims and sought redress. While these petitions are not transparent and were often written with the assistance of local philanthropists, they do embody Aboriginal perspectives and aspirations more than most other sources from this era. Understood in their political and cultural contexts, petitions provide valuable clues to Aboriginal people's understandings of colonial power and authority.

Aboriginal petitions have been of considerable interest to historians in recent years.[5] Here is a close look at the mid–nineteenth century, a crucial period in Aboriginal–settler relations. In the 1850s, most aspects of colonial governance, including Aboriginal policy, shifted from Britain to the Australian colonies, with the exception of Western Australia, which gained self-government much later, in 1890. Through the system of "responsible government," developed especially through Britain's relations with her Canadian colonies and then applied in Australia, Britain retained control over foreign policy and defense, and the right to veto colonial legislation it judged contrary to its imperial interests, but handed over all other matters to local legislatures. Under this system, the division of power and authority between the Colonial Office in Britain and local legislatures was by no means clear or settled, necessitating continual negotiation. Despite their loss of power, governors remained important as the link with the British Colonial Office, transmitting legislation for approval, and as the representative of the Crown, fulfilling important ceremonial functions. Aboriginal people seeking redress in this period were thus confronted by governors, Chief Secretaries, ministers of the Crown, missionaries and protectors, local authorities and police, and even royal visitors, all of them representing different and yet legitimate sources of authority.

Aboriginal campaigners were hindered by the fact that, unlike indigenous peoples in other parts of the world, they had no formal treaties of cession on which to base their claims.[6] Nor could they hope to put much meaningful pressure on colonial governments. The partially elected legislative councils that made up the organs of representative government in the 1840s and early 1850s often reflected the views of the very pastoralists who were seizing Aboriginal land. The bicameral parliaments and expanded male suffrage that came with responsible government in 1856 were not much better.[7] Colonial legislatures, now in control of Aboriginal affairs, were often openly unsympathetic, seeing Aboriginal people as a nuisance in the present and a "dying race" without a future. Yet these governments could not completely ignore imperial and humanitarian pressures; a space was thus created in which Aboriginal petitioners could sometimes make their claims heard. This chapter focuses on four of Britain's Australian colonies—Tasmania, Victoria, South Australia, and New South Wales—and draws attention to their differences as well as their commonalities. In the other two colonies, Queensland and Western Australia, frontier violence raged until much later, and petitioning appears to be a twentieth- rather than a nineteenth-century phenomenon.

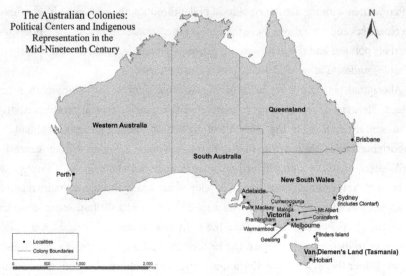

The Australian Colonies:
Political Centers and Indigenous
Representation in the
Mid-Nineteenth Century

N

Queensland

Western Australia

Brisbane

South Australia

New South Wales

Perth

Adelaide

Cumeroogunja

Sydney
(includes Clontarf)

Point Macleay Maloga

Mt Albert

Victoria

Coranderrk

Framlingham

Melbourne

Warrnambool

Flinders Island

Geelong

Van Diemen's Land (Tasmania)

Hobart

Localities
Colony Boundaries

0   500   1,000   2,000
Kms

This map shows the missions where indigenous petitions were created and the colonial
cities where they were presented in mid–nineteenth century Australia. *Drawn by Nathan
Wales (School of Geosciences, University of Sydney) in collaboration with Ann Curthoys and Jessie Mitchell
(School of Philosophical and Historical Inquiry, University of Sydney, Australia), 2010*

Petitioning

Petitioning is a very old and widespread form of nonviolent claim making. A petition
is a request for redress of grievance, sent from a subordinate person or group to a superior. It is usually written in a humble tone, acknowledging the disparity of power,
but also emphasizing that the ruler or government has an obligation to respond.[8] Its
rhetoric is typically deferential; using juridical and religious metaphors, a petition is, as
Edmund S. Morgan puts it, "a request, a prayer, a supplication from an inferior to a
superior."[9] Petitions shed light on the identity of both the petitioner and the authority
they are approaching; they are, in Ravi de Costa's words, "implicit descriptions of the
moral worlds in which particular claims are sensible and legitimate."[10]

From the middle ages, petitioning was *the* standard means by which Britons approached
the authorities. David Zaret demonstrates how the English Civil War and the development of printing caused petitioning to shift, from the seventeenth century onward, from
private and local messages to a form of public campaigning.[11] After the Restoration, petitioning was discouraged, but by the early nineteenth century it had once again become
a common part of political life. This was due partly to the growth of the Evangelical
movement, with its emphasis on pamphleteering, lecturing, lobbying, and mobilizing
the public—petitions were common, for example, in the campaigns against slavery—and
partly to the rise of Chartism in Britain between 1838 and 1848, when tens of thousands

of petitions were produced, with millions of signatures, addressing a range of grievances. Interestingly, while the power of the monarchy was declining at this time, many petitions continued to address the Crown—as Paul Pickering argues, "it would be a mistake to underestimate the residual popular belief in the benevolent role of monarchy."[12] Thus, for the period from the 1830s to the early 1880s, petitions were recognized as a major means of expressing, influencing, and creating public opinion.

The influence of petitioning stretched throughout Britain's empire. It was widespread in the American colonies in the seventeenth and eighteenth centuries, and in Upper Canada, during the turbulence of the early 1830s.[13] Its popularity was also growing in Australia by the 1840s, as Pickering has shown, thanks to the arrival of immigrants influenced by Chartism who used this technique to call for an end to transportation and for more representative or responsible government.[14] However dissatisfied they were with particular British powers or policies, colonists insisted their petitioning was a quintessentially British activity, part of a long lineage of popular constitutionalism.[15] This did not mean, however, that only colonists of British origin used petitioning. It was also used, for example, by the Indian handloom weavers of colonial Andhra in the late eighteenth and early nineteenth centuries,[16] and by those First Nations peoples in British North America who journeyed to London to appeal directly to the Crown, employing the familial language of "great white mother" or "great father" to express their sense of the obligations owed to them by the imperial center.[17] In the 1860s and 1870s, both they and Māori in New Zealand used petitions to assert rights to land and autonomous government.[18]

In this context, then, it is not surprising that Aboriginal peoples in the Australian colonies adopted petitioning as a favored form of activism. While their political influence was slight, they did have several rhetorical grounds for appeal. They could assert that settler society owed them something for their loss of land. Although most colonists did not recognize Aboriginal land *rights*, there was sometimes, as Richard Broome puts it, "a paternalistic sense of duty to 'the original owners of the soil'".[19] They could appeal to the humanitarian and evangelical desire to convert them to Christianity, promising to conform to British notions of civilized behavior in return for security, dignity, and free association. Sometimes they could also shame individuals who had mistreated them. Over time, Aboriginal people found some cracks in the colonial edifice that settlers had built to exclude them, and they made their case. And sometimes their claims succeeded.

Flinders Island, Van Diemen's Land, 1847

Aboriginal petitioning began during the era of direct British control. The earliest known examples occurred in Van Diemen's Land (renamed Tasmania in 1856). In the early decades of the nineteenth century, this colony saw bitter land wars between colonists and Aboriginal people, and in an effort to halt the violence Lieutenant Governor George Arthur sent George Augustus Robinson on a "friendly mission" around the colony in the early 1830s, to persuade the survivors to retreat to government-sponsored reserves. Henry Reynolds has argued that Robinson negotiated an unwritten treaty of sorts, promising the people peace, protection, material goods, and the right to keep visiting their homelands.[20] Certainly, the surviving Oyster Bay and Big River peoples, when they famously walked into the capital city of Hobart with Robinson's party in January 1832, seemed to regard themselves not as prisoners but as free agents. They met confidently with the lieutenant governor before boarding a ship for Bass Strait, understanding, as the local newspaper, the *Colonial Times,* put it, "that they were to be sent to a place where there is plenty of kangaroo and no work."[21] Instead, Arthur sent them to Flinders Island, where they were gathered together in an institutional environment under government officers keen to control and "civilize" them. Most of them would never be able to return home.

By the late 1830s, the people on Flinders Island (mostly the descendents of the Ben Lomond, Big River, and western communities) were becoming discontented and angry about their poor living standards, lack of autonomy, and distance from home. At first, they expressed their anger through disobedience and passive aggression, but later they began to protest more directly.[22] During 1845 and 1846, the residents, usually via the advocacy of community leaders Walter George Arthur and Mary Ann Arthur, appealed to Robinson, to the lieutenant governor, and finally to Queen Victoria to improve their living conditions and get rid of their bullying new commandant, Dr. Jeanneret. Walter George Arthur complained to Robinson of government officers treating the Flinders Island people with arrogance and neglect.

> The natives are having been treated shamefully just like savages . . . the people (white people) I mean, use the natives as they please and they dare not speak one word in their own defence and why, because Doctor Jeanneret carrys his pistols in his pockets and puts the blacks in jail.[23]

Appeals to representatives of the Crown were less forthright in tone but expressed the same feelings. The residents asserted that they were a free people who had negotiated a peaceful withdrawal from the mainland and were therefore entitled to be protected from tyranny and to enjoy the rights of white men.[24] They addressed the lieutenant governor as "Father," using paternalistic language that both acknowledged imperial supremacy and, as Reynolds notes, deployed their own language of kinship.[25]

On February 17, 1846, the residents drew up the first petition to a reigning monarch from an Aboriginal group in the Australian colonies.[26] The island's white Christian teacher, Robert Clark, assisted them, but both he and they insisted that they understood the process, and there is no reason to suppose the Flinders residents were ignorant of the broad structures of power in the British world; they had had various connections with colonial authorities and individual settlers over the years. Superintendent Dr. Joseph Milligan, who encouraged their efforts in 1846, commented that petitioning was a right held by all the queen's subjects, and expressed pleasure that the Aboriginal people were coming to appreciate this aspect of civilized government.[27]

Addressed to Queen Victoria, this petition had a specific objective: to exclude Dr. Jeanneret from the island. It also articulated wider views, reminding the Crown that the people had negotiated with the authorities and lived peaceably on the island, and that Jeanneret had abused his position, using violence and threats, mismanaging their supplies, and putting them in jail "for talking to him because we would not be his slaves." Using language that evoked both equality and paternalism, they assured the queen that, "we are your free children . . . we were not taken prisoners but freely gave up our country to Colonel Arthur then the Governor after defending ourselves."[28] They voiced their pleas in appropriate, formal language, not challenging Britain's right to rule, but, rather, appealing to humane imperialism. "As a tactical document," remarks literary critic, Penny van Toorn, "it played British colonial authorities at their own moral game."[29]

To an extent, the petition worked. A furious Jeanneret imprisoned Walter George Arthur, one of the leaders, and tried without success to make him renounce the petition. Arthur responded by calling for Jeanneret to be charged with "falsely putting me in Jail"; he demanded the same justice as "a white man and a free man."[30] The matter was referred to the Colonial Office in London, where Undersecretary James Stephen considered the petition sympathetically. On Colonial Office advice, Lieutenant Governor William Denison dismissed Jeanneret in 1847, closed the institution, and ordered the removal of the survivors to Oyster Cove, on the Tasmanian mainland not far from Hobart. Not all colonists, however, welcomed this decision. Some protested furiously, arguing that the Flinders Island people would resume their attacks on settlers, and seeing both the return of the Aborigines and the continuation of convict transportation as signs of an authoritarian and irresponsible government. Once these antitransportationists achieved the self-government they were seeking, it seemed, the Aboriginal survivors would have less chance than ever of a sympathetic hearing.[31]

From the Protectorate to the Board:
Seeking Land in Victoria, 1835–1863

As it turned out, Aboriginal petitioning survived the advent of responsible government; indeed, in some areas it increased. It was most extensive in the colony of Victoria, across the Bass Strait from Van Diemen's Land and originally part of New South Wales and known as Port Phillip. Aboriginal people there began negotiating with Europeans even before dispossession had truly begun, when in 1835 representatives of the Port Phillip Association tried to purchase their land by treaty, an attempt overturned by the Sydney-based government on the grounds that the land in question was Crown land and not Aboriginal people's to sell.[32] By the mid-1840s, a swift and devastating invasion was occurring, leading to many deaths through disease, loss of food sources, alcoholism, and violence. Nonetheless, some Aboriginal people tried to deal with the new authorities. They sought out relationships with missionaries, sympathetic colonists, and government-appointed protectors, explaining to them the boundaries and importance of their traditional country and the harm they were suffering through loss of land and colonial hostilities. While not always embracing Christianity, they hoped that the new missions and protectorate stations might enable them to stay in their country, and they were willing to adhere to mission life, to some extent, to achieve this. Wesleyan missionary Francis Tuckfield, for example, told the Wesleyan Methodist Missionary Society in 1840 that Aboriginal people from around Geelong were asking him for a mission of their own, lamenting "Our country all gone."[33] In the same year, the Daungwurrung people of the Goulburn River district were dismayed by the resignation of their sympathetic protector James Dredge and promised him that if he could secure some land in their country, they would build him a house and work on his farm.[34] In 1843, Woiwurrung leader Billibellary told the Melbourne-based protector William Thomas that his people were too miserable to survive as they were but would become sedentary farmers if only they had a reserve on the Yarra. Even the people who drank and begged around Melbourne told Thomas, "give us all land in our own country and we live like Whites."[35] In these scattered moments are the origins of an emphasis on land in exchange for "living like Whites" that would grow stronger in decades to come.

After the colony gained separation from New South Wales in 1850 and responsible government in 1856, Aboriginal activists began to address the new local legislature. In 1859, a delegation of senior Woiwurrung and Daungwurrung men visited William Thomas (now the Guardian of Aborigines, a position created when the Protectorate wound up in 1849) and asked for a reserve near the Goulburn river. He accompanied them to meet with the Surveyor-General and the Commissioner for Crown Lands, a meeting the press described as serious and dignified.[36] These advocates then led Thomas around their country, showing him the mountains and waterfalls near Mt. Albert and dividing up their land, cutting "AB"—"Black (Aboriginal)"—into the trees with their tomahawks.[37] However, they soon found themselves thwarted by hostile neighbours and the Central Board to Watch Over the Interests of the Aborigines, established in 1860, the first such board under colonial government control. Woiwurrung advocates invited the Daungwurrung to join them on a new reserve in their country, for which they lobbied the board, helped by Thomas and their new Scottish

Presbyterian missionary, John Green. In March 1863, still without an answer, the Greens and a party of forty Kulin trekked to the desired land, named it Coranderrk, and began a campaign to make it permanent.[38]

Soon after settling on Coranderrk, the Kulin had an opportunity to take their claims to a higher authority. The board granted their request to take part in the governor's levée (a formal reception held in honor of Queen Victoria's birthday) in order to congratulate the newly married Prince of Wales and send gifts to the queen. William Thomas and Robert Brough Smyth (secretary to the Board) assisted in preparing their address. On May 24, 1863, a Kulin deputation of fifteen men and five boys, dressed in European clothes and traditional possum-skin cloaks, walked forty miles to Melbourne and delivered presents. For Queen Victoria, they gave an elaborate possum rug, two reed spears, a basket, a "hurling stick," and a firestick, and for the Prince of Wales a shield, two spears, a boomerang, and a "bludgeon." They specified that most of the gifts should go to the queen and "to the son who has just got married," but hoped her other sons would also have a share.[39] The men also presented to the queen a "loyal address," inscribed on a parchment with sketches of native animals, Aboriginal families, weapons, and native plants. Its language suggested both a grasp of colonizer discourse and Aboriginal people's own ideas of obligation and kinship.[40] The address stated that the Woiwurrung, Boonwurrung, and Daungwurrung people "send very many thanks to the Great Mother Queen for many many things," and promised they would "throw away all war-spears. No more fighting but live like white man almost." They used a familial language referring to the queen's son, and to "you, his Great Mother, Victoria." In turn, Governor Barkly promised to pass the message on to "the Queen their 'great mother,' as they call her, and her son" and assured them that she loved all her subjects and would be glad that they loved her.[41]

This document made no specific political requests, but its context makes it impossible to separate from the surrounding campaigns for a reserve. Both the Kulin and the Board seized an opportunity to advance their claims. For the Kulin, as Penny van Toorn puts it, the address was an occasion where Aboriginal people used writing to "carry their voices over the heads of local officials so they could be heard by higher authorities to whom the locals were accountable."[42] For the board, it was a chance to assert its own authority over Aboriginal affairs, which was new and contested; the previous three years had seen many arguments with colonists over funding, employment of officials, and placement of reserves. At the levée, the secretary took the opportunity to speak about the Board's hard work and meager funds and possibly hoped to advertise the success of their "civilizing" schemes.[43] If the Aboriginal presentation was groundbreaking, it was both facilitated and perhaps hemmed in by the power of the board—a power that would become stronger and less benevolent in years to come.

A month later, the government gazetted the land at Coranderrk, and messages arrived on behalf of the queen thanking them for their gifts and loyalty and expressing concern for their well-being. The Kulin concluded that appeals to the governor and the Crown could be effective and worthwhile.[44] They developed a powerful narrative of entitlement, voiced during conflicts over Coranderrk in later decades, where they portrayed the station as a grant in their traditional country delivered to them by Governor Barkly and Queen Victoria. Richard Broome comments that Aboriginal Victorians had "a powerful moral view of the world," seeing themselves as "a free people like other British subjects." In this view, a sense of connection with the Crown was immensely strengthened; "Queen Victoria, her government and settlers owed Aborigines a living because whites had occupied Aboriginal land and because Aboriginal people had agreed to "settle down" under the Queen on reserves."[45]

Meeting Prince Alfred, 1867–1868

Aboriginal people soon had a chance to get closer to royalty than they had ever been before. The Woiwurrung in 1863 had been pleased to hear that Prince Alfred, now the Duke of Edinburgh, might visit them, and five years later, he did indeed travel through the Australian colonies as part of his global journey onboard the HMS *Galatea*.[46] In each colony visited, Aboriginal people sought to make presentations to and conduct performances for the prince, indicating just how keen they were to forge stronger links with the Crown, increase their local status, and present themselves as dignified figures and equal subjects.

As it turned out, though, five years was a long time in colonial politics. In Victoria, the Central Board to Watch Over the Interests of the Aborigines had assumed greater powers by this time, and it banned Aboriginal people from townships during the royal welcomes.[47] Ostensibly, this was to prevent public drunkenness and violence, but perhaps the board also wished to avoid political demonstrations. The year before had seen successful protests by Aboriginal people around Warrnambool against the board's plan to close their station at Framlingham, while the Kulin peoples at Coranderrk had already shown their keenness to speak to the Crown.[48] As a result of the board's caution, only a few individual Aboriginal Victorians met the prince. In Tasmania, too, there was only a meeting with individuals, when Prince Alfred was greeted in Hobart by William Lanney and Truganini, who were introduced as the only surviving people of full Tasmanian descent; the "last of their race." They do not seem to have been able to make any public statements, and the people of mixed descent living in the Bass Strait islands were not considered at all.[49]

However, in several other colonies, Aboriginal people did present gifts, petitions, and performances to the prince. This took a particularly striking form in South Australia.

Founded in 1836, this colony had a reputation for being more controlled and orderly than many others; there was no convict system, and it was designed originally around the planned import of labor and sale of land. An Aboriginal protectorate had been established, along with several missions, and some Aboriginal nations, especially the Kaurna around Adelaide, had a history of friendly meetings and performances for the governor. At the same time, though, there were bloody struggles over land, as colonists spread outward with the pastoral and copper mining industries and pushed north toward the salt lakes by the 1850s. Despite some attempts at more humane governance, dispossession and depopulation continued to occur.[50]

At the same time, Aboriginal activism was emerging, comparable to that at Coranderrk in Victoria. This became especially notable at the Point Macleay Congregationalist mission, south of Adelaide, set up by George Taplin in 1859 among the Ngarrindjeri, the confederated peoples of the Lower Murray lakes. Unlike their counterparts in Victoria, the Ngarrindjeri were able to welcome Prince Alfred in November 1867. When the royal party stopped near the mission, about five hundred Ngarrindjeri gathered from the surrounding districts. Many dressed up for the occasion, the older people wearing traditional cloaks, the younger ones in European dress. They greeted the royal party with flags and cheers, and the school children gave demonstrations of weaponry and songs. The people had also written and signed an address, read out by an adolescent boy called George Pantuni, which welcomed the duke and wished him a safe journey. It explained that the old men were going to dance for him the way they used to before the white people came, but that he must not misunderstand this and think that they were "wild blacks." In fact, Pantuni continued, they had had a Christian education and gathered every Sunday "to pray to the same God and hear of the same Jesus as your Royal Highness does." He went on:

> Some have given up native customs and become real Christians, and many others are learning the way. Many of us got an honest living by working like white people. We have often been told about the Queen your mother, and we hope and pray that God will always bless her.

The duke replied that he was impressed by their progress and hoped they would continue to embrace "civilized" habits.

Later, the men painted themselves and danced for hours before a fascinated crowd. As Michael Parsons has explored, there was a long-standing practice in South Australia of Aboriginal people performing for British audiences, sometimes for money but also as a conciliatory gesture, especially toward the governor and the Crown.[51] On this occasion, the Ngarrindjeri asserted their people's connection to the monarchy, their dignity and equal subjecthood, and their engagement with missionary models of paternalism. Also apparent, however, were ongoing tensions with neighboring colonists. Taplin noted with annoyance that several settlers, notably the powerful local pastoralist John Baker, treated the Aboriginal participants dismissively, trying to control their performances and keep them away from the royal landing. Later, during a women's dance, the performers were offended when one colonist, possibly Baker, called on them to take off their clothes. "What for blackwoman do that," one asked in reply, "when whitewomen no do it?"[52] When Baker also prevented the Ngarrindjeri men from taking Alfred on a kangaroo hunt, they complained furiously to Taplin, "John Baker been steal our prince."[53]

Yet the aborted kangaroo hunt was nothing compared with the disappointment and astonishment of the Aboriginal people who gathered in Sydney to meet the prince a few months later. They, too, had been keen to meet him. George Thornton, a member of the NSW Legislative Assembly and a former Mayor of Sydney, noted their eagerness. "There are," he wrote to the Colonial Secretary in February 1868,

> a great many Native Blacks—who have come from various parts of the colony to see "the Queen's Son"—they have a great desire to see, and also to be seen by him . . . they are also desirous of being permitted to show His Royal Highness one of their "corrobborees."[54]

A month later, the New South Wales government organized a feast for Aborigines, to coincide with Prince Alfred's return to Sydney after a visit to Brisbane.[55] About three hundred men, women, and children from a variety of tribal groups had gathered, some from hundreds of miles away. The press described it as the largest Aboriginal grouping the current generation of colonists had ever seen in Sydney. On March 12, the prince visited Clontarf, on the north side of Sydney Harbour, for a picnic, at which, among other events, he would dispense gifts of clothes and blankets and watch a "corroborree."[56] Fifty years earlier, Governor Macquarie had conducted similar "native feasts," so this was something of a revival of a long-lapsed tradition.[57] Much to the dismay and anger of many Aboriginal people, the feast was disrupted in a most unexpected way, when a renegade Irishman burst out of the crowd and shot and wounded the prince.[58] The *Empire* reported that the "excitement and anger of the aborigines were as great, and more strongly expressed, than those of their white visitors."[59] A chance to assert their special connection to the Crown had been lost.

Thus, the prince's tour shows four different sets of relationships between Aboriginal people and government at work: in Victoria, a controlling protectionism; in Tasmania, the sense of impending extinction and the exclusion of mixed-race people from the category of "Aboriginal"; and in South Australia, the importance of the mission in a district where colonization was relatively thin. In New South Wales, where older practices of paternalism and protection had long fallen into disuse under the belief that Aboriginal people would soon be extinct, a government had to revive older practices for the royal occasion. Throughout it all, however, was the common feature of Aboriginal people's interest in a stronger relationship with the monarchy.

Petitioning for Land, 1870s and 1880s

During the 1870s and early 1880s, as political struggles over land intensified, various Aboriginal groups petitioned the governors of their colonies for land, sometimes with success. In South Australia in early 1872, Taplin and the Point Macleay residents, backed by the local Aborigines' Friends Association, lobbied the Commissioner of Crown Lands to expand their station, and when this failed (partly because of settler opposition), they petitioned Governor James Fergusson, "praying for the land which the committee has applied for."[60] Frustratingly, very few details of this petition—the first of its kind in South Australia—appear to have survived. Accompanied by lobbying from the AFA, however, it seems to have succeeded, as the government granted a new license for the land requested at Point Macleay in July 1872.[61]

Meanwhile, in the colony of Victoria, the struggles of the Coranderrk residents were continuing. From the late 1860s onward, they fought repeated interference by the Aboriginal Protection Board (which had replaced the earlier board). This body was becoming ever more dismissive of Kulin peoples and cultures and more sympathetic toward the pastoralist lobby, some members of which were calling for the reserve to be flung open for their own selection.[62] In their efforts to secure the land and assert their autonomy, the residents proved to be skillful and determined activists. When the board in 1874 forced popular missionaries, John and Mary Green, off the station, the residents lobbied board members, politicians, the press, and sympathetic colonists for over a decade.[63] Between 1875 and 1881, four delegations walked the sixty kilometers to Melbourne, sometimes without food or in poor health, to complain about their treatment.[64] The board often received them rudely, even threatening them with expulsion from Coranderrk. Indeed, this activism so irked the board that it twice hired detectives in an attempt to prove that the residents had not written the letters and petitions themselves. The documents proved genuine.[65]

In July 1881, the new government, led by Bryan O'Loghlen, responded to residents' complaints by ordering a parliamentary inquiry.[66] Twenty-two Aboriginal witnesses, many of them senior members of the community, spoke assertively to the inquiry about the poor diet and living conditions at Coranderrk, their wish to retain the land, and their demand that John Green be allowed to return. In addition, they sent two petitions and eleven written statements.[67] One of the petitions was signed by fifteen men, and the other by forty-six people, twenty of them women; Penny van Toorn suggests that traditional distinctions of gender and age influenced who signed which petitions, and the order of names.[68] The document stated:

> We want the Board and the Inspector, Captain Page, to be no longer over us. We want only one man here, and that is Mr. John Green, and the station to be under the Chief Secretary; then we will show the country that the station could self-support itself.[69]

Richard Broome has argued that mutuality and "right behavior" were vital on Coranderrk and informed their political campaigns.[70] When former chief minister, Graham Berry, left Victoria in 1886, he was bid farewell by a group from Coranderrk, who walked into Melbourne again to present him with gifts of weapons and handicrafts—the tactics of 1863 were still in evidence. One of their white supporters, Annie Bon, pointed out that it had been twenty-three years since these people made their presentation to the governor and the queen, and that not enough had been done since to support them. An address was read out, apparently dictated by Woiwurrung leader William Barak, reiterating how Berry had helped them when "the board would not give us much food and clothes and wanted to drive us off the land . . . you gave us the land for our own as long as we live."[71] Thus, connections with senior politicians and the Crown remained personal, strategic, and significant.

As in Tasmania over thirty years earlier, the petitioners won the battle but not the war. The inquiry criticized the board's running of the station and recommended keeping Coranderrk open with improved conditions. It also recommended, however, that the "half-castes" be sent away to work. This was a way of cutting the budget and removing many younger activists. This trend culminated five years later in the 1886 Aborigines Protection Act, which required all "half-castes" over the age of thirteen to leave the settlement, thus splitting up families and weakening the community.[72]

Petitioning in New South Wales

In New South Wales, there was not the same tradition of petitioning as in the other colonies. After the introduction of responsible government in 1856, there was minimal government policy of any kind, in an expectation that Aboriginal people would disappear altogether, and indeed, population decline had been catastrophic. Since the closure of a number of missions in the 1840s, there had been little of the desire to control and civilize Aboriginal people that had been so apparent in Victoria and South Australia. Apart from an annual blanket distribution and some small medical aid, governments did very little.

There were, nevertheless, the beginnings of petitioning in the 1860s. In 1865 and 1867, several Aboriginal people, probably of the Yuin nation on the South Coast, unsuccessfully petitioned for boats for fishing.[73] The next petition for a boat—from "Currigan, or Captain, Aboriginal" of the Cooks River—was granted, probably because it was made in the context of Prince Alfred's visit to Sydney.[74] After this, requests for boats increased, and some of them succeeded.[75] There appears to have been a pattern of the petitioners working with local sympathetic settlers to help them formulate the request and send it to Sydney.

In 1881, when petitioning and protest by the Aboriginal residents at Coranderrk were at a peak, New South Wales saw its own petition for land, one that was later to become the most well known of them all. This was the Maloga petition, addressed to the governor of New South Wales by the Yorta Yorta people resident at the Maloga Mission, on the New South Wales side of the Murray River. As in the other colonies, the petitioners worked with a missionary. Daniel Matthews had begun the Maloga mission as a private venture in 1874, intermittently at first but permanently from 1876. The people he attracted were mainly Yorta Yorta from the Murray-Goulburn-Edwards river basin. Where the Kulin at Coranderrk were by this time experiencing too much official intervention from the Victorian authorities, the Yorta Yorta at Maloga were encountering almost complete indifference from the government of New South Wales. The mission relied on public donations and the earnings of the Aboriginal men at nearby sheep and cattle stations. Occasionally it ran out of money completely, and Matthews was forced to ask the men to leave, to survive through fishing or working on neighboring stations. Keen to keep the mission together, Matthews lobbied the Sydney government hard for support. On one visit in October 1878, he instigated the Committee to Aid the Maloga Mission, a body that eighteen months later became the more broadly defined Aborigines Protection Association (APA). It succeeded in gaining some small government grants for Maloga, but nothing substantial or continuing.[76] On April 1, 1881, Matthews wrote in his diary, "Our store is frequently empty."[77] Something had to be done.

In April, the men at Maloga drew up a petition to Governor Augustus Loftus requesting land. Though they identified themselves on the document in European terms as "members of the Moira and Ulupna tribes" (referring to local pastoral stations), many of them were Yorta Yorta and some were Pangerang.[78] Most of the forty-two signatories signed their names; only one used his mark.[79] The petition began with a grievance:

That all the land within our tribal boundaries has been taken possession of by the Government and white settlers; our hunting grounds are used for sheep pasturage and the game reduced and in many places exterminated, rendering our means of subsistence extremely precarious, and often reducing us and our wives and children to beggary.

It went on to offer a promise:

> We, the men of our several tribes, are desirous of honestly maintaining our
> young and infirm, who are in many cases the subjects of extreme want and
> semi-starvation, and we believe we could, in a few years support ourselves by
> our own industry, were a sufficient area of land granted to us to cultivate and
> raise stock.

The promise was not only one of being self-sufficient, but also of behaving in a respectable British manner:

> We have been under training for some years and feel that our old mode of life
> is not in keeping with the instructions we have received and we are earnestly
> desirous of settling down to more orderly habits of industry, that we may form
> homes for our families.

In what appears to be a clear reference to the success of Coranderrk, the petitioners reminded the governor that when Aboriginal people in other colonies had been granted suitable land, they had "proved capable of supporting themselves."

The petitioners and Daniel Matthews each had reasons for wanting the grant of land adjoining Maloga mission. For Matthews, it would lay the foundation for a more secure institution, with stronger official backing. For the Yorta Yorta petitioners, it would guarantee them a future on their own land, and possibly freedom from Matthews' interference in their lives and cultural practices. Knowledge of whom to petition and how to frame a petition came most likely from Matthews, but probably also from Coranderrk activists visiting or living at Maloga.[80] William Barak, the senior man who had led the Coranderrk deputations to Melbourne, was visiting Maloga when the people there were formulating their petition; indeed, one of the signatories, David Berrick, was his son.[81]

Preparing the petition was one thing; putting it in the hands of the relevant authorities quite another. The Governor of New South Wales was much further away (around five hundred miles by land; a three-day journey by train and wagon) than the mere sixty miles separating the Victorian government and the Coranderrk residents. Unable to present the petition themselves, as Aboriginal delegates often preferred to do, the Maloga residents had to entrust the document to Matthews, who made the long journey to Sydney. He took the petition to the *Sydney Morning Herald*, which printed it with supportive comments on July 2, and to the *Daily Telegraph*, also sympathetic, which printed it on July 5, the same day he presented it to the governor.[82] After much pressure, and perhaps in response to the newspaper publicity, government officials finally received an APA deputation, which drew attention to the petition to the governor and "the necessity for a grant of land for the blacks at Maloga."[83] However, when a second deputation visited the Minister for Lands on July 18, they found him entirely unsympathetic.[84] No grant of land was forthcoming, and it seemed the petition had failed.

Within two years, however, in response to APA pressure and the evident need of the increasing number of Aboriginal people moving into Sydney, the New South Wales government began to develop policies closer to those of the southern colony of Victoria. The government appointed a Protector of Aborigines and promised to establish reserves for Aboriginal protection, education, and civilization.[85] On April 9, 1883, a reserve of eighteen hundred acres on the requested land was announced in a gazette.[86] This land became the site of a government station, Cumeroogunja, soon to become one of the most successful in southeastern Australia. Many Maloga residents moved there throughout the 1880s, and it replaced the Maloga mission altogether in 1888.

Much more recently, this petition became famous in the context of the failed *Yorta Yorta* Native Title claim. Under the Native Title Act of 1993, the Yorta Yorta claimed traditional land on both the northern and southern sides of the Murray River (which separated Victoria from New South Wales). The Federal Court rejected their application in 1998, and the High Court their appeal in 2002. In their original application, the Yorta Yorta had quoted the 1881 petition to support their claim of continuous occupation of the land in question, and as evidence of a long history of their efforts to obtain land. The strategy backfired when Judge Olney took the view that the petition proved that by the 1880s the Yorta Yorta had ceased to observe those laws and customs based on tradition that were necessary for a successful native title claim. The judge concluded that while "there can be little doubt that Matthews would have played a part in the composition and presentation of the petition," there was no suggestion that it misrepresented the views or aspirations of the Maloga residents themselves.[87]

Judge Olney's reading is open to question. The Maloga petition is a complex multivalent text, articulating a number of different grievances, histories, and desires. When it accuses "the Government and white settlers" of taking the land and undermining the people's means of subsistence, reducing them to semistarvation and beggary, it represents both the Yorta Yorta and Matthews. When it seeks a grant of land enabling self-sufficient farming, not as part of "our old mode of life" but to enable the growth of "more orderly habits of industry," it melds the petitioners' desires for autonomy and independence with the missionary desire for a new, civilized, and Christian mode of life. While the petition is not in itself evidence of what traditional practices did or did not survive on Maloga, it does point to the continuing importance of family, identity, security, and freedom.

Conclusion

Aboriginal petitioners of the middle decades of the nineteenth century were constrained by their dispossession and deprived circumstances, but still they managed to assert their demands, sometimes successfully. They learned where power lay, and they never lost sight of those authorities closest to them, seeking to draw them into patterns of mutual and personal obligation. At the same time, they attempted to venture as high up the British hierarchy as possible, appealing to a sense of compassion and responsibility from the governor and the monarch. They knew that these higher authority figures could sometimes press lower and local ones into action, even when it was the latter who held primary responsibility. The petitions combined local Aboriginal cultures, with their emphasis on reciprocity, family relationships, and mutual obligation, with an expectation (also held by other indigenous peoples worldwide) that support was more likely to come from the imperial center than from local settlers and officials. In Australian Aboriginal petitions are traces of the appeals to paternalism and obligation, combinations of assertiveness and submissiveness, and uses of Christian language that were features of claim making that had occurred, and was still occurring, in many other imperial settings. These documents and performances were shaped by mixed elements of global Britishness, Christianity, and Aboriginal cultural distinctiveness. In these mid–nineteenth century petitions are the origins of strategies of appealing to international opinion, legal bodies, and the British monarchy that Aboriginal Australians continue to use to this day. In their maintenance of community, family, and identity, they have asserted a discursive and symbolic power in modern Australian society, and they have not allowed a generally rapacious and uncaring settler society to destroy them.

NOTES

1. *Argus*, May 27, 1863: 5.
2. In this essay, we identify people by their particular locations and clans wherever possible. When referring to Australian indigenous people in general, or where more precise terms are unknown, we have used the term "Aboriginal".
3. Louise Hall and Jessica Mahar, "How Willie Wombat Charmed the Block," *Sydney Morning Herald (SHM)*, January 20, 2010. See also J. L. Cohen, "Pemulwuy (c. 1750–1802)," *Australian Dictionary of Biography (supplementary volume)* (Melbourne: Melbourne University Press 2005), 318–319.
4. As Jane Lydon comments, for Aboriginal people, "meetings constituted performances"; dancing with strangers "expressed a formal relationship and was a key form of communication." Jane Lydon, *Eye Contact: Photographing Indigenous Australians* (Durham: Duke University Press, 2005), 27.
5. Bain Attwood, *Rights for Aborigines* (Sydney: Allen and Unwin, 2003); Diane E. Barwick, *Rebellion at Coranderrk* (Canberra: Aboriginal History Inc, 1998); Diane Barwick,

"Coranderrk and Cumeroogunga: Pioneers and Policy," *Opportunity and Response: Case Studies in Economic Development*, ed., T. Scarlett Epstein and David H. Penny (London: C. Hurst and Company, 1972); Ravi de Costa, "Identity, Authority, and the Moral Worlds of Indigenous Petitions," *Comparative Studies in Society and History*, 48(3) (2006): 669–698; Lydon, *Eye Contact*; Henry Reynolds, *Fate of a Free People* (Ringwood: Penguin, 1995).

6. See Stuart Banner, *Possessing the Pacific: Land, Settlers, and Indigenous People from Australia to Alaska* (Cambridge, MA: Harvard University Press, 2007), esp. 1–46; Bain Attwood, *Possession: Batman's Treaty and the Matter of History* (Carlton, Victoria, Australia: Miegunyah Press, 2009), 2, 4, 18–32, 94.

7. While the constitutions of Victoria, New South Wales, South Australia, and Tasmania did not explicitly exclude Aboriginal men from voting, in practice Aboriginal men were deterred by isolation, disinformation, and low literacy, as well as electoral laws excluding itinerant men and recipients of charity. See John Chesterman and Brian Galligan, *Citizens without Rights: Aborigines and Australian Citizenship* (Cambridge: Cambridge University Press, 1997), 14; Anna Doukakis, *The Aboriginal People, Parliament & "Protection" in New South Wales 1856–1916* (Sydney: Federation Press, 2006), 5; Julie Evans, Patricia Grimshaw, David Phillips, and Shurlee Swain, *Equal Subjects, Unequal rights: Indigenous Peoples in British Settler Colonies* (Manchester: Manchester University Press, 2003), 70; Murray Goot, "The Aboriginal Franchise and Its Consequences," *Australian Journal of Politics and History*, 52(4) (2006): 520–521.

8. See Susan Zaeske, *Signatures of Citizenship: Petitioning, Antislavery and Women's Political Identity* (Chapel Hill: University of North Carolina Press, 2003), 3–4.

9. David Zaret, "Petitions and "Invention" of Public Opinion in the English Revolution," *The American Journal of Sociology*, 101(6) (May, 1996): 1497–1555, quote on 1514.

10. de Costa, "Identity, Authority, and the Moral Worlds," 670.

11. Zaret, "Petitions and "Invention" of Public Opinion."

12. Paul Pickering, "Loyalty and Rebellion in Colonial Politics: The Campaign against Convict Transportation in Australia," *Rediscovering the British World*, eds., Philip Alfred Buckner and R. Douglas Francis (Calgary, Alberta, Canada: University of Calgary Press, 2005), 87–107, quote on 102. See also, David Nicholls, "Addressing God as Ruler: Prayer and Petition," *British Journal of Sociology* 44, 1 (1993): 138; Paul A. Pickering, "'And Your Petitioners &c": Chartist Petitioning in Popular Politics, 1838–48," *English Historical Review*, 116, 466 (2001): 368–88, esp. 371; Paul Pickering, " 'The Hearts of Millions': Chartism and Popular Monarchism in the 1840s," *History*, 88, 290 (2003): 227; Alex Tyrell with Yvonne Ward, " "God Bless Her Little Majesty": The Popularising of Monarchy in the 1840s," *National Identities* 2, 2 (2000): 118; Carol Wilton, *Popular Politics and Popular Culture in Upper Canada, 1800–1850* (Montreal and Kingston: McGill-Queen's University Press, 2000), 55; Zaeske, *Signatures of Citizenship*, 21–22.

13. Stephen A. Higginson, "A Short History of the Right to Petition Government for the Redress of Grievances," *The Yale Law Journal*, 96, 1 (1986): 142–166; Wilton, *Popular Politics and Popular Culture*.

14. For some examples, see J. B. Hirst, *The Strange Birth of Colonial Democracy: New South Wales 1848–1884* (Sydney: Allen & Unwin, 1988), 25, 46; Terry Irving, *The Southern Tree of Liberty: The Democratic Movement in New South Wales before 1856* (Sydney: Federation Press, 2006), 42–49; Pickering, "Loyalty and Rebellion in Colonial Politics," 87–107.

15. Wilton, *Popular Politics and Popular Culture*, 21–22, 60–62.

16. Potukuchi Swarnalatha, "Revolt, Testimony, Petition: Artisanal Protests in Colonial Andhra," *International Review of Social History*, 46(2001): 109, 121, 128.

17. Jim Miller, "Petitioning the Great White Mother: First Nations Organizations And Lobbying in London," *Reflections on Native-Newcomer Relations: Selected Essays*, ed., Jim Miller (Toronto: University of Toronto Press, 2004), 217–241.

18. Ian Radforth, "Performance, Politics and Representation: Aboriginal People and the 1860 Royal Tour of Canada," *Canadian Historical Review*, 84, 1 (2003): 19–22; M. P. K. Sorrenson, *A History of Maori Representation in Parliament* (Wellington, 1986), 24–26.

19. Richard Broome, "'There were vegetables every year Mr Green was here': Right Behaviour and the Struggle for Autonomy at Coranderrk Aboriginal Reserve," *History Australia*, 3, 2 (2006): 43.1–43.16, quote on 43.4.

20. Reynolds, *Fate of a Free People*, 156–157. For a different evaluation of Robinson's promises, see James Boyce, *Van Diemen's Land* (Melbourne: Black Inc, 2008), 284–296.

21. *Colonial Times*, January 11, 1832, 2. See also N. J. B. Plomley, *Friendly Mission: The Tasmanian Journals and Papers of George Augustus Robinson* (Launceston, Australia: Queen Victoria Museum and Art Gallery, 1966), 605.

22. Reynolds, *Fate of a Free People*, 156–162; Lyndall Ryan, *The Aboriginal Tasmanians* (Sydney, Australia: Allen and Unwin, 1994), 179, 185.

23. Walter George Arthur to George Augustus Robinson, February 1, 1847, also Arthur to Robinson, July 5, 1843, *Weep in Silence: A History of the Flinders Island Aboriginal Settlement*, ed., N. J. B. Plomley (Hobart, Australia: Blubber Head Press, 1987), 1014–1015. Spelling and grammar from the original.

24. Reynolds, *Fate of a Free People*, 7–8.

25. Walter George Arthur to G.W. Walker, December 30, 1845, Mary Ann Arthur to Colonial Secretary of Van Diemens Land, December 30, 1845, Walter George Arthur to Colonial Secretary of V.D.L., June 15, 1846, *Struggle for Aboriginal Rights: A Documentary History*, eds., Bain Attwood and Andrew Markus (NSW: Allen & Unwin, 1999), 38–41; Reynolds, *Fate of a Free People*, 12, 25.

26. Ryan, *The Aboriginal Tasmanians*, 201.

27. Reynolds, *Fate of a Free People*, 9–19; Ryan, *Aboriginal Tasmanians*, 197.

28. Reynolds, *Fate of a Free People*, 7–8.

29. Penny Van Toorn, *Writing Never Arrives Naked: Early Aboriginal Cultures of Writing in Australia* (Canberra, Australia: Aboriginal Studies Press, 2006), 122.

30. Reynolds, *Fate of a Free People*, 14–15; Ryan, *The Aboriginal Tasmanians*, 201–202.

31. Ryan, *The Aboriginal Tasmanians*, 203.

32. Barwick, *Rebellion at Coranderrk*, 20–25; Attwood, *Possession*, 36–58.

33. Francis Tuckfield to General Secretaries, September 30, 1840, Wesleyan Methodist Missionary Society, *Archive: Australasia 1812–1889 (WMMS)*, Mp2107 (Record ID: 133095), reel 2, National Library of Australia (NLA); Francis Tuckfield to the General Secretaries, WMMS, June 31, 1840, in Francis Tuckfield, *Journal, 1837–1842 (FTJ)*, MS11341, Box 655, State Library of Victoria (SLV).

34. James Dredge, November 27, 1841, December 4, 1841, *James Dredge, Diaries, Notebook and Letterbooks, 1817–1845 (JDD)*, MS11625, MSM534, SLV.

35. William Thomas to G. A. Robinson, December 1, 1843, PROV VPRS4410 unit 3, 1843/78 (reel 2), Public Records Office of Victoria.

36. *Argus*, March 9, 1859, 4; Barwick, *Rebellion at Coranderrk*, 40; *Geelong Advertiser*, March 9, 1859, 2; *Ovens and Murray Advertiser*, March 10, 1859, 3.

37. William Thomas, February 28–29, 1859, March 4, 1859, March 16–18, 1859, March 23, 1859, April 13, 1859, June 5, 1859, June 10–11, 1859, *William Thomas Journal and Papers, 1850–59, (WTP)* ML MSS 214/5 (microfilm CY3127), Mitchell Library; William Thomas, March 2–4,

1859, March 13–19, 1859, *William Thomas Reports 1845–62*, ML MSS 214/6–7 (microfilm CY3078), Mitchell Library.

38. Attwood, *Rights for Aborigines*, 9; Barwick, *Rebellion at Coranderrk*, 41, 51, 58; Richard Broome, *Aboriginal Victorians: A History Since 1800* (Sydney, Australia: Allen & Unwin, 2005), 124–125; William Thomas to the Commissioner of Lands and Survey, March 4, 1859 and William Thomas to Robert Brough Smyth, October 5, 1860, *The Struggle for Aboriginal Rights*, ed., Attwood and Markus, 41–43; William Thomas, July 11–12, 1859, July 19, 1859, August 6–8, 1859, August 12–13, 1859, *WTP*, ML MSS 214/5 (microfilm CY3127); *Victoria: First Report of the Central Board Appointed to Watch Over the Interests of the Aborigines in the Colony of Victoria* (Melbourne, Australia: John Ferres, 1861), 5.

39. *Argus*, May 27, 1863, 5; *Age*, May 27, 1863, 4; *Herald*, May 27, 1863, 2; Robert Brough Smyth to William Thomas, May 22, 1863, and William Thomas to Robert Brough Smyth, May 27, 1863, in *William Thomas Correspondence, returns etc*, 1863, ML MSS214/19 microfilm CY3104, Mitchell Library; William Thomas, May 25–26, 1863, *William Thomas Journal and Papers*, 1860–1867, ML MSS214/5 microfilm CY3128; *Victoria: Third Report of the Central Board Appointed to Watch Over the Interests of the Aborigines in the Colony of Victoria* (Melbourne, Australia: John Ferres, 1863), 11.

40. Barwick, *Rebellion of Coranderrk*, 66; Attwood, *Rights for Aborigines*, 16; Lydon, *Eye Contact*, 39–43.

41. *Argus*, May 27, 1863, 5; William Thomas, May 26, 1863, *WTJ*, 1860–1867, ML MSS 214/5.

42. Van Toorn, *Writing never arrives naked*, 125.

43. *Argus*, February 18, 1864, 5, May 27, 1863, 5; *Herald*, May 27, 1863, 2; *Leader: A Weekly Journal of News, Politics, Literature and Art*, no. 387, vol. X, May 30, 1863, 6–7.

44. Barwick, *Rebellion at Coranderrk*, 66; Van Toorn, *Writing never arrives naked*, 6.

45. Broome, *Aboriginal Victorians*, 129. See also, Barwick, *Rebellion at Coranderrk*, 66; Van Toorn, *Writing Never Arrives Naked*, 125.

46. Cindy McCreery, "A British Prince and a Transnational Life: Alfred, duke of Edinburgh's visit to Australia, 1867–8," *Transnational Ties: Australian Lives in the World*, eds., Desley Deacon, Penny Russell, and Angela Woollacott (Canberra, NZ: ANU E-press, 2008), 57–74; Cindy McCreery, "'Long may he float on the ocean of life': the first royal visit to Tasmania, 1868," *Tasmanian Historical Studies*, 12 (2007): 19–42; Cindy McCreery, "The Voyage of the Duke of Edinburgh in HMS Galatea to Australia, 1867–8," *Exploring the British World*, eds., Kate Darian-Smith, Patricia Grimshaw, Keira Lindsey, and Stuart Macintyre (Melbourne, Australia: RMIT Publishing, 2004): 959–978.

47. *Argus*, October 28, 1867, 5; Ian D. Clark, "The northern Wathawurrung and Andrew Porteous, 1860–1877," *Aboriginal History*, 32 (2008): 97, 101–107; *Victoria: Sixth Report of the Central Board*, 1869, 34.

48. Jan Critchett, *Our Land Till We Die: A History of the Framlingham Aborigines* (Warrnambool, Australia: Deakin University Press, 1980, this ed. 1992), 14.

49. McCreery, "Long may he float," 37; *Mercury*, January 10, 1868, 2.

50. Peggy Brock, "South Australia," *Contested Ground: Australian Aborigines Under the British Crown*, ed., Ann McGrath (St. Leonards: Allen & Unwin, 1995), 208–222; Robert Foster, "Feasts of the Full-Moon: The Distribution of Rations to Aborigines in South Australia, 1836–1861," *Aboriginal History*, 13 (1989): 63–78.

51. Michael Parsons, "The tourist corroboree in South Australia to 1911," *Aboriginal History*, 21 (1997): 46–69.

52. Account reproduced in the *Argus*, November 19, 1867, 5; George Taplin, *Diaries*, November 3–11, 1867, PRG 186-1/12, vol. 6, fiche 4 of 5 (in the Edith Gertrude Beaumont Papers, State

Library of South Australia). Also, Graham Jenkin, *Conquest of the Ngarrindjeri* (Adelaide: Rigby, 1979), 85–95, 151; J. D. Woods, *The Native Tribes of South Australia* (Adelaide, Australia: E.S. Wigg & Son, 1879), 111–113.

53. Taplin, *Diaries*, November 11–13, 1867. See also Jenkin, *Conquest of the Ngarrindjeri*, 83–86; David Sampson, *Strangers in a Strange Land: The 1868 Aborigines and other Indigenous Performers in Mid-Victorian Britain* (Ph.D. thesis, University of Technology Sydney, 2000): 141, http://adt.lib.uts.edu.au./public/adt-NTSM20050509.160844.

54. Quoted in Sampson, *Strangers in a Strange Land*, 141.

55. In Brisbane, too, the prince was greeted by Aboriginal people, painted and carrying traditional weapons, invited by the organizers. Constance Campbell Petrie, *Tom Petrie's Reminiscences of Early Queensland* (Brisbane, Australia: Watson, Ferguson & Co., 1904, this ed. 1981), 210–212; *Queensland Daily Guardian*, February 25, 1868, 2; *Queenslander*, February 29, 1868, 2.

56. *Argus*, March 30, 1868, 1 supplement; April 1, 1868, 5; *Brisbane Courier*, March 4, 1868, 2; *Sydney Mail*, March 14, 1868, 4; *Sydney Morning Herald*, March 12, 1868, 4. Concerning the clothes and blankets, see George Thornton to Colonial Secretary, February 27, 1868, Colonial Secretary's In Letters, no 68/1137, State Records NSW, 4/619.

57. R. H. W. Reece, "Feasts and Blankets: The History of Some Early Attempts to Establish Relations with the Aborigines of New South Wales, 1814–1846," *Archaeology and Physical Anthropology in Oceania*, II, 3 (October 1967): 190–206.

58. *SMH*, March 13, 1881.

59. *Empire*, undated, as reproduced in the *Argus*, April 1, 1868, 5; *SMH*, March 13, 1868. See also John Milner and Oswald W. Brierly, *The Cruise of HMS Galatea, Captain H.R.H. the Duke of Edinburgh, K.G., in 1867–1868* (London: WH Allen and Co, 1869), 406.

60. Aborigines' Friends Association, *The Fourteenth Annual Report of the Aborigines' Friends' Association* (Adelaide, Australia: John Thomas Shawyer, 1872), 4; Jenkin, *Conquest of the Ngarrindjeri*, 45, 79, 128–129; Taplin, *Diaries*, April 30, 1872, PRG 186-1/12, vol. 7, 5/10 fiche.

61. Jenkin, *Conquest of the Ngarrindjeri*, 128–129.

62. Attwood, *Rights for Aborigines*, 12–13; Lydon, *Eye Contact*, 18.

63. *Argus*, February 24, 1876, 5; Attwood, *Rights for Aborigines*, 10–12, 15–21; Barwick, *Rebellion at Coranderrk*, 88, 105, 108, 128; Broome, *Aboriginal Victorians*, 169–170, 175, 180; Broome, "There were vegetables every year Mr Green was here," 42.13; Penny van Toorn, "Authors, scribes and owners: The sociology of nineteenth-century Aboriginal writing on Coranderrk and Lake Condah reserves," *Continuum*, 13, 3 (1999): 335, 340.

64. Van Toorn, "Authors, scribes and owners," 35; Barwick, *Rebellion at Coranderrk*, 107, 128, 161, 178.

65. Van Toorn, "Authors, scribes and owners," 336.

66. Broome, *Aboriginal Victorians*, 172.

67. Broome, "There were vegetables every year Mr Green was here," 43.6.

68. Van Toorn, "Authors, scribes, and owners," 338; Van Toorn, *Writing Never Arrives Naked*, 131–132.

69. Victoria Board appointed to enquire into, and report upon, the present condition and management of the Coranderrk Aboriginal Station, *Coranderrk Aboriginal Station: Report of the Board appointed to etc* (Melbourne, Australia: John Ferres, 1882), 98, petition dated November 16, 1881.

70. Broome, "There were vegetables every year Mr Green was here," 43.2–43.7.

71. *Argus*, March 25, 1886, 7.

72. Attwood, *Rights for Aborigines*, 28; Broome, *Aboriginal Victorians*, 171–172; Broome, "There were vegetables every year Mr Green was here," 43.5–43.6; Lydon, *Eye Contact*, 20–22; Victoria, Board, *Coranderrk Aboriginal Station*, for example: iii–v, 6–9, 14–18, 22, 25, 28, 69.

73. The Minister for Lands, Robertson, in refusing the petition, had commented that there was real doubt "whether the petitioners would be capable of taking care of a boat." Minister for Lands, memo attached "Nanny" and "Lucy" to Sec. Lands, undated, Lands In Letters no 65/6042, State Records NSW, 3693.

74. Petition "Currigan, or Captain, Aboriginal," to Governor Belmore, June 5, 1868, Colonial Secretary's In Letters, no. 68/2995, State Records NSW, 4/626.

75. Thomas Grieve, Senior Constable, Nowra, to Officer-in-Charge-of-Police, June 23, 1876, Colonial Secretary's In Letters, no. 76/4523, encl. with no 76/4876, State Records NSW, 1/2335.

76. *SMH*, October 15, 1878, February 17, 1880.

77. Daniel Matthews, *Seventh Report of the Maloga Aboriginal Mission Station, Murray River, New South Wales* (Echuca: Riverine Herald, 1882), copy in Matthews Papers, National Library of Australia, MS 2195.

78. Barwick, *Rebellion at Coranderrk*, 255.

79. Nancy Cato, *Mister Maloga: Daniel Matthews and his Maloga Mission* (Brisbane, Australia: University of Queensland Press, 1976), 386.

80. Barwick, *Rebellion at Coranderrk*, 302; Attwood, *Rights for Aborigines*, 27. See entry for April 19, 1879, Matthews Diaries, quoted in Cato, *Mister Maloga*, 121.

81. Barwick, *Rebellion at Coranderrk*, 255, esp. n.52.

82. Entries for May 25 and June 30, 1881, Matthews Diary; Report of APA meeting, July 7, in *SMH*, July 9, 1881; *Daily Telegraph* (Sydney), July 5, 1881.

83. Report on NSW Aborigines Protection Association meeting, July 8, *SMH*, July 9, 1881.

84. Entry for July 18, 1881, Matthews Diary.

85. See Ann Curthoys, "Good Christians and Useful Workers: Aborigines, church and state in NSW 1870–1883" in Sydney Labour History Group, *What Rough Beast? The state and social order in Australian History* (Sydney: George Allen & Unwin, 1982), 31–56.

86. Cato, *Mister Maloga*, 131.

87. Members of the *Yorta Yorta* Aboriginal Community v Victoria & Ors [1998] Federal Court of Australia 1606 (December 18, 1998), para. 121, accessed September 3, 2010, at http://www.austlii.edu.au/cgi-bin/sinodisp/au/cases/cth/FCA/1998/1606.html?stem=o& synonyms=0&query=Members%20of%20the%20Yorta%20Yorta%20Aboriginal%20 Community%20v%20Victoria.

9

THE NATIVE LAND COURT
MAKING PROPERTY IN
NINETEENTH-CENTURY NEW ZEALAND

Christopher Hilliard

The Native Land Court began hearing cases in 1865, after the most important of the wars that gave real substance to British sovereignty over New Zealand.[1] There had been small communities of non-Māori—whalers, sealers, traders, missionaries—in New Zealand for decades before the British annexed it in 1840, and the exiguous military and financial resources of the colonial government meant that indigenous authorities continued to prevail in most places. Nevertheless, after 1840 there was a steady influx of colonists, and pressure on the government to make more land available for them. Under the Treaty of Waitangi, the basis for annexation by Britain, only the government could buy Māori land, so as to minimize the problem of fraudulent or predatory land deals. This made land even more of a national political issue than it would otherwise have been. By the late 1850s, land sales were being resisted by individual chiefs and by the Kīngitanga, a pantribal movement led by a Māori "king," which opposed further land sales within its borders and functioned as a quasi-state, with its own police force, Māori-language newspaper, and postage stamps.[2] The Kīngitanga's lands, in the Waikato region south of Auckland, were among the most fertile in the country. For the colonial government as well as the Kīngitanga, land and authority were entwined, and when the government invaded the king's territory in 1863 and ultimately forced the tribes under the Kīngitanga's banner to quit the Waikato, it took the most important step toward effective authority over the islands of New Zealand.[3]

The New Zealand Wars closed off what Richard White, in a North American context, has called "the middle ground"—a system of "accommodation" in which white people "could neither dictate to" the indigenous people "nor ignore them."[4] Land was confiscated from tribes involved, and the government's monopoly on land purchases was abandoned. In peacetime, the colonial land transfer system had to reckon with indigenous forms of tenure. The Māori population in the North Island had sizable concentrations and could not be treated as nomadic. Indeed, this is really a story about only one of New Zealand's two main islands. Questions of land and settlement in the sparsely populated South Island were broadly comparable to those in other parts of the second British empire, and the South Island was cited alongside New South Wales when those making policy for the East Africa Protectorate later in the nineteenth century considered the dangers of squatting and land monopolism.[5]

The Native Land Court apportioned shares in a particular block of land on the basis of competing histories narrated to the court by interested tribes and kin groups. At first, under the rules of the court's architect, Francis Dart Fenton, title was vested in ten tribal owners with the intention of shoring up the authority of established chiefs.[6] In the early 1870s, Fenton's rival, the Native Minister Donald McLean, overhauled the court. The Native Land Act of 1873 replaced the ten-owner system with one of complete individualization of title. A memorial of ownership recorded all the "shareholders" in a block. If one member of a larger tribal grouping went to court to secure title with a view to selling land, representatives of other families and tribes were compelled to join in the proceedings lest they lose their interests in the land.[7] Judges would weigh the competing histories and then allocate shares in the block. Fenton was the only judge appointed in the 1860s and 1870s to have a legal training; most of the others were Europeans with histories of interaction with Māori communities (which Fenton also had).[8] The judges were assisted by interpreters, Māori-speaking clerks, and Māori "assessors"—chiefs who sat on the bench to advise, and help legitimate, the European judges. Claimants at a hearing had to establish their connection to the land in question through recitations of *whakapapa* (genealogy) or detailed descriptions of "how they and their recent ancestors had lived on the land—indicating burial places, cultivations, houses and other signs of settlement."[9] The records generated by the process were later used by anthropological researchers, and many New Zealand anthropologists active between the 1880s and the 1920s cut their teeth on work for the court.[10]

This "unique institution" was a state application of ethnographic knowledge quite different from those most familiar in the historiography of imperialism and anthropology: attempts to police, or formulate, categories such as race and caste; and efforts to adjust policies on labor or public health in the light of indigenous custom or the purported psychological traits of particular tribes or peoples.[11] Despite its distinctive character, the Native Land Court's ethnographic nature appears quite unremarkable to New Zealand researchers who, in academic work and in investigations undertaken as part of the Treaty of Waitangi claims process (as the Waitangi Tribunal and other government and quasi-governmental bodies investigate alleged historical breaches of the Crown's treaty obligations to Māori), have produced a corpus of extraordinarily concrete and nuanced work on the operations of the court.[12] The Native Land Court's ethnographic quality also passes without comment in the American legal scholar Stuart Banner's comparative study, *Possessing the Pacific*.[13] These historians seldom register any surprise that tribal narratives and the rehearsal of local knowledge became central to the resolution of property claims (or rather, to the process of enabling land to be claimed *as* property) in a settler colony *after* the middle ground had closed, when settlers' willingness to accommodate indigenous ways in the areas of law, medicine, and education was greatly diminished.

This chapter is an attempt to make sense of the interactions of Māori self-representations and colonial law in the Native Land Court. The first section places the framing and operation of the court in the context of race and politics in nineteenth-century New Zealand. Next, the chapter focuses on a particular case to bring out the ethnographic nature and cross-examination procedures of the court. The final section explores the relation of the court's jurisprudence to Māori, common-law, and international law concepts.

Settler ("Pākehā") politicians and officials of different persuasions agreed that transforming Māori land holdings into alienable property was crucial to the civilizing project as well as to the progress of European settlement. The most self-conscious discussion of the anticipated relationship between the Native Land Court process and the Europeanization of Māori was Henry Sewell's speech, as Minister of Justice, to fellow members of the New Zealand parliament's upper house in 1870.[14] "The object of the Native Lands Act," Sewell said, "was two-fold":

> to bring the great bulk of the lands of the Northern Island which belonged to the Natives, and which, before the passing of that Act, were *extra commercium*— except through the means of the old land purchase system, which had entirely broken down—within the reach of colonization. The other great object was the detribalization of the Natives.[15]

It was the first goal—to make Māori land available for settlers to purchase—that was paramount. Assimilation was not as forcefully articulated an ambition of the New Zealand legal machinery as it was in the case of the Dawes system of individuating Indian land in the American West.[16] However, some, including Sewell, saw the Native Land Court as an engine of assimilation. As he explained, "detribalization" meant "destroy[ing], if it were possible,"

> the principle of communism which ran through the whole of their institutions, upon which their social system was based, and which stood as a barrier in the way of all attempts to amalgamate the native race into our own social and political system. It was hoped that by the individualization of titles to land, giving them the same individual ownership which we ourselves possessed, they would lose their communistic character, and that their social status would become assimilated to our own. That was taking place to a great extent, but the result had not as yet attained, and would not be attained for many years.[17]

These comments suggest an untroubled belief in the link between property owner-ship and the sorts of responsibility and judgment that Victorians in New Zealand as well as in Britain bundled into the word "character." As he went on, however, Sewell made it clear that he did not believe that the individuation of land ownership would quickly or automatically induct the Māori into a European "social and political system." The Native Land Court might assign fee-simple title to individual Māori, but "under-lying those individual rights were those tribal communistic interests which were still existing." A tribe that wished to sell some of its land had to go before the court and have "its lands vested in certain Natives by name as individual proprietors, though the real intention of the transaction was to vest the lands in them as administrators only."[18] As Sewell moves from programmatic statement to the details of the court process and land purchases, the assimilative possibilities of individuating collective title become less convincing.

In this speech, Sewell in effect placed the Native Land Court in the tradition of as-similative measures whose heyday was the 1840s and 1850s, between the beginning of formal colonization and the outbreak of the first Taranaki War in 1860. In these years a rickety colonial state, especially under the governorship of George Grey, pursued policies of racial "amalgamation," the political and legal aspects of which were the sub-ject of Alan Ward's landmark 1973 study of Māori and the colonial state, *A Show of Justice*, and whose intimate, "race-mixing" dimensions are the subject of Damon Iere-mia Salesa's important new book.[19] The word "amalgamate" lingers on alongside "as-similated" in Sewell's speech, but the terms of relations between indigenous people and settlers had changed fundamentally by 1870 as a result of the wars and subsequent confiscations. The assisted immigration and public works schemes of the 1870s worked to translate military victory into lasting conquest. Roads and railways "opened up" hitherto isolated—and independent—Māori-held territory in the North Island, and the conversion of tribal lands into alienable blocks facilitated Pākehā purchase of land in step with the extension of transport networks. Negotiations and conflicts between Māori and settlers continued, but in many parts of the North Island, the progress of colonization had become capillary rather than a matter of dramatic confrontation. In this setting, assimilation or amalgamation mattered much less to the settler state than it had when relations with Māori were the central concern of the colonial government. As in other settler polities, what New Zealand's colonists and the state needed most from the indigenous people was their land, not their labor.[20]

In any case, while "detribalization" might be a prerequisite for "assimilation," it did not necessarily lead to it. The Native Land Court did have the effect of undermining, or recasting, tribal relations, but without profoundly assimilative consequences. "Detrib-alization" is an inadequate term for several reasons, not the least of which is that two Māori words—*hapū* and *iwi*—were subsumed under the one English word. *Hapū* is often glossed as "subtribe" and *iwi* "tribe." Before the late nineteenth century, however, the *hapū* was the primary form of tribal organization, and the *iwi* a more figurative body. As Angela Ballara remarks, the sales made possible by the court's determination "contributed to the loss of small hapū as viable corporate units" and their surviving members' incorporation into, or "redefinition" as members of, other tribal groups— "those they were living with, or, more usually, the major hapū, both larger and older established, from which the smaller hapū was genealogically derived."[21] The court process fragmented and dislocated many *hapū*. As Ballara writes, "the strength of small, pre-Land Court Māori communities lay in their common economic and social interests." The legal process disrupted those interests, not only by tempting individual chiefs and part-owners with the rewards of going against the collective, but also because it replaced overlapping or ambiguous entitlements to land and resources such as cultivations and eel weirs with clear divisions.

The *hapū* was not a colonial category, but it *was* modified by the colonial state, as judges sought to impose more fixity on family and tribal connections that some-times were fluid. Some *hapū* were linked with more than one *iwi*, but the court's conception of Māori society required that *hapū* be treated as "subtribes" of a single *iwi*. In the first few decades of the court's operation, "thousands of little hapū were identified and assigned a place as sections of the paradigm of tribes recognised by the court."[22] Many *hapū* names appeared for the first time in the court's minute books. A judge would ask the name of the ancestor from whom the litigants claimed descent and thereby entitlement to the land. The minutes would refer to the claim-ants as descendants of—"ngā uri a"—the ancestor X, and after a few references, "ngā uri a X," would give way to the shorthand "Ngāti X"—most tribe names beginning with "Ngāti."[23]

A colonial state reordering indigenous categories for its own purposes of governance is a familiar phenomenon in imperial history—one thinks of Thomas R. Metcalf and Nicholas B. Dirks' work on India and Ann Laura Stoler's far-reaching programmatic essays.[24] As far as assimilation is concerned, it is worth pointing out that even as the court worked to undermine *hapū* as viable social and economic units, the court pro-cess's emphasis on genealogy and tribal histories reinscribed the owners *as* Māori or "natives." Even when, as usually happened, the court process and ensuing sales—and the further sales routinely needed to pay for legal costs—undermined the economic and territorial base of a *hapū*, the individuals pried loose from those places remained clearly marked as "natives" or "Māori" (a word that came into common use as a term for New Zealand's indigenous people only in the mid-nineteenth century; before col-onization, "māori" simply meant "ordinary"). They might be drawn into the Pākehā economy, especially in extractive industries or timber milling outside the larger towns, but racial distinctions remained legible.

The point may be illustrated by panning forward to a land purchase in 1920 involving a block in the Bay of Plenty that had passed through the Native Land Court at the end of the nineteenth century. Ben Keys, a bilingual land-purchasing agent working for a Bay of Plenty law firm, traveled several hundred miles to "search out some Natives living in the southern portions of this Island in order to obtain their signatures to the deed." These were Māori whose names were on the Native Land Court's memorial of ownership, stakeholders in the block. Keys and the Māori man who was working with him, Eru Nikorima, traveled by train to Foxton, where they obtained their first signature. In a village further on, "after long delay, we located another one of our Māoris working at a flaxmill." They drove him to Levin, where he signed the deed in front of a witness and was paid by Keys. That afternoon, Keys and Nikorima moved from village to village in search of "a woman who owned an interest in a piece of land near Ngongotaha" (also in the Bay of Plenty) and eventually "located her in the house of an ancient half-caste named Ransfield," who, trying Keys' patience, made "a long speech of welcome (in Maori)" and "manfully stuck to the duties dictated by Maori customs of hospitality."[25]

Each of these transactions involved Māori scattered far from the tribal land in which the Native Land Court had recorded an interest, but each was able to be traced through other Māori using Nikorima's contacts and knowledge of Māori social organization and custom. Though in some senses "detribalized," these Māori were still enmeshed in intertribal "Māori" networks—and, at least in the case of the woman in Ransfield's house, living in recognizably traditional "Māori" ways. One part-owner of the land, however, had married a Pākehā and proved difficult to trace through Nikorima's Māori contacts. Keys and Nikorima knew that "one of the Natives of whom we were in search" was somewhere in Wellington, "but the only clues we had to work upon were that she was the wife of a European named Jones, and that she was at one time employed in a laundry." While Nikorima tried to find her using his own methods, Keys began making inquiries by telephone and quickly found Mrs. Jones in a laundry in one of Wellington's inner suburbs.[26]

To examine the court's procedure, take as an example the case of the Waimana Valley, on the edges of the Bay of Plenty and Urewera regions. In March 1880, a Native Land Court was convened in the nearby town of Opotiki, with judge Henry A. H. Monro presiding. The case was a rehearing of a case decided by different judge in 1878. It involved ownership of land at Waimana and took place after several years of wrangling over land surveys and attempts by different parties to lease some of the land to Pākehā. Families of Ngatiraka and Ngaituranga, both of them *hapū* of the Tuhoe *iwi*, and Upokorehe, a *hapū* of Whakatohea, had been living together on the land for some time, and the court now had to extract clearly defined property rights from a complicated history of occupation and use of the land. Upokorehe based their case on continuous occupation since the time of their ancestor Raumoa; the two Tuhoe *hapū* claimed that the land was theirs by right of conquest, and that Upokorehe "had never been permitted to return as owners; and that such of them as are now residing on Waimana are there only by permission, and in virtue of their matrimonial relationships to the dominant owners, the Tuhoe."[27] (This passage, like others quoted in this chapter, comes from the judge's notes on the hearing: like many of the early judges of the Native Land Court, Monro spoke Māori, and he took notes on testimony in court, translating as he went.)

In the 1880 hearing, it was the evidence of actual use of the land over successive generations that was decisive, rather than disputed conquests further back in the past. Witnesses were asked to specify where in Waimana they had laid cultivations, and did so, providing the names of cultivations as well as their locations.[28] And they were asked to give the names of their dead who were buried on the block. When Te Whiu Takurewa, a Tuhoe witness who chose to "affirm" rather than swear on a Bible, was asked to "give the names of any of your dead who are buried on this land," he answered: "There may lie 200. My ancestor Mapae was buried in this land just outside the block." Counsel for the other tribe pressed him to name others. "My own mother is buried at Maungarewarewa, on the block."[29]

Such evidence persuaded Monro that Tuhoe were the "paramount owners" of the block:

> Whether Upokorehe were forcibly expelled (as is alleged) or no, it is plain to the Court that Tuhoe are in paramount occupation; and that they possess extensive cultivations within the limits of the Waimana Block; and cemeteries in which some hundreds have been interred; of whom many have never been disturbed, although the bones of others have been removed to their more inland seats at Maungapohatu. Much stress is laid on the interment [in] Waimana of [the chief] Maungahaaruru whose eminently sacred rank precludes the removal of his bones, as proof of their owners[hip] of the land in which such a man was buried.
>
> The Upokorehe, on the contrary, cannot point to any of their dead lying at Waimana except some children buried there within the last few years. . . . Such inability contradicts the assertion of a continuous occupation during many genera[tions]. . . . whatever traditional rights the descendants of Raumoa may have once asserted, they had been long extinguished; and that the Urewera, or Tuhoe, had been the undisputed and paramount owners, and actual occupants, before upwards of fifty years before the present time.[30]

The information about burial places and cultivations emerged through the examination of witnesses in the familiar adversarial common-law manner. While the restructuring of the Native Land Court in the early 1870s was intended in part to make the institution somewhat more like a commission of inquiry than a court, with the "examination of witnesses and the investigation of title" to be "carried on by the presiding Judge without the intervention of any counsel or other agent," the 1873 legislation permitted the involvement of lawyers if the claimants were unable "to select one of themselves to act as their spokesman to conduct the case in their behalf."[31] In the Waimana hearing, both parties employed Pākehā lawyers, but only the lawyer for Upokorehe, J. A. Tole, handled the cross-examination himself. Tole appears to have worked through an interpreter, though given the detail of tribal history he was able to go into, Tole clearly had some of the cross-cultural facility that the Native Land Court process depended on.[32] Cross-examination on matters of tribal history was apparently beyond the lawyer for Tuhoe, John Richard Rushion, and the questioning of the other side's witnesses was undertaken by two Tuhoe leaders, Netana Piki (a man) and Huhana Te Waihapuarangi (a woman). They often asked questions about very recent events, such as the surveys and negotiations with prospective buyers and lessees, and accused the Upokorehe witnesses of "dishonestly" accepting money from a Pākehā, Captain Swindley, and of deceitfully trying to take Tuhoe land. "Have the Urewera [i.e., Tuhoe] ever disturbed you in the occupation of your land? Then why do you now come to disturb me in the Court yard of my house?"[33] The Māori advocates used the courtroom to press on with the contemporary dispute, whereas Tole was keener to delve further into the "traditional" past.

Tole used tribal history in two ways. First, with the evidence of burial sites and cultivations favoring Tuhoe's claim of "paramount occupation," as the judge called it, Tole sought to shore up Upokorehe's case that they had never been conquered by Tuhoe and so had been a continuous presence, at least, in Waimana for many generations. Second, by grilling Tuhoe witnesses about their knowledge of their genealogy and matters of tribal history not immediately relevant to the present case, Tole worked to cast doubt on their authority as custodians of tribal knowledge. He began his cross-examination of Huhana by inquiring about the provenance of her narrative of the Tuhoe conquest of the land. He then pressed her on details of her ancestry, asked her about the circumstances under which Upokorehe currently lived on the block, and repeatedly circled back to the details of the conquest:

> TOLE: Where did you learn this story from?
> HUHANA: From my grandmother's brother, also from Mohi Tai[,] Tuahine and Te Marama.
> TOLE: They told you about the Raumoa having been driven away?
> HUHANA: Yes.
> TOLE: Did you learn from your mother also?

HUHANA: Yes.

. . .

TOLE: Do you claim through Te Awamate?

HUHANA: Yes.

TOLE: Te Awamate was a woman?

HUHANA: Yes, she had two husbands.

TOLE: Who was the first?

HUHANA: Pukeahunoa.

TOLE: Who was the other?

HUHANA: Te Rangihiaroa.

TOLE: Who is your Ngaituranga ancestor?

HUHANA: I cannot g[ive] my genealogy from Ngaituranga.

TOLE: Can you give children of Pukeahunoa?

HUHANA: Ye[s]—i Hunga and others.

TOLE: Who was the wife of Te Wanui?

HUHANA: I don't know.

TOLE: Who were the children?

HUHANA: Tamehau.

. . .

TOLE: Did you not state in Court that your anc[cestors] lived on the land but did not claim it?

HUHANA: I said my claim commenced from the time of Touo Kino.

TOLE: Did you give a different ancestor at last Court?

HUHANA: No.

TOLE: Are there any of Raumoa on the land now?

HUHANA: Yes but not as Raumoa, they live under the Ngaituranga and Ngati-raka, being connected with them.

TOLE: Did you ever hear that the descendants of Raumoa gave the Uriwera [i.e., Tuhoe] leave to live on Waimana?

HUHANA: No.

TOLE: Have you heard it stated?

HUHANA: At last Court I heard it.

TOLE: Did you never hear it before?

HUHANA: No.

TOLE: What was the battle between Ngaituranga and Raumoa called?

HUHANA: Orupe.

TOLE: What was the name of the chief who was killed?

HUHANA: There were many killed. Tauapaua was the one I heard of.

TOLE: Did the Ngaituranga and Ngatiraka never quarrel?

HUHANA: Yes, small squabbles but not about land.

TOLE: You say the Upokorehe have no claim on the land?

HUHANA: None so far as I know.

TOLE: Do you know a place called Otenaku?

HUHANA: Yes. It was a pa [fortified settlement] of Ngatiraka, not on this land.

TOLE: [Was] there any quarrel about the land before [the] murder?

HUHANA: Yes. Manuauware trespassed he went on to the others land to plant *hue* [gourds] and was murdered—on that account.

TOLE: Where did he come from?

HUHANA: Otenaku.

TOLE: You live at Whakatane?

HUHANA: Yes, the Waimana river runs into Whakatane.[34]

The Waimana case was decided on the grounds of the practical roots that the two Tuhoe *hapū* had put down on the land, not on more remote issues of tribal history. However, Tole's questions about whether Tuhoe had ever driven Raumoa's descendants, the Upokorehe, out of Waimana, meant that the Native Land Court hearings generated a written corpus of accounts of a moment in the area's past. Monro's notes record multiple versions of the story. The first account that the court heard was that of the Tuhoe witness Te Whiu Takurewa:

Ngati Tuhoe fought the Raumoa tribe and dispossessed them. The fighting took place in the time of Murakarake and also of Tuhoe. The first fight was an attack by Raumoa on Manuauware. That is[,] the Raumoa murdered him. When Tuhaki heard of it, he arose to avenge it. He came to Ohope, a pa belonging to the Raumoa, with his war party. He enquired where Tauwhakarewa was. The Raumoa said he had gone to Ohiwa. Tauwhakarewa was a chief of the Raumoa. Tuhaki asked where Tauapaua was[.] They said he was at te Paoa, another pa of the Raumoa, outside the block [i.e., Waimana]. Tuhaki and his army went to the Pa & found Tauapaua there. He took the pa[,] killed Tauapaua and brought his head to Orupe. The Raumoa fled to Waimana after this and s[tayed] away ever since.[35]

Te Whiu's testimony was a touchstone for several Upokorehe witnesses, who disputed his claim that Manuauware belonged to Tuhoe. He was, they insisted, a descendant of Raumoa and so a member of *their* tribe. Manuauware had, however, quarreled with his own people and sought the aid of Te Awatope, a chief from another tribe—Tuhoe, said one witness; Ngatiawa, said another—to take over some Raumoa land. The Upokorehe elder Heremaia Te Marama flatly contradicted Te Whiu: "I heard Te Whiu say that they o[wn] the land by conquest. I deny it. Manuauware [was] killed on the block. He belonged [to] Upokorehe and was slain [because he] wished to take the land." Heremaia went on to describe the events in more detail than any of the previous witnesses. Manuauware and Te Awatope

> came from Whakatane to the Parau stream. They planted *hue* seeds there, then Awatope said, let us return to Whakatane. Manuauware said no let me finish planting my seed. Awatope spoke a proverb, "Awatope to manu whiti tua. Koukou to manu au ware[.]" The meaning was that Manuauware was foolish to neglect his advice. The result was Awatope went away & was saved. Manuauware stayed and was killed by Tawhakarewa. Tawhakarewa thrust the body into a pit. The pit was called Te Waimana Ka Kuru, from which this block took its name. After this Awatope brought a war party of Ngatiawa and Ngai-terangi. They came to Waiotahi. Kahutai of Raumoa sent a messenger to Tau-whakarewa for assistance. When it came they attacked the forces of Awatope and routed them. The battle was called te Waiwhero. Waiwhero is a stream between the Orupe and Tuhua pas. The stream was reddened with blood, down to its junction with the Waiotahi—hence the name [*wai* = water, *whero* = red]. Tawhakarewa came back to his pa at Orupe. Te Morehu of Awatope's party was saved by Kahutai because he was related to him. The Raumoa continued to live on the land after this.[36]

The case notes record two other versions of this episode. The accounts quoted here are more than sufficient to show the texture and variousness that attracted students of Māori culture to the court's ethnographic archive. It was not such a leap from Native Land Court minute books to the *Journal of the Polynesian Society*. The stylizations characteristic of early anthropologists' renderings of tribal histories—which owe more to the fabricated Gaelic sagas of James Macpherson's "Ossian" than to any "noble savage" tradition—were already present in the ways the judges thought about the witnesses before them. Ossian-style archaisms appear even in Monro's scribbled case notes: "The Ngatiraka and Ngaituranga were grieved at the murder and they rose and smote the Ngatiraumoa."[37] Two of the handful of judges who wrote books on Māori history observed that one of the fringe benefits of sitting on the Native Land Court bench was the "Māori stories" it enabled them to collect.[38]

Contemporaries differed over the extent to which the Native Land Court was, or should be, a tribunal analogous to other institutions with the name of "court." Preem-inent among the doubters was the former Chief Justice, Sir William Martin, who wrote in a memorandum in 1871 that "The chief business of the Court is in fact the business either of a Commission or of a jury. Why keep up the resort to English counsel in a Court which is not constituted for the administration of English law, but only for the ascertainment of Native custom, and of the facts of occupation and ownership?" The "main business" of the court, he wrote, was "simply the collecting and estimating of evidence, requiring not so much legal knowledge as a certain degree of skill or acuteness in the officer collecting it, and honesty in estimating it."[39] Martin was advising the Native Minister, McLean, as he worked to replace Fenton's Native Land Court rules with a new set of procedures, which were enshrined in the Native Land Act of 1873.

Fenton firmly believed that the Native Land Court *was* a court, and he succeeded, briefly, in having its judges appointed on terms similar to judges of the Supreme Court, rather than the magistrates of the district courts.[40] Writing to the Native Minister in 1867, after the court had been in operation for two years, Fenton wrote: "a reasonable confidence in the Government, and a desire to abandon strife and accept British law administered in open Courts, has followed the operations of the Land Court wherever its sittings have been held." He cited the hearing over which he presided at Cambridge in the Waikato, a case involving important Kīngitanga tribes: "the great majority of the persons present were constituted tribes which have been the heart of the rebellion from the commencement. It is true that there was a silent impressive contest during the first day as the old chiefs refused to be sworn or to affirm; but their moral force was not equal to ours, and they yielded. The victory of law and order was complete, and when subsequently the disturbances were renewed at Tauranga these tribes kept aloof, although intimately interested in that part of the country, and in single individuals who joined the rebels."[41] What Fenton is celebrating here is respect for a European legal process, not substantive common-law doctrines. In the phrase "law and order," the first term collapses into the second.[42]

When McLean moved to reorganize the court, Fenton appealed for reports from his judges to show the value of the existing system. Monro obliged with a testimonial in tune with Fenton's own thinking. The court was more successful in facilitating the acquisition of Māori land than the old system of Crown preemption had been, he told Fenton, "but when to this we add the increased reverence for law, and increased confidence in the judicial tribunals which are intrusted with its administration, it is difficult to calculate the value of the system in its effects upon the Native mind."[43] Though not a lawyer, Monro nevertheless declared that the court's "revolutionary" objective was "the exchange of a communal and often-disputed tenure of lands held as the property of all the free members of a tribe, for one definite, personal, and subjected to at least the broader principles, if not in all cases to the technical niceties, of the real estate law of England."[44] This is to move a good deal of English property law from the "broader principles" column to the "technical niceties" column. For Monro, as for Fenton, the court taught respect for the order that English law could bring, rather than an understanding of English law and the notions of freedom, responsibility, and agreement it could be presented as standing for.

In some early statements, Fenton claimed an English pedigree for the tribunal he was proposing. In an 1859 sketch of a "Scheme for the Partition and Enfranchisement of Lands Held under Native Tenure," Fenton envisaged that a magistrate would hear competing Māori claims to land "as an enquiry before the Commissioners under an Act for inclosing lands of common would be conducted in England."[45] He buttressed his claim that this scheme was "somewhat analogous to the system pursued by our Anglo-Saxon forefathers" with a endnote to Henry Hallam's *Constitutional History of England* (1827), and as further support he cited figures on the acreage of common land brought into cultivation under the Enclosure Acts from 1760 to 1834.[46] In the Native Land Court's Kaitorete hearing, Fenton remarked that, "The character attached by the English authorities to the wild lands of the colony up to this period, seems to resemble very much that of the folcland or public land of the Saxons."[47] However, this was a case between the Ngai Tahu *iwi* and the Crown about "waste lands" and aboriginal title in the South Island, and as such turned on issues different from most Native Land Court cases, which involved disputes between rival *hapū* and *iwi*. The history of enclosure and the doings of "our Anglo-Saxon forefathers" offered little guidance in these cases. And the main grounds or *take* (literally, "roots") for property claims that the Native Land Court recognized were hardly common-law concepts.[48]

Chief among these *take* was *take rapuatu*, or conquest. The court's understanding of "conquest" derived partly from judges' impressions of Māori society and partly from the law of nations—a more or less "colloquial" knowledge of international law, to use Lauren Benton's word. Fenton declared in an 1866 judgment in the Compensation Court, a tribunal set up to hear cases arising the postwar confiscations, that "the great rule which governed Māori rights to land was force ie., that a tribe or association of persons held possession of a certain tract of country until expelled from it by superior power, and that on such expulsion, if the invaders settled upon the evacuated territory, it remained theirs until they in their turn had to yield it to others."[49] Fenton went on to outline a position that would quickly become one of the governing principles of the Native Land Court as well as the Compensation Court[50]: the court would not recognize any "conquests" occurring after the assertion of British sovereignty in 1840. "[H]aving found it absolutely necessary to fix some point of time at which the titles, as far as this Court is concerned, must be regarded as settled, we have decided that that point of time must be the establishment of the British Government in 1840."[51] As the historian Bryan D. Gilling writes, "the Court concluded that while it could continue to recognize changes in land ownership deriving from events such as inheritance or gift, it could not recognize changes made by force after the nominal superimposition of British sovereignty in 1840."[52]

Gilling sees the origin of the "1840 rule" as a mystery: "why *should* the Native Land Court need such a commencing point?" If it did need one, "the question arises of why the Court could not determine ownership of Maori customary land as at the date of the Court's sitting on each individual case."[53] Thinking of the 1840 rule in the context of the law of nations makes it less mysterious. Gilling locates the rule's origins in Colonial Office and local officials' concerns to give substance to British sovereignty within New Zealand. Conquest, being an international law concept, could not be held to occur after British sovereignty was asserted, turning tribes from quasi- (or de facto) sovereign bodies into Queen Victoria's subjects. A conquest is a conquest only if it involves sovereign entities; otherwise it is trespass.[54] In his published judgments, Fenton did not discuss the international-law pedigree of the idea of conquest, but the relevant jurisprudence was not unknown in New Zealand. In an 1864 pamphlet, Henry Sewell quoted a long passage from *Worcester v. Georgia* (1832) in which Chief Justice John Marshall discussed the legal effects of conquest.[55]

Continuous occupation supported property claims in Roman law, but in Native Land Court jurisprudence occupation was associated with Māori custom: "Keeping one's fires burning, the principle of ahi kaa, was regarded by the Court as crucial to any claim to that land."[56] Government lawyers of an intellectual bent such as Sewell and Fenton did not rationalize this use of Māori custom in the court's procedure or (in Fenton's case) explain how it was compatible with the notion that the court was schooling Māori in English legal traditions. Dependence on using Māori knowledge was a given of the New Zealand situation. The settler state needed Māori land brought into the market, and so, of course, required Māori landholders to enter the market as at least grudgingly willing participants.

However, the court's use of Māori concepts such as *ahi kaa* does not, of course, mean that the adjudication of claims was substantially conducted "according to Native custom and usage," as the legislation had it.[57] Fenton's belief in the primacy of "force" rather than *whakapapa* in relationships between people and land[58] ran counter to indigenous people's understandings of their culture. And, as previously shown, the court's adherence to its *iwi–hapū* model of tribal organization applied a fixative to fluid social arrangements. David V. Williams speaks for a number of critics when he says that, "despite statutory assertions to the contrary, there was no application of Māori custom to the Court's ascertainment of rights to title. Rather, a distorted version of 'Māori custom' was invented by the Land Court judges."[59]

Implicit in this judgment, and indeed throughout Williams's book, is a counterfactual of a more respectful Māori–Pākehā relationship. Yet, given the constitution and *raison d'être* of the Native Land Court, it would be unrealistic to expect its treatment of Māori custom to be more "bicultural." At least, it would be unrealistic to expect that of an institution established after the 1850s. Benton has argued convincingly that legal pluralism was in retreat elsewhere in the British Empire—New South Wales and the Cape colony are her case studies—after the early nineteenth century.[60] As Damen Ward has shown, the 1830s and 1840s were a time of active debate within the Colonial Office and in exchanges between London and the colonies of New Zealand, South Australia, and Western Australia, between advocates of the "strict application" of British laws and exponents of temporary "exceptionalism," tolerating indigenous laws and sanctions, especially in disputes between indigenous people themselves.[61] It was during this period that the most ambitious New Zealand experiment in legal pluralism was launched. This was the resident magistrates system in the 1840s and 1850s, in which legal officers in predominantly Māori districts sanctioned Māori practices such as *muru* (plundering raids) as remedies for theft and other crimes (or crimes that had, in effect, become torts, since the colonial state did not monopolize punishment and redress).[62] The wars of the 1860s retrenched the initiatives in legal pluralism and "amalgamation" of the previous two decades.

So when *whakapapa*, tribal history, and details of cultivations, burials, and sites of special significance came before the Native Land Court, they did so as evidence rather than as "laws" or even as laws of evidence. That this state of affairs was neither legal pluralism nor the respectful and reciprocal alternative history Williams presupposes does not make it unremarkable. The court's level of reference to "Native custom and usage," distortions notwithstanding, stands in contrast to other state institutions in the second half of the nineteenth century. After the wars of the 1860s, government policies on Māori customs were usually geared toward undermining them. Māori children were not encouraged to learn the Māori language and, indeed, sometimes were punished for speaking it at school.[63] Efforts were made to weaken the influence of traditional healers.[64] This is a position characteristic of a "mature" settler colony, one in which the middle ground has been closed. Yet, while other aspects of indigenous knowledge were actively suppressed, Māori historical thinking and conceptions of social organization remained the empirical—as distinct from legal—basis for adjudicating property claims.

NOTES

1. My thanks to all the participants in the workshop at the University of Sydney that led to this volume, and in particular to Saliha Belmessous, Andrew Fitzmaurice, and Mark Hickford. I am grateful to Kate Jordan for research assistance and Jeff Abbott of the Waitangi Tribunal Library for making unpublished reports available to me.
2. J. E. Gorst, *The Maori King*, ed., Keith Sinclair (1864; Hamilton, New Zealand: Paul's Book Arcade, 1959).
3. On the New Zealand Wars and their consequences, see James Belich, *The New Zealand Wars and the Victorian Interpretation of Racial Conflict* (Auckland: Oxford University Press, 1986).

4. Richard White, *The Middle Ground: Indians, Empires, and Republics in the Great Lakes Region, 1650–1815* (Cambridge: Cambridge University Press, 1991), x, xv.

5. See M. P. K. Sorrenson, *Origins of European Settlement in Kenya* (Nairobi, Kenya: Oxford University Press, 1968), chap. 3.

6. Francis Dart Fenton to Donald McLean, August 28, 1871, in H. Hanson Turton, ed., *An Epitome of Official Documents Relative to Native Affairs and Land Purchases in the North Island of New Zealand* (Wellington, NZ: Government Printer, 1883), part G, 23, 49.

7. "Memorandum by Sir William Martin on the Operation of the Native Land Court," January 18, 1871, in Turton, *Epitome*, part G, 35.

8. Bryan D. Gilling, *The Nineteenth-Century Native Land Court Judges: An Introductory Report* (Wellington, NZ: Waitangi Tribunal, 1994), 7–25.

9. Jeffrey Sissons, *Te Waimana: The Spring of Mana: Tuhoe History and the Colonial Encounter* (Dunedin, NZ: University of Otago Press, 1991), 60.

10. See ibid., pp. 4, 5, and, more generally, M. P. K. Sorrenson, *Manifest Duty: The Polynesian Society over 100 Years* (Auckland: Polynesian Society, 1992).

11. The quotation is from Donald M. Loveridge, *The Origins of the Native Lands Acts and Native Land Court in New Zealand* (Wellington, NZ: Crown Law Office, 2000), 8.

12. Loveridge, *Origins of the Native Lands Acts and Native Land Court*; Richard Boast, *Buying the Land, Selling the Land: Governments and Māori Land in the North Island 1865–1921* (Wellington, NZ: Victoria University Press, 2008); David V. Williams, "*Te Kooti Tango Whenua*": *The Native Land Court, 1864–1909* (Wellington, NZ: Huia Publishers, 1999); Angela Ballara, *Iwi: The Dynamics of Māori Tribal Organisation from c. 1769 to c. 1945* (Wellington, NZ: Victoria University Press, 1998), chs. 7, 17. The Waitangi Tribunal investigates historical breaches of the treaty. Loveridge's lengthy report was undertaken as part of the tribunal process, and the books by Boast and Williams owe much to their authors' involvement in the researching of the Treaty of Waitangi claims and counterclaims; Ballara is now a member of the tribunal. On the treaty claims process and its historical revisions, see Miranda Johnson, "Making History Public: Indigenous Claims to Settler States," *Public Culture* 20, no. 1 (2008): 97–117; Giselle Byrnes, *The Waitangi Tribunal and New Zealand History* (Auckland, NZ: Oxford University Press, 2004), as well as Jim McAloon's critique, "By Which Standards? History and the Waitangi Tribunal," *New Zealand Journal of History* 40, no. 2 (2006): 194–213, and the replies by Byrnes (ibid., 214–229), Michael Belgrave (ibid., 230–250), and W. H. Oliver (ibid. 41, no. 1 [2007]: 83–87).

13. Stuart Banner, *Possessing the Pacific: Land, Settlers, and Indigenous People from Australia to Alaska* (Cambridge, MA: Harvard University Press, 2007), chap. 3. See also Simon Young, *The Trouble with Tradition: Native Title and Cultural Change* (Sydney, Australia: Federation Press, 2008), 170–178.

14. For contrasting views of the significance of this speech, see Peter Spiller, Jeremy Finn, and Richard Boast, *A New Zealand Legal History* (Wellington, NZ: Brooker's, 1995), 147–148, and Williams, *Te Kooti Tango Whenua*, 87–89. I agree with Williams on this point.

15. *New Zealand Parliamentary Debates*, 12 (1870): 361 (Legislative Council). Compare "A Report, by Walter L. Buller, Esq. R. M., on the Partition and Individualization of the Kaiapoi Reserve, in the Province of Canterbury," *Appendices to the Journals of the House of Representatives* (1862), E-5, 11.

16. See Patricia Nelson Limerick, *The Legacy of Conquest: The Unbroken Past of the American West* (New York: Norton, 1987), 195, 197–199; Patrick Wolfe, "Land, Labor, and Difference: Elementary Structures of Race," *American Historical Review* 106, no. 3 (2001): 888.

17. *New Zealand Parliamentary Debates*, 12 (1870): 361 (Legislative Council).

18. Ibid.

19. Alan Ward, *A Show of Justice: Racial "Amalgamation" in Nineteenth Century New Zealand*, 2nd ed. (Auckland, NZ: Auckland University Press, 1995); Damon Ieremia Salesa, *Racial Crossings: Race, Intermarriage, and the Victorian British Empire* (Oxford: Oxford University Press, 2011).

20. See Wolfe, "Land, Labor, and Difference"; Caroline Elkins and Susan Pedersen, "Introduction: Settler Colonialism: A Concept and Its Uses," in Elkins and Pedersen, eds., *Settler Colonialism in the Twentieth Century: Projects, Practices, Legacies* (New York: Routledge, 2005), 8.

21. Ballara, *Iwi*, 252.

22. Ibid., 271, 275.

23. Ibid., 271.

24. Thomas R. Metcalf, *Ideologies of the Raj* (Cambridge: Cambridge University Press, 1994); Nicholas B. Dirks, *Castes of Mind: Colonialism and the Making of Modern India* (Princeton: Princeton University Press, 2001); Ann Laura Stoler and Frederick Cooper, "Between Metropole and Colony: Rethinking a Research Agenda," in Cooper and Stoler, eds., *Tensions of Empire: Colonial Cultures in a Bourgeois World* (Berkeley: University of California Press, 1997), 1–40; Ann Laura Stoler, "Tense and Tender Ties: The Politics of Comparison in North American History and (Post) Colonial Studies," *Journal of American History* 88, no. 3 (December 2001): 829–865.

25. Ben Keys, diary for 1920, 79–80 (May 11, 1920), Ben Keys Papers, MS Papers 407–432, Alexander Turnbull Library, National Library of New Zealand, Wellington.

26. Ibid., 103 (May 11, 1920). See also Christopher Hilliard, "Licensed Native Interpreter: The Land Purchaser as Ethnographer in Early-20th-Century New Zealand," *Journal of Pacific History* 45, no. 2 (September 2010): 229–245.

27. H. A. H. Monro, "Opotiki: 8 March 1880" (file of case notes), 95–96, H. A. H. Monro Papers, MS 366, box 3, folder 12, Auckland War Memorial Museum Library.

28. Ibid., 5, 29.

29. Ibid., 3, 5.

30. Ibid., 96–97.

31. Native Land Act 1873, s. 44.

32. As well practicing law, Tole was a member of the House of Representatives, where he acted as a lieutenant to the former governor turned member of parliament, Sir George Grey. *The Cyclopedia of New Zealand: Industrial, Descriptive, Historical, Biographical Facts, Figures, Illustrations*, 6 vols. (Wellington, NZ: Cyclopedia Co., 1897–1908), 2:107–108.

33. Monro, Opotiki case file, 28, 34.

34. Ibid., 11–13. Italics indicate underlining in the original.

35. Ibid., 4.

36. Ibid., 44–46. Italics indicate underlining in the original.

37. Ibid., 11.

38. Gilbert Mair, *Reminiscences and Maori Stories* (Auckland, NZ: Brett, 1923), 54; T. W. Porter, *Legends of the Maori and Personal Reminiscences of the East Coast of New Zealand* (Christchurch, NZ: L. M. Isitt, 1925), 61. Other books by Native Land Court judges are John Alexander Wilson, *Sketches of Ancient Maori Life and History* (Auckland, NZ: Brett, 1894); Francis Dart Fenton, *Suggestions for a History of the Origins and Migrations of the MaoriPeople* (Auckland, NZ: Brett, 1885). See also Grant Young, "Judge Norman Smith: A Tale of Four 'Take,'" *New Zealand Universities Law Review* 21, no. 2 (2004): 311; Ballara, *Iwi*, 92 and chap. 8.

39. "Memorandum by Sir William Martin on the Operation of the Native Land Court," January 18, 1871, in Turton, *Epitome*, part G, 35.
40. Gilling, "Native Land Court Judges," 34. Despite its name, the Supreme Court was the superior court of first instance. New Zealand's highest court was the Privy Council in London.
41. Fenton to the Hon. the Native Minister [J. C. Richmond], July 31, 1867, in Turton, *Epitome*, part G, 31.
42. See also F. D. Fenton, *The Laws of England: Compiled and Translated into the Maori Language, by Direction of Thomas Gore Browne: Ko Nga Ture o Ingarani* (Auckland, NZ: Williamson and Wilson, 1858), 45. Compare Damen Ward, *"Savage Customs and Civilised Laws": British Attitudes to Legal Pluralism in Australasia, c. 1830–48* (London: Menzies Centre for Australian Studies, 2003), 26.
43. Henry A. H. Monro to Fenton, May 12, 1871, in Turton, *Epitome*, part G, 54.
44. Monro to Fenton, May 12, 1871, ibid., 53.
45. F. D. Fenton, *Observations on the State of the Aboriginal Inhabitants of New Zealand* (Auckland, NZ: W. C. Wilson, 1859), 43–44.
46. Ibid., 42.
47. Native Land Court, Kaitorete hearing, Christchurch, May 5, 1868 (Chief Judge Fenton), in [F. D. Fenton, ed.] *Important Judgments Delivered in the Compensation and Native Land Court* (Auckland, NZ: published under the direction of the chief judge of the Native Land Court, 1879), 33–34.
48. Boast, *Buying the Land, Selling the Land*, p. 93; Gilling, "1840 Rule," 136–137.
49. Compensation Court hearing on Oakura, New Plymouth, June 1866 (Chief Judge Fenton and Judges John Rogan and Henry A. H. Monro), in Fenton, *Important Judgments*, 9. The Compensation Court "seems to have been, in effect, more or less the same institution as the Native Land Court. . . . Both institutions were presided over by Francis Dart Fenton as Chief Judge, and other judicial personnel (such as Judges Rogan and Monro) also overlapped. Much of the body of precedent later applied in the Native Land Court was first created by the Compensation Court." Spiller, Finn, and Boast, *A New Zealand Legal History*, 148.
50. Gilling, "1840 Rule," 161.
51. Compensation Court hearing on Oakura, New Plymouth, June 1866 (Chief Judge Fenton and Judges Rogan and Monro), in Fenton, *Important Judgments*, 10.
52. Gilling, "1840 Rule," 137.
53. Ibid., 157–159.
54. "At first the Maoris were regarded by the Crown as an independent and organised state, capable of forming a treaty . . . " Native Land Court, Kaitorete hearing, Christchurch, May 5, 1868 (Chief Judge Fenton), in Fenton, *Important Judgments*, 32.
55. Henry Sewell, *The New Zealand Native Rebellion: Letter to Lord Lyttelton* (1864; Dunedin, NZ: Hocken Library, 1974), 5–9.
56. Gilling, "1840 Rule," 137; Native Land Court, Aroha hearing, April 1871 (Judges F. E. Maning and Henry A. H. Monro), in Fenton, *Important Judgments*, 109–110.
57. Native Land Act 1873, ss. 7, 31, 45, 51, 56, 57.
58. Māori describe themselves as *tangata whenua*, the people of the land. *Whenua* is the word for "placenta" as well as the word for "land."
59. Williams, *Te Kooti Tango Whenua*, 73–74. Saying that "a distorted version" of Māori custom was "invented" by the court implies that its jurisprudence was more coherent than it was. Grant Young has argued convincingly that the widespread belief that the court

systematically applied four *take* to the cases that came before it derives from an influential twentieth-century text that retrospectively imposed order on "nineteenth-century chaos." "There were no clear and fixed rules defining 'take' and when they might apply to certain circumstances." Cases became increasingly complex and could appear *sui generis*. The court's judgments were not formally reported, which hindered the development of a system of precedent. (Young, "Judge Norman Smith," 329–330.) However, the fact that the court did not develop its own consistent and procrustean version of Māori custom does not, of course, mean that it followed "Native custom and usage."

60. Lauren Benton, *Law and Colonial Cultures: Legal Regimes in World History, 1400–1900* (Cambridge: Cambridge University Press, 2002), chap. 5.

61. Ward, *"Savage Customs and Civilised Laws."*

62. Ward, *Show of Justice*; Alan Ward, "Law and Law-enforcement on the New Zealand Frontier, 1840–1893," *New Zealand Journal of History* 5, no. 2 (1971): 128–149.

63. See Judith Simon and Linda Tuhiwai Smith, eds., *A Civilising Mission? Perceptions and Representations of the Native Schools System* (Auckland, NZ: Auckland University Press, 2001), chap. 5; *Report of the Waitangi Tribunal on the Te Reo Maori Claim* (1986; Wellington, NZ: GP Publications, 1996), 8–10.

64. Derek A. Dow, "'Pruned of its Dangers': The Tohunga Suppression Act 1907," *Health and History* 3, no. 1 (2001): 41–64.

10

AFRICAN AND EUROPEAN INITIATIVES IN THE TRANSFORMATION OF LAND TENURE IN COLONIAL LAGOS (WEST AFRICA), 1840–1920

Kristin Mann

In the port of Lagos on the West African coast, the encounter between indigenous and European land claims began before British colonization in 1861. Prior to that time, trade, diplomacy, immigration, and missionary activity had already created new uses for landed property, given it new value, and introduced new ideas about the kinds of rights that could exist in land and buildings. Moreover, the bitter conflicts that developed around land claims in late-nineteenth and early-twentieth century Lagos brewed as much within the African population as between it and the British colonizers. This chapter investigates the impact of African actions on the ground in the emergence of a new system of land tenure in and around the town between the 1840s and the 1910s. While adjudication in the courts and its attending articulation of claims and counterclaims played an important role in this process, they were preceded by decades of less well-studied changing practices in the granting, buying, selling, mortgaging, and bequeathing of real estate that laid the foundation for what took place in law courts.

The relationship between land claims and political sovereignty constitutes a central theme of this volume. At Lagos, as elsewhere throughout European empires, conflict over rights in land was bound up during the colonial period with protests against the loss of political autonomy. Indeed, anticolonial struggle created opportunities in Lagos for certain chiefs and their families to reassert rights in land against not only the British but also the local monarch. Although initially unsuccessful, changed imperial priorities around the turn of the twentieth century opened the way for one such family and its supporters to win a major legal victory in the courts that also carried great political weight within the community. For decades, local people had already been adapting foreign-inspired land transactions to their own requirements, sometimes to the bewilderment or consternation of British officials. The new land law that developed in Lagos during the colonial period was shaped as much by African initiative as it was by British colonial policy and jurisprudence. Long-term changes in Lagos land law were rooted in broader economic, political, and social transformations taking place within the town.

As the Atlantic slave trade entered its last, largely illegal phase during the first half of the nineteenth century, the small Kingdom of Lagos on West Africa's Bight of Benin became one of the leading centers of the commerce north of the Equator. The external slave trade transformed the kingdom's capital, also known as Lagos, which was located on two small islands at the center of a vast lagoon, from a crossroads of regional trade into an Atlantic port linking Africa, Europe, and the Americas, especially northeastern Brazil. Income from the slave trade increased the wealth of the town's Ọba, head of a ruling dynasty that had been introduced from the Kingdom of Benin to the east in the late seventeenth century, as well as that of certain chiefs, primarily of the war grade, who along with the Ọba dominated the role of commercial middleman in the slave trade. However, the new wealth from the slave trade simultaneously exacerbated rivalries within the royal lineage and tensions between the Ọba and other chiefs, some of them called Idẹjọs and said to be descended from the town's earliest settlers.

Beyond its internal effects, the growth of the Atlantic slave trade at Lagos also led in 1851 to the kingdom's bombardment by the British Royal Navy. At that time, a strong king, Kosoko, was deposed and driven into exile, and a weaker if constitutionally still independent British ally, Akitoye, was installed in the palace. A decade later, Britain forced Akitoye's successor, Ọba Dosunmu, and four of his chiefs to sign a treaty that ceded Lagos to the queen, and much of the territory formerly occupied by the kingdom subsequently became a British Crown Colony. The stated reasons for the annexation were the abolition of the external slave trade and the better protection of the inhabitants of the area. However, abolition was bound up at Lagos with the development of a new export trade in palm produce, for which industrialization and urbanization were creating important new markets in Europe. By the time Britain annexed Lagos in 1861, British policy makers had come to believe that new types of commerce capable of reforming Africa from the sins of the slave trade could not develop along that part of the coast under indigenous rule but, instead, required civilized, British command.

With the establishment of a British presence at Lagos after 1851 came Christian missionaries and European merchants, as well as growing numbers of repatriated former slaves from Brazil and Sierra Leone. The missionaries and repatriated slaves introduced new Christian religious beliefs and practices, as well as Western education and other external influences, including new ideas about land ownership.

British colonization in 1861 resulted in Lagos's permanent loss of sovereignty, and its slow development as a British imperial capital as well as an Atlantic port. Within only a few years, colonial officials had established a strong executive branch and new courts presided over by British judges, which began hearing disputes among locals, as well as

Europeans, Sierra Leoneans, and Brazilians. This lean colonial state ruled the colony directly despite only modest growth until the 1890s.[1]

Land in Precolonial Lagos

By the time evidence began to be recorded about landholding practices in the mid–nineteenth century, the question of who owned the land in and around Lagos had already acquired great political importance and become hotly contested. Within months of the signing of the Treaty of Cession in 1861, by which Ọba Dosunmu did "give, transfer, and . . . grant" Lagos to the British queen, a number of the Idẹjọ chiefs protested on the grounds that land in the kingdom belonged to them and the Ọba did not have the right to give it away.[2] In subsequent decades, as land became a scarce and more valuable resource, the issue took on major economic significance, as well.

Both written records and oral traditions pertaining to precolonial land tenure in Lagos have been framed in the context of specific political and economic transformations by actors—European and African—who had clear interests and advocated particular outcomes. In the early decades of the twentieth century, for example, British administrators in Africa favored upholding local traditions regarding land and other matters, unless they were repugnant to "natural justice, equity, and good conscience," in the interest of preserving precolonial authority, managing change, and making the nation's vast new colonies on the continent easier to rule, although they had earlier pursued a quite different policy. Aware that colonial governments were committed to preserving tradition, actors on all sides subsequently invoked and often invented "custom" to support their interests.[3] Untangling precolonial norms and practices from the skein of conflicting evidence in both colonial documents and oral traditions regarding land ownership in Lagos thus presents a difficult challenge. Two general observations should guide the process. First, norms and practices regarding land rights in Lagos have long been dynamic. There was no static precolonial or even precontact regime. Second, customary land law as articulated in the colonial period emerged from a dialogue between the colonial state and its African subjects, which took place in a number of arenas—administrative, judicial, political, and academic.[4]

According to an important local myth, the Ọlọfin, or first ruler of the settlement, divided the waters of the surrounding lagoon and the land on the two islands at the kingdom's center, as well as parts of the nearby mainland, among a number of men. These individuals are said to have received titles derived from the name of the territory where they exercised authority, been allowed to wear distinctive white caps as part of their insignia of office, and become the first Idẹjọ chiefs. By the mid–nineteenth century and possibly before, an idea existed that the Idẹjọ or the families they headed owned all of the land in the town of Lagos and its vicinity, as well as the fishing rights in the lagoon, by virtue of lineal succession from the first *Idẹjọ*.[5] One of the earliest documented expressions of this belief occurs in a letter that the first colonial governor, H. S. Freeman, sent the British foreign secretary reporting the *Idẹjọ's* opposition to the Treaty of Cession, which stated, "[The White Capped chiefs] are the rightful possessors of the land. . . . [T]he King and War-men hold no rights unless by grant from the White Capped chiefs."[6]

The origin of the idea that the *Idẹjọ* or their families owned all Lagos land is uncertain. It may date from the time of colonization by Benin, when the occupying warlords and subsequently the new ruling dynasty accommodated the heads of local communities by recognizing their rights to land.[7] No matter what its origin, the belief gained new salience in the first two decades of the twentieth century for two reasons. First, the *Idẹjọ* chiefs, who had been unable to uphold their claim to land in the opening decades of colonial rule, renewed their fight as its value increased with the rapid growth of the colonial and commercial capital from the mid-1890s.[8] Second, the conviction that the *Idẹjọ* families owned all Lagos land provided an ideological basis for challenging claims by the colonial government that absolute ownership of land in Lagos, as well as sovereignty over it, had passed to the British Crown under the Treaty of Cession. For if the *Ọba* had never enjoyed rights in Lagos land, then how could he have ceded ownership of it to the British Crown? The changing interests of the *Idẹjọs* and their families coincided with growing alarm among educated Africans about Britain's land policies in West Africa discussed below. Influential members of these two groups made common cause, the struggle over land rights became a form of anticolonial protest, and the idea that the *Idẹjọ* chieftaincy families owned the land in Lagos won widespread popular support.[9]

In practice, however, a larger number of extended families (*idile*) had exercised communal rights in land at least as early as the mid–nineteenth century. This group included the families of other types of chiefs, as well as of the *Idẹjọs*, but it was not limited to them. Neither local traditions nor early colonial observers attempted to explain the discrepancy between the popularly held idea that the *Idẹjọ* families owned all Lagos land and the empirical fact that other families also exercised ownership rights in it, beyond the *Idẹjọ's* assertion that all other owners had obtained their land from them.[10]

The diffusion of rights of communal land ownership at Lagos can perhaps best be explained by reference to the process through which the settlement grew and incorporated new groups into itself. Early settlers and their descendants claimed land by virtue of being the first to occupy, clear, and develop it. The heads of these families exercised authority over land, which they retained as institutions of centralized government developed and the most important of them were integrated into the changing political system as *Idẹjọ* chiefs.

Little evidence survives that illuminates land tenure during these early years. In the first decades of colonial rule, however, Lagosians reported that male and female members of these families enjoyed rights to use and participate in the management of town and rural family land, as well as rooms in town compounds. Females sometimes exercised their rights in landed property less actively than males because women normally lived with their husbands after marriage. In addition, farming and gathering tree crops were men's work, in which female family members had limited direct participation. Children commonly succeeded to farm plots and town housing that had been occupied by their fathers or mothers. If they needed additional property to use, they requested a further allocation from the head of the family. So long as land in the town and surrounding countryside was plentiful, male and female family members had little difficulty obtaining as much of it as they needed.[11]

The Beni viceroy and chiefs who had settled at Lagos by the mid–seventeenth century, founding the royal dynasty and the administrative and military classes of chiefs, apparently occupied land for their own use and subsequently exercised ownership rights in it that differed little from those enjoyed by earlier inhabitants. They did not, however, immediately claim wider authority over land. As the young Kingdom of Lagos grew and good, unclaimed land on Iddo island, Lagos island, and the nearby mainland ceased to exist, later immigrants obtained both town and rural land to use by requesting it from a local chief or the head of a lesser landowning lineage. Alternatively, strangers sometimes asked, initially, to be allowed to live in the compound of a prominent Lagosian and only later requested land on which to build or farm. Chiefs usually accommodated strangers wanting access to landed property because it enabled them to increase the number of their followers. Many observers insisted, however, that chiefs and the heads of lesser lineages could grant land to strangers only with the consent of their families as a whole.[12]

Prior to the development of Lagos as an Atlantic port in the nineteenth century, the idea that land could be permanently alienated did not exist. Nor was there a market in land, although a highly developed system of market exchange existed for many kinds of goods. The heads of landowning families did not grant land to strangers in perpetuity; rather, they extended only certain usufruct rights in it.[13] Yet in Lagos, as in many other places in precolonial Africa, the value of followers generally exceeded that of land, so that landowning families normally allowed strangers to retain town and rural plots, so long as they fulfilled basic obligations. These responsibilities included deference, allegiance, contributions to family religious and life-cycle ceremonies, and conformity to fundamental social norms. Migrants granted both rural land and town housing were also supposed to make an annual payment of farm produce or other commodities to the family head. This prestation did not constitute rent, as its monetary value was usually small and bore no relationship to the value of the land; rather, it symbolized that the occupier acknowledged the ongoing claim of the landowning family to the property and owed allegiance to its head. Failure to fulfill any of these duties was regarded as grounds for ejection from land or housing, as was a propensity to cause trouble within the family.[14] So long as strangers lived up to these expectations, however, they were usually permitted to retain use of the landed property they had been granted.[15]

When strangers who had been granted access to land died, their heirs were commonly allowed to continue using the property, although in theory only with the permission of the head of the landowning family. Such occupants were not supposed to allocate portions of the land to others without the consent of the head of that family.[16] Restrictions also limited what strangers could do with farmland they were granted. In most rural areas, they were not supposed, for example, to harvest palm or other tree crops growing on it. Nor were they to plant crop-bearing trees, rights in which tended to be identified with ownership of rural land.[17]

Despite widespread acceptance of these normative ideas about the obligations that strangers who were granted land or space in urban compounds owed the landowning family, performance of such obligations sometimes fell into abeyance. Changes of this kind generally occurred either because the newcomers were in time absorbed into the landowning family as kin or because they successfully asserted their independence from it. Furthermore, despite the restrictions commonly said to exist on what strangers could do with the landed property they occupied, grantees or their descendants sometimes began exercising full rights in it, such as granting portions to others or planting crop-bearing trees on rural land. By negotiating such changes, strangers often came in time to regard themselves and to be regarded by others as the owners of the land they occupied. In this way, communal landownership gradually diffused from the lineages of the first settlers to others founded later. Redefining their rights in land was an integral part of the larger process through which immigrants transformed themselves from strangers into community members.

Few questions about Lagos attracted greater interest in the colonial period than the rights of the Ọba in land because of the matter's relevance to Britain's claim to own all of the territory ceded by Dosunmu, not just to exercise sovereignty over it. By the early twentieth century, most local commentators, and even the king himself, maintained that the Ọba had no rights in land beyond that occupied by his family for its own use. Thus, the *Eleeko*, as the Ọba was then called, told government officials investigating land tenure in 1912 that, "The fundamental law . . . in and around Lagos was that all land was in the hands of the Idejo chiefs. The king had no control over land."[18] T. W. Johnson, who as court interpreter from 1876 to 1909 had heard most of the important litigation involving land, stated during the same inquiry, "The king had no control in land matters . . ."[19] Buchanan Smith, the Assistant Commissioner of Lands responsible for the investigation, concluded, "Most of the witnesses allege[d] that the king had no direct control over land, except that which belonged to him personally or to his family."[20] British officials, on the other hand, sought to construct and preserve, in the face of shifting judicial opinion on the subject, a legal argument that the Ọba had nonetheless enjoyed some kind of authority over land. An often quoted dictum of Justice Smalman Smith's tried to resolve the matter by acknowledging that the king had not enjoyed absolute ownership of land, but nonetheless claiming for him and his council a "national proprietary right" in land that entitled the Ọba to alienate it.[21] This point of view continued to persuade many British representatives even after the Privy Council, in its famous 1921 decision in *Amodu Tijani v. The Secretary, Southern Nigeria*, upheld the Crown's ultimate title to land but ruled that it did not impair the rights of the *Idẹjọ* chiefs and other local landowners.[22]

There is no evidence that in the precolonial period the Ọba received a share of the prestations that strangers gave landowning families in recognition of permission to occupy different kinds of landed property.[23] Data do indicate, however, despite local representations of custom to the contrary, that by the first half of the nineteenth century and perhaps before, Ọbas were exercising authority over land and, in some instances, granting it independently to outsiders. In a revealing moment, the *Eleeko* told the 1912 land inquiry that the king had given certain chiefs their land, although he then reversed himself after protests from the chiefs present exclaiming, "What I mean when I say that the king gave these chiefs their land is this: the king asked the Idejos to give them land."[24] Akinṣemoyin, Oṣinlokun, and Kosoko, three important late-eighteenth or mid–nineteenth century Ọbas, all enlarged their factions by urging powerful allies from neighboring towns and rural areas to move to Lagos with their followers and then ensuring that they received land on which to build compounds. Traditions of origin of several chieftaincy families recount that when their founders migrated to Lagos, *Idẹjọ* granted them land at the behest of the Ọba.[25] The chief of a leading *Idẹjọ* family indicated, moreover, that such grants were not always made voluntarily.[26]

Furthermore, when Europeans and Brazilians began settling at Lagos in the era of the slave trade, some of them looked to the Ọba for help obtaining land and housing. J. B. Wood, who collected Lagos traditions in the nineteenth century, claimed that European slave traders had bought land at Lagos and that the king had received one half of the proceeds, while the White Capped chiefs took the other half.[27] A letter from the Brazilian slave trader José Lourenco Gomez pleaded with Ọba Kosoko to grant him "with ink and paper" a house that had formerly belonged to another Brazilian.[28]

Wood maintained that the *Idẹjọ's* authority over land diminished in the first half of the nineteenth century, while that of the Ọba increased.[29] As the wealth and power of Lagos's kings grew in the era of the slave trade, they apparently sought to extend their authority over land as a means of strengthening their position vis-à-vis the *Idẹjọs* and certain other chiefs. The fact that *Ọbas* in Benin, unlike those in most Yoruba states, claimed ownership of all of the land within their kingdom may have helped inspire and legitimize the changing policy of Lagos's *Ọbas* in land matters.[30]

Ọbas Akitoye and Dosunmu, who reigned in the 1850s, took advantage of developments during that decade to consolidate their authority over land. Many Brazilian and Sierra Leonean repatriated slaves as well as European merchants, missionaries, and consular officials who arrived in Lagos following the bombardment turned to the *Ọba*, not the *Idẹjọs* or other prominent chiefs, for grants of the land they needed, and the kings met their requests. An agreement that Akitoye signed with European merchants in 1852 stated that the *Ọba* would allow them to erect storehouses on the eastern point of the island and choose their places of residence. None of the four chiefs signing the agreement with Akitoye was an *Idẹjọ*, and there is no evidence that he consulted them about its contents.[31] Moreover, the Church Missionary Society agent C. A. Gollmer obtained from *Ọba* Akitoye grants to five large plots, although in this case the grants were made by the *Ọba* "with his chiefs," and three *Idẹjọ* and ten other chiefs put their marks to the document.[32] Subsequently, Benjamin Campbell applied to the king for land on which to build a British consulate.[33]

At the end of the decade, the *Ọba* confidently told Robert Campbell, an Afro-Caribbean exploring the region as a site for possible settlement by American blacks, that "so far as his dominions extended . . . emigrants might select land suitable to their purpose, and he would gladly give it" to them.[34] But the most decisive evidence of the *Ọba's* growing authority over land can be found in seventy-six written grants that Dosunmu, who succeeded Akitoye in 1853, made to Brazilians, Sierra Leoneans, and a few others. Only six of the earliest grants say that they were made "with the advice and consent" of the chiefs. The rest mention no authority but the *Ọba's*.[35]

More far-reaching changes, however, soon overtook the *Ọbas* in their efforts to extend control over land. As repatriated slaves and a few Europeans settled in the community toward the end of the precolonial period, they introduced new ideas about how to own land and obtain access to it. Europeans regarded the slightly elevated ground along the waterfront on the south side of Lagos island as the "airiest" building sites, freest from the "miasma and fever" they believed were so deadly to them. Land there also provided easy access to the harbor and was a safe distance from the "filthy" African quarter to the northwest, also prone to devastating fires because of the thatch used to roof local buildings.[36] The CMS missionaries encouraged their disciples among the Sierra Leonean repatriated slaves to obtain land and build houses nearby on the southeastern corner of the island in a neighborhood that became known as Olowogbowo, while the Brazilian freed slaves settled in the interior of the island, developing Campos Square and Bamgbose Street.

As early as the 1850s, fierce competition existed for land in these areas.[37] Familiar with private property rights in land and houses through residence in Brazil and Sierra Leone, many liberated slaves, as well as European missionaries and merchants, treated their land grants from the Ọba as giving them fee-simple title-free of restrictions on alienation and of obligations under local tenure, although it is doubtful that this is what Akitoye and Dosunmu had intended to confer.[38] Those who could not obtain grants from the Ọba to property they wanted soon began buying it from locals or other immigrants who had earlier received land grants, and a market quickly developed for real estate in choice locations. When a British merchant J. G. Sandeman, for example, failed to obtain a parcel he had hoped for from the Ọba because the CMS already claimed it, he bought a different plot nearby.[39] To cite further examples of early land sales, a Brazilian bought a plot in 1854 from Dagra, one of the king's slaves, while the following year a Sierra Leonean woman who had been granted land died, and her plot was sold at public auction.[40] Robert Campbell wrote after visiting Lagos that rural land could be obtained in the area, "as much as can be used, 'without money and without price,'" but that town plots already cost "from $2 to $50 and even $100."[41]

Ọba Dosunmu apparently grasped something of the increasing value and changing significance of land and wanted to retain authority over its allocation. When forced by the British to sign the Treaty of Cession, one of the two concessions he negotiated was that "In the transfer of lands, the stamp of Docemo affixed to the document will be proof that there are no other native claims upon it."[42]

Colonial Transformations in Land Tenure

There can be no doubt that by the time Great Britain annexed Lagos in 1861, the alienation, commercialization, and privatization of land on the island were already well underway. These processes speeded up following the cession, and by the end of the century they had spread to parts of the mainland. H. S. Freeman observed that, "in consequence of the rise in the value of land in Lagos, the settlers have not only claimed the land they were occupying . . . but have taken possession of other land, and in some cases have sold it."[43] The sale of land did not stop with Sierra Leoneans and Brazilians, moreover, but rapidly spread to chiefs, family heads, and occupants enjoying only usufruct rights in it, as well. Sir Mervyn Tew remarked in his *Report on Title to Land in Lagos* that after the annexation Africans began to sell land for monetary compensation, while T. C. Rayner commented in an earlier report that by the final decades of the nineteenth century land was "freely bought and sold in . . . Lagos."[44] The concept of private ownership of land simultaneously took hold, and rights acquired through purchase were widely regarded as absolute by educated and uneducated Africans alike. Justice Osborne observed that "A purchaser from a family

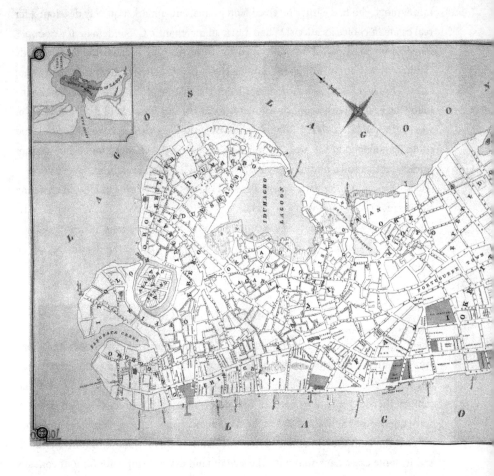

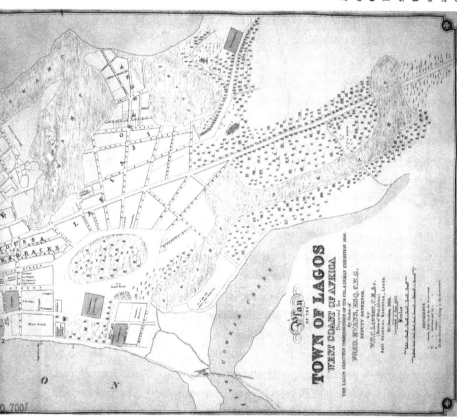

Plan of the Town of Lagos, West Coast of Africa, prepared for the Executive Commissioners of the Colonial and Indian Exhibition by Fred Evans, 1885, shows areas of African settlement on the northern and southwestern sides of the island and the European quarter along the southern waterfront.
Courtesy of the National Archives UK

acquire[d] an absolute interest," while Tew quoted the war chief Aṣogbon as stating that since the cession a grant of land by natives for monetary consideration was intended to convey absolute ownership, the deciding factor being "the payment of money for land."[45]

Throughout most of the second half of the nineteenth century, British officials in London and Lagos assumed that the commercial growth and prosperity of the young colony depended on the continued development of private property rights in land. For one thing, many of them subscribed to an evolutionary view of human history in which the development of private property rights in land was associated with higher stages of civilization. However, practical considerations also influenced the views of officials. Lagos's developing export trade in palm produce, on which, most agreed, the future of the colony depended, was conducted largely on credit. From the 1850s, European and Sierra Leonean merchants began requiring the Africans to whom they made commercial loans to pledge land or houses as security, and soon many African traders adopted the practice. Although Lagosians sometimes mortgaged land in which they enjoyed rights as family members or that to which they had been granted access by overlords, a presumption existed among merchants, traders, and officials that only privately owned property should be pledged to cover debts. Both at the time of the annexation and afterward, officials sought to promote and protect the development of private property rights in land in part to shore up credit, the basis of the colony's international trade.[46]

Early colonial land policy in Lagos was shaped, however, not by a clearly articulated vision from above, but piecemeal by the efforts of local administrators to respond to what was happening among Africans on the ground. The growth of the market for privately owned land in and around Lagos initially ran ahead of government efforts to promote and regulate it. The market was fueled not only by the widespread desire of Lagosians for real estate that they could mortgage to obtain credit, but also by other changing uses of landed property. By the 1850s and 1860s, a market had emerged for rental property, which in time spread from Europeans and Sierra Leonean and Brazilian immigrants to other sectors of the population, as well. The rental market generated valuable cash income. In addition, escalating real estate prices soon made landed property an excellent and relatively secure speculative investment.[47] Land and dwellings remained important to Lagosians for the reasons they always had been—as sites of economic enterprise, places of domestic shelter, and centers of family religious, social, and political activity. Within two decades of the 1851 British bombardment, however, real estate ownership had also acquired significant new meaning and value as both a major form of wealth and a primary path to it. Yet if British colonial land policy did not drive the transformations in land tenure taking place in Lagos, it did profoundly shape how the messy and complex process unfolded.

During the closing decades of the nineteenth century, the colonial government took the view that under the Treaty of Cession ultimate ownership of land in Lagos had passed to the British Crown. Governor Freeman's letters of commission empowered him to "make and execute in Our name and on Our behalf . . . grants and dispositions of any lands . . . within Our . . . Settlement."[48] Soon after his arrival, the governor began issuing land grants to some people and refusing them to others. Protests to the Colonial Office on behalf of a number of Sierra Leoneans whose claims had been denied led officials there to encourage the governor to ascertain what land in Lagos had been granted away and to whom, and what remained at the disposal of the Crown.[49] In response perhaps to this instruction, officials in Lagos hastily enacted a fateful ordinance, No. 9 of 1863, which provided for the appointment of three commissioners to ascertain "the True and Rightful owners of the land within the settlement of Lagos."[50] The long-term consequences of this legislation far outweighed the care and consideration that went into its enactment.

The law called upon the commissioners to sit for about a year and inquire into "the titles by which . . . all the lands within the Settlement are held, occupied, or laid claim to." It empowered the three men to summon anyone "having or pretending to have any right or title to lands within [the] Settlement, either by Grant or otherwise," along with their witnesses and the "books, papers, or other documents . . . upon which . . . they found . . . their claim." In cases where the commissioners concluded that persons had "good and valid" titles, they were to grant them certificates. In those where the commissioners believed that titles were invalid or without proof, they were to tell the claimants that they had no right to the property and record the fact.

Only one of the first three commissioners had any legal background, and only one other had much prior experience at Lagos. Whether the men summoned occupants of land or waited for inhabitants to approach the commission is unclear, but the three of them soon began validating some claims to land and denying others.[51] Instead of issuing certificates of title as stipulated under the ordinance, however, the commissioners made recommendations to the governor, who in approved cases issued documents that came to be known as Crown grants. Sir Mervyn Tew, who had access to the records of the land commissioners, found that they systematically favored claims based on grants from Ọba Dosunmu, demise by will, purchase, gift, and long occupation, sometimes unsupported by any written documentation.[52]

The commissioners could not, of course, complete the work of inquiring into titles to land in Lagos within one year. The government reenacted the ordinance twice more, and it continued the practice of issuing Crown grants even after the legislation expired in August 1866. A subsequent ordinance, No. 9 of 1869, allowed anyone who had "been in possession by himself or by his tenant" of property within the settlement for a period of three years, "without the payment of rent, or anything in the nature of rent, and without any acknowledgment of title to any person," to apply to the administrator for a grant of the land. This legislation also authorized the executive to declare as reverted to the Crown the property of anyone who did not obtain a grant within six months of being ordered to do so. It further provided that disputes over land should be settled by a colonial court, rather than an indigenous tribunal.[53] The language of the ordinance, which was gendered male, reveals implicit British assumptions about who landowners in the colony should be. To encourage draining swamps and improving land, the government introduced further ordinances that required owners to fill swamp land and remove "rubbish, ordure or filth," under penalty of sale at public auction. It continued to issue Crown grants to persons who filled swampland until the end of the nineteenth century.[54]

All of this early colonial land legislation gave Lagosians new ways of obtaining rights in land, and it profoundly influenced the terms in which they subsequently articulated claims to land.[55] By the time the government stopped issuing Crown grants after the turn of the twentieth century, almost four thousand such documents had been executed, 75 percent of them to land on Lagos Island.[56]

The Ọba and some of the chiefs resisted the colonial government's land policies, but to little avail. In the early 1860s, Dosunmu petitioned the British Parliament, arguing that he had ceded sovereignty over Lagos under threat of force and that "the course . . . adopted by the Executive, with regard to real property, should be changed." In land matters, the petition stated, the Ọba should be allowed to "use his seal according to the deed of cession."[57] Following the Idẹjọ's failed protest against the Treaty of Cession on the grounds that the Ọba did not have the right to grant Lagos lands away, Administrator Glover deposed two of them, perhaps as a consequence.[58] Subsequently, many of the chiefs apparently continued to protest the government's land policy silently by rejecting Crown grants. Tew maintained that some of the chiefs, such as Aṣogbon, initially responded positively to Glover's encouragement to apply for Crown grants but then changed their minds when warned by "foreigners"—probably Sierra Leonean repatriates—that the documents meant that the government was claiming all Lagos land.[59]

Dosunmu took out a few grants, including to the land on which the palace stood, but many of the Idẹjọ and other Lagos chiefs did not obtain Crown grants to most of the land that they and their families occupied. There is no reason to think that the land commissioners rejected applications by the chiefs, who in most cases would have had no difficulty establishing their title to land. The failure of so many of the chiefs to obtain Crown grants can be explained only by assuming that they did not apply for them. The chiefs' rejection of Crown grants probably stemmed from multiple factors: fear of what the documents meant or opposition to them, aversion to dealing with the new colonial government, disinclination to pay the fees necessary to obtain grants, and stubborn belief that for important chiefs and their families the grants were unnecessary.

Beyond what Crown grants communicated about the authority that the new colonial state was assuming over land, the meaning of the documents was ambiguous. None of the legislation that led the state to issue grants defined the rights they conferred. Government officials awarded them to validate title to land, but of what kind or on the basis of which rights was not specified. Administrators made the grants, however, in the name of individuals, not families or other groups. Throughout the early colonial period, most British officials regarded African ideas about land ownership as antithetical to progress, and they assumed that colonial rule and economic development would eventually transform them. Until the administration of the Yoruba interior confronted the colonial state with new political and social imperatives after 1893, most British officers in Lagos believed that the demise of communal ownership by families was inevitable and would be a good thing. E. A. Speed, acting chief justice of the Lagos Supreme Court, expressed this view as late as 1909, when he wrote in an important legal decision:

[F]amily ownership is gradually ceasing to exist [in Lagos]. In a progressive community it is of course inevitable that this should be so.[60]

Despite the legal ambiguities of Crown grants, many British officials and African observers alike in Lagos maintained that the documents conferred a fee-simple title. Yet some government officers and one influential African lawyer also acknowledged that the state had originally intended the grants to confirm a preexisting right of occupancy, which might rest on family as well as individual ownership. When disputes arose in the colonial courts between grantees and others claiming rights in the property, judges—who under the 1876 Supreme Court ordinance were supposed to decide disputes among locals according to their own law and custom, unless doing so violated the repugnancy clause or was incompatible with local statute—sometimes upheld family or other collective ownership.[61]

It is harder to know how the recipients of Crown grants themselves understood the documents. Judging from the names of the persons to whom they were issued, which indicate origins only imperfectly, about 70 percent of the Crown grants went to Sierra Leonean, Brazilian, or other Atlantic emigrés in the period 1863 to 1866. These recipients generally treated the documents as giving them fee-simple title during their lives, and they sold, mortgaged, or otherwise disposed of the property as they saw fit. But in 1869, to cite a later year that was not atypical, about half of the grants issued went to local people, and this more democratic distribution continued as the century progressed. If the chiefs generally eschewed Crown grants, other members of the indigenous community did not.[62]

Some locals took out Crown grants as representatives of families or other groups that occupied the land and continued to regard it as collectively owned, even after obtaining the grant. In such cases, many or all of the adult members of the family or other collectivity continued to exercise rights in the land. But other local people obtained grants to family-owned land, sometimes without the knowledge of their kin, and subsequently treated the property as though it were privately owned. At the end of the century, Lagosians complained that there was a growing tendency for persons who had taken out Crown grants as representatives of families to claim private ownership of the land.[63] Thus, the legal effects of Crown grants remained uncertain. In a very real sense, the documents conveyed whatever rights in landed property the recipients could use them to exercise.[64] Despite this ambiguity, Crown grants offered Lagosians an important new means of asserting rights in land, and they were widely identified with private rather than communal ownership. The acquisition of a Crown grant commonly became the first step in exercising rights of private property in land or a house.[65]

If the land commissioners had accepted purchase, gift, long occupation, and demise by will as evidence of title to land and justification for issuing Crown grants to it, so the colonial courts and the public sometimes interpreted these practices as conferring rights of private property in land, whether or not a Crown grant had been obtained. Purchase, gift, inheritance, and long occupation without acknowledging the rights of a grantor all became additional means by which Lagosians could obtain fee-simple title to landed property. Documents from the Lagos Supreme Court established in 1876 show that while judges sometimes refused to uphold the sale of family land without the consent of kin, they treated sales as conferring absolute ownership if consent had been obtained or if the property was privately owned.[66]

Following the annexation, Lagosians could also be given privately owned landed property. When the donors executed deeds of gift or otherwise made their intentions very clear, as commonly occurred among Sierra Leonean and Brazilian immigrants, these transfers proved relatively unproblematic.[67] Locals and immigrants from the interior and elsewhere on the coast, however, much more commonly obtained access to land through the grants of usufruct that indigenous peoples had long made. Both the colonial courts and many local authorities eventually took the position that absolute ownership of family land could not be granted away without the consent of the family.[68] Yet in the nineteenth century, the Lagos Supreme Court sometimes treated long occupation of land without the performance of ritual or economic obligations to an overlord as evidence of absolute ownership, and Lagosians themselves occasionally adopted this perspective. If those who occupied landed property could hold on to it and over time cease paying the grantor the homage, prestations, and service associated with usufruct, then they could often redefine their rights in the property and assert fee-simple title to it.

Inheritance offered another means of obtaining privately owned land in Lagos, though less common than Crown Grants, purchase, and the gradual redefinition of rights during long occupation. Inheritance practices illustrate clearly, however, that the changes taking place in land tenure within the African population were not linear—from communal African to privately owned European. Instead, they had a dynamic of their own. After the introduction of English law and establishment of the colonial legal system, individuals could have wills written that provided for the disposition of their landed property. While not the norm, some of those who adopted the practice employed the documents to leave real estate to individuals or groups of people in fee-simple or according to other specifications.[69] In a development that deviated from the evolutionary expectations of British officials and led them to grumble about the "peculiar" state of land law at Lagos, however, most land and houses in which individuals exercised fee-simple title during their lives in fact devolved to heirs as communally owned family property.[70] Indeed, many Lagosians who left wills, even educated Christians, used them to ensure that their self-acquired land and houses would pass down to subsequent generations as family property. In time, this type of succession, which transformed privately owned landed property into family-owned property on the death of the person who had acquired it, came to be accepted as local custom. Buchanan Smith noted that in Lagos Colony "a Crown grant often becomes after the first generation . . . a piece of inalienable family land" and that the "native who purchases [land] at a sale can sell it again if he so chooses, but that, if he fails to do so, at his death it becomes vested in his descendants as a whole." He observed, moreover, that in Lagos persons often bought real estate "with the view that on their death it should pass in bulk to their descendants and be considered family land, and as such be inalienable."[71]

As this brief discussion of inheritance makes clear, communal ownership of land and buildings by families did not die out in Lagos following the growth of a market for land or the introduction of private property rights in it. Rather, family ownership remained dominant in the sense that more people continued to exercise rights in land that way than any other, even while the selling of land and buying of it by individuals continued apace. Buchanan Smith called the "tenacity" of "ownership by the family, under the control . . . of its head," even in cases where the proprietor had an undoubted freehold title vested in himself personally, one "of the most curious features" of Lagos's modern system of land tenure.[72] Sir Melvyn Tew concluded in 1939, "I do not believe . . . that even in Lagos today family ownership can be said to be a dying institution."[73]

During the scramble for Africa at the end of the nineteenth century, Great Britain acquired vast new territory inland from the coast, behind Lagos and in other parts of the continent. The expansion of the British Empire in Africa changed the imperatives facing colonial governments in southern Nigeria and elsewhere. As a consequence, officials in London, Lagos, and other administrative centers started to rethink land policies and retreat from encouraging the development of private property rights in land. Once it became clear that Britain would rule its vast new inland empire through local authorities, government officials began to fear that changes in land tenure that undermined the control of chiefs and elders over such a vital resource would threaten their power and jeopardize the stability of colonial administrations. During these years, officials also began thinking more explicitly about the organization of production for export, and, in Nigeria, they committed themselves firmly to the path of African agriculture rather than large-scale foreign plantations. By the 1910s, some local officials had begun to worry that a market for land and private property rights in it were spreading north from Lagos Colony into the Yoruba Protectorate and would dispossess local farmers from the means of rural production. Policy makers feared that this process would drive landless peasants into the capital city, where they would become a "burden on the nation," descending into vagrancy and crime if males and prostitution and polyandry if females.[74]

The details of the evolution of colonial land policy in the twentieth century are beyond the scope of this study, and they have, in any case, been analyzed elsewhere. Suffice it to say that the colonial government soon resolved to uphold communal ownership of land as a means of preserving the authority of local rulers and protecting the access of African farmers to land.[75] Places such as Lagos, where a market in land was already well developed and rights of private property had long made their mark, soon became sources of irritation and inconvenience. The realities of land tenure in Lagos and certain other West African coastal towns and cities did not fit well with Britain's revised development plan for its now larger and much more important empire inland from the Atlantic.

By the turn of the twentieth century, the market for land in Lagos was too deeply entrenched to be eliminated, but even there Britain slowly and unevenly shored up communal tenure and the rights of certain chieftaincy families to land in and around the town. The shift occurred in fits and starts, largely through judicial decisions such as that in the landmark case *Amodu Tijani v. The Secretary, Southern Nigeria*, but occasional legislation reinforced what was taking place in the courts.[76] It is ironic that imperial exigencies and a ruling by the highest court of the British realm had secured by the 1920s the rights of major Lagos chieftaincy families in large swaths of land in or near the city, a claim raised, in part, as a political challenge by a number of the *Idẹjọ* chiefs at the moment of annexation roughly sixty years before. The roots of memory and of anticolonial protest ran deep in Lagos, such that the legal victory in *Amodu Tijani* was widely experienced as a political triumph as well. The reinvigoration of communal tenure in the early decades of the twentieth century, however, did not forestall further conflict and litigation over land rights. Lagosians had learned well, and they continued to invoke history and custom in support of competing claims to land, as they contested social identities and political relationships.

Conclusion

A study of the messy and contested history of land tenure in colonial Lagos shows that it was shaped by a dialogue between the colonizers and colonized, but that contrary to what might be expected, major transformations in land rights and land use were driven by the practices of Africans on the ground and later in colonial courts, rather than by the policies of British colonial rulers. The data also show that changes in land tenure and land law were in no sense unidirectional.

Before Britain's annexation of Lagos as a Crown Colony in 1861, a market in land had already begun to develop in the African community, and rights of private property in land and houses had started to emerge where they had not existed before, as freed slaves from Brazil and Sierra Leone and soon local peoples themselves looked for new ways to obtain access to town real estate and stake claims in it. After the annexation, colonial land policies sought to catch up with developments on the ground and to regulate them. To be sure, colonial administrators threw their weight behind the development of private property rights in land, which they regarded as necessary to commercial development and Christian civilization. On the other hand, British magistrates and judges were committed to settling disputes in colonial courts among indigenous peoples over land and other resources according to "native law and custom," which exercised a countervailing influence.

Furthermore, Africans, both repatriated slaves and local peoples, who acquired through purchase, government grant, or other means individually owned land, which they could freely sell or pledge as collateral for credit, quickly began on their deaths, through written wills, and oral instructions, to pass land and houses on to their heirs collectively as inalienable, communally owned family property, mimicking indigenous land tenure. Colonial authorities regarded this reversion to African practices in the second generation of ownership as contrary to both their evolutionary expectations and their long-term goals for development, yet the weight of local behavior was such that officials could not alter the trend. Although not examined in this essay, local landholders, in addition, used the colonial courts to articulate new kinds of land rights, which they represented as indigenous, to maintain control over different sorts of dependents.[77]

Finally, this essay has shown that as Britain moved inland from the coast in the 1890s and colonized the interior, colonial officials changed their minds about the desirability of promoting the development of a market and private property rights in land. Land alienation had already begun to spread north from Lagos, and colonial officials became concerned that if indigenous rulers there lost control over land it would undermine the policy of indirect rule through which Britain sought to govern its growing African empire inland from the coast. The commercial exchange and private ownership of land that had taken hold at Lagos and were championed by literate Africans as rights to which Britain's colonial subjects were entitled suddenly became a major threat to be contained on the grounds that they were not "customary."

NOTES

1. For a fuller discussion of these themes, see Kristin Mann, *Slavery and the Birth of an African City: Lagos, 1760–1900* (Bloomington: University of Indiana Press, 2007).
2. The Treaty of Cession is reprinted in Robert S. Smith, *The Lagos Consulate, 1851–1861* (Berkeley: University of California Press, 1979), 140–141. For a report of the Idẹjọs' protest, see Freeman to Russell, March 5, 1862, encl. in British National Archives, Colonial Office Records, Original Correspondence, Lagos Colony (hereafter CO 147) 1, Freeman to Newcastle, March 8, 1862.
3. Terence Ranger, "The Invention of Tradition in Colonial Africa" in Eric Hobsbawm and Terence Ranger, eds., *The Invention of Tradition* (Cambridge: Cambridge University Press, 1983), 211–262; Martin Chanock, *Law, Custom and Social Order: The Colonial Experience in Malawi and Zambia* (Cambridge: Cambridge University Press, 1985), 145–216; Sara Berry, *No Condition is Permanent: The Social Dynamics of Agrarian Change in Sub-Saharan Africa* (Madison: University of Wisconsin Press, 1993), 22–42; Richard Roberts and Kristin Mann, "Introduction" in Kristin Mann and Richard Roberts, eds., *Law in Colonial Africa* (Portsmouth, NH: Heinemann, 1991), 20–36; Sara S. Berry, *Chiefs Know Their Boundaries: Essays on Property, Power, and the Past in Asante, 1896–1996* (Portsmouth, NH: Heinemann, 2001), 7.
4. Sally Falk Moore, *Social Facts and Fabrications: "Customary" Law on Kilimanjaro, 1880–1980* (Cambridge: Cambridge University Press, 1986); Martin Chanock, "Paradigms, Policies, and Property: A Review of the Customary Law of Land Tenure," *Law in Colonial Africa*, 62; M. P. Cowen and R. W. Shenton, "British Neo-Hegelianism and Official Colonial Practice in Africa: The Oluwo Land Case of 1921," *Journal of Imperial and Commonwealth History* 22 (1994): 217–250.
5. J. Buckley Wood, *Historical Notices of Lagos, West Africa* (Exeter: James Townsend, n.d.), 3–14; John B. Losi, *History of Lagos* (Lagos: Tika Tore Press, 1914), 3. See also the testimony of Lagosians printed in West African Lands Committee, Committee on the Tenure of Land in West African Colonies and Protectorates (hereafter WALC), "Correspondence," 222–244; and Sir Mervyn Tew, *Report on Title to Land in Lagos* (Lagos: The Government Printer, 1947), 6–9.
6. Freeman to Russell, March 5, 1862, encl. in CO 147/1, Freeman to Newcastle, March 8, 1862. See also, J. A. O. Payne, *Table of Principal Events in Yoruba History* (Lagos: Andrew W. Thomas, 1893), 6.
7. Wood, *Historical Notices*, 17; Losi, *History*, 12.
8. For evidence of the Idẹjọs' renewed interest in land during the early twentieth century, see *Amodu Tijani v. The Secretary, Southern Nigeria, The Law Reports (Appeals)* (1921) vol. II, p. 399 ff, reprinted in C. K. Meek, *Land Tenure and Land Administration in Nigeria and the Cameroons* (London: HMSO, 1957), 77–84; and Tew, *Report*, 5.
9. Omoniyi Adewoye, "The Tijani Land Case (1915–1921): A Study in British Colonial Justice," *Odu* 13 (1976): 21–39; Richard L. Sklar, *Nigerian Political Parties: Power in an Emergent African Nation* (Princeton: Princeton University Press, 1963), 42–44; Pauline H. Baker, *Urbanization and Political Change: The Politics of Lagos, 1917–1967* (Berkeley: University of California Press, 1974), 94–97; Berry, *No Condition Is Permanent*, 105.

10. WALC, "Correspondence," 229. See also Tew, *Report*, 6.

11. Information on land tenure in precolonial Lagos comes from WALC, "Correspondence," 223–245. Additional data can be found in judges' notes on land cases brought before the Lagos Supreme Court. Many of the most important cases, or excerpts from them, are reprinted in WALC, "Minutes," 522–528; Robert Forsyth Irving, *A Collection of the Principal Enactments and Cases Relating to Titles to Land in Nigeria* (London: Stephens and Sons, 1916), 201–319; and *Nigeria Law Reports* (hereafter NLR), vols. 1–2. Other relevant documents include T. C. Rayner and J. J. C. Healy, *Reports on Land Tenure in West Africa (1898)*, Colonial Office Library, West Africa Pamphlet, No. 19; A. G. Hopkins, "A Report on the Yoruba, 1910," *Journal of the Historical Society of Nigeria* 5 (1969): 84–85; Tew, *Report*; and Meek, *Land Tenure*. The literature on Yoruba land law is voluminous. For a start, see P. C. Lloyd, *Yoruba Land Law* (London: Oxford University Press, 1962); T. Olawale Elias, *Nigerian Land Law and Custom* (London: Routledge and Kegan Paul, 1951); and G. B. A. Coker, *Family Property among the Yorubas* (London: Sweet and Maxwell, 1958). Sandra T. Barnes, *Patrons and Power: Creating a Political Community in Metropolitan Lagos* (Bloomington: Indiana University Press, 1986) provides long-term perspective on the significance of land and houses in Lagos.

12. WALC, "Correspondence," 229. Also interviews in Lagos with Prince A. L. A. Ojora, October-November 1984, and Chief S. B. A. Oluwa, January 1985.

13. WALC, "Correspondence," 227.

14. T. C. Rayner, "Land Tenure in West Africa," in Rayner and Healy, *Land Tenure*, 1; J. J. C. Healy, "Land Tenure in the Colony of Lagos," in Rayner and Healy, *Land Tenure*, 1; WALC, "Correspondence," 142, 224, 227, 232–238; Hopkins, "Report on the Yoruba," 13–15; Meek, *Land Tenure*, 63, 72, 115, 156, 189–191; interviews with Prince A. L. A. Ojora, Chief S. B. A. Oluwa, and Alhaji A. W. A. Akibayo (February 1985); Rhodes House Library, Oxford (Colonial Records Project), Mss.Afr.L15, W. Fowler, "A Report on the Lands of the Colony District."

15. *Ajose v. Efunde and others*, excerpted in WALC, "Minutes," 525.

16. WALC, "Correspondence," 229.

17. Rayner, "Land Tenure," 3; WALC, "Correspondence," 142, 219, 224, 228–229; Meek, *Land Tenure*, 130, 175; Alfred Burdon Ellis, *The Yoruba-Speaking People of the Slave Coast of West Africa* (London: Chapman and Hall, 1894), 188–189. See also Elias, *Nigerian Land Law*, 185.

18. WALC, "Correspondence," 179.

19. *Ibid.*, 238.

20. *Ibid.*, 224.

21. Quoted in W. Buchanan Smith, "Report. Land Tenure in the Colony of Lagos," WALC, "Correspondence," 224. For the text of Justice Smith's decision see *Ajose v. Efunde*, WALC, "Correspondence," 246–248. Elias, *Nigerian Land Law*, 6–28, discusses changing views of the impact of the Treaty of Cession on land ownership in Lagos Colony. Meek, *Land Tenure*, 64–65, observes that the rights of the Ọba in land were "much discussed in numerous land cases." Chanock, "Paradigms, Policies," and Cowen and Shenton, "British Neo-Hegelianism," locate the issue in broader imperial perspectives.

22. See, for example, Tew, *Report*, 7–9.

23. WALC, "Correspondence," 228–230, 239.

24. *Ibid.*, 179.

25. Interview with Chief S. B. A. Oluwa; Losi, *History*, 14; Takiu Folami, *A History of Lagos, Nigeria* (Smithtown, NY: Exposition Press, 1982), 107, 112, 114, 118. Ọba Ọṣinlokun or Ọba Idewu Ojulari also granted land in Lagos to refugees from Gun territory. *Fanojoria v.*

Kadiri, 22 June 1881, Judges' Notebooks, Civil Cases, the Lagos Supreme Court (hereafter *JNCC*) 3, 265–275.

26. *Callamand v. Vaughan*, quoted in Meek, *Land Tenure*, 53. See also WALC, "Minutes," 525.

27. Wood, *Historical Notices*, 18.

28. House of Lords Sessional Papers, 1852–1853, 22, Gomes to Kosoko, February 4, 1850, 347.

29. Wood, *Historical Notices*, 18.

30. On the rights of Benin's *Qba* in land, see WALC, "Minutes," 184, 391–392, and "Correspondence," 166; and Meek, *Land Tenure*, 158–159, 162, 181, 229.

31. PP 1862.LXI.339, Papers Relating to the Occupation of Lagos, Agreement with the King and Chiefs of Lagos, February 28, 1852, 342. For a description of how the British merchant J. G. Sandeman sought to obtain land in Lagos, see Sandeman to Fraser, January 8, 1853, encl. in British National Archives, Foreign Office Records, Slave Trade Correspondence (hereafter FO 84) 920, Fraser to Malmesbury, March 1853.

32. FO 84/976, Campbell to Clarendon, May 28, 1855, plus encls. For the voluminous correspondence regarding Akitoye's grants to Gollmer, see FO 84/950, 976, and 1002; and Smith, *Lagos Consulate*, 37, 80–81, 97–98.

33. FO 84/976, Campbell to Clarendon, April 4, 1855.

34. Robert Campbell, "A Pilgrimage to My Motherland," in M. R. Delany and Robert Campbell, *Search for a Place: Black Separatism and Africa, 1860* (Ann Arbor: University of Michigan Press, 1969), 164.

35. British consuls recorded a number of Dosunmu's grants, and those that survive can be found in a bound volume in the Strong Room at the Lagos Land Registry.

36. FO 84/920, Martin to Fraser, December 27, 1852; FO 84/950, Campbell to Clarendon, May 1, 1854; CO 147/6, Freeman to Newcastle, March 26, 1864.

37. FO 84/920, Martin to Fraser, December 27, 1852, and Fraser to Malmesbury, March 11, 1853; FO 84/950, Campbell to Clarendon, May 1, 1854; FO 84/976, F.O. to Campbell, May 24, 1855, and Campbell to Clarendon, September 1, 1855.

38. Meek, *Land Tenure*, 55. Information about land ownership in Freetown, Sierra Leone comes from Christopher Fyfe, *A History of Sierra Leone* (London: Oxford University Press, 1962), 143–144 passim; and about that in Bahia comes from B. J. Barickman, *A Bahian Counterpoint: Sugar, Tobacco, Cassava, and Slavery in Recôncavo, 1780–1860* (Stanford: Stanford University Press, 1998), 107–108, 190–195; and personal communication from João José Reis, July 18, 2000.

39. Sandeman to Campbell, August 28, 1855, encl. in FO 84/976, Campbell to Clarendon, September 1, 1855.

40. Tew, *Report*, 13. Also *Amuleye v. Thomas*, February 19, 1879, JNCC, 2, 70.

41. Campbell, "Pilgrimage," 243.

42. Treaty of Cession, August 6, 1861, reprinted in Smith, *Lagos Consulate*, 141.

43. CO 147/5, Murdock to Elliot, July 24, 1863.

44. Tew, *Report*, 11; Rayner, "Land Tenure," 1. See also A. W. Osborne, "Memorandum," WALC, "Minutes," 522–528; "Memorandum by Sir Walter Napier on the Principles of Native Land Tenure in the Gold Coast and Southern Nigeria," WALC, "Draft Report," Appendix C, 149; and Smith, "Report," 223–227.

45. Osborne, "Memorandum," 522; Tew, *Report*, 11. See also Rayner, "Land Tenure," 4.

46. Chanock, "Paradigms, Policies," 62–63; A. G. Hopkins, "Property Rights and Empire Building: Britain's Annexation of Lagos," *Journal of Economic History* 40 (1980): 777–779; Mann, *Slavery*, 264–265.

47. Mann, *Slavery*, 266–269.

48. Quoted in Tew, *Report*, 13. The Letters Patent issued in 1886, when Lagos was separated from the Gold Coast, contained similar language, as did those issued in 1906 and 1913 on the creation of the colonies of Southern Nigeria and Nigeria. Meek, *Land Tenure*, 57, 62.

49. CO 147/2, Emigration Office to Elliot, November 22, 1862; CO 147/3, Freeman to Newcastle, February 5, 1865; CO 147/5, Emigration Office to Elliot, July 24, 1863, Buxton to Newcastle, April 18, 1863, plus encls., and Freeman to Newcastle, July 24, 1863.

50. This ordinance is reprinted in Irving, *Collection*, 3–5.

51. CO 147/3, Glover to Newcastle, July 10, 1863.

52. Tew, *Report*, 12–14.

53. Irving, *Collection*, 9–11. See also Meek, *Land Tenure*, 59.

54. Healy, "Land Tenure," 3. Also Tew, *Report*, 14–16; and Meek, *Land Tenure*, 61.

55. Although beyond the scope of this essay, I have analyzed the rhetoric of shifting land claims in *Slavery*, chaps. 7–8.

56. One further government action had long-term implications for land ownership in the town of Lagos. An anti-European uprising at Abeokuta in 1867 led many Egba Christians to flee south to the British colony. Administrator J. H. Glover obtained for these refugees land at Ebute Metta, on the mainland across from Lagos Island, from Chief Oloto, the *Idẹjọ* with authority over the area. Glover had the territory laid out in blocks, and he then entrusted the headman of the group with settling each refugee and "his family" on a plot and obtaining a ticket to the land for him. A few of the approximately seven hundred settlers who obtained land in this way subsequently applied for Crown grants to their parcels, but the majority did not. Much of the land in the government layout remained unoccupied following settlement by the Egba refugees, and as the population of the city subsequently grew, others acquired plots there through a variety of means—squatting, government allocation, and sale or grant by ticket holders or members of the Oloto family. In time, the question of who owned the land in this section of the city and how they owned it became very complicated and gave rise to "bitter conflict and much litigation," the more so because a Land Commissioner at some point burned the government's copies of the "Glover tickets," and many ticket holders lost or destroyed theirs. Tew, *Report*, 13–25; Meek, *Land Tenure*, 58–62; Stanhope Rowton Simpson, *A Report on the Registration of Title to Land in the Federal Territory of Lagos* (Lagos: Federal Government Printer, 1957), 37. Bound volumes recording the government's Crown grants can be found in the Strong Room of the Lagos Land Registry. On the uprising at Abeokuta, see S. O. Biobaku, *The Egba and Their Neighbours, 1842–1872* (Oxford: Clarendon Press, 1957) 83–84; and J. F. A. Ajayi, *Christian Missions in Nigeria, 1841–1891: The Making of a New Elite* (London: Longmans, 1965), 200–203.

57. Just what the *Ọba* meant by this request is unclear, because the Treaty of Cession stated only that in the transfer of lands the King's seal would be proof that "there are no other native claims on it." Col. Ord maintained after interviewing Dosunmu that the king wanted, by fixing his seal, to establish the *Ọba's* title to land belonging to deceased natives. PP 1865.XXXVII.287, Report of Col. Ord on the Condition of the British Settlements on the West Coast of Africa, 312–313, and Appendix C, "The humble Petition of Docemo . . . to . . . Parliament . . .," n.d., 330.

58. For references to Glover's deposition of the two chiefs, see *Callamand v. Vaughan* and *Ajose v. Efunde*, WALC, "Minutes," 524–525.

59. Tew, *Report*, 12. Also *Ajose v. Efunde*, 247. The registers of Crown grants at the Lagos Land Registry show that the Aṣogbon did, indeed, obtain a single grant in 1863 but then abruptly abandoned the practice until 1868, when he received two more. Ladega, a member of the

Aṣogbon family who subsequently became chief, also took out a number of Crown Grants in his name beginning in 1868.

60. *Lewis v. Bankole* (1909) 1 *NLR*, 83. Chanock, "Paradigms, Policies," (62–66) briefly discusses the early colonial idea that African land tenure was primitive and needed to evolve to recognize private property, but his analysis focuses primarily on a later colonial period when the preoccupations of colonial administrators changed and the doctrine of communal ownership took hold. See also Anne Phillips, *The Enigma of Colonialism: British Policy in West Africa* (London: James Currey, 1989), 59–84; Berry, *No Condition Is Permanent*, 101–110; and Berry, *Chiefs*, 1–34. The literature on colonial land policy generally pays insufficient attention to the promotion of rights of private ownership in the nineteenth century and subsequent changes in policy as governments extended their authority inland from the 1890s.

61. Rayner, "Land Tenure," 4; WALC, "Correspondence," 38, 225, "Memorandum by Napier," 14, and Smith, "Report," 223–227; Tew, *Report*, 17; Meek, *Land Tenure*, 61. See also T. Olawale Elias, *The Nigerian Legal System* (London: Routledge and Kegan Paul, 1963), 3–5, 12–14; and Omoniyi Adewoye, *The Judicial System in Southern Nigeria, 1854–1954* (Atlantic Highlands, N J: Humanities Press, 1977), 25.

62. These data come from an analysis of Crown Grants at the Lagos Land Registry.

63. *Lagos Weekly Record*, October 3, 1891, 3, c. 2–3. Also Smith, "Report," 26; and Meek, *Land Tenure*, 63.

64. Sara Berry, *No Condition Is Permanent*, 101–103, has shown how official policy and local practice combined to make land rules ambiguous and subject to ongoing reinterpretation in twentieth-century Africa. She has argued that, as a consequence, peoples' access to land has depended on their participation in processes of interpretation and adjudication. What Berry says of the twentieth century was true in Lagos by the closing decades of the nineteenth century. Since then judges, administrators, scholars, and the public have all expended much time, energy, and—in the case of the public—money contesting the meaning of Crown grants. For brief introductions to this subject, see Tew, *Report*, 16–23; Elias, *Nigerian Land Law*, 21–28; and Coker, *Family Property*, 182–216 passim.

65. The government defined the rights conferred by Glover tickets no more clearly than it did those vested in Crown grants. Over time, however, judges and officials treated the tickets much the way they did Crown grants—as conveying fee-simple title subject, in certain cases, to family rights. In the 1920s, the Oloto family stepped up efforts to reassert its rights to land within the Glover layout, inspired perhaps by changes in land policy after the turn of the century, as well as by the Privy Council's 1921 decision in *Amodu Tijani v. The Secretary, Southern Nigeria*. The family had little success, however, with plots that had been allotted to the Egba refugees. Tew, *Report*, 29–31.

66. *Brimah Balogun and another v. Oshodi* (1931) 10 NLR 36; *Re Public Lands Ordinance, 1876* (1899), excerpted in WALC, "Minutes," 523. From before the annexation, British officials had encouraged registration of conveyances, leases, mortgages, and deeds of gift at the consulate and later at the colonial Land Registry established for the purpose. In 1883, an ordinance made registration of such documents compulsory, but many land transfers continued to occur without the creation, much less registration, of any written documentation. The fees for registration alone were enough to discourage many Lagosians from registering land records. See, for example, Lagos Colony, *Blue Books*, 1880, 1885.

67. For examples of Deeds of Gifts, see Charlotte Davies to Victoria Davies, December 24, 1863, 2, 236; Susannah Turner to Rebecca Johnson, trustee for Christiana Abigail Johnson,

June 12, 1869, 8, 437; and Ladipo to Rebecca Johnson, June 3, 1870, 10, 288, all recorded at the Lagos Land Registry. Fee-simple title seems to have been given in particular to educated girls, often with the provision that after marriage their husbands should have no rights in the property.

68. Elias, *Nigerian Land Law*, 186–187; Meek, *Land Tenure*, 130–131; Coker, *Family Property*, 113–114, 118–120.

69. This observation is based on a reading of wills at the Lagos Probate Registry. See, for example, the testaments of S. A. Crowther, May 3, 1881, 1, 162; Jane Dorcas Sawyer, December 15, 1892, 1, 218; Sunmonu Animaṣaun, August 21, 1895, 1, 357; A. Alberto, April 25, 1895, 1, 394–396; J. Ayorinde, May 16, 1898, 2, 60–64; and C. R. Cole, January 13, 1910, 3, 192–199.

70. Rayner, "Land Tenure," 4; WALC, "Minutes," 254, 516, and "Draft Report," 63–64; Tew, *Report*, 39.

71. WALC, "Correspondence," 226. See also Rayner, "Land Tenure," 3; and "Memorandum by Napier," 150. The courts finally held in the twentieth century that only self-acquired property and not family land could be affected by wills because individuals did not enjoy alienable rights in the latter. Elias, *Nigerian Land Law*, 268; WALC, "Minutes," 516, 526.

72. WALC, "Correspondence," 223.

73. Tew, *Report*, 19. See also Meek, *Land Tenure*, 64, 116, 132, 136–137.

74. WALC, "Minutes," 151–152, 243, 252–253, "Correspondence," 190, "Draft Report," 64, and "Memo by Napier," 151–153.

75. Phillips, *Enigma*, 59–84; Berry, *No Condition is Permanent*, 24–42, 106; and Berry, *Chiefs*, 5–8. Chanock, "Paradigms, Policies," analyzes discourse that shaped British colonial land policy during this period.

76. See, for example, *De Cruz v. De Cruz* (1892) and *Oloto v. Dowudu* (1894), excerpted in WALC, "Correspondence," 248; *Re Public Lands Ordinance, 1876* (1899) and *Ayorinde v. Asiatu and others* (1899), excerpted in WALC, "Minutes," 523, 525; *Oloto v. Dawuda and others* (1904) 1 NLR 57; *Lewis v. Bankole*, 81; and "Memorandum by Napier," 149–150. See also Elias, *Nigerian Land Law*, 207; and Coker, *Family Property*, 164–166, 200–201 passim.

77. For an analysis of this phenomenon, see Mann, *Slavery*, 258–262, 274–276.

AFTERWORD
THE NORMATIVE
FORCE OF THE PAST

Duncan Ivison

One of the most provocative suggestions the essays in this book make is that recovering the "hidden transcripts" of the legal claims made by indigenous peoples against European practices of dispossession and subjugation has important implications for our understanding of indigenous peoples' rights today. Indeed, in her Introduction to this volume, Belmessous puts this point very clearly:

> contemporary rights arguments have a foundation in native legal understandings that date from before colonization itself. In debates over indigenous rights, many scholars and activists have questioned whether the Western legal instruments that were employed so effectively to dispossess indigenous peoples are not tainted. Can those same legal conventions be used now to deliberate objectively over the future of indigenous rights? Our study reveals the terrible mistake that could be made in assuming that legal debate at the time of contact was conducted in exclusively Western terms.

At the same time, historians are usually also deeply concerned to avoid anachronism and to not impose present-day concerns upon our understanding of the past. So how do we square these two claims? One thing the essays in this book demonstrate is the extent to which indigenous peoples were engaged in the business of *making* claims—of engaging in what political philosophers might call the practice of mutual justification. A claim is thus an appeal to a certain set of reasons—or to a standard of justice or right—but also presupposes a picture of human agency. To demand justification for the exercise of power over oneself is to assert one's agency or standing as a moral and/or political agent. It is to assert that might is not right and that any exercise of power must be accompanied by *reasons*, and not just any reasons, but reasons that one could plausibly accept. Of course, a crucial philosophical question is to establish the validity of what kinds of reasons would count as justifying or justifiable in this sense. And it is a fascinating historical question to establish the historical limits and contexts within which certain justificatory schemes—certain sets of justificatory reasons—acquire their normative force or power. Thus, what we might call the "uptake" of indigenous peoples' claims in contemporary political discourse is deeply shaped by the way in which the history of their struggle has been understood. Recovering the hidden transcripts of their legal struggles, understood as far as possible in their own terms, is to rediscover the political agency and standing of indigenous polities.

Still, this leaves some important and often perplexing philosophical questions to consider. At the most basic level, one of the key premises underlying the project this book represents raises the question of the relationship between history and normativity. Does the way we understand the context in which people acted in the past shape our judgments about what should be the case today? This might seem an overly general question (with an obvious answer), but it is a particularly important one, when we consider the role of scholarship in contemporary debates over the situation of indigenous peoples today. In Australia, for example, there have been fierce public debates over aboriginal history—the so-called "history wars"—in which it seemed very clear that judgments about the past were directly related to judgments about what needed to be done now. Debates about the meaning of history are difficult to conduct in the hyperactive and attention deficit media-sphere of liberal democratic public cultures today. They do not lend themselves to the careful weighing of evidence and patient reconstruction of arguments characteristic of (at least most) academic history seminars or monographs. Nevertheless, the general question of what a changed historical view means for the formation of normative judgments in the present is an important and challenging one. It is particularly acute in the case of indigenous peoples, for whom, in many cases, it can be said that the "the past" is hardly past.

All the chapters in this volume address, at some level, the historical context in which indigenous peoples acted at the time of European settlement around the globe, and the way European conceptions and practices of law, politics, and culture were applied to their situation and, more importantly, how they reacted and not only (physically) fought back but *argued* back. Many of the chapters also seek to recover a much richer and less Eurocentric context in which we might be able to grasp the intensions and meanings of indigenous actors and their actions in their own right—including the concepts, conceptions, and theories they were invoking to explain and justify their behavior. The challenges of doing so should be familiar to most historians: there are problems of looking for and assembling the right kind of evidence to support claims about what was intended and why. And there is a need to resist what Andrew Fitzmaurice, in his chapter, calls "ethnological ventriloquism": of imposing Eurocentric conceptions—however indirectly and inadvertently—on explanations of indigenous peoples' claims as either mere projections of European arguments, or as graspable only within European conceptual schemes. The worry is that the depth of misunderstanding that often characterized the actual relations between European settlers and the indigenous inhabitants at the time of contact will extend to the historical grasp of those relations today.

The chapters in this volume make important contributions in addressing many of these historiographical challenges in innovative ways. They offer imaginative redescriptions—based on innovative archival and textual research—of indigenous peoples' claims that draw on a wealth of both European and indigenous sources. They offer subtle interpretations, for example, of extant treaty documents, putting them into rich historical context that brings out much more clearly the voice(s) of indigenous political agency. And they offer subtle and complex reconstructions of European imperial discourses that demonstrate the extent to which various imperial legal and political norms were shaped by a diverse range of legal, political, and cultural sources, including indigenous ones. As I have suggested, one of the most powerful themes that emerges is the extent to which indigenous peoples not only had their own rich political and legal theory upon which to draw in contesting European assertions of *dominium* and *imperium*, but also constantly asserted it in the face of European incursions. Physical resistance and normative counterargument went hand in hand. War is the continuation of politics by other means.

But how should we understand the normative upshot of this broader project of providing a richer and more accurate historical picture of indigenous peoples in the history of early modern imperialism? What does this history have to do, if anything, with the situation of contemporary indigenous peoples?

There are, at least, three possible responses. First, beyond the (still important) platitudes of understanding one's history in order not to repeat it, the suggestion might be that history has no normative import whatsoever for contemporary claims. Normative argument and justification is one thing, history another. One is a truth-seeking exercise—or at least a fact-seeking one—and the other, a justificatory one. Although understanding the history of injustice, for example, helps us to understand the context of the claims indigenous groups make today (and perhaps also the anger and frustration underlying them), the validity of those arguments does not ultimately rest on history. Their validity will rest on the cogency of the arguments for justice in the here and now and in light of contemporary standards of what justice requires. Telling the history of conquest and settlement and of displacement and resistance might well be important in helping to forge more realistic and sympathetic modes of public discourse and collective identity. But this is distinct from the justification of the claims themselves.

A second response might be a more narrowly legal one. Insofar as establishing occupation and use, for example, is crucial to the determination of contemporary land claims (as it is in Canada and Australia), then history has a very direct role to play in the contemporary situation of indigenous peoples. The landmark *Mabo* judgment in

Australia, for example, is replete with historical claims that clearly shape the overall thrust of the judgment.[1] Contemporary native title claims require a range of historical materials and evidence that are often crucial in determining the validity of a native title.

A third response is both more subtle and radical. First, consider two different models of normative power—that is, the source of normative authority for the critique of social and political arrangements. In one, the normative power of critique lies in the connection between the experience of oppression or unfreedom and conceptions of justice, freedom, recognition, or fairness that individuals and groups appeal to in making their claims for redress. The appeal to general principles helps to articulate and generalize the pain or vulnerability experienced by the individual or group concerned and translates that experience into claims others (ought to) feel bound to address.

According to the second model, the normative power of critique is not tied to general principles or norms but, rather, arises through a genealogical unmasking of historically and socially contingent social and political arrangements. General principles themselves are subject to critique, as no regulative ideal can be said to transcend the particular and hence the need for critique and dialogic revision. Thus, the normative power of critique in this second model derives from the very fact that there are no foundations immune from critique and that provide a vantage point from which to look down on (or out over) relations of power.

According to this third approach then, the current "frames" of our normative arguments may seem immutable, but in fact, they are much more historically contingent than often supposed. Although it is impossible to put everything into question at once, properly conceived, a historical approach can contribute to loosening long-held assumptions that fix certain crucial parts of our political discourse—and thus our imagination—in place.

I want to consider the first and especially the third argument in more detail below. The aim is to explore some of the philosophical issues underlying many of the claims in the essays in this volume, especially those, as Belmessous suggests, that are about revealing the claim-making force of indigenous legal arguments. The first approach seems too narrow but raises some thorny philosophical questions. The third is attractive but requires elaboration. My suggestion will not be that historians need to transform themselves into normative theorists, but rather that a certain way of conceiving of the very normativity of our concepts is informed by a historical approach.

Consider the first response, that to confuse history and normativity is to commit a category mistake. For philosophers, the worry here is one of committing the *genetic fallacy*: confusing a claim about the origins of something with its truth-value. The philosopher, of course (or at least some philosophers), tries to keep the distinction between the descriptive and the normative (or between facts/values, is/ought) as clean as possible. Unveiling the historical specificity of an argument says nothing, in itself, about its ultimate validity. It may denaturalize a concept and perhaps make it seem more contingent, but this does not, in itself, refute it. Contingency does not entail arbitrariness. Exposing hitherto unnoticed historical origins of a concept or conception may well refute certain *beliefs* we have about it, but it may not.[2] A genealogy of a concept, or a particular language of politics, can be debunking, but also vindicatory.[3] It will depend on how that genealogy sits within the self-understanding of the tradition or community of interpreters involved, or for whom the concept or conception has significance. Even Nietzsche, for example, although he hoped that his genealogy of the origins of morality would engender a change in the beliefs people have about moral value, did not think it literally *entailed* the falsity of morality.

A more radical criticism of the tendency to separate pure normative theory from "history" is that it makes for a hopelessly abstract approach to understanding politics, in particular. Raymond Geuss, for example, claims that contemporary analytic political philosophy, especially under the guise of Kant, has fallen prey to a kind of fetishism of pure normativity.[4] Although he does not deny that in many particular instances keeping clear the distinction between facts and norms is important and useful, he does not think it should be granted absolute priority, as it often is. Geuss argues that we should avoid attributing to a set of human-conceptual inventions an absolute or timeless status that somehow entitles them to float free of context. This means embracing what he calls a "realist" approach to political philosophy, which is centered on

> the study of historically instantiated forms of collective human action with special attention to the variety of ways in which people can structure and organize their actions so as to limit and control forms of disorder that they might find excessive or intolerable for other reasons. This is a historically specific study if only because the concepts of "order" and "intolerable disorder" are themselves variable magnitudes.[5]

Of course, it is one thing to criticize the *projection* of particular political or cultural forms as universal; it is another to deny there are any universals at all. The latter does not necessarily follow from the former, as Geuss seems to suggest.

Geuss's emphasis on the historically contingent nature of many of our conceptual frameworks draws, in large part, on the work of Quentin Skinner and the so-called "Cambridge School" of the history of political thought. The upshot of Skinner's methodological approach is that what historical reflection can do is help debunk the seeming obviousness of many of our assumptions about what seem to be both the limits and possibilities of our conceptual schemes—which in turn shape the limits and possibilities of possible course of political *action*. The historian of political thought, argues Skinner, can help us appreciate "how far the values embodied in our present way of life, and our present ways of thinking about those values, reflect a series of choices made at different times between different possible worlds."[6] In doing so it does not necessarily provide a new set of answers to our problems as much as a new set of questions that can help "liberate us from any one hegemonic account of those values and how they should be interpreted."[7] Skinner is careful to bracket the whole question of truth claims. Although it is part of his approach that what it is rational for someone to hold as true will vary with the totality of her beliefs, it is another thing to say this of truth in general. Truth is not reducible to rational acceptability; however, the intellectual historian—at least according to Skinner—should be primarily interested in the latter, not the former.[8]

So an appreciation of the historicity of our conceptual schemes and the way various clusters of values have formed and come to be understood over time open up space for critical reflection on those values. Skinner has famously applied his approach to revealing what he claims is an occluded aspect to our thinking about liberty; namely, a "neo-Roman" conception of negative liberty.[9] But this same approach has also been applied to the situation of indigenous peoples, to which we now turn.

Perhaps the most significant attempt to apply the Cambridge approach to the situation of indigenous peoples has been by James Tully. The reason for examining Tully's work here is that it deals explicitly with some of the underlying issues about the potential normative force of recovering the "hidden transcripts" of indigenous political agency at the heart of many of the essays in this volume.

Tully casts his approach as a form of "public philosophy" that is distinct from the usual "analytic," "historical," and "genealogical" approaches in the field. What is distinctive about Tully's notion of public philosophy is its fundamentally *practical* nature. Thus, theory loses its privileged place, not only in terms of the position of the theorist, understood as floating free of practical debates, but also in the orientation of the activity of political theory itself. The elaboration of this shift is complex but involves moving away from the construction of systematic, abstract theories that are meant to validate or redeem practical claims made in political argument, to engaging with (by seeking to understand, clarify, compare, and contrast) the *actual* claims and practices themselves. This should not be confused with a demand that political philosophy become more empirical or "practical" in the sense of "applied political theory." Rather, drawing on diverse sources, but especially the work of Wittgenstein and Foucault, it means taking activity and practice as prior to theory and placing the particular language games at issue in context and examining them from the ground up, so to speak. Instead of seeking constantly to universalize the terms of the game we find ourselves in (whether in relation to justice, citizenship, or freedom), we have to learn to situate it as one among any number of possibilities.

Here then is the crucial role of history for the political theorist, and especially what Tully calls "historical survey." One way of gaining critical distance on our particular language games, including the way we formulate problems in the first place, is through historical and conceptual *comparison*. We do this by listening to others and the way they understand their practices, looking for similarities and dissimilarities across different games, drawing analogies, offering (re)descriptions for further analysis, and looking for ways of speaking and acting differently. Historical surveys are a crucial aspect of this form of analysis. There are two parts to this approach. First, there is the task of excavating the different "languages" and theories of political thought out from underneath the dominant modes of seeing the world:

> Political theorists in the past are seen as questioning, testing and challenging
> some of the accepted conventions of their age in various ways . . . This kind of
> survey of the history of political thought shows how the mainstream system of
> judgments was gradually put in place, often over centuries, as the stage-setting
> of reflective disputes and debates, the reasons that were given for and against it,
> and the alternatives displaced.[10]

But, in addition, there is a need to provide historical surveys of the *nondiscursive* features of the various practices of "government" (understood in the broadest sense, drawing on the work of Michel Foucault) that have become institutionalized and legitimated and which shape people's conduct. What other forms of government were displaced in the process? To what extent do the practices of government to which we are subject today depend on features that escape critical attention because they are taken as "given" or "natural"?

So historical surveys have a critical as well as historical function. Of course, history needs no other justification than the inherent value of understanding history for its own sake. But for Tully—and I think for many people committed to exploring the history of European imperialism and its consequences for indigenous peoples today, including many of the authors in this book—history also has a crucial political function. These historical surveys, Tully argues, can be offered to theorists and citizens to help further "horizon-expanding reasons and re-descriptions" for their consideration and response. History helps develop a "critical orientation" to the background conventions of contemporary practices and challenges.[11]

The philosophical insight here draws on Wittgenstein's now famous analysis of the indeterminacy of rule-following,[12] Tully sees a close analogy between the inherent linguistic freedom that Wittgenstein's argument implies (i.e., the possibility of going on differently always being present in any language game), and the practical extralinguistic freedom of "enactment and improvisation within the inherited relations of power in which the vocabulary is used."[13] This is nothing less than the "civic" or democratic freedom of citizens: the freedom to enter into dialogue with those who govern and to call the prevailing norms of recognition and action coordination to which they are subject into question.

So despite the pervasiveness of imperialism in the contemporary world—at least as far as indigenous peoples are concerned, but not only them—another world is not only possible, but actual.[14] And it's the methodology of historical survey and comparative analysis at the heart of the Cambridge approach to political thought that can help us see this, or so Skinner and Tully claim. Just because "western imperialism," Tully argues, governs through indirect and informal means and so depends (to some extent) on the active collaboration of those subject to it, another world of pluralism persists within the "interstices of globalization." And one of the most astonishing examples of this is the survival and resurgence of indigenous peoples around the world today.

Tully discusses the situation of indigenous peoples in two papers that reflect his distinctive vision of a "public philosophy" and his historical approach to the nature of imperialism.[15] In "The Negotiation of Reconciliation," he outlines the contours of both an alternative history of and normative framework for relations between aboriginal and non-aboriginal peoples (the comparative/historical approach goes hand in hand with the normative throughout Tully's argument). In the very next chapter, "Struggles of Indigenous Peoples for and of Freedom," the tone is somewhat bleaker, given his focus on some of the main obstacles that remain for negotiating reconciliation today.

Very broadly speaking, over the past four centuries, two important modes of interaction between indigenous and nonindigenous peoples have been *treaty-based* and *colonial* relations. As the essays in this book demonstrate, these two modes often become intertwined and indistinguishable, but for analytic purposes, at least, it is useful to distinguish between them. From the earliest period of contact (not everywhere, but in many places), treaties have been an important part of indigenous and nonindigenous relations. Despite often being carried out in the midst of a "sea of strategic relations of power, force and fraud," treaties provide a normative prototype for a just relationship between two or more peoples.[16] Indeed, it was upon the basis of this complex mode of interaction that in 1996 the Canadian *Royal Commission on Aboriginal Peoples* (RCAP) put forward a new framework for reinterpreting aboriginal/non-aboriginal relations, grounded in five basic principles: mutual recognition, intercultural negotiation, mutual respect, sharing, and mutual responsibility. The idea lying behind this approach is that each principle can be defended from within the respective worldviews of both parties and thus forms something like an "overlapping consensus"—to draw on a phrase from the American philosopher John Rawls—subject to ongoing critical assessment from each side.[17] So, for example, the principle of mutual recognition requires that indigenous peoples be recognized by the rest of Canada (and the international community) as equal "First Nations," and thus any exercise of sovereignty over them must be adequately justified, which means democratically legitimated. Equally, indigenous First Nations must recognize that nonindigenous Canadians have legitimate interests in the land and institutions that have developed since settlement. Both these perspective must be incorporated into any new arrangements that are agreed to.

However, at the same time as treaties structured relations between indigenous and nonindigenous peoples—as many of the essays above make clear—"colonial" relations were also ever present. In Canada, for example, the *Indian Act* cast aboriginal people as primitive wards of the state, incapable of consent and whose societies and ways of life were doomed to extinction. It also asserted prior sovereignty over aboriginal peoples and presumptively subjected them to the authority of the state and its laws and institutions. This legal and normative framework, combined with changing facts on the ground—including demographic changes, shifts in strategic alliances, and so on—and the consolidation of the imperial international order, all worked to undermine the rough normative promise of treaty relations.

For many indigenous peoples, these colonial and imperialist relations persist into the present. Even when principles or norms are found that could frame new relations (such as those provided by RCAP), they can be turned around and used in contrary ways. For example, a narrowing of the meaning and scope of the recognition of "aboriginal rights" in Canadian constitutional law has ended up restricting the freedom of indigenous peoples in unanticipated ways.[18] The principle of self-determination in international law was extended to former colonies in Africa and Asia but was denied to indigenous peoples, since it was assumed they already enjoyed internal self-determination within the states in which they were forcibly included.[19]

The problem, Tully and others claim, lies with two crucial "hinge propositions" that secure the system of ongoing colonization of indigenous peoples. The first is the claim that exclusive jurisdiction over indigenous peoples is not only legitimate but effective, and the second is that there is basically no viable alternative. Either the state exercises exclusive jurisdiction, or indigenous peoples must overthrow it or secede and establish their own. These propositions are woven so deeply into the structure of modern politics, so the argument goes, that they are almost impossible to dislodge directly. Instead, they have to be put into question through a multiplicity of immanent critiques and techniques that challenge and modify them from within. They are as much struggles *of* freedom as *for* freedom.

But how do these struggles of freedom amount to a genuine alternative to imperialism? More specifically, how can we distinguish between forms of contestation that *modify* an imperial relationship—leaving the underlying structures intact—from one that *transforms* it? For example, how can we identify forms of treaty relations that transform the colonial structure of aboriginal/nonaboriginal relations from those that merely entrench it? How can the language of self-determination and self-government, or of "aboriginal rights" or "aboriginal title" be turned around and used against the very forces constraining them? Unlike some critics who advocate a radical break with all such apparently intercultural concepts, Tully thinks this is premature. And here we can see how the essays in this volume offer valuable guidance. As Belmessous points out (and Fitzmaurice, Hickford, Hilliard, and Mann also suggest), once we understand how indigenous legal arguments shaped European responses—as much as European arguments shaped indigenous responses—then our conceptual inheritance becomes more complex in potentially interesting ways.

This returns us to the basic issue of the relation between history and normativity. For Tully, the normative power of critique and the ability to "think differently" stems from the space—the freedom—opened up by historical critique and the debunking of the dominant language games of politics. No single theory or approach can capture the critical vantage point from which to form normative judgments about how the world ought to be. In fact, political theory itself should be carried out not so much as the search for transcendental rules or norms that can structure political community, but as a form of public, practical philosophy: no norm is immune from reflexive critique, including the very norms that motivate public philosophy itself. The only test for "reasonableness" (or unreasonableness) is the democratic one of deliberation and contestation over the terms at issue, including the very norms that are supposed to govern the way we argue about those norms.

Philosophers will argue about whether this is as truly "anti-foundational" as Tully claims. The norm that no norm is immune to critique seems grounded in a claim about democracy, which in turn seems grounded in a set of claims about the kind of justification owed to people conceived of in a particular way (as possessing dignity, or respect, and thus as being owed reasons for any exercise of authority over them). I will not consider this debate here. But it does point to deep and interesting questions about the role history plays in normative debate more generally. Historians need not become political theorists, and political theorists are usually (with some notable exceptions) bad historians. But principles and norms are always formed against the backdrop of contingent discursive and nondiscursive practices. Beliefs about conceptions of right or justice can shift and change in light of the emergence of new groups and the need to address different political problems. The general presuppositions that inform the constitutional rules of a society and that inform the understanding and the justification of exercises of power can change over time. In other words, even normativity has a history.

NOTES

1. *Mabo v Queensland* (No. 2) [1992] HCA 23; (1992) 175 CLR 1 (June 3, 1992).
2. Telling the history of a concept or conception may involve simply bracketing claims about its truth-value in general, instead of having any necessary relation to its ultimate validity. I return to this issue in a moment.
3. Bernard Williams, *Truth and Truthfulness* (Princeton: Princeton University Press, 2002).
4. Raymond Geuss, *Philosophy and Real Politics* (Princeton: Princeton University Press, 2008).
5. Geuss, *Philosophy and Real Politics*, 22.
6. Quentin Skinner, *Liberty before Liberalism* (Cambridge: Cambridge University Press, 1998), 116.
7. *Ibid.*
8. Quentin Skinner, "Interpretation, rationality and truth," *Visions of Politics, vol. 1: Regarding Method* (Cambridge: Cambridge University Press, 2001), 51–53.
9. Quentin Skinner, *Hobbes and Republican Liberty* (Cambridge: Cambridge University Press, 2008).
10. James Tully, *Public Philosophy in a New Key, vol 1.: Democracy and Civil Freedom* (Cambridge: Cambridge University Press, 2009), 33.
11. Tully, *Public Philosophy*, 34.
12. Ludwig Wittgenstein, *Philosophical Investigations*, trans. G.E.M. Anscombe (Oxford: Basil Blackwell, 1958).
13. Tully, *Public Philosophy*, 245.
14. In the next few paragraphs I draw on Duncan Ivison, 'Another world is actual: Between imperialism and freedom', *Political Theory* 39, 1 (2011) 131–7.
15. Tully, *Public Philosophy*, chap. 7–8.
16. Tully, *Public Philosophy*, 226.
17. John Rawls, *Political Liberalism* (New York: Columbia University Press, 1993).
18. Michael Asch, "From Calder to Van der Peet: Aboriginal Rights and Canadian Law 1973–1996" in Paul Havemann, ed., *Indigenous Peoples' Rights in Australia, Canada and New Zealand* (Oxford: Oxford University Press, 1999), 428–446.
19. Tully, *Public Philosophy*, 276–287.

CONTRIBUTORS

Rolena Adorno is the Reuben Post Halleck professor of Spanish and Portuguese literature at Yale University. She researches and teaches in colonial Spanish American literary and cultural history and the nineteenth-century origins of Hispanism in the United States. Her books include *De Guancane a Macondo: estudios de literatura hispanoamericana* (2008), *The Polemics of Possession in Spanish American Narrative* (2007), *Álvar Núñez Cabeza de Vaca: His Account, His Life, and the Expedition of Pánfilo de Narváez* (1999), and *Guaman Poma: Writing and Resistance in Colonial Peru* (1986). She has won book prizes from the Modern Language Association, the American Historical Association, the Western Historical Association, and the New England Council of Latin American Studies. In 2009 she was appointed by President Barack Obama to the National Council on the Humanities, the advisory board of the National Endowment for the Humanities.

R. Jovita Baber is the Director of Research at Illinois Facilities Fund. Previously, she was an assistant professor of history at the University of Illinois Urbana-Champaign. She has expertise in Colonial Latin America, Early Mordern Iberia. She recevied numerous awrds for her history research, including a National science Foundation (NSF)grant, three Fulbrights and an Andrew W. Mellon Fellowship in Latin American History.

Saliha Belmessous is a senior research fellow at the University of New South Wales. Her research interests include European colonial history and policies towards indigenous peoples. She has held fellowships in the United States and Australia. Her books include *D'un préjugé culturel à un préjugé racial: la politique indigène de la France au Canada* (Lille, France, 2000) and *Assimilation and Empire: Uniformity in French and British Colonies, 1541–1954* (Oxford: Oxford University Press, 2013).

Lauren Benton is a professor of history at New York University. She researches and writes about the comparative legal history of empires in world history. Her books include *A Search for Sovereignty: Law and Geography in European Empires, 1400–1900* (Cambridge University Press, 2010), and *Law and Colonial Cultures: Legal Regimes in World History, 1400–1900* (Cambridge University Press, 2002), which was awarded the World History Association Book Award and the James Willard Hurst Prize.

Ann Curthoys is a Honorary Associate at the University of Sydney. She has written widely in the fields of Australian history, in areas including indigenous-settler relations, print journalism, television, the Cold War, racial thought, feminist history, and national identity. Her recent publications include *Rights and Redemption: History, Law, and Indigenous People* (2008); and *How to Write History that People Want to Read* (UNSW Press, 2009).

Andrew Fitzmaurice is an associate professor of history at the University of Sydney. He specialises in the ideology of European colonisation. He is the author of numerous books and articles, including *Sovereignty, Property and Empire, 1500–2000* (Cambridge University Press, 2014) and *Humanism and America: An intellectual history of English colonisation, 1500–1625* (Ideas in Context; Cambridge University Press, 2003). He is also the co-editor of *Shakespeare and Early-Modern Political Thought* (Cambridge University Press, 2009).

Mark Hickford is a Crown Counsel at the Crown Law Office in Wellington and adjunct lecturer in law at Victoria University of Wellington. He has appeared in the Waitangi Tribunal, the Māori Land Court, the Environment Court and the ordinary courts. He has published on native title, legal and constitutional history, the politics and law of Crown-Māori relations and the Treaty of Waitangi. He is the auther of *Lords of the Land: Indigenous Property Rights and the Jurisprudence of Empire* (Oxford University Press, 2011).

Christopher Hilliard is a professor in history at the University of Sydney. His research interests include Modern British cultural and intellectual history, and New Zealand history. He is the author of *English as a Vocation: The 'Scrutiny' Movement* (Oxford: Oxford Universwity Press, 2012), *To Exercise Our Talents: The Democratization of Writing in Britain* (Harvard University Press, 2006) and *The Bookmen's Dominion: Cultural Life in New Zealand, 1920–1950* (Auckland University Press, 2006).

Duncan Ivison is professor of political philosophy at the University of Sydney. He specialises in political theory, ethics and the history of political thought. He is the author of *Rights* (Acumen and McGill Queens Press, 2008), *Postcolonial Liberalism* (Cambridge University Press, 2002) and *The Self at Liberty: Political Argument and the Arts of Government* (Cornell UP, 1997). He is also the co-editor of *Political Theory and the Rights of Indigenous Peoples* (CUP, 2000, reprinted in 2002).

Kristin Mann is professor of history at Emory University. She has published widely on slavery and legal issues in African history. She is the author of *Slavery and the Birth of an African City: Lagos, 1760–1900* (Indiana University Press, 2007) and *Marrying Well: Marriage, Status and Social Change Among the Educated Elite in Colonial Lagos*

(Cambridge University Press, 1985). She is also the co-editor of *Rethinking the African Diaspora: The Making of a Black Atlantic World in the Bight of Benin and Brazil* (2001) and *Law in Colonial Africa* (1991).

Jessie Mitchell is an indipendent scholar. She specializes in the imperial and racial aspects of nineteenth century Australian political life and the history of nineteenth-century missionaries in the colonies. She is the author of *In Good Faith? Governing Indigenous Australia through God, Charity and Empire, 1825–1855* (ANU E-Press, 2011).

Craig Yirush is an associate professor of history at the University of California Los Angeles. His scholarship focuses on the early modern British Atlantic, the question of Amerindian rights in the first British Empire, and the connection between law and political theory in early-modern Europe. He is the author of *Settlers, Liberty, and Empire: The Roots of Early American Political Theory, 1675–1775* (Cambridge University Press, 2011).

INDEX

abolition, of slave trade, 224
Aboriginal petitioning, 182, 185, 187, 198
   interest in, 183
   for land, 193–94
   in New South Wales, 194–97
   as phenomenon, 183
Aboriginal protectorate, 191
Aborigines, 189, 198n4. *See also* Central
      Board to Watch Over the Interests of
      the Aborigines; *Royal Commission on*
      Aboriginal Peoples
   Broome on, 185, 190
   colonial perspective on, 183
   government and, 192–93
   population decline among, 194
   Prince Alfred and, 190–93
   reserves for, 197
Aborigines' Friends Association (AFA), 193
Aborigines Protection Act, 194
Aborigines Protection Association, 195, 197
Acadia, 121
   French cession of, 110, 127n41
accommodation, system of, 204
acquisition, of empires, 20–21
AFA. *See* Aborigines' Friends Association
African land tenure system, 9, 223, 227, 239
agency
   of indigenous actors, 56–57, 57, 145, 167,
     248–51
   political, 145
agōn, as a metaphor, 153–55, 175
agriculture, in West Africa, 240
ahi kaa, 217
Akitoye, 224, 230–31
Alexander VI, 45
Alfonso X, 51
Alfred, Prince
   Aborigines and, 190–93
   Ngarrindjeri and, 191
Algonquian peoples. *See also* Native
     Americans; Powhatans
   language of, 9

political structure of, 92
   Spelman, H. on, 94–95
alienation, right of, Richmond on,
   157–58
Almagro, Diego de, rebellion of, 68
Amerindian cultures, 63
Andeans, 5
   affiliation detachment by, 67
   classification of, 76
   designation of, 68
   Guaman Poma on, 76
   history, 70, 74–80
   as hopeful, 80
   kin unit of, 66–67
   low-born, 70
   restitution to, 74, 78
   as submissive, 79
Andean claims, 64f
Andean sovereignty
   las Casas on, 74
   reclaiming, 74–80
Anglicus, Alanus, on crusades, 95
antimeridian, 28f–29f
Apess, William, 144
Argall, Samuel, 90
   metaphysical beliefs of, 91
Arney, George, 163
Arrowsic Conference, 121
Arthur, George, 186
Arthur, Walter George, 186
   imprisonment of, 187
Arundel, Peter, 90
Ashurst, Henry, 138–39
Aṣogbon, 234, 236
assimilation, 206
   detribalization and, 207–8
audience, question of, 14
Australia. *See also* New South Wales;
     Queensland; South Australia;
     Tasmania; Victoria; Western
     Australia
   colonies of, 183, 184f

www.ingramcontent.com/pod-product-compliance
Lightning Source LLC
Chambersburg PA
CBHW020800300725

30249CB00040B/623